The Enjoyment of Theatre

The Enjoyment
of Theatre

sixth edition

Kenneth M. Cameron

Patti P. Gillespie

PEARSON

Boston | New York | San Francisco
Mexico City | Montreal | Toronto | London | Madrid | Munich | Paris
Hong Kong | Singapore | Tokyo | Cape Town | Sydney

Executive Editor: Molly Taylor
Editorial Assistant: Michael Kish
Marketing Manager: Mandee Eckersley
Editorial Production Service: Omegatype Typography, Inc.
Manufacturing Buyer: JoAnne Sweeney
Cover Administrator: Kristina Mose-Libon
Interior Design: Carol Somberg
Electronic Composition: Omegatype Typography, Inc.

For related titles and support materials, visit our online catalog at
www.ablongman.com.

Between the time Website information is gathered and published, some
sites may have closed. Also, the transcription of URLs can result in
typographical errors. The publisher would appreciate being notified of any
problems with URLs so that they may be corrected in subsequent editions.

Library of Congress Cataloging-in-Publication Data

Cameron, Kenneth M.
      The enjoyment of theatre / Kenneth M. Cameron, Patti P. Gillespie—6th ed.
         p.   cm.
      Includes index.
      ISBN 0-205-37551-0 (alk. paper)
      1. Theater.   I. Gillespie, Patti P.   II. Title.

   PN2037.C27 2004
   792—dc21

                                                            2003041905

Printed in the United States of America

10   9   8   7   6   5   4   3   2   1   08   07   06   05   04   03

Contents

Preface

For the sixth edition of *The Enjoyment of Theatre,* we have made significant changes. On the one hand, we have heavily revised five chapters, more lightly revised all others; on the other hand, we have worked to increase the book's eye appeal, both with new design and with new color photos of Broadway productions by New York's finest theatrical photographers. In connection with this improvement, we have quadrupled the number of color pages.

Textual changes include deep revisions aimed at placing the theatre in cultural and business contexts. We had previously treated the theatre primarily as an art; however, with the loss of confidence in art generally, we decided this time to place the theatre culturally and economically. The results have been widespread and varied—for example, a major revision of Chapter 2 to emphasize theatre in culture and business, and a completely rewritten chapter on commercial theatre, now Chapter 18. In the historical section, this approach has led to extensive revision to get at overall flow and big movements, noticeable particularly in the 1800s and 1900s; the individual historical chapters are now mostly shorter and punchier.

As well, we have placed the theatre within the more general category of performance. New discussions of performance mark the substantially rewritten Chapter 1, and the idea of performance now occurs throughout the book. We have also beefed up the discussion of playwriting.

Users familiar with earlier editions will not find the old final chapter on world theatre; important as it was in earlier editions to include world theatre separately, we now believe that awareness of the world has increased so profoundly that theatres outside the West should be integrated for study. Therefore, major Eastern theatres—Noh, Kabuki, Kathakali, Beijing Opera—now appear with their historical contemporaries of the West, and each historical chapter includes materials on Eastern theatres. The effects of colonialism are now in Chapter 18; the recent theatres of Africa are in Chapter 19.

New features in this edition include several "stories of the play," summaries of great plays that are used as examples. Also new are discussions, with both color and black-and-white images, of computer-aided design (CAD) and of "corporate theatre," an important new direction in the application of design. We have kept such older features as "Thinking About the Theatre" and "Links," the latter, in particular, updated to follow changes in media and the Internet. We have also kept our in-depth illustration captions, which have long been praised by users for their ability to teach, not merely to decorate. The extensive glossary continues to give quick definitions of key terms and ideas.

The question of eye appeal has proved a vexing one. Today's students take as given a sophistication of design that is commonplace in advertising and television but sometimes difficult if not impossible in books. Matters of budget, of time lag (a revision takes a year to write and another year to produce), but most of all of density of material make the glitz and glamor of pop media uncongenial: a double-page advertising spread can give its message with one dynamic visual and five words, but a complex idea (e.g., the director's staging of a text) takes hundreds of words and, if there is space, many visuals. Modern advertising and TV design sell sizzle; perhaps regrettably, this book sells steak—and sometimes fairly tough steak, at that—because learning is not a matter of one-liners and sound bites; it is a matter of complex understanding. We hope the new color and the new design do appeal to student eyes—but the fact remains that the text has to be read and understood.

We are indebted to many people for their help, including all those who permitted the use of photographs. Individuals who were of particular help to us were Michael Kish of Allyn and Bacon, Norman Hart, Stacey Stewart, Michelle Washington, Jim Patterson, Tim Donohue, Nancy Hereford of the Mark Taper Forum, and Heidi Holtz at Syracuse Stage.

Allyn and Bacon would like to thank the following reviewers for their valuable suggestions and useful comments: Lynne Greeley, University of Vermont; Ann Klautsch, Boise State University; Michael M. O'Hara, Ball State University; Marilyn I. Scharine, Westminster College; and Michael D. Whitlatch, Buena Vista University.

Locating Theatre, Experiencing Plays: Theory and Criticism

Part I focuses on ways of looking at theatre, ways usually called *theory* and *criticism*. *Theory* is an attempt to explain the nature of something, such as theatre or drama. It tries to answer such fundamental questions as, what is it? how does it work? *Criticism* is an attempt to explain specific instances of something, not theatre in general but *a* play or *a* performance. What does this particular play mean and how does it convey that meaning by its form and structure? How does this particular production present the play to this audience? Why were these particular choices about acting and directing and design made? How does this production try to communicate its ideas to the audience? How well did it succeed? Part I ends by considering some of the people who use theory and criticism as they work with today's theatre.

Theatre: Performance and Art

When you have completed this chapter, you should be able to

■ Define *performance* and list traits shared by performances

■ Define *art* and list traits shared by arts

■ Discuss how theatre differs from other kinds of performance (e.g., lectures, games, parades, rituals)

■ Discuss how theatre differs from other kinds of arts (e.g., painting, sculpture, opera, dance)

■ Discuss, using specific examples, similarities and differences between art/life; performance/life; dramatic character/real person; dramatic character/actor; performing art/visual art; performing art/sport

■ List and explain the traits that comprise theatre

■ Explain in what sense theatre is a system of relationships (rather than a thing)

■ Explain how theatre resembles and yet differs from film and television

People choose to go to the theatre for many reasons. It is part of theatre's richness that it appeals to people in many different ways simultaneously. Part of theatre's appeal is social: It's a good place to meet people and be with friends. Part of its appeal is sensual, for theatre pleases the senses through the talent of its actors, the spectacle of its visual display (scenery, costumes, lighting), and the beauty of its language and music. It appeals too by engaging the imagination with its stories and characters, which offer us experiences that we have never had—and may never have—but which we recognize as possible for us: exotic yet familiar, good and evil, funny and sad. And theatre appeals intellectually because the issues raised by its plays are the human issues that we confront daily and that our forebears confronted in their time. What is theatre that it can appeal to so many people in so many different circumstances?

Theatre is both a *performance* and an *art,* and theorists have explored theatre from both points of view. Most of today's theoretical work views theatre as a kind of performance, whereas earlier theories of theatre treated it as a kind of art. Both views are correct. By shifting emphasis between the two, we can understand more about the theatre than would be possible from either view alone.

Theatre as Performance

Performance is an activity where some people do something while other people watch. Many different kinds of performance exist on a continuum from humdrum and everyday to formal and special. People perform roles in everyday life—that is, they shift their

FIGURE 1.1 **Street Performance.**
A mime performs in the Piazza Navona in Rome. Notice how he has used costume and makeup to identify himself as a performer and how he has marked off his performance space. (Note, too, that he hopes to earn money.) (Photograph courtesy of Michelle Washington.)

actions, and sometimes even their appearances, depending on what they are doing and for whom. For example, a man giving a speech to a group of businessmen behaves and dresses differently from the same man teaching his son to kick a soccer ball. A woman behaves and dresses one way in front of a jury as she argues her case and a different way when she stands in a grocery line. They perform roles as salesman and father, lawyer and consumer for certain people in certain situations; they will perform a myriad of other roles in other situations, in the presence of other people.

Other performances of life are more formal, more clearly structured, and they may seem even more special because they do not happen every day. In such performances as church services or weddings, for example, there are usually agreed-on sequences of events and predetermined sets of words. In games and sports, there are rules that must be followed and time constraints that must be observed. More highly structured still are such performances as circuses and fairs, where people come together on special occasions to watch trained people do things for their enjoyment. Most formal of all are performances of the sort found in theatre, opera, and dance, for, in these instances, people gather to watch specially trained people perform in highly structured works of art, hence the name *performing arts* to describe this special group.

Traits Shared by Performances

All performances, both informal and formal, share certain traits. They have

- Doers (performers, actors)
- Something done (a speech, ritual, or play)
- Watchers (spectators, audiences)
- Performance sites (a stadium, church, theatre, or street)
- Movement through time (they have beginnings and ends)

In a fight resulting from road rage, the fighters are the doers (performers or actors); fighting is the something done; the crowd that gathers to watch is the audience, the watchers or spectators; the performance **site** is the street where the fight is taking place. The fight begins and ends. In a theatrical performance, the actors do a play for an **audience,** usually in a theatre building, and the performance takes time.

The relationship between the doers and watchers leads to one of performance's greatest appeals—its immediacy. Because it happens in real time, with the performer and spectators brought together in the event, performance has a compelling sense of NOW.

The same interaction that gives performance this power of immediacy, however, also makes it ephemeral—fleeting, nonrecoverable. In performances, as in life, events happen and are gone, never to be recaptured. Although a storyteller (another kind of *performer*) may repeat a story for different audiences, the storyteller is a human being and not a machine. For this reason, each time a storyteller works, the performance is different, the more so because audiences affect performance and audiences change at every performance. (There is an exception to this generalization, that is, when performances exist in such media as radio, film, television, and video. Such *mediated performances* exist physically on film stock as images or as electronic impulses and so can be recovered exactly as they were made and repeated unchanged many times.) Except for mediated formats, performances do not leave a record. Exact copies do not exist. They cannot be played over and over without change. When the moment in performance is gone, it is entirely gone. Thus, performance is ephemeral.

Traits Causing Differences among Performances

Different types of performances, although sharing some traits, do not share all; that is, performances are not identical. They differ according to their

- Purposes (the reasons for which they are done)
  Church services are held so that people can worship; games, so that someone can win; auctions, so that people can exchange goods and money.
- Relationships between doers and watchers
  At spectator sports, the watchers (fans) interact often with one another—talking, buying Cokes—but they seldom interact with the players, except indirectly, to hurl abuse for a player's mistake or to cheer for a score. At an auction or a parade, on the other hand, doers and watchers interact often and directly. At an auction,

FIGURE 1.2 **Sport as Performance.**
Basketball games (like other spectator sports) are performances (doers, watchers) bound by strict time limits and complicated sets of rules. Spectators come purposefully to cheer their team to victory. Here, players from the University of Maryland, national champions in 2001. (Photograph courtesy of University of Maryland Campus Photo Services.)

spectators call out to the auctioneer and talk to their neighbors. At a parade, spectators watch for a while and march for a while or even leave to do other things, coming back only in time to catch the end of the parade. In a mediated performance (radio, film, TV), performers and spectators aren't even at the same site: they don't occupy the same time or place and so cannot interact.

■ Organizing principles (the reasons performances begin and end and seem all to be part of the same event)

Auctions are organized by the things to be bought and sold; they begin when the auctioneer holds up the first item for sale and end when the last item has been sold. A church service is held together neither by rules (like a game) nor by items (like an auction) but by a schedule determined by custom, symbolism, and doctrine.

■ Self-awareness (the degree to which the people involved know that they are at a performance and why)

In street fights, spectators do not come together purposefully; they encounter the fight by accident; but people come to a boxing match or circus specifically to watch trained people perform marvelous feats. Boxing matches and circuses, then, are self-aware in a way that street fights are not.

Obviously, none of these traits (purpose, relationship, organizing principles, and self-awareness) is better than another; each is simply different, and from different combinations of these differences come different types of performances. A final, extended example of one kind of performance may clarify how traits can combine differently to produce a certain kind of performance. We have chosen ritual as the example because rituals are performances occurring in all cultures, even though they are perhaps most closely associated in the popular mind with certain social and religious forms in Africa, pre-Columbian America, Southeast Asia, and parts of the Pacific.

Rituals share many elements across these cultures. They often incorporate such elements as masks, costumes, dance, music, and some sort of text, although the texts are often improvised and transmitted orally rather than in writing. They usually have as their purpose some sort of cultural outcome—to heal, to honor, or to mourn. An identifying element is the community bonding of those present; that is, one of the results of a ritual is to bind a community together. Such bonding is probably enhanced because ritual lacks any clear separation between performers and audience—those attending participate regularly and directly in the activities. Rituals typically lack a dedicated space. Although rituals often take place in spaces configured for them at the time, the space is seldom permanently altered and no effort is made to suggest a location for the ritual different from the actual location in which it unfolds. Because rituals can take place over several miles of countryside and extend over several days, the event often has a very diffuse quality, with some people able to catch only an occasional glimpse of what is unfolding.

To sum up: theatre is a kind of performance that shares some traits with other sorts of performances: it has doers and watchers, a place of performance, and movement through time; it is immediate and ephemeral. Although resembling other kinds of performances, it is not identical with any of them; it has its own purposes, relationships, principles, degrees of self-awareness, and relation to time.

FIGURE 1.3   **Ritual as Performance.**
Rituals typically intermix performers and audience, unfold in an actual location, and regularly incorporate masks, costumes, music, and dance, as this re-creation of a healing ceremony of the Iroquois False Face Society shows. (Painting by Ernest Smith, photograph by the Rochester, New York, Museum of Arts and Sciences. Courtesy of Donald G. Cameron.)

Theatre as Art

In addition to being a kind of performance, theatre is also a kind of art. Just as there are many different kinds of performances, there are many different kinds of art—poetry, novel, painting, sculpture, architecture, music, dance, theatre, to mention only the most obvious.

Traits Shared by Arts

Just as all performances share some traits, all arts, however different they may be in some ways, share certain traits. For example, all art

- Is artificial, that is, art is made rather than natural (existing in nature)
    This idea is at first difficult to grasp because we often prize art for how closely it resembles nature, thrilling to a portrait or a painting precisely because it so closely resembles the thing it copies. Still, an artist makes art; it does not just happen.

- Exists for itself, not needing any practical use in real life

   An advertising jingle may be arresting and tuneful, but it is not considered a work of art because its purpose is to sell something; a piano sonata has no practical use in the world and may not even be hummable, but it is an example of musical art.

- Is self-aware

   Artists know in a general way what they are trying to do, and they possess a preparation and a discipline that allows them, within limits, to accomplish what they attempt.

- Produces a certain kind of response—an aesthetic response—in the audience

   Again, the exact meaning of *aesthetic response* has been endlessly debated, but we would not be far off if we agreed that an aesthetic response includes an appreciation of beauty and some understanding that goes beyond the merely intellectual or the merely entertaining.

Traits Causing Differences among Arts

Although all arts share certain traits, they also differ in certain ways, and it is these differences that allow us to distinguish among the kinds of art. Arts differ in

- Their relationship with time and space

   Some arts unfold through time; for example, music or novels require time to move from their beginnings to their end. Other arts exist in space; a building or a piece of sculpture occupies space and does not move from a beginning to an end over time; it is best seen by walking around it, looking at it from several sides.

- Their principles of organization

   Some arts are organized by stories; in them lifelike characters seem to be thinking and talking and doing things very much like what we do in real life. Other arts do not use stories but instead are organized by patterned sounds (music) or patterned colors (painting).

- Their idea of audiences

   Novels and paintings, for example, assume they will be enjoyed by solitary individuals; opera and dance, on the other hand, assume that groups of people will assemble to enjoy them. The ways by which arts reach their audience also differ.

- Their mode of presentation

   Some arts, like novels, are transmitted by the printed page; others, like film, rely on mechanically produced images; still others, like opera, dance, and theatre, require live performers in the presence of a live audience.

Theatre's Relationship with Other Arts

Theatre's relationship with other arts is extremely complex. Sometimes it contains them, other times it merges with them, and often it transforms other arts for its own purposes

FIGURE 1.4 **Theatre: Performance and Art.**
Dedicated to bringing together actors, puppets, music, and dance in a single artistic performance, Figures of Speech Theatre offers its audiences a complex aesthetic experience. (Courtesy of Figures of Speech Theatre.)

(and vice versa). For example, scenery and costumes routinely use techniques of painting and sculpture, and within plays there are so often songs and dances that we even have the expressions *theatre music* and *theatre dance.* Works like *Porgy and Bess* or *Sweeney Todd* so completely merge opera with musical theatre that they are performed by both theatre companies and opera companies, and such songs as "The Impossible Dream" become famous simply as songs, having lost all association with the play in which they first appear. Sometimes, too, the same story rests at the center of several different arts. For example, *Romeo and Juliet* has been staged as a play, a ballet, an opera, several films, and *West Side Story,* a Broadway musical. In each case, the artists made quite different choices, selecting from Shakespeare's story those elements that could be best communicated through their own art. For opera, the composer selected those moments best communicated through music; for dance, the choreographer selected the moments best communicated through movement, and so on. Such choices focus the audience's attention in different ways. Shakespeare's play leads us to watch and listen to the actor speak Shakespeare's poetic dialogue, but opera leads us to listen to the music, perhaps barely following the story, and dance may ask us to watch movement only, almost ignoring story and character.

FIGURE 1.5   **Theatre and Other Arts.**

Costuming and scenic design in theatre make use of techniques shared with arts like painting and sculpture, and many productions include music to underscore mood. Here, Shakespeare's *Romeo and Juliet*. (Courtesy of Bowling Green State University, directed by F. Scott Regan, designed by Bradford Clark.)

Each art, by selecting and focusing the audience's attention, can make a completely different point through the very process of selection and focus. To take a single example, when *The Singular Life of Albert Nobbs* was changed from a short story to a play, the basic (true) story and characters remained the same: For much of her life, a young woman disguised herself as a man, Albert Nobbs, in order to get a job, make money, and be independent—at a time when women rarely were able to do any of these things. The story (written by a man) treated the tale as an extraordinary example of the human imagination and resilience, a tale of one person's bizarre life. The play (written by a woman) added a male narrator, rearranged a very few scenes, and caused the visual elements in the play to comment on the story itself so that the play became a feminist exploration of women's condition within a patriarchal culture.

To sum up, theatre resembles other arts in being artificial and self-aware and in intending to evoke an aesthetic response rather than to produce an immediately useful item. It differs from other arts in its relation to time and space, its principles of organization, its anticipated audience, and its mode of presentation, and it has a quite complicated relationship with many other arts.

Theatre as Performing Art

From what we have understood about theatre as a particular kind of performance and a special kind of art, we can now say more about the major characteristics of theatre.

- Theatre uses a special kind of performer—an actor.

  An actor is a performer who impersonates, that is, a performer who uses the pronoun "I" and means somebody other than him- or herself. Thus, actors differ from streetfighters, priests, and football players, who neither intend to perform nor pretend to be someone other than themselves. Actors differ even from jugglers and music-video stars; although these people intend to perform, they do not say "I" and mean someone other than themselves.

- In theatre, live actors perform in the presence of a live audience

  A *live* actor in the sense used here is not the opposite of a dead actor but is rather *an actor who is in the physical presence of the audience.* Thus, theatre actors differ not only from other kinds of performers but also from other kinds of actors. *Theatre* actors differ from actors in film or television, for example, because in those media the picture or image of the actor (rather than the actual actor) is offered to the audience.

  Theatre actors must *both impersonate and be physically present,* for it is these two traits—impersonation and presence—that separate them from various other performers, on the one hand, and from actors in other media, on the other.

- Because in theatre actors and audiences share the space and time, theatre is both immediate and ephemeral; that is, it has a strong sense of NOW, and it cannot be repeated exactly.

- Theatre depends on action (which for now we can think of as stories and characters) to organize and bind the theatrical event.

  We can think of stories as worlds created for artistic purposes, worlds that resemble (but are distinct from) the actual world in which we live, *virtual worlds,* an expression that recalls the invented worlds of the computer's virtual reality. Part of the reason that theatre's virtual worlds resemble our own real world so convincingly is that these virtual worlds are inhabited by *characters.* Characters might be thought of as virtual people, because characters are artistic creations intended to resemble people. Well-created characters are often so compelling, so lifelike, that we can feel as if we know them personally. We may even begin to talk of them *as if* they were real people. But characters are not real people; they are created by a playwright for the play, just as the virtual world is created.

- Theatre's virtual world is more intense and concentrated than the world in which we live.

  Because everything on stage has been selected and placed there by someone for a purpose, everything on stage is important—it has meaning for an audience. Thus, everything on stage gains a significance that it may lack in real life. For example, it is not unusual for theatre audiences to be captivated by an on-stage scene when an actor cooks a meal or uses a washing machine. Obviously, cooking or using a washing machine is not very interesting in real life, but, on stage, these simple actions can provoke excitement because theatre transforms them from ordinary to meaningful activities.

The real art of theatre lies, then, not in copying life, but in presenting heightened visions of life within the special conditions of artistic performance: actors, action, audience, flowing time, and real space.

- The theatre uses a real performance space, but usually with artificial (that is, made-for-the-purpose) settings.

  Theatre uses a defined performance space that is physically in the presence of the audience and limited by existing architecture. It can give us representations, replicas, of actual places (e.g., outer space), but it can give them only on a scale appropriate to its own scale and to the actors working in or in front of the scene. Film, on the other hand, can take us anywhere and show us images of actual places, even on a vast scale (the Grand Canyon, outer space). Because film shows *images* of places rather than real places, it can range far in its presentation of objects and spaces.

  Many kinds of activities easily shown on film (horse races, car crashes) are difficult or impossible to show on stage. Film and television can show not only races and crashes, they can also show selective close-ups that direct our attention and heighten our enjoyment of the events: speeding hooves, snorting nostrils, exploding gas tanks, collapsing fenders. Theatre has no close-up, no medium shot.

  Because of the nature of its space, when theatre tries to stage a large event like a horse race (as it did in the late nineteenth century), it has to compromise. By putting horses on treadmills (on which they could run while staying in place) and placing a painted cloth moving on rollers behind them, stage designers made horses seem to race. But common sense told the audience that there had to be treadmills and moving scenery.

  Nonetheless, theatre audiences love such scenes, even though they know they are seeing an obvious trick; they seem to appreciate the skill required to make the illusion. Indeed, it is one of theatre's paradoxes that the very restrictions of theatre's real space seem to increase the audience's enjoyment of difficult scenes produced there.

- Theatre proceeds at its own pace through time.

  We cannot play a performance over, nor can we play it backward, nor can we fast-forward it to see how it will come out. We cannot put a theatrical performance aside for a while and pick it up later. If we don't like a performance, we cannot turn a dial and get another station or hit a button and change channels. If we don't understand a moment in the theatre, we cannot stop and go back to it, hoping to grasp its significance the second or third time through. In other words, as members of a theatre audience we do not control the way the theatrical performance unfolds as we can control the pace at which we watch a videotape or read a poem or novel. For better or worse, the theatre performance proceeds at its own pace and must be followed at that pace.

FIGURE 1.6 **Theatre's Heightened Visions of Life.**
Although theatre resembles life, it is more intense, more concentrated, more purposeful. Part of the actor's challenge is to offer strong emotions believably. Shown here, scenes of anger and joy in a production of *Fences,* at Hampton University.

■ By now it should be clear that theatre is not a thing (an object) but a process, a system of relationships—a system of constantly altering relationships—among actor, action, audience, time, and space.

Changing even one of these relationships changes the whole. We might be tempted to think that a play in the theatre and a play on film are separated only by rather mechanical differences. But a filmed play is not just theatre recorded on strips of acetate. Obviously such a mechanical difference is important, but this change in mode of presentation—from live actor in front of live audiences to a se-

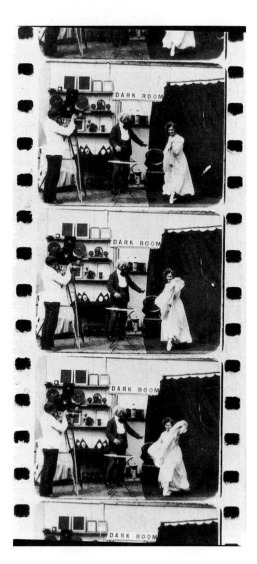

FIGURE 1.7   Film.

Film, like theatre, often uses actors and scripts; unlike theatre, it gives its audiences projected images, not actual people, and film, unlike theatre, can be shown repeatedly without change. (The Animated Picture Studio, 1903, from the collection of Kemp R. Niver and J. P. Niver in the Motion Picture, Broadcasting and Recorded Sound Division of the Library of Congress.)

ries of moving images of actors on acetate—causes other major shifts. Making plays on film depends on camera work, editing, and juxtaposing images, things impossible in the theatre. As a result, the very structure of a film—the way the action moves forward—is vastly different from that of a play; a film gives its information differently and so communicates with audiences differently.

■ Theatre is lifelike, but it is not life.

Because theatre is an art, it is artificial—made by artists. Theatre's artificiality is sometimes more difficult to see than the artificiality of other arts, however, because theatre is also a performance. Theatre uses real human beings pretending to be other human beings engaged in actions that look very much like those we see in life. So convincing is it that sometimes people have confused it with real life. There are many apparently true stories about people attending their first play who have rushed on stage to save a character who is being threatened, like the man who tried to save Desdemona from Othello.

Theatre in fact sometimes seems so lifelike that it has often been used as a metaphor for life. The most famous example of the metaphor is probably Shakespeare's "All the world's a stage/and all the men and women merely players," but there are others, such as "This world is a comedy to those that think, a tragedy to those that feel." There is even the expression *theatre mundi*—theatre of the world—used throughout the Middle Ages by scholars and poets who saw the strong resemblance between theatre and life.

We need to remember, however, that a metaphor is a special kind of comparison, one that implies, but does not use, the words *like* or *as.* We know that the real sense of these quotations is that the world is *like* a comedy or *like* a tragedy. And clearly the metaphor comparing life and theatre is apt. Life and theatre move forward through time. Just as life has a past, a present, and a future, plays have a beginning, middle, and end, and in plays, as in life, these stages are defined through time. Life and theatre exist in space; that is, men and women in life take up space and move through space, like actors on a stage. Life and theatre have men and women doing and saying things: While some people act and speak, others listen and watch. Those who act and speak in life are *like* actors in the theatre, while those who listen and watch in life are *like* audiences in the

Thinking About **Theatre**

"All the world's a stage,
And all the men and women merely players:
They have their exits and their entrances;
And one man in his time plays many parts, . . ."

—William Shakespeare, *As You Like It,* II, vii.

Make a list of the many "roles" that a typical college student "plays" in life. What "roles" will likely be added and which dropped?

theatre. And the lives of real people that we know often don't seem very different from the actions or stories that we see when we go to a play.

Despite such similarities, however, life and theatre are different in many ways, only a few of which need be suggested. Most lives last for years; most theatre lasts a few hours. Life often seems diffuse, confused, and inexplicable; theatre appears concentrated, orderly, and meaningful. Life may be dangerous, but theatre is safe in a special way. Although theatre may bring us up close to a human activity (like a murder) that is terrifyingly *like* life in its immediacy, we as audience are separated from it and so can watch it in relative safety, experience it without physical danger.

Taking Stock

Obviously, there is no simple definition of theatre, just as there is no simple definition of performance or of art or of life. Still, there's no reason to despair. The only purpose of defining a word is to call to mind those recurring clusters of traits to which it seems to refer—traits that set it apart from other, often closely related things, activities, or ideas. The point of trying to define *theatre*—or anything else—is not to put it in a box, to confine it and deaden it. The point, rather, is to understand it better so as to appreciate its power better.

Links to More About Theatre

 Luigi Pirandello, *Six Characters in Search of an Author.* Appearance and reality, the theatre and life.

 Suzanne Langer, *Feeling and Form,* 1953. Aesthetics for a linear world.

Richard Schechner, *Performance Theory,* 1988. For the postmodern world.

Victor Turner, *From Ritual to Theatre: The Human Seriousness of Play,* 1982.

 <www.vl-theatre.com/list14.shtml> A list of links.

KEY TERMS

Check your understanding against this list. Brief definitions are in the Glossary; page references there will direct you to appropriate pages. (Persons are page-referenced in the Index.)

aesthetic response	mediated performance
art	performance
criticism	performing art
ephemeral art	theory
impersonation	

Theatre: Cultural Expression, Business, and the Role of Audience

When you have completed this chapter, you should be able to

- Describe ways in which theatre audiences are social

- Explain how the size and arrangement of audiences affect their ability to be social units

- Explain how permission and self-image promote the social quality of audiences

- Explain how theatre audiences are interactive

- Explain why theatre audiences can serve as an index to culture

- Describe how business and theatre interact

- Explain the fundamental tension between theatre as art and theatre as business

- Explain what is meant by *asymmetric transnationalism*

- Describe funding patterns in today's theatre in the United States

Theatre is not only a performance and an art, it is also an expression of the time and place that produce it, an expression of its *culture*. Often, too, theatre is a business, and, in our own time, a very big business.

We have seen that theatre through its plays offers human actions that depend on characters (artificial human beings) who live in virtual worlds. These characters experience conflicts, make decisions, and succumb to powerful emotions in their world, while audiences watch and react. Theatre presents such plays, such characters in action, by using human actors in front of live audiences, and the audiences watch and react to the performance as well as to the play. Said another way, theatre provides a connection both between the audience and the play and between the audience and the performers. In these two connections, theatre binds the world on stage to the world of the audience. This powerful link between stage and audience, virtual world and real world, makes theatre a window through which can be glimpsed the world outside the theatre—the culture of the time. Theatre's audience is a key to opening this window.

But theatre binds the stage world to the real world in yet another important way. Through much of its history, theatre audiences have enabled performances by being willing to pay for the pleasure of attending them. By buying tickets, audiences have footed the bills for theatre, providing the means to pay actors, build scenery and

FIGURE 2.1 **Theatre's Audiences.**

Theatre connects the audience both to the play and to the performers. To enhance the connection, some productions devise ways of bringing performers into the audience, as do these ramps for the production of *The London Merchantperson*, a feminist rendering of George Lillo's *The London Merchant*. Directed by Catherine Schuler. (Courtesy of the University of Maryland.)

costumes, and rent and maintain performance spaces. Audiences are thus the financial engine that drives the performance. Theatre audiences are again a key, this time a key to understanding theatre as a business.

As keys to culture and engines of finance, audiences are central to understanding both how theatre works as an expression of its culture and how it works as a business. For this reason, we begin by discussing this important part of every theatrical performance, its audience.

The Nature of Theatre Audiences

Theatre Audiences Are Social

Most people enjoy the companionship of others—they are social beings who enjoy feeling themselves to be members of a group. Every good theatre audience is a group in which the response of each audience member depends both on the performance and on the responses of other members of the group. If a theatre audience fails to coalesce as a group, the performance itself will be unsuccessful. A sense of groupness in the audience, then, is crucial to the enjoyment of theatre. Although there are no hard-and-fast rules about how to build an audience's sense of itself as a group, several factors are at work.

Size and Arrangement

Both size and seating arrangement are important. One person in a theatre audience is not enough. To enhance a performance, a theatregoer's response needs to be amplified, joined by the responses of others. Forty thousand people won't work in a theatre either, because so many people can't relate intimately with the stage. Although there's no magic number for a theatre audience, some numbers are clearly too small and others are too large. Probably the number is about right if the audience fits well within the space, and each person can easily hear and see the performance. The best audience space for a theatre is, therefore, one small enough to define an audience (help it see itself as part of a group) but not so small as to confine it (make it physically uncomfortable). A hundred people in a very large theatre will feel uncomfortable, but the same number in a small space will happily enjoy the play. Also, the arrangement of seats interacts with the number of spectators and the size of space to affect the audience's sense of itself as a social unit. A person sitting in the midst of other people feels more comfortable than those sitting at the end of a row; a person sitting in the middle of an otherwise empty section lessens membership in the group.

Permission

There is an unspoken agreement in theatre between actors and audiences that what the actors embody on stage is not real life and that it is permissible to respond to it in unusual ways (laughing out loud at a character who is crying, for example, or applauding when a sympathetic character shoots one who threatens). This agreement gives audiences permission to respond in safety to whatever transpires on the stage; that is, no audience member will be harmed by on-stage threats or sanctioned for responding to on-stage actions. This shared permission contributes to shaping the audience into a social unit. Permission is thus a social phenomenon that bolsters theatregoing as a social experience.

Self-Image

Each theatre audience develops a self-image, which also enhances the audience's sense of itself as a group. An audience's self-image influences its behavior, including its dress. Part of the self-image comes from society's expectations. Members of a theatre audience do not wear pajamas, although they watch television in them comfortably. Audience members do not carry beer and hot dogs into the theatre, although they carry both to a baseball game. Part of the self-image comes from specific expectations set up by the particular theatre or production, often as a way to enhance the enjoyment of a performance. For a special celebration in the theatre or a special play, for example, the theatre might encourage audience members to dress formally, but for another kind of play at a different theatre, audience members might be encouraged to wear sportswear or even jeans. These two audiences would likely expect different experiences from their night out at the theatre, and they will behave accordingly.

Theatre people try to assure that audiences form a social unit because it is so important to the success of a performance. Only when theatre audiences work as social units, groups, rather than merely collections of individuals can theatre artists shape the meaning of plays and performances by providing cues that are salient for the group. Performances are not successful if people attending them behave as individuals—or worse, a mob—because, under such circumstances, theatre artists have lost control of the performance. Unable to shape the responses of the whole, artists are unable to guide the play's meanings and significance. This link is important not only to theatre artists; it is also important to theatre students and scholars, for it allows us to make tentative judgments about the beliefs and values of the audience.

Theatre Audiences Are Interactive

Audiences are not just social units; they are *interactive* social units, with individual audience members interacting both with the performers on stage and with one another. Obviously, no one can say for certain precisely how an audience will respond during a play or how any individual in an audience will respond at a given moment. Performances differ, audiences differ, and individuals in audiences differ.

When performances are successful, however, most members of the audience behave similarly much of the time. That an audience is a group rather than a collection of individuals or a mob suggests that audience members will respond to many of the same things in roughly the same ways—and indeed they do.

To show approval, audiences usually *applaud* (clap their hands). At the end of a play, actors *take a bow* for as long as the applause continues (although to *milk the audience*—

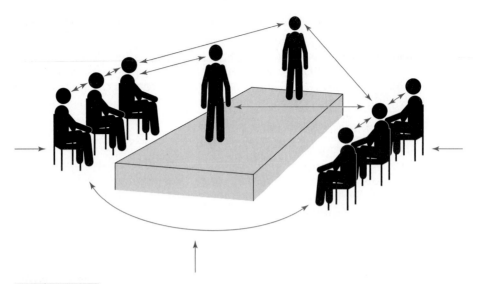

FIGURE 2.2   Theatre's Interactive Nature.

Audience members affect each other; actors affect and are affected by them; all relate to the outer society of which they are a part.

try to make the audience extend its applause—is considered bad form). In past times, audiences might clap so long that actors gave an *encore* (repeated a piece), just as opera singers do today. To show exceptional approval, audiences may stand and applaud (give a *standing ovation*). When something is funny, audiences usually laugh, anything from a belly laugh to a snicker. (Sometimes audiences will laugh because they're uncomfortable—nervous laughter. Actors dread hearing this kind of laughter because it shows the performance is not working right.) When something is sad, audiences may cry, although today's theatre audiences do not shed tears as easily as they once did— or as easily as they now laugh. Although we associate applause, laughter, and tears with success, silence is often a sign of a very successful performance. "You could hear a pin drop." Especially at the end of a well-performed serious play, silence is often the audience's response, as if applause were too frivolous for the moment.

To show disapproval, audiences may simply withhold the usual responses of approval. More likely, though, they will become noisy. Coughing, shuffling feet, whispering, rattling programs are all signs of unease or boredom; each person may think he or she is being quiet, but many people moving at once, however unconsciously, can become quite loud—and horribly revealing. More aggressive signs of disapproval come when members of the audience boo or leave the theatre. (In some ages, audiences were even more aggressive—yelling at the actors and even throwing things on stage.)

An audience's disapproval most often signals a bad performance (about which we say more in Part II of this book), but it may signal instead an audience that fails to en-

FIGURE 2.3 Audience Response.

Theatre, because of its immediacy, can have powerful effects on audiences. Scenes like this one from *Suburban Motel* may provoke disapproval or discomfort in some audiences. (The Ulysses Theatre Company, Chicago. Zeljko Djukic, director; Natasa Djukic, designer; Jason Holmes, photographer.)

ter into the virtual world prepared by the playwright and the actors. Occasionally such an audience just doesn't understand theatre well enough to enjoy it. (Such an audience will improve with experience.) More often, though, an audience refuses to enter the virtual world because they are alienated from this particular performance. Sometimes they are encountering a performance that they did not expect from reading the play's title or the reviews of the performance. More likely, members of the audience are embarrassed, shocked, or angered to find a play whose political, religious, or ethical views they deplore. They may be reacting to particular scenes whose language, violence, or nudity they find shocking.

The interactivity of audiences is important as a way of increasing the enjoyment of theatre. The responses of audiences allow performers to adjust their performances to increase appropriate responses and decrease unwanted ones. The responses are important to students and scholars of theatre, too, for when we see how an audience responds, we gain valuable clues about how the audience views a play and a performance. These clues, in turn, allow us to make tentative judgments about the people seated in the theatre and the culture of which they are a part.

Theatre as Cultural Expression: The Role of the Audience

The idea of culture is a very complex one. For our purposes, *culture* is that set of beliefs, values, and material goods that a group shares. For example, early in the twentieth century, there was a rather clear division between *high culture* (the behavior and preferences among people of enlightenment and good taste, those trained in intellectual and aesthetic pleasures) and *low culture* (the behavior and preferences among uneducated and "unrefined" members of society, those who lacked acquaintance with the fine arts and the humanities). This once potent division has all but disappeared, although ghosts of it can still be seen in the split between those who regularly attend opera and those who prefer television. Various pundits have dubbed the culture of the twenty-first century in the United States a consumer culture (one that values the acquisition of goods), a popular culture (one that prefers *People Magazine,* television, rock, and football), a communication culture (one saturated with the means for sharing ideas), and a mass culture (one produced by the media and intended for the greatest number of people). The point is that there are always several layers of culture—cultures within cultures. Still, it is possible to distinguish in a general way American culture from, say, Afghan culture or Ugandan culture. An earlier writer has argued that "language is culture." As we use the word *culture,* then, we are trying to suggest a complex web of traits that compete, merge, and exist alongside one another and that comprise a recognizable cluster—a *gestalt* or world view.

We are now ready to tie an audience's major traits to its role as a conveyor of information about culture. That theatre audiences are groups is important because it allows us to infer that the behavior of the group is the behavior of most of its members. Because their behaviors comprise their self-image, the behaviors can offer clues about the permission that exists between them and the performers. That theatre audiences are interactive allows us to infer that the behaviors of individual audience members are related, that they are generally acceptable to the group, and that they influence the performance in important ways. By identifying an audience's responses, we gain insights into their reactions to the performance, whether they were engaged or bored and, if engaged, whether they approved or disapproved of what they saw. When we see the behaviors of the particular audience, we can begin to draw conclusions about the culture from which this audience came, because theatre audiences are necessarily drawn from the larger society of which they are a part.

An example may make the relevance of this idea clearer. The strong connection between stage and audience has implications for the practice of theatre. In preparing their art, theatre artists will make decisions to assure the groupness of audiences and to enhance their enjoyment; that is, they will take their probable audience into immediate account as they plan their art. In deciding what play to produce, producers will consider the preferences of the likely audience; in deciding where to produce it, they will match the size of the likely audience with the configuration of available spaces. Playwrights must imagine what real audiences will come to the theatre to see and then write plays that will bring audiences into the theatre and affect them after they get there. Designers and directors must figure out ways to guide the responses of audiences through visual cues, so that the play "means" for audiences what they want it to "mean," that is, they must provide visual clues that give the play appropriate cultural resonances. Actors must imagine how audiences will respond to moments of performance and then perform in ways that prompt appropriate responses, based in part on shared cultural understandings of voice and movement. Actors, after all, want to hear applause, not booing or nervous laughter.

From the outset, then, theatre artists work to ensure that the performance and the audience in the theatre share cultural values that will make the audience want to enter the virtual world prepared for it. Through the choices they make—the plays they produce, the spaces they select, their scenery, costumes, and performances—theatre artists inevitably reveal how they envision their likely audience. And this likely audience is, of course, a microcosm of a larger culture. By studying both the choices of theatre artists and the responses of the audience, we can glimpse something about the world existing outside theatre—the culture. Through the choices made by the theatre artists, we can begin to infer what they think their audiences—and therefore the larger culture—seem to want or need. It is in this way—and because of these linkages—that theatre, probably more than any other art, *expresses and partakes of* the culture of which it is a part. For such reasons, theatre has been called, metaphorically, "a mirror of life."

FIGURE 2.4 **Theatre, Audience, and Culture.**
Here, visual cues suggest a production aimed at children and an audience that can recognize and gain meaning from signals like playing cards and dice. *Alice in Wonderland.* (Directed by Sharon Ammen, at Saint Mary-of-the-Woods College.)

But we must be cautious in any conclusions that we draw, for several reasons.

First, theatre is at the center of some cultures but quite peripheral to others. Cultures in which theatre was central include those of Greece in the fifth century B.C.E. and of western Europe in the Middle Ages. Here theatre performances were special events, parts of major civic and religious festivals that were held only occasionally. At these times the whole community was involved, and most citizens attended and supported the festivals, including the theatrical performances that were embedded in them. Today, by contrast, most people don't attend theatre regularly. Many can't afford it, some don't have access to it, a few don't like it. Were we to study theatre in an attempt to understand the cultures of fifth-century B.C.E. Greece or western Europe during the Middle Ages, we could be fairly confident that the audience in the theatre fairly represented most other citizens living in that same time and place. Studying theatre to grasp traits of our own culture, however, would require us to remember that theatre now appeals to only a limited group, and so its audience may represent only a small subset of today's larger culture. Still, by the very act of asking the question, "Who goes to the theatre and why?" we can glean something about a culture's values and interests.

Second, although theatre is "a mirror of life," we must remember that a mirror can be a fun-house mirror as well as a bathroom mirror. A bathroom mirror shows a person his or her physical appearance, and some theatres do seem to show life more or less as it is lived at a particular time and place. A fun-house mirror, however, stretches, compresses, and otherwise distorts the image; and some theatres show the audience just such a distorted image of itself, highlighting its horrors or poking fun at its foibles—interpreting and critiquing rather than merely presenting the culture. The point is that theatre can offer important insights into people and cultures, so long as inferences are drawn carefully, cautiously, and tentatively.

How theatre can serve as a guide to changes in culture can be suggested by sketching how theatre audiences themselves change over time. Theatre audiences today tend to be from the mainstream of middle- and upper-middle-class society: most are under thirty-five, affluent, gender-mixed, and relatively new to theatre. Patterns of class, age, and gender were not always as they are now, however. In the late 1600s, aristocrats dominated theatre audiences, and they insisted on plays that displayed "propriety" and so reflected an idealized view of upper-class behavior. Audience members dressed elegantly, in part because they went to the theatre as much to be seen as to watch the performance; they represented high culture. During the early 1800s, in contrast, working-class audiences attended theatres in great numbers, and the young men among them were notorious for their raucous behavior. They liked melodramas and plays filled with spectacular special effects. They interrupted plays, drowning out bad performances with stomping and boos and cheering good ones, often until the play came to a standstill. Their theatre was decidedly low culture. By the 1900s, working men were replaced by families whose behaviors were altogether more subdued and who preferred plays that represented middle-class, urban domestic life; theirs was a culture dubbed middle-brow.

Changes in audiences, theatres, and cultures are connected. When performances are free or inexpensive, all classes may attend, a circumstance that influences the choice of play, for example. When a single ticket costs several hundred dollars (as they occasionally do in today's theatres), affluent patrons will probably be overrepresented in audi-

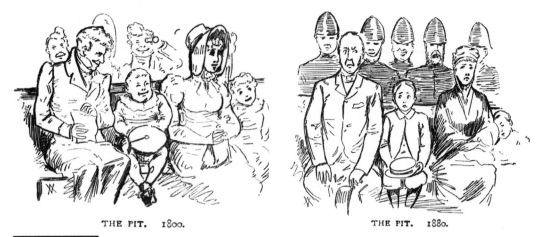

THE PIT. 1800.   THE PIT. 1880.

FIGURE 2.5 **Theatre, Audience, and Culture.**
Audiences shift over time with shifts in culture. As shown here, a theatre audience of the early nineteenth century both dressed and behaved differently from an audience of the late nineteenth century.

ences, again influencing the choice of plays for production. When men and women are equally free in a culture, both can be expected in theatre in roughly equal numbers, but in cultures where women are thought to need protection (in the 1800s in the United States, for example), gender differences within audiences may be striking. Race and ethnic heritage may also figure importantly, both because all cultures do not prize theatres equally and because some people may be segregated or denied access to theatres based on race or ethnicity. Then, too, theatre audiences expect different things from theatre, often related to their general level of education. Audiences are therefore to a degree self-selected; that is, some people want to see musicals; others, situation comedies; still others, plays that are politically challenging or sexually free. All such factors, and more, must be weighed before generalizing about the relationship between a theatre's audience and its culture.

In sum, because theatre audiences are interactive social units, theatre artists shape performances in ways calculated to achieve certain responses from them. For the same reason, we can use theatre as one probe into the culture of a particular time and place.

Links to More About Theatre

<library.websteruniv.edu> The Eden-Webster Library on the Internet. Click on "Net resources by subject," then "theater and costume," then "comprehensive lists of sites" for many areas of theatre.

Thinking About **Theatre Audiences** ────────

In 1964, Marshall McLuhan, a scholar of media, explained that *"Hot media . . . are low in partici-pation, and cool media are high in participation or completion by the audience."* Assume that

McLuhan is correct. Prepare a computer graphic (or a sketch) that shows where dance, film, opera, radio, television, and theatre fall along a continuum between hot and cool media.

Theatre as Business: The Role of the Audience

Just as audiences are important to theatre as a form of cultural expression, audiences are also important to theatre as a business. In a commercial theatre, the audience pays the bill. For much of theatre's early history theatre was not a business in the usual sense of the word; that is, it was not a commercial enterprise that people undertook to make a living. Rather, theatre was a communal celebration in which volunteers did most of the work and bills were paid by the community, church, or wealthy citizens as their religious and civic duty.

Since the Renaissance (c. 1500s), however, most theatres in the Western world have been a business—subsidy has given way to pay-as-you-go, and audiences have pro-vided the money that pays the bills. Some people fear that a commercial theatre places too much power in the hands of audiences, those who pay the bills. But someone has to pay, and it has yet to be demonstrated that the effects of commercialism on theatre are worse than the effects of patronage, when the king or church subsidized performances by paying the bills. Other people argue that business in theatre is a false force, one that should be ignored. But ignoring it is simply not possible, and probably it should not be ignored. After all, actors and playwrights have a right to make a living in the same way as bankers and secretaries, and keeping audiences coming to theatre and enjoying it is surely as important as other decisions made surrounding production.

The role of audience in the business of theatre sets up tensions almost at once with its role in the performing art of theatre. As we have seen, for theatrical performance to work, a theatre audience must have a sense of itself as a social group. But a major force in theatre tugs against this idea of a coherent group, and that force is money. The eco-nomics of theatre demands that the audience be big enough to pay for the scenery and costumes, to pay the actors and all the support personnel, the rent on the building, the author's royalties, the maintenance of the space, and on and on. A desire for profit—income over and above expenses—demands that audiences be bigger still: bigger au-dience, more profit. Thus, although the art of the theatre may suggest that the best-sized audience for a particular play in a particular space is two hundred, the busi-ness of the theatre may demand an audience of three thousand, a size that will almost certainly degrade the audience as a social unit. Some compromise between theatre as art and theatre as business is almost inevitable.

FIGURE 2.6   **Theatre and Money.**
Many European countries subsidize theatres, but in the United States, theatre has always
been a for-profit activity, except during the Great Depression of the 1930s, when the federal government established the Federal Theatre Project (FTP). FTP productions typically
used large casts (to relieve unemployment among actors) and relied on scenery and
costumes that substituted imagination for dollars. Here, an FTP production of George
Bernard Shaw's *Androcles and the Lion* in Los Angeles. (Courtesy of the National Archives
of the United States.)

Such a compromise, however, must be a careful one. In a commercial theatre,
some minimum number of customers is needed to pay the bills, or theatre will cease
to exist. As we have seen, however, too many people in the theatre may not form a social unit. So, although the needs of the business of theatre call for as many people as
possible to attend a performance, the needs of the performing art of theatre limit that
number to as many people as can develop a sense of themselves as an interactive
group.

The Business of Theatre

"The business of America is business." These words of Calvin Coolidge help explain why
patterns seen in business appear also in the arts.

The values of business now suffuse almost every part of the culture, and the language of business dominates talk about wholly unrelated fields. It is not uncommon to hear students described as consumers at a university, and the graduates described as the university's products. We routinely speak of "spending" or "saving" or even "banking" time. We ask governments and doctors to be more efficient, and we expect agents for athletes to negotiate mega-salaries and advertising contracts. The talk and decisions around theatres now, not surprisingly, are as much about profit, loss, bottom line, and labor relations as about the meaning of plays and the aesthetics of production.

Similarly, business executives now lead all sorts of organizations, including those not usually considered businesses. Such people bring with them the outlook and skills of corporations, and they often resemble one another far more than the people whom they lead. Their skills in policy-making and management often allow them to transfer from one sort of enterprise to another: first CEO of a corporation, then governor of a state, and later president of a university or health-maintenance organization. University presidents are now seldom drawn from the world of scholarship, for example, and managers of hospitals may or may not have training in medicine. Just so, Broadway theatres are run by a loosely tied group of executives drawn mostly from business and real estate, many of whom have little experience in theatre.

Businesses now take considerable interest in the arts for their possible commercial benefit. They, or the foundations growing out of them, give major support to the visual, musical, and performing arts. Texaco underwrites weekly radio broadcasts of the Metropolitan Opera, for example, and The Ford Foundation funds a program to support emerging playwrights. Businesses routinely support theatres in cities around the country, buying blocks of tickets and advertisements in the programs, or awarding grants for specific projects, or even sponsoring selected productions. Not only are such ventures believed to be excellent advertisement for products, they are also thought to be good ways of demonstrating that businesses are good corporate citizens, contributing members of their community. As a bonus, having a professional symphony, ballet, and theatre company in a city, businesses have come to believe, makes it easier to recruit managers and executives to work in such cities.

The business economy is now a global, or transnational, one. Just so, theatres around the world are producing many of the same plays. *Waiting for Godot*, a play written in French by an Irishman, is now produced in the United States and in Korea, for example, and *A Doll's House*, written by a Norwegian, finds production in India. Even the same productions can be seen in more than one country, when language is not an insurmountable barrier. *Les Miserables*, a musical based on a novel by a Frenchman, was conceived in Paris and opened in London before transferring to New York for a long run.

But the transnationalism practiced by both business and art is asymmetric. Western art and Western businesses tend to dominate, a culmination of trends begun about a hundred and fifty years ago and solidified by the emergence of the United States as the world's only great power. For this reason, seeing productions of Shakespeare in Japan is more likely than finding performances of Japanese dramas in England, and seeing plays by Molière in Africa is more common than encountering productions of francophone African plays in France.

FIGURE 2.7 **Global Theatre.**
Samuel Beckett's *Waiting for Godot,* directed by Young-Woong Lim, Echo Theatre Company, Seoul, Korea. *Neela,* based on Henrik Ibsen's *A Doll's House* and Ingmar Bergman's adaptation of it, in India, with Swatilekha and Rudraprasad Sengupta. (Photographs courtesy of Seoul Performing Arts Festival and Farley Richmond/Nandika Theatre of Calcutta.)

Changing Patterns in Business and Theatre

Just as audiences changed over time to embody a changing culture, so too has the business of theatre shifted to mirror changes in business practices outside theatre. For example, when businesses outside the theatre were small and often home-based, theatre companies were centered on one or two families who put on plays and shared expenses, income, and work. Such *sharing companies* were among the earliest ways that theatre organized itself to do business.

When cities grew large enough to house a theatre company more or less permanently, several unrelated people formed larger and more complex sharing companies, with the most valuable members of the company owning several shares and the least valuable owning a share or less. Members of such companies tended to specialize, performing only certain kinds of roles or undertaking only certain tasks of production, such as playwriting or costuming. Such companies even hired other people, paying them a salary rather than allowing them to join the company. The theatre company in which Shakespeare worked was of this sort. He owned shares in the company as well as in the building in which the company performed, making him (like the other shareholders) both businessman and theatre artist.

By the late 1800s, business outside of theatre had changed its ways of organizing, and so had theatre. In some countries, such as Germany, theatre had come to be thought of as a cost of government, and so all major German cities subsidized—and continue to subsidize—theatres, allowing tax dollars to join with ticket sales to pay expenses. In several countries, notably France and England, government-supported theatres existed alongside commercial theatres.

The United States set a different pattern. Here, private enterprise mostly ruled. The old sharing system, where theatre artists participated directly in the business of the company, gave way to a system of for-profit corporations headed by entrepreneurs who saw theatre mostly as a way to make money. Business people (as distinct from theatre people) began to invest money, sometimes in a theatre company but more often in a single production, and they expected to recover their investment, with interest, from ticket sales. When, outside the theatre, great monopolies formed in railroads and steel, and the so-called robber barons (such as the Carnegies and the Rockefellers) dominated the economy in the United States, theatres also became monopolies headed by powerful men. In New York and on the road, these *producers* controlled theatre buildings and the productions playing in them. This producer typically located needed investors, planned and produced the show, and paid the theatrical personnel (who then were mere employees). By this time, ticket sales were needed not only to pay the bills but also to make a profit for the investors, who were no longer theatre artists themselves. As ticket sales alone proved unable to equal the rising costs of production, paid advertising and public relations became an important part of theatre's business, just as they had become important tools of other businesses.

When, in the early 1900s, government trust-busting broke up the monopolies outside theatre, forces inside theatre broke the monopolies of the most powerful producers, and so business practices changed yet again. Starting about fifty years ago, severe pressures on the commercial theatre led to cautious experimentation in ways of producing theatre other than as a strictly profit-making enterprise. For the first time, the U.S. government set up an agency that could be a funding stream to the arts: the National Endowment for the Arts (NEA). Individuals and groups in cities, mostly outside New York, began to experiment with organizing theatre as non-profit, rather than for-profit, corporations. Educational institutions transferred theatre study and practice from extra- or co-curricular activities to full-fledged academic units.

Recently, the costs of production have escalated so dramatically that ticket sales and paid advertisements alone no longer provide enough money, and so the sale of film, television, and video rights have become increasingly important sources of funding. Business people and mid-level managers increasingly assumed responsibility for producing theatre, bringing with them the ideas and techniques of business and management. Too, these business people, lacking experience in theatre, transferred much of the artistic power—once belonging to actor-sharers—to directors and designers. At about the same time, the once centralized power of the producer was dispersed among others—the director, the general manager, and other co-investors, many of whom were now major entertainment corporations (like Disney) rather than, as previously, wealthy individuals. At the beginning of the twenty-first century, most countries have some combination of subsidized and unsubsidized, profit and not-for-profit, and professional and amateur theatres.

FIGURE 2.8 **Professional Theatre.**
Musical theatre, the most popular kind of theatre in the United States today, is also often
the most expensive to produce, requiring large casts, many scenes, and an orchestra.
Shown in production here, *Flower Drum Song* at the Mark Taper Forum, Los Angeles.
(Photograph by Craig Schwartz, courtesy of Mark Taper Forum.)

To sum up, since the 1500s, most theatres in the west have been run as businesses,
a focus that places theatre audiences in the crucial role of providing the money needed
for productions. Because the needs of theatre-as-business often conflict with its needs
as art, compromises are necessary. Just as the values of business now pervade Western
cultures, they also permeate theatres' cultures.

KEY TERMS

Check your understanding against this list. Brief definitions are in the Glossary; page references there will direct you to the appropriate pages. (Persons are page-referenced in
the Index.)

applause
culture
encore
high culture
milk an audience

National Endowment for the Arts (NEA)
producer
sharing company
standing ovation
take a bow

How to Read a Play

When you have completed this chapter, you should be able to

■ List and explain Aristotle's six parts of a play

■ Explain the interrelationships among the six parts

■ Describe different kinds of plot

■ Explain "wholeness of action"

■ Distinguish among tragedy, comedy, tragicomedy, melodrama, and farce

Seeing a play and reading a play are different experiences. They require different tools and different approaches. Seeing a play is the only complete theatrical experience. Reading a play sensitively means understanding what it is and how it works.

First, a play is not theatre; that is, reading a play from a book offers a very incomplete experience. Because of the incompleteness of the written text, some theatre artists talk of the playscript as a "notation" for production, others as "a pretext rather than a text." To make an analogy with music: a written play is like musical notes written on a page; the performed play is like the music that comes when a musician turns the notes into music. The incompleteness of the written play makes reading a play different from reading a newspaper or a novel. The newspaper and novel are both complete in themselves; their language fills them out. A play, on the other hand, is only a part—although a very important part—of a different kind of experience.

Second, reading a play means understanding that playwrights create plays by making choices. The playwright, to be successful, must persuade an audience, convince it of the truth of the play. A playwright's goal is not simply to tell a story but to tell it in a certain way, a way that causes the audience to derive some meanings but not others, to experience some kinds of pleasures but not all kinds. To say it another way, the playwright, using only words, must shape characters and actions that allow actors to perform and designers to design so as to produce certain effects in audiences. Playwrights, then, are always shaping, although indirectly, the meanings and pleasures that audiences glean from the play. Both of these traits have implications for how to read a play.

Because the play is intended for performance, its written text leaves large areas blank. The play reader must learn to fill in these blanks through clues embedded in the text (such clues are, in fact, clues to performance). For example, in a novel, many paragraphs may be devoted to describing the place where the novel takes place; in plays, such lengthy descriptions are absent, because the place of the play will be shown visually, through scenery, in the theatre. A play reader must visualize the place from clues.

Because the playwright, through choices, is constantly shaping the perception of the audience, a reader's job is to discover how. That is, a reader must locate the choices made by the playwright and from these choices try to infer what the playwright wanted to do to audiences, using actors. The task is not always easy, because the tendency of any reader is to "believe" the story, to see it as "the way things are." To guard against this tendency, a reader might remember that every play begins as a stack of blank paper and that any story can be told in several different ways, each having quite different results. It is the task of the reader to discover which way the playwright decided to tell the story and what the anticipated results of that decision are.

Reading a play means making the effort—and knowing how to make the effort—to understand the play, both how it will appear in the theatre and what choices the playwright made and why. These ideas are often hard to keep in mind because the written play can be read with pleasure *as if* it were self-sufficient, and it can be so convincing that it is hard to imagine its being any other way. But it is important to remember that the written play is only one part of theatre (a play is not self-sufficient) and that the play results from choices made by a playwright specifically to affect audiences in certain ways.

Reading a play then requires techniques of critical thinking that can be learned. We will examine the process of play reading in three stages: preliminary work, play analysis, and organizing a coherent response.

FIGURE 3.1   **The Mind's Eye: Environment.**
If a stage direction says only, "The Forest of Arden," the reader may start with a mental schematic (*above*) and fill it in as the play supplies details (*left*). An actual stage setting (*right*) may be quite different: *As You Like It* at the University of South Carolina. (Directed by Jim Patterson, SSDC; setting by Dennis C. Maulden; lighting by Ann Courtney; costumes by Rebecca

Preliminary Work

Before beginning to read the play, some preliminary work will more than repay the time. The idea here is to get ready to enter a new world: what does the world look like? who are the "people" living in this world?

Title

Reading begins at the beginning—with the title, the first piece of information. The author believed that it said something important about the play; therefore, it is a clue to at least one important part of the play. Titles like *Richard II* and *Cats* are very straightforward; on the other hand, titles like *Half Off* and *Top Girls* are mysterious until well into the play.

Cast of Characters

This list gives vital information on the size and traits of the cast—their names, ages, sexes, and relationships. Introductions are as important in reading a play as they are in entering a room at a party.

Opening Stage Directions

The description of the play's setting (the place where the play takes place) is usually given here as are descriptions of the play's opening moments. In plays that have been produced, these stage directions often reflect the actual Broadway or London production; in other plays, they give the playwright's vision. Reading them, we may be able to visualize (and hear) the play's opening.

Time for Questions

The reader should think about the information so far and begin to ask questions. What kind of theatre is being used? What is the historical period of the play? What did buildings, furniture, clothing look like in this period? What is the opening mood—joyful or somber, tense or relaxed? How do characters get on and off the stage? Is the setting indoors or outdoors? Are there doors, and if so, where? Where do the characters enter from? And other like questions.

First Reading

Then, with the beginning as strongly visualized as possible, the reader begins to read the play, underlining and making notes on:

- What happens in the play?

- Who makes things happen and who tries to stop things from happening; also, what is the relative importance of the characters?

- What key words, images, and ideas run through the play (including, what is the relevance of the title)?

FIGURE 3.2 The Mind's Eye: Interiors.

"A living room," the stage direction may say, or a character may describe a room. The reader must build it mentally from the necessities of staging as he or she reads: doors that work; chairs for two people or five or seventeen; a window an actor can lean out of or jump through or comically be unable to reach. Possibilities here include a real room (*right*), a realistic stage setting of 1893 (*below*), a setting of fabric and soft sculpture for *The Importance of Being Earnest* at Bowling Green State University (*above left*), and an almost abstract setting by Emil Pirchan (*above right*).

Ending

It is important to pause briefly over the ending to determine what the system of rewards and punishments was for the play. Were the rewards serious or playful? Who ended the play better or worse off than they began it?

After the first reading, the reader is familiar with the play and has a sense of what it is about and of what happens in it, as well as of who its characters are. The next stage aims at an orderly and informed analysis of the play. Such an analysis may finally result in a judgment about the play.

Play Analysis Using the Parts of the Play

Plays can be analyzed for many different sorts of information. A historian, for example, may read a play in order to discover something about the period in which it was written; a linguist may read it in order to study ways in which language is used or ways in which the use of language has changed over time. Many critical methods are available to help with an analysis of plays, and several will be discussed in the later chapter on criticism.

For now, however, let us agree that a theatre person most often reads a play for information about how it will appear in the theatre. One useful method of extracting this sort of information was first offered by the Greek Aristotle, whose ideas are adapted here for modern use.

Aristotle identified the following six parts of a play:

1. Plot

2. Character

3. Idea

4. Language

5. Music

6. Spectacle

Two important points need to be made here. One, the order of the parts is important because it suggests the precise nature of the relationship among them. Two, the six parts should not be thought of as boxes into which sections of the play are placed; rather, they are parts of a system, a network of interrelationships so connected that a change in any one can have important effects on all others. These relationships are exceedingly complex, but, in brief, reading down the list gives a sense of control (the nature of the plot controls the kinds of characters that must appear in it; the kinds of characters control the kinds of ideas possible in the play, etc.). Reading up the list suggests source (music, in the sense of sounds, is the material out of which language is made; ideas are the materials out of which characters are made, etc.).

Although very old, this breakdown is still useful. We can go through almost any play and show how every aspect of the play—every speech, movement, event—relates to these six parts.

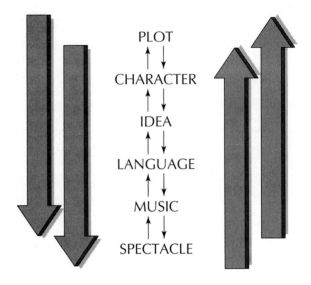

FIGURE 3.3   **Parts of a Play.**
The six parts of a play comprise a system; a change in any one changes all the others. As the arrows show, the relationships are reciprocal: e.g., plot determines the kind of character needed; character is the stuff out of which plot is made.

PLOT

CHARACTER

IDEA

LANGUAGE

MUSIC

SPECTACLE

Plot

Plot is the ordering of the incidents in a play. This means that plot is not only *what* happens in the play; it is also the *order* in which things are made to happen and the *reasons* why things are put in that order by the playwright.

Parts of Plot

Plot is itself made up of many parts. Aristotle and later critics have offered names for the most common of these parts.

Exposition—the giving of information about past events. The greatest amount of exposition often comes at the beginning of the play, when audiences know least about events and characters. In some plays, however, important exposition is delayed until very late; in a murder mystery, for example, the most important facts about past events ("whodunit") come at the end.

Point of Attack—the place in the *story* where the playwright begins the *plot*. Greek playwrights tend to begin their plots late in the story and so are said to have a late point of attack; Shakespeare tends to begin his plots toward the beginning of his stories and so is said to use an early point of attack.

Action—the central chain of events in the play, particularly as those events are the central character's attempt to achieve an important goal. Action and character are tightly bound and are understood through each other, so that an answer to the question "What is the play's action?" always requires the inclusion of character.

Successful action in most plays has wholeness, that is, it has a beginning, a middle, and an end (in terms of logic, not time). The beginning of a play means that nothing

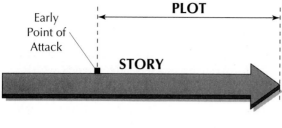

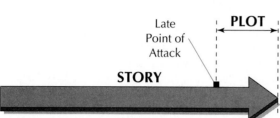

FIGURE 3.4 **Plot and Story.**
Plot is the arrangement of the incidents, the way the story is told. When plot and story begin at about the same point, the play has an early point of attack. When the plot begins late in the story, the play has a late point of attack.

necessary comes before it. A play's action usually begins when a character makes a *discovery* (passes from ignorance to knowledge). When characters discover, they usually are led to decide (to act). Discovery therefore propels action and moves a play from its beginning to its middle, during which characters will make other discoveries, some of which will result in a *reversal* (a change in the direction of the action, usually occasioned by a discovery that is contrary to the character's expectation). The end of a play comes when no necessary action remains.

If the action is not a logical whole, the play will not be understandable to the audience as a work of art. Wholeness is fundamental. It is one of the most important aspects that distinguish art from life, which it imitates.

Unlike a play, a life is not perceivable as a whole, especially while it is being lived. Our lives are diverse and complicated; we carry on several "actions" of which we perceive only dimly (and often incorrectly) the beginnings; the ends are always over life's horizon. People often say they do not understand their lives; they are confused or have lost control or are having an identity crisis. They do not see the whole of their lives.

In a play, on the other hand, wholeness is visible and allows the audience to understand, and so to learn. A dramatic *character* may be confused or out of control or in an identity crisis, but the audience sees the whole of the situation (beginning, middle, and end) and so is not confused. It is important to remember that drama is able to reveal life to us because it is an invention and not real life.

Complication—the opposing or entangling of the action. Often at the beginning of the play, the action seems simple: a character desires to accomplish something. This desire is then complicated by obstacles, particularly by the efforts of other characters to frustrate the action, or even to destroy the central character. Complications are most often revealed as discoveries by characters and reversals in the course of the action.

Conflict is a common kind of complication, one that is central to most (but not all) plays. In situations where one or more characters try to thwart the ideas and actions of another, conflict results. Conflict between characters may provide an easily understandable moral or philosophical opposition (good *versus* evil), but other conflicts are between a character and a force (such as society, fate, or gods, which may be personified).

Most plots have many complications. Each complication changes or threatens to change the course of the action because the character must deal with the complication before pursuing the original goal. Complications are either caused (by some agency like another character or a god or a force) or accidental (the result of something like a storm, a flood, or a chance meeting of characters). Caused complications are usually thought to be better than accidental ones, especially in serious plays.

Rising Action—action of increasing complication.

Crisis—derived from the Greek word for decision, *crisis* means "decisive moment," a turning point in the action. Crisis usually results when the play's major discovery leads to the major reversal. We expect to find rising action from complication to crisis; after the crisis, we anticipate falling action.

Falling Action, Resolution, or *Dénouement*—"the untying"—the unraveling of complication, the declining action as crisis is passed and complication is resolved.

Kinds of Plot

In one sense, there are as many kinds of plots as there are plays, but some basic patterns tend to repeat and so have been given names. Two in particular may be cited.

1. *Causal plot* (also known as *linear,* or *climactic,* or *antecedent-consequence* plot). The incidents of linear plot can be seen to lie along a line of causality from beginning to end. The word *climactic* is sometimes used because such plots build to a *climax,* the most exciting moment of the plot for the audience. (Note that the term

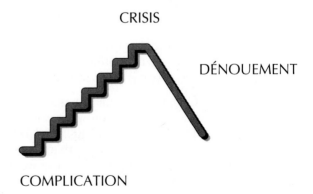

FIGURE 3.5 **Complication, Crisis, and Dénouement.**
Rising action typically comprises many smaller complications. The turning point (crisis) initiates the falling action (dénouement).

CRISIS

DÉNOUEMENT

COMPLICATION

differs from *crisis; climax* refers to an audience's response to plot and not to a part of the plot.)

Causal plots are of two major types: *single line of development,* with no subordinate lines (for example, Sophocles' *Oedipus the King*) and *multiple lines of development,* consisting of a major line and several subordinate ones, often called "subplots" (for example, Shakespeare's *Hamlet*).

2. *Episodic plot* (also known as *contextual* or *thematic* plot). The incidents (episodes) of episodic plot do not follow each other because of causality; rather, they are usually ordered by the exploration of an idea. Social-problem plays and plays by Bertolt Brecht often use this kind of plot, with each scene exploring a new aspect of a social problem or enlarging the study made to that point. An extreme example is a nineteenth-century play (Georg Buechner's *Woyzeck*) for which the author never settled on a final ordering of scenes.

Remember, however, that only the imagination of playwrights limits the way plots are organized. Many nontraditional and experimental arrangements are constantly being tried, and old organizations, like plots of spectacle, language, or character, are occasionally still used.

Character

A dramatic character and a real human being are not the same thing. Dramatic characters are inventions of playwrights. The fact that dramatic characters pursue human goals, speak human words, and embody human responses means only that dramatic characters are part of an artistic creation that is about life, not that it is life itself. Dramatic character is, at best, an imitation of selected aspects of humanity.

In addition to being imitations of people, dramatic characters are also functions within a plot. That is, they were created by the playwright to perform certain tasks

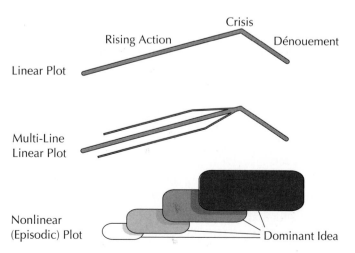

FIGURE 3.6 **Kinds of Plot.** Greek tragedy typically had a simple linear plot; Shakespearean tragedy a multilinear plot. Many contemporary plays have episodic plots.

Linear Plot

Rising Action

Crisis

Dénouement

Multi-Line Linear Plot

Nonlinear (Episodic) Plot

Dominant Idea

within the plot. Each character can be analyzed in every scene for its function, using the play's parts: for example, to further the plot, to reveal information about character, to express ideas, to contribute to spectacle.

Dramatic characters, as imitations and functions, have no existence before the play and no future after the play is over. They are no more than what the playwright has created for the play and for us.

Dramatic characters are performed by actors to create a convincing imitation of real people.

Kinds of Characters

Some kinds of characters repeat often, and so critics and scholars have designated them as follows:

Protagonist—the central figure in the main action

Confidant(e)—a character in whom the protagonist or another important character confides

Antagonist—in a play with conflict, the character who opposes the protagonist

Raisonneur, or *author's character*—one who speaks for the author, directly giving the author's moral or philosophical ideas; usually not the protagonist

Foil—one who sets off another character by contrast: comic where the other is serious, stupid where intelligent, shrewd where naive

In many plays, authors divide characters into sympathetic and unsympathetic, the former created to appeal to audiences, the latter to repel them. The fate of these groups at the end of plays usually embodies the major moral stance of the play and so should be noted.

Sources of Character

Because playwrights cannot describe characters to us directly, we must seek clues about their appearance, motivations, and behaviors. A reader must remain alert for such clues, especially noting places such as these:

- *Stage directions*—although some playwrights do not discuss characters in stage directions
- *What other characters say*—however, we must understand these other characters in order to know how to interpret what they say
- *What the characters say about themselves*—with the same problem of interpreting what they say
- *What the characters do*—their acts
- *Relationships among characters*—under increasing complications, the real nature of relationships—hate, love, friendship, dependence, forgiveness—shows more clearly
- *Most important, the plot itself*—for example, decision reveals character; complication forces decision. Characters often change as the plot develops; leading characters of-

FIGURE 3.7 **The Mind's Eye: Character.**
The play reader may get only a name or sex and age but must
visualize such characters as Pantalone (*left*), a Southern judge
(*above*), or an Irish farmer (*above right*). Professional actors like
Walt Witcover (*right*) go far beyond such mental pictures.
(Photograph courtesy of Walt Witcover; top right courtesy of the
Department of Rare Books and Special Collections, the University
of Rochester.)

ten behave and think differently at the end of the play; they have "learned." Ac-
counting for such changes helps one gain understanding of both character and play.
Some critics even say that "the play is understood by its ending," a great oversimpli-
fication but often a useful notion.

Idea

No play is without meanings. A play does not have to be filled with intellectual speeches
to offer meanings, and a careful reader learns how to find and understand them. Even
the silliest comedy has meaning because it imitates human action and because it expresses a time and a society. Not all playwrights set out to teach, but we can extract
meaning from their plays nonetheless.

Plays seldom offer single, simple meanings. The best offer many meanings, and
any attempt to reduce these to "the idea of the play" or "the theme of the play" greatly
oversimplifies the work. Meanings fall into two major categories: *idea*—meanings
contained entirely within the play; and *extrinsic meaning*—those meanings (perhaps

FIGURE 3.8 Idea.

A reader must think about how an idea will be conveyed in production. In this production of *Hair*, a 1960s musical depicting a counterculture that cries out for peace but sometimes breeds violence, both ideas are captured visually by transforming the well-known symbol of peace (*above*) into the equally recognizable tableau of crucifixion (*below*). (*Hair*, directed by Norman Hart at Montgomery College [Maryland].)

wholly unintentional) in the society and the period of which the play is an expression. We are concerned here with idea.

Sources of Idea

The play's idea comes in part from its *plot.* We tend to generalize from example, and the playwright, by choosing and ordering events, has created an example (the play). We then may generalize from that example, seeing that (in this playwright's view) certain causes lead to certain (good or bad) events.

In plays organized by conflict, the victor in the conflict embodies the "good" way of behaving, while the loser embodies the "bad." They are rewarded or punished accordingly, through (for example) money, love, promotion, or pardon. For example, comedies often end with the formation of a new society; by discovering who is included and who excluded from this society, a reader can often grasp the major idea of the play by asking questions: Why were these people included and those excluded? What were the traits of each group? The behaviors of each group?

The play's idea comes also from *character.* In a good play, the major ideas are embodied in the character and action of the protagonist. If the character is positive (approved by the author, "good"), then the protagonist embodies a good. These "goods" and "bads"—the defining elements of the play's moral world—are best understood through the system of rewards and punishments in the play. Typically, the protagonist explains his or her own idea near the play's crisis; rewards and punishments usually appear in the play's dénouement.

The play's *language* itself can reveal idea. Important characters' speeches before and after crises are especially revealing, as are important characters' speeches when they are on stage alone or with a confidant(e). The speeches of *raisonneurs,* especially when close to the complications and crises, often reveal idea, as do many speeches during the *dénouement* when the playwright (through the characters) is tying up questions and resolving issues raised by the play.

Language

As we have seen, language through the speeches of characters is an important carrier of meaning in the play.

But language as an act, separate from the meaning of the words, can also reveal idea, as, for example, whenever words or images repeat often in a play. The frequent appearance of the word *death* in a play about love would suggest that the play's idea is probably *not* "Love conquers all." Similarly, repeated images or metaphors carry meaning. One such image in *Hamlet* is of weeds, which support an idea about the protagonist as fighting against an evil, choking, destructive environment.

As an "act" separate from the meaning of the words, language is also one of the most revealing clues to character. The choice of words and the length of sentences can tell the reader something about the circumstances of a character—social class, level of education, complexity of thought, for example. As well, the rhythm of a character's speech may indicate something about mood or lifestyle.

Thinking About **Plays**

Early in the twentieth century, Alexander Woollcott, an American critic, remarked, *"To say of a bad play that some of it is pretty good is a little too much like saying of an unpleasant egg that at least part of it was fresh."* Explain in what sense this statement is accurate. Refer to specific pages in this chapter and in Chapter 1 that support Woollcott's claim.

Music

In musical plays, the importance of music to character, mood, and rhythm is clear.

In nonmusical plays, the reader must understand that the language itself embodies music, because language in plays is intended to be spoken aloud, not read. Oral language inevitably has pitch, rhythm, and so on; that is to say, oral language is musical.

Like language, music reveals clues about plot, character, and idea. For example, regular, slow rhythms create very different moods from sharp, staccato ones. Verse, especially rhymed verse, is usually more formal than prose; in serious plays verse seems to add weight to the action, whereas in comedy it often enhances the wit of a line by accentuating a word or nuance.

Spectacle

In reading, it is especially important to try and visualize the action so that the contribution of spectacle to the performance can be imagined. To be sure, much of the spectacle in today's theatre is the work of designers, whose individual genius cannot be predicted from the page. The cues for their work are there, however, in the same text that the reader uses. The imagination must work to keep spectacle in the mind's eye while reading.

Spectacle, like language, can embody idea, clarify character, and forward plot. A burning cross on stage captures a racial situation that needs no words to describe; two female characters, one dressed in red and the other in pink, predispose us to think of them as differing in their degree of "feminine propriety"; a pistol drawn from a purse may be enough to cause the antagonist to retreat in defeat and the protagonist to prevail, without any words being spoken because in this instance what is seen (the spectacle) is enough to communicate the idea.

Spectacle—which on stage is always working on the sense of sight—is the hardest of the six parts to understand from the text. It is necessary to imagine it as fully as possible, but the imagined spectacle of the reader will probably prove quite different from the actual spectacle of performance, although both should probably suggest the same meanings.

Organizing a Response

The result of a play analysis should be an organized response to the text. An organized response should be *informed* (based on a knowledge of drama and theatre), *orderly* (consistent and well-reasoned), and *defensible* (based on the evidence offered by the text and capable of explanation to somebody else).

Response Based on the Parts of a Play

Analysis should reveal how the parts work together in the play. A response probably should not simply begin with plot and then move to each part in turn, but any response will want to be based on answers to questions based on the parts, questions like

- Is the plot internally consistent? What kind of organization does it display? What is its point of attack? Its crisis? Its major complications?

- Is each character active, interesting, and consistent? Does each have a function throughout?

- Are the play's ideas important, and are they embedded in character and plot?

- Is the language interesting and expressive?

- Does the play's music (including its spoken language) support and enrich character and idea?

- Is the spectacle interesting and appropriate? Does it support rather than overwhelm the other parts of the play?

Response Based on Genres

The word *genre* means simply a *kind* or *type*. In general literature, the word customarily refers to types such as novel, poetry, or drama. Within drama, the word is used to distinguish recurring types (specifically recurring *forms*) of drama—tragedy, comedy, and so on.

Generic criticism is a major branch of dramatic criticism, so much so that whole books have been written about, for example, the nature of tragedy. Our understanding of genres often changes under historical pressure, so that within any one category we can have several kinds—Neoclassical tragedy, Romantic tragedy, heroic tragedy, and so on. Here it is possible to give only the broadest useful definitions of five major genres:

1. Tragedy—a work of the highest seriousness, with a serious protagonist in a serious action with serious consequences. Human decision is central to tragic action.

2. Comedy—a work whose issues are usually social and mundane (rather than spiritual or moral), with a protagonist involved in an action without deeply serious

FIGURE 3.9 **Genre.**

Genre is often visible in production as well as in text. Facial expressions and body positions make clear that *Home*, by Samm Art Williams (*left*) is funny while *Macbeth*, by William Shakespeare (*right*) is serious. (Produced by the Black Theatre Workshop at University of Missouri-Columbia; Clyde Ruffin director and costume designer; scenic design by Patrick Atkinson, lighting by R. Dean Packard.)

consequences. Usually, as well, human decision is limited, comic characters being comic because they are locked into types or into intense self-interest.

3. Tragicomedy—a work that mixes elements of tragedy and comedy, often by giving otherwise serious plays a happy ending, or vice versa, but often by conferring a degree of seriousness on characters and subjects usually not so treated.

4. Melodrama—a work of apparent seriousness with issues cast in terms of extremes (good and evil), the actual issues being less profound than the language suggests. Endings often show good rewarded and evil punished, in keeping with characters who are aligned according to morality; good (hero, heroine) and evil (villain).

5. Farce—a comic work whose aim is laughter, from a non-English word meaning "to stuff," indicating that farce is stuffed with laughter-producing elements. The typical protagonist in farce pursues a mundane, often trivial action, and characters often lack decision. Both the characters and the plots of farce have been called *mechanical,* and it is in the working out of its machinery that farce often provokes its best laughter.

Using an analysis based on the parts of a play and its genre, a reader should be able to organize an informed, orderly, and defensible response, either in speech or in writing. Such a response should go beyond personal response to the play (although personal response is important). It should demonstrate an understanding of the play and how it might work in the theatre; it should not be merely a gut reaction. Part of the enjoyment of theatre depends on gut reaction—but only part.

Links to More About Theatre

Louis Catron, *The Director's Vision*, 1989.

Ronald Hayman, *How to Read a Play*, 1977.

James Thomas, *Script Analysis for Actors, Directors, and Designers*, 1992.

KEY TERMS

Check your understanding against this list. Brief definitions are in the Glossary; page references there will direct you to appropriate pages. (Persons are page-referenced in the Index.)

action	exposition
antagonist	foil
causal plot	generic criticism
character	genre
climax	idea
complication	plot
confidant(e)	point of attack
conflict	protagonist
crisis	raisonneur
dénouement	reversal
discovery	spectacle
episodic plot	

How to See a Play

When you have completed this chapter, you should be able to

- Describe major differences between reading and seeing a play

- Explain how an experienced audience member can both participate in and observe a performance

- Explain differences between actor and character and between real person and dramatic character

- Explain differences between plot and story

- Explain differences between dramatic and theatrical style and discuss how they may be related

Reading a play and watching a performance are different sorts of activities. The play text comes to us only as words on a page. The performance that we see results from putting together several arts—the written text, the actors, the scenery, costumes, and lighting. Text is repeatable, but performance is not—we watch it moment by moment, responding to many stimuli (sensual, emotional, and intellectual) and unconsciously fusing them into a whole. The written text appeals to our intellect and emotions; performance in the theatre appeals most immediately to our senses and only through them to our intellect and emotions.

Studying a play is therefore different from studying a performance. In studying a play text, we analyze—we take a play apart to see how it *might* work on stage. In studying a performance, we "take it in" through our senses (mostly sight and hearing) and see/hear how it *does* work on stage. In analyzing a play, we can stop and think, or return to a difficult passage and reconsider it. In studying a performance, we watch and hear a moment go by—in real time; later we can only *recall* (not retrieve) that moment.

For such reasons, criticism of performance requires an approach somewhat different from that of play analysis.

Performance criticism can use, cautiously, Aristotle's six parts of a play text, but with the understanding that the nature of theatre radically alters the relationships among these parts. For example, spectacle is primary, because theatre is visual. (Modern theatre especially has endowed spectacle with great meaning—in light's ability to focus attention and create mood, in setting's and costume's ability to give information about time and place, and so on.) In the analysis of a play text, plot, character, idea, and language dominate. But in the analysis of a performance, these four parts (residing mostly in the play) *are submerged within and expressed through music and spectacle, through being spoken by actors and appearing physically on stage.*

An example can clarify this point: character in a play text is revealed only through written words and intellectual constructs called *decisions*. Character in performance, however, is revealed through the work of the actor, for whom the written text (and its six parts) is the basis of the artistic creation but is not the artistic creation itself. Character in performance depends not only on what the words of the play *say* but also on

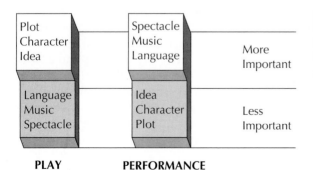

PLAY   PERFORMANCE

FIGURE 4.1   **Parts of Performance.**
In reading the play, plot, character, and idea claim first attention; in watching a play, spectacle, music, and language dominate.

what the actor *does*—with voice, body, costume, and makeup. To discover character in performance (to understand what the actor is doing with and to the text) means to ask not only the questions asked during play analysis but another set as well, including such questions as these: How does the actor say the words? How does the actor react to the words and actions of others? How does he or she stand? move? wear costumes? create rhythms? create images?

Performance criticism thus introduces a whole new set of questions to textual analysis: What are the arts of the actor, the scenic designer, the costume designer, and the lighting designer? And how are these arts fused with the written play?

Play analysis examines only the art of the playwright; performance criticism, however, examines the arts of the other theatre makers as well. For this reason, Aristotelian analysis remains a good starting point for thinking about performance, but it is only a starting point; it must be supplemented.

Performance criticism means looking in two directions at once—at the play and at the audience, because performance binds the written play to a particular audience. Play analysis and performance analysis are thus inevitably linked, but they are very different.

In analyzing plays, we saw that playwrights made decisions aimed at shaping the perceptions of the reader. In analyzing productions, we see that each theatre artist is also making such decisions. That is, actors build their performances through a series of decisions, each aimed at promoting a certain understanding and eliciting a specific response from the audience. Designers envision and then build their costumes and settings, their stage lighting and sound tracks, so as to communicate certain ideas to their audiences and to evoke certain kinds of responses from them. Whereas playwrights have only a general audience in mind, theatre artists must prepare their productions for specific audiences that will be physically present in the theatre. Just as play analysis requires an effort to remember that a playwright is trying to persuade the reader to a certain point of view about a series of events, a performance analysis requires us to remember that theatre artists are trying to persuade us to embrace *their point of view of this production.*

Any play carries within it possibilities for many different productions, some similar, others wildly different. One production might try to reproduce the play more or less as the playwright created it; another production might try to modernize the play, bringing its appearance and approach more in line with contemporary values; still another might use the elements of production to comment on or even critique the world of the play, the world created by the playwright, exposing its ideas as unworthy or unjust. Just as play analysis requires an effort to discover and understand the choices of the playwright, performance analysis means trying to see and understand the choices made by theatre artists, who want us to accept the performance as they have envisioned it. Just as play analysis requires us to think critically about what we read, performance analysis requires us to think critically as we watch the performance unfold in the theatre. We can consider the techniques of performance criticism in three parts: preliminary work, performance analysis, and organizing a response.

FIGURE 4.2 **Director's Approach.**
The same scene from Molière's *Tartuffe*—Orgon watches as Tartuffe tries to seduce Elmire. The scenes look different because the two productions approached the play differently. (*Above*, directed by Jim Patterson, SSDC, University of South Carolina; *below*, directed by Suzanne Burgoyne, University of Missouri, Columbia, scenic design by Cheryl Black, costume design by Kerri S. Packard, lighting design by Charles Willis.)

Preliminary Work

The preliminary work of performance criticism begins before the audience member arrives at the theatre and continues to the opening of the curtain. The preliminary work includes considering

- The art of theatre itself
- The nature of the work itself
- The program distributed to the audience
- The clues offered by the theatre's physical surroundings

The Art of Theatre

Analyzing a performance means in part knowing enough to do so. Knowing the role of each theatre artist, for example, enhances the ability to understand a performance. Understanding the role of the theatre audience in performance—that it can affect performance and so has some responsibility to "work" with actors in creating the event—suggests a need to consider responses as a part of the critique of performance.

Thus, a knowledge of the art of theatre supports a critique of any single performance. Attending theatrical performances, taking courses in theatre arts, and reading books about theatre provide this general knowledge. In a lifetime of attending plays and reading about theatre, a person becomes a knowledgeable member of an audience and so is better equipped to engage in performance criticism.

The Work Itself

An audience member should take the time to learn something about the material to be performed before arriving at the theatre. Some people like to read a play before seeing it; others prefer simply to learn something about it through reviews and advertisements. From whatever source, audience members should arrive at the theatre with a general idea of what they are going to see—because expectations will affect the way a performance is perceived. Just because *Cat on a Hot Tin Roof* has a funny-sounding title does not make this play a comedy, and anyone arriving at the theatre expecting a comedy may be angered or confused by the performance. Taking children to see *Who's Afraid of Virginia Woolf* because it sounds like a children's story will probably result in an unhappy shock.

The Program

An audience member should read the program before the play begins. It almost always indicates the place or places where the action will unfold and introduces the characters who will appear on stage, giving their names and major relationships. Programs often include a synopsis of the play's major action, highlighting the most important mo-

University of Maryland Dept. of Theatre
April 30, May 1-3, 6-10 at 8 pm
May 4 and 11 at 2 pm

Pugliese Theatre • 301/405-2201 (V/TTY)
Reg. Tickets $10 • Students, Senior Citizens $7

PETER
PANSY'S
excellent ADVENTURe

FIGURE 4.3 **Expectation.**
"Preliminary work" may sometimes mean simply responding to publicity or word of mouth. Here, an attention-grabbing flyer advertising a feminist version of *Peter Pan*.

ments and thereby suggesting where the audience's attention should focus. Sometimes in the program there will be notes written by the director, designer, or dramaturg. Such notes may be especially helpful, for they sometimes point to the major issues with which the production grapples or explain the director's special point of view in staging this play. (Programs also often offer helpful, if inessential, information, like what good restaurants are close to the theatre and what attractions are coming next to that theatre.)

The Physical Surroundings

An audience member will be repaid for spending a few minutes looking around the theatre and listening to sounds, because theatre artists will often try to establish a proper mood for a play even before it begins. Country and western music in the background probably reveals something important about the production and sets a mood quite different from that established by a Bach concerto or a rap song. Lighting may be used to establish mood, and scenery (where visible) may suggest things like time, place, and social class.

Sometimes oddities (for example, small platforms with scenery or lighting stands) appear in an area normally reserved for audience seating. Such spaces alert an audience member that the performance may spill over from the stage and into the auditorium, a signal that the play may be unusual in other ways as well.

The purpose of the preliminary work is to become prepared for the moment when the performance itself begins. The more prepared for the performance, the better able the audience is to follow the performance as it moves at its own rate through time.

Performance Analysis

The goal of performance analysis is to reach greater enjoyment through understanding—not merely a statement like "I really liked that," or "I was bored." Rather, the audience member needs to be able to *explain* the reasons behind such responses. These reasons usually have to do with the selection of the play, the appropriateness and skill of the actors, the suitability of the visual elements, and so on. Much of the rest of this book will deal with ways of understanding and evaluating the several arts involved in performance. The purpose of this section, however, is to offer a way of looking at the contributions of these arts, to serve as an introduction to issues involved in the complex problem of performance analysis.

To analyze a performance, an audience member must do two things at once: *participate in the performance* (entering into the action, empathizing with the characters, and so on); and *watch the performance* ("standing back" from the story and characters in order to observe how the effects are being achieved). This dual view of performance is as rewarding as it is difficult to achieve, but with practice any audience member can learn to participate and observe simultaneously. Again, if carefully used, Aristotle can help us think through this dual view, and the vocabulary in Chapter 3 can, with adaptation, serve us here as well.

Part of learning to maintain a dual view is understanding how the performance appeals through both the play and the specific performance of that play. The play's central values in performance are its story, characters, and ideas, reached through language, music, and spectacle, as expressed in acting, scenery, costumes, lighting, and sound.

Values of the Play

Drama, as imitation of human action, allows audience members to generalize from particular stories, characters, and ideas to more general human truths. Because the stories, characters, and ideas are invented and concentrated for the play, they seem even more important than similar events (unselected and unfocused) seem in real life. Thus, the concentration of theatre art accounts for much of its power, but that same concentration complicates the task of performance analysis.

Story

Plays, as imitations of human actions, are compelling because they tell stories. *Stories* are similar to, but not identical with, Aristotle's *plot*. While experiencing theatre, we cannot analyze plot—we cannot perceive the ordering of the incidents and the reasons for that ordering—we can only follow and respond to the story of the play, to the tale of "what happened."

Stories are made up of incidents that have coherence; that is, the incidents seem to follow one another for a reason. Stories are not only compelling in themselves (we are interested in what happens); they are also compelling because they serve as the framework within which the characters, words, ideas, and values of the play unfold. In a sense, then, we understand the characters, ideas, and values of a performed play through the story that it tells.

Stories in theatre gain much of their interest through their use of *suspense* and *surprise.*

Suspense is the unfolding of events in such a way that audiences want to know what happens next. "And then what happens?" they ask. Suspense requires preparation—curiosity must be created. And suspense must be satisfied—the audience must learn what happens, and what happens must be understandable in terms of what the audience expected might happen. *Suspense, then, requires preparation, connectedness, and resolution.*

Surprise is a happening that is unexpected at the time but quite logical when viewed in retrospect. Therefore, surprises, to work, must be prepared for within the world of the performance; that is, surprises are not the same as mistakes or accidents. For example, if during a love scene on stage a bed collapses, it is a surprise if the bed was supposed to collapse (perhaps for purposes of comedy); if the scenery simply broke down, it is not a surprise but an accident.

In the first case, an audience would delight in the added comedy as the actors, through dialogue and action, swiftly incorporated the collapse into the overall story of the play, thus revealing that the collapse was intentional. An audience in the second instance would become uncomfortable as it became clear that the bed broke because of inadequate stage carpentry. If, for example, the bed broke during the scene in Shakespeare's tragedy where Hamlet confronts his mother, the audience's discomfort might lead it to laugh in extreme embarrassment because it would be swiftly apparent that the bed's collapse was not part of the planned performance.

Some surprises come from the merely unexpected—something happens that we simply did not anticipate (the bed collapses). Some surprises come from reversals of the expectation—something happens when we had expected something quite different would happen (we had expected the husband to arrive but the priest arrived instead). Some surprises are a slight twist of an otherwise expected event—something happens that is similar to but not quite the same as what we had expected (we thought the butler committed the murder but discovered that the maid did).

Characters

In performance, characters and story are interrelated, as characters and plot are in a play. We understand each through the other, although they remain independent. But characters in performance, unlike characters in a play, are created by the actors' choices of vocal and physical traits as well as by the words printed on pages of a play. Characters in performance are therefore very complex creations that are based on the characters in the play but are nonetheless different from them.

Audiences respond to characters for different reasons. Often a character is appealing because audiences can identify with it. "I recognize myself in that character," or "I can

FIGURE 4.4 Character.

Contrast the actor's appearance (costume, makeup) for the character of the tutor in *Electra* (*left*) with actors' appearance in *Asinamali!* (*right*). The first suggests an approach that seeks the universal and mythic, whereas the latter suggests the stuff of everyday life. (*The Tutor,* designed by Irene Corey, from *An Odyssey of Masquers: The Everyman Players,* Anchorage Press Plays, Louisville, photograph by Orlin Corey. *Asinamali!* photograph by Laine McCall, courtesy of the Mark Taper Forum.)

identify with her" are strong sources of pleasure or suffering in the theatre. We like to see the mirror held up so that we can watch those like ourselves. Some characters are said to have universal appeal (or to be a universal character); the appeal of such characters is that they are recognizably like human beings of many different times and places.

Some characters, although we do not identify with them, appeal to feelings deep within us. Such characters, we say, appeal to us at a subconscious level, through some subconscious reference. For example, the Greek tragedy *Oedipus Rex* has survived for 2000 years and given us a psychological term (the *Oedipus phase* or *complex*) that explains much of its power. One critic said it causes us to "think the unthinkable"—a man who has children by his mother and murders his father. All these things are in the play

Thinking About **Performance**

Barbara Stanwyck, an American film and TV actor, remarked: *"My only problem is finding a way to play my fortieth fallen female in a different way from my thirty-ninth."* Explain this quotation in terms of the relationship between character in play and character in performance; between character and actor; between character and genre (see Chapter 3).

text. In performance, however, they are given a terrible immediacy that gives them life, size, and horror—*this* man and woman, *this* bloodshed, *this* scream.

Still other characters appeal because we recognize others in them, a trait especially clear in the case of historical characters. Seeing an actor portray a character we think we know offers a special treat for audiences, who will often flock to see an actor portray former luminaries in works like *Abe Lincoln in Illinois* or *Picasso at the Lapin Agile.* Here the delight is not only in enjoying the character in the performed play but also in watching to see how closely the actor meets our preconceptions of the real person. To take advantage of this associative response, the performance must depict people with whom the audience has strong ties and must present them in convincing—and perhaps visually recognizable—ways.

It is important to stress that characters in performance, like characters in a play text, are not real people. They are *like* real people. Because in performance we hear and see live actors actually speaking and moving before us, we need to be clear that, although the actors are real, the characters are invented, with no existence outside the performance itself.

Idea

Generally the ideas that are revealed through a performance are given the least thought while we sit in the theatre and watch, but they are often the aspect of the production that we talk most about once we leave the theatre. There is a good reason for this phenomenon. Performance is transitory; theatre is "the home of the Now." When we leave the theatre, the vividness of the acting, the onstage images and sounds fade. We seldom remember sensory stimuli clearly; afterward we can only describe them. We are therefore left with the intellectual content of the play in performance, which is verbally expressible and so may remain fresh and sharp in our minds.

In fact, the ideas within the performance may become more important with the passing of time. If experiencing the immediacy of the performance has moved us, it has become part of our lives, and now we want to know what it means *to us.*

Ideas are embedded in all play texts and performances. Some ideas are more interesting and more important than others, to be sure, but ideas exist in all. Whereas the ideas of play texts come mostly through the plot and dialogue, however, ideas in performance come most immediately through the specific choices made by the actors and designers (of scenery, costumes, lighting, and properties). For example, images in performance can communicate ideas vividly, even without words (although words of course deepen and extend the ideas). For example, an actor with a shaved head, wearing paramilitary garb, quite clearly communicates an ideology even before he speaks. A set that positions a computer so that it looms menacingly above the actors makes a clear (although nonverbal) statement of a power relationship, a statement that the actors' words and performance enhance and modify. It is through such means that specific *performances* of Shakespeare's *Julius Caesar* have offered ideas about Nazi Germany and South American dictatorships, even though the *play's* ideas were about the nature of rule in Republican Rome and, perhaps, Elizabethan England.

Ideas that are not well integrated into the performance are distracting and theatrically unsatisfying. Indeed, to update an old theatrical adage, "If you want to send a message, use a fax." The saying means that ideas are not the end-all or be-all of performance. Ideas are only one important element of judging the importance of a play in performance, even though they tend to dominate later discussions of performance, lingering after the immediate, sensory elements of performance have faded from memory.

Idea in performance succeeds only if other, theatrical, values of the play succeed—because ideas come to audiences through the other elements of specific performance.

Values of the Specific Performance

Story, character, and idea reside mostly in play text; music (what we hear) and spectacle (what we see) reside in performance. Indeed, the word *theatre* literally means *seeing place* and *auditorium* literally means *hearing place;* spectator is one who watches, audience one who listens. Therefore, audience members will also want to ask questions about the elements of performance that may be distinct from the play text itself. Three such elements are central to understanding most performances: the given circumstances of the performance, its theatrical conventions, and its style.

Given Circumstances

We may define the *given circumstances* of a performance as those basic traits that determine the world of the stage: the age, sex, social class, and physical health of the characters; the time and place of the action; the mood established on the stage; and so on.

Usually the written play determines the given circumstances, but not always. For example, the play *Everyman* comes from the English Middle Ages, and so the performance usually proceeds *as if* it were unfolding then and there. But a director may wish to emphasize the timelessness of this action and so perform it *as if* it were taking place in England of the 1990s or in the Western United States during the gold rush. In producing a French comedy of the 1660s, a director might want to do it "authentically," making it as close as possible to what the original production might have been. Or the director might decide that the fun within the play is more important than the circumstances of its original production and so select materials based on their brightness and color, even using techniques of cartoons or caricatures as guiding principles. Clearly all such decisions will necessarily affect not only the visual aspects of the production but also the sounds selected as background and the techniques used by the actors.

FIGURE 4.5   **Given Circumstances.**
This strong evocation of a busy newsroom clues the audience to both the time and place of the action and the sort of people involved. (Production is *The Front Page,* director, Harold Tedford; designers, Darwin Reid Payne [scenery], Mary Wayne-Thomas [costumes], and Jon Christman [lighting], at Wake Forest University.)

Whatever the decision about given circumstances, the circumstances for every production must be made clear to the audience through the visual aspects of production (scenery, costumes, lighting, properties), the sounds and music of the production, and the work of the actors. An audience member engaged in performance criticism must determine what the given circumstances of production are and then examine how those circumstances were communicated through the arts of production. Only then can some evaluation of this aspect of production be made, through answering questions like these:

- What seemed to be the source and purpose of the production's given circumstances?
- Were the circumstances clear?
- Were they consistent throughout the production?

Conventions

A *convention* can be thought of as a contract between theatre artists and audiences, an agreement to do things a certain way for the good of all. It is a shortcut between what is meant and what is done. Each of the arts within theatre has conventions. Several examples can clarify.

FIGURE 4.6   **Convention.**

One convention of this production of *Into the Woods,* a musical by Stephen Sondheim, is that the world of the stage differs from the real world—that the shape, material, and color of trees' foliage is magical rather than literal. (Production from Bowling Green State University, directed by Michael Ellison, designed by Bradford Clark.)

In today's theatre, it is a convention that months or years can pass between the acts of a play, even though common sense tells us that, in fact, only a few minutes have passed.

A convention in scenic design is the agreement between actors and audience that when a setting depicts a room of a house, a door in that room leads to another room of the house or to the outdoors. Common sense tells us that the door actually leads to an area backstage. Another sort of scenic convention allows a yellow cardboard circle hung aloft to represent the sun.

An acting convention from the eighteenth century was that a hand raised to the forehead, palm out and the eyes cast upward, indicated suffering.

In musicals, characters sing their emotions. This use of music is a convention, because common sense tells us that music neither accompanies our lives nor changes as we shift activities and moods.

Such agreements between artists and audiences serve to enhance performance and so work for the good of both. Audience members trying to understand and evaluate a performance need to watch for the conventions operating in a production:

- Are the conventions clear?

- Are the conventions similar to other, familiar theatrical conventions? To conventions on television? Or are they in some way distinctive?

■ Do the conventions seem aimed at promoting the view that the onstage world is quite like real life, or do they aim rather to call attention to the differences of the stage from life?

Style

The word *style* is one of the most useful and yet one of the most confusing that is applied to any art. Part of the confusion comes from the word's being used in so many ways in daily life: clothes are "stylish"; there is "New Orleans style" jazz, different from "Chicago style"; there are kosher-style dill pickles; many performers are said to have their own personal "style."

In art, including theatre art, the word *style* is used to describe a recurring cluster of traits that seem to set one type off from another type of the same art—two styles of painting, for example, or two styles of music. Dramas (written texts) have style, and so do performances. It is therefore possible to speak both of dramatic style and theatrical style.

Generally, a play written in a particular style will also be performed in that style; that is, the dramatic and theatrical style are the same. But in some instances (for reasons which we will return to later), theatre artists may decide that the performance should be in a style different from that of the written play.

Styles tend to change over time. For example, seventeenth-century plays and productions displayed something we now call a Neoclassical style, while early nineteenth-century plays and productions generally showed what we call a Romantic style. Contemporary theatre is marked by its tendency to use many different styles among its productions, but, for a single production, there is usually a single style.

Style can be analyzed by considering ways in which various elements are expressed and combined. Different cooking styles emphasize different sorts of foods and different spices. Different styles within visual arts differ in their preference for certain ways of manipulating mass, line, color, and texture. Different styles within literary arts tend to prefer certain kinds of language, characters, and plots over others. The ways in which individual elements are manipulated are related to style.

It is not possible to study style in detail here, but some of its major areas of difference can be suggested. Three—abstraction, detail, and material—interact to help define a style.

Abstraction. *Abstraction* is *removal from observable reality.* An artist may choose any point along a continuum from quite abstract to wholly lifelike. For example, a painting that is simply a splash of red interrupted by dots of black is quite abstract, whereas a near-photographic portrait of Marilyn Monroe is quite lifelike.

Similarly, a theatre artist can either *reproduce observable reality,* or render parts of reality as *generalized but understandable shapes,* or *abandon reality* almost entirely. For example, scenic designers might choose to reconstruct a room onstage, making it as much like a real room as possible; or they might make all walls transparent and use furniture specially made of steel; or they might choose to show only an open space with platforms and geometric shapes. Lighting designers might, through color and angle, suggest real

FIGURE 4.7   **Style: Abstraction.**

The costume rendering for a production of Molière's *The Miser* (*left*) offers a lifelike body, with many details of fabric, texture, and color. The machine-like costumes (*right*) depart from reality (are abstracted) by covering the faces and limbs with metal cylinders, thus hiding details of the human body and reducing details of color, texture, and so on. (Rendering by Martin A. Thaler, University of Vermont; machine costumes from Huntley Carter, *The New Spirit in the European Theatre, 1914–1924*.)

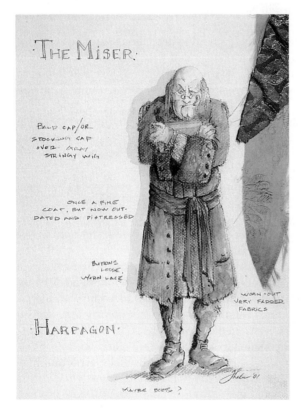

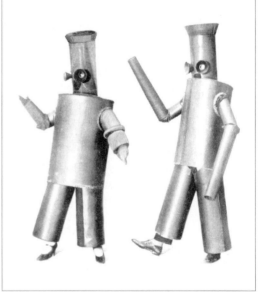

sunlight, or they might choose to flood the acting area with blue light. Costume designers might use real clothes taken from a thrift shop, or they might construct a covering of metal and cardboard in such a way as to disguise the shape of the human body.

Decisions about the level of abstraction are choices about style and are themselves often closely related to the selection and use of detail.

Detail. At issue here is both the *amount* of detail and the *kind* of detail. Again, an artist can choose anything along a continuum from no detail to overwhelming detail, and along various continua of kinds of detail: natural/artificial, expensive/cheap, urban/rural, and so on. For example, the abstract painting could be a splash of solid red with a single black dot, or it could be highly textured layers of many shades of red with numerous black dots of varying textures. The portrait of Marilyn Monroe might show her dressed in a solid fabric or in a highly patterned one, wearing no jewelry or bedecked in brooches and rings.

Similarly, theatre artists can make choices about amounts and kinds of details. An actor, for example, can move often, crossing the stage, sitting and standing, gesturing nervously (much detail); or she may remain quite still, using no gestures, and speak in a monotone (little detail). A scenic designer may fill a room with furniture and bric-a-brac (much detail) or leave the same room utterly unadorned except for a single chair stage center (little detail). The costume designer may choose a rich silk dress covered with dollar signs sewn in brilliants (much detail) or a plain black leotard (little detail).

Again, all such decisions are matters of style, and they often interact with the materials selected for rendering the details.

Material. Choosing materials means making decisions about such things as mass, line, color, and texture. Different materials produce different effects. An oil painting differs from a charcoal sketch; a building in stone differs from one in brick.

In theatre, too, certain kinds of materials predispose audiences in certain ways. For example, a setting built entirely of aluminum tubing calls on an audience's association with science or industry, perhaps, and invites a sense of detachment, coldness, cleanness. Such a setting is different from an otherwise identical setting made of bare wood, which an audience might associate with an earlier time and so derive a sense of tradition, comfort, and warmth. Similarly, costumes made of burlap will "say" something to an audience quite different from otherwise identical costumes made of satin or wool or cotton, each of which encourages its own set of associations for an audience.

In examining visual elements in production, performance critics must therefore ask questions like these:

- Are the colors pastel or saturated?
- Are the textures smooth and shiny or rough and pocked?
- Are lines curved or jagged?
- Are masses large and unbroken or broken up?

FIGURE 4.8 Style: Materials.

Industrial materials are used for the setting of the musical *Godspell*. (Directed by Frank Mundy, designed by George Epting, South Carolina State University.)

Although more difficult, similar kinds of questions, applied to actors, can lead to an understanding of their style in a performance.

- Are the actors *seeming to be* real people involved (unknowingly) in a real situation, or are they clearly aware of themselves as performers (perhaps they address the audience directly from time to time)?

- Are the actors using many small details of voice and movement, or are they relatively still, both vocally and physically?

- What materials of voice and body have the actors selected for the performance (soft or loud voices, erect or slouching posture, and so on)?

Again, all such questions are questions relating to style. An audience member functioning as a performance critic will want to notice the choices made with respect to level of abstraction, the amount and kind of details, and the choice of materials. And he or she will want to evaluate the appropriateness and consistency of the choices—and if possible infer why these rather than other choices were made.

Links to More About Theatre

James H. Clay and Daniel Krempel, *The Theatrical Image,* 1967. How to see in images.

Organizing a Response

The result of critiquing a performance should be an organized response to the performance itself. Because most performances are based on plays, a piece of performance criticism will most often need to address two related questions:

- What are the major values of the play?
- How are these values revealed or transformed through performance?

As with a play analysis, performance criticism should be *informed* (based on knowledge of theatre), *orderly* (consistent and well reasoned), and *defensible* (based on evidence offered by the performance itself and capable of explanation to someone else).

Good performance criticism often *synthesizes* the values of play and performance; that is, the critic does **not** usually begin with a discussion of story, characters, and idea and then move to a discussion of given circumstances, convention, and style. Rather, the critic tries to communicate how the performance (the work of the actors, director, and designers) reveals the story, characters, ideas, and values of the play. In the course of the discussion, many of the questions given earlier in this chapter will be answered for the particular production.

Some other guiding questions might be the following:

- Are the *given circumstances* of the production clear? How do they relate to the given circumstances of the play itself? How are these given circumstances made clear?
- What are the *conventions* of the production? Do they seem to work with those of the play? How or how not?
- What is the *style* of the production, and how is that style achieved? Is it the same style as that of the written play (if that question is answerable)? Are the various theatrical arts in the same style?
- Is the *story* clear? How do the several elements of production enhance its suspense and surprises?
- Are all *characters* clear? Are they interesting? How has each actor made the character clear? Interesting? How have the several elements of design contributed to these goals?

FIGURE 4.9 Style.

The Greek tragedy, *Prometheus,* is here produced in different styles. Masks, costumes with simple but strong lines, and geometric scenery lead toward abstraction (*above*). Unmasked actors, scantily dressed, with chains and earrings call up ordinary life, with a hint of punk rock. (*Above,* directed by Richard Scammon, photograph courtesy of Indiana University and Vera Scammon Broughton; *below,* directed by Michael Robertson, University of Northern Iowa.)

- Are the *ideas* clear? Compelling? What elements of production have worked to further these goals?

- Did the *audience* seem attentive and appreciative, and how did the audience responses fit with my own?

Check your understanding against this list. Brief definitions are in the Glossary; page references there will direct you to appropriate pages. (Persons are page-referenced in the Index.)

abstraction	story
auditorium	style
convention (dramatic, theatrical)	surprise
given circumstances	suspense

Mediators and Gatekeepers

When you have completed this chapter, you should be able to

- Explain what comprises a good theory

- Discuss the kinds of questions that theorists ask

- Explain how theory can affect production

- Distinguish between a critic and a reviewer

- Discuss what a dramaturg does

- Describe what experts in pubic relations, advertising, and marketing do

- Describe the role of theatrical agents

- Compare modernism and postmodernism

There is a final group of people who shape audiences and performance. *Gatekeepers* influence which plays and performances are available; *mediators* influence how people read plays and see performances. These people seldom work directly with performances in the theatre, but they nonetheless help shape the perceptions of audience members, and sometimes those of theatre artists as well. These are people who both produce and use theory and criticism, sometimes to explore intellectual possibilities, sometimes to sell tickets. Their influence can vary from the enormously important to the quite trivial. They are the theorists, critics, reviewers, dramaturgs, public relations people (including for our purposes those charged with advertising and marketing), and agents.

Theorists

A theory is an intellectual construct that seeks to explain a phenomenon. In theatre, there are two kinds of theories:

Dramatic theory, which deals with plays (Aristotle's theory of tragedy, for example)

Performance theory, which deals with live performance and which has as yet no comparable example

Theorists seek to answer questions such as: What is theatre? What is drama? They may seek to answer questions on genre: What is tragedy? What is comedy? They may seek to answer social or political questions: What role has theatre played in the maintenance of the status quo? How is drama implicated in racism?

An ideal theory meets several requirements. It would be

- *Systematic* (reasoned and orderly)
- *Internally consistent* (one part of a theory would not contradict any other part)
- *Sufficient* (the theory would give all the information necessary to understand the phenomenon)
- *Congruent* (the theory would account for all available evidence and contradict none)

Theories are deemed better still when they offer their dense explanations both briefly and clearly (e.g., $e = mc^2$).

Theatrical Theories Today

As a study of the history of theories shows, there are no ideal theories. Theories of drama and theatre have multiplied in the postmodern period (that is, the period since about World War II, when many previous assumptions about the nature of truth as "scientifically verifiable" and "objective" came under serious attack). Most postmodern theories rest on new assumptions of the world and people's place in it, which the following comparisons may help clarify:

Modernism rests on:	*Postmodernism* rests on:
The industrial age	The information age
Reason, science	Nihilism, meaninglessness
Hierarchy	Participation, dialogue
Autonomous individuals	Socially shaped people
History as progressive	History as nonlinear, discontinuous
Dualities, opposites	Differences rather than opposites

The multiplication of theories of drama and theatre is itself an expression of postmodernism, where difference and contingency are prized. It is also worth noting that today's theories of theatre and drama are theories that were developed in fields other than theatre and then applied to theatre. They were not developed, as was Aristotle's, specifically to explain the nature of theatre and drama. This telling shift may signal a change in theatre's position within today's culture, from central to peripheral.

Among the most important current theories are the following:

Feminist theory, an amalgam of film theory and a branch of psychoanalytic theory (Lacanism), with various goals: for example, to study a historically male theatre vis-à-vis women, to examine gender in performance, to define a feminist aesthetic

Marxist theory, an attempt to explain links between art and economics by asking some version of questions such as these: "Who profits by the current arrangements for publishing and producing plays?" "Why do audiences approve of plays and productions that acquiesce in an oppressive status quo?" and "How can audiences be persuaded to see and act on their own oppressions?"

Semiotics, the study of signs, an attempt to understand how audiences make meanings from the auditory and visual clues given in a performance; a potentially very powerful theory for explaining theatre and its effects because it partakes of the essence of theatre as a *seeing* and *hearing* place

The Importance of Theories

Theories and theorists of theatre are important because they influence the practice of theatre by noting what is and is not acceptable; in so doing, they affect not only what audiences see but also what audiences expect to see. Granted, it is not easy to say which comes first—the theory or the practice; that is, it is unclear whether theory leads practice, by urging theatre artists in one direction or another; or whether theory follows practice, by codifying after the fact what plays and production practices are now satisfying to audiences; or whether theory and practice simply change along parallel paths, both influenced by some larger force.

For our purposes, the answer to the question doesn't much matter, because, once established, theories and theatre practices seem tied together in ways that influence both the kinds of play produced and the conventions governing their production. In the

FIGURE 5.1   **Modern and Postmodern Productions.**

Two plays written in roughly the same historical period, one given a modern (illusionistic, historically and spatially recognizable) and the other a postmodern (ahistorical, fragmented, disorienting) production. (*The Tempest* at Wake Forest University. Director, James Dodding; designers, Darwin Reid Payne [scenery], Mary Wayne-Thomas [costumes], and Jon Christman [lighting]. Photograph by Bill Ray III. *Tis Pity She's a Whore*, directed by JoAnne Akalaitis at the Public Theatre. Photograph by Martha Swope.)

Links to More About Theatre

Jill Dolan, *The Feminist Spectator as Critic,* 1988.

Kenneth Tynan, *Curtains,* 1961. Exemplary reviews by a man who loved the theatre.

1600s, for example, plays that did not follow certain rules prescribed by theorists were almost never produced. Acceptably written plays, when produced, followed almost formulaic conventions of acting, scenery, and costuming. In our own time, for another example, both the plays and theories popular in the early 1900s have fallen into disfavor; the plays are seldom produced because they now seem old-fashioned and uninteresting, too predictable and too contrived. When a once-accepted theory begins to fall into disfavor, competing theories and practices jostle about until some new theory gains widespread acceptance, after which, patterns of plays and productions again begin to coalesce. Until a new theory gains dominance, however, both plays and productions are remarkable for their blend of forms and styles. We are living in such an age.

Theatrical theories are also important because they can illuminate the culture that embraces them. Aristotle's theory of drama, for example, clearly establishes the play as the most potent force in the theatrical experience and envisions a play where actions have predictable consequences. Theories in our own time propose the centrality of audiences in the experience and envision plays where actions are as often episodic as causal. Such shifts point to larger cultural changes where a single point of view (the play) is replaced by multiple points of view (individuals in an audience) and a world of causality is replaced by a more chaotic world, one where "stuff happens."

The creation of theory, then, is an activity of major importance, one now located mostly in universities, where whole courses are sometimes devoted to the work of a single theorist: "Aristotle on Tragedy," "Suzanne Langer's Aesthetics of Drama." From universities, theories filter into the general consciousness through the work of other mediators and artists—not always in a form that the theorists themselves would recognize.

Critics

Criticism is the careful study of a play or group of plays, usually by applying theory. The line between criticism and theory is not always clear, however, because many theorists are also critics, and many critics make theoretical statements.

Like theory, criticism has two branches: dramatic criticism (the study of plays) and performance criticism (the study of performances). Probably because theories of drama are more fully developed than theories of performance, dramatic criticism continues to be the more widely practiced. Today, different dramatic critics focus on quite different subjects—a play's form and structure, its image and metaphor, its politics and sexuality, and so on—depending usually on what theories guide their inquiries. They and their criticisms are often labeled by the issues they address—formal critic(ism), Marxist critic(ism), feminist critic(ism). Most performance critics, absent well-developed theatrical theories, seek either to describe and explain the complex impacts of discrete moments of performance or to apply theories drawn from sociology and anthropology to compare theatrical with social and cultural performances.

Criticism today, both dramatic and performance, unfolds mostly in university classrooms and academic publications. Like theory, criticism is a serious intellectual undertaking. Its need for reflection militates against deadlines and pressures. For this reason, most of the best modem critics have academic connections; only a few of today's best critics are also theatre artists.

Because of its academic home, criticism might be expected to affect mostly scholars and students. But criticism reaches a larger public—theatre audiences—because theatre artists (especially directors and dramaturgs) routinely read criticisms of past productions to help them think about the play they are preparing to mount. Through such research, criticism affects the work of theatre artists directly and, through them, audiences. Because today's audience members seldom read criticism, its influence on them is indirect, filtered through theatre directors and dramaturgs. Occasionally the influence comes from what directors and dramaturgs write (in program notes, for example), but more often it comes from what they put on stage. Like theorists, then, critics are important because they influence theatrical practice and so, indirectly, audiences, both how audiences see plays, and what plays they see.

Critical practices, like theories, change through time, and so criticism, like theory, can be a key to changes in culture. Criticisms of Shakespeare's plays written during the past four hundred years are extremely revealing about changes in attitude. To read criticisms of *The Merchant of Venice,* for example, is to track changing views of Jews from Shakespeare's time to our own; criticisms of Shakespeare's romantic comedies offer tantalizing clues about how different societies have viewed young love and cross-dressing.

Reviewers

Reviewers are men and women who see plays and then write about them. Their orientation is toward consumer protection; that is, presenting themselves at best as an "ideal audience," they recommend or warn against performances on the basis of a taste shared with their readership.

Reviewers are seldom critics. They do not rely consistently on theory; they rarely pretend to objectivity. They lack the time to reflect on what they have seen, their work usually appearing in a daily or weekly publication. Often, their format is so limited (one minute on radio or television) that little can be said at all.

Reviewers are reviewers of both drama and performance. They do not attempt to tell readers or listeners what performance is or how it works, but they do tell them whether or not the performance is likable within certain limits.

FIGURE 5.2 **Critics.**
Some critics of the twentieth century were so powerful and famous that theatres were named for them. Here, the Brooks Atkinson Theatre.

Thinking About **Mediation**

In *The Critic*, a play by Richard Brinsley Sheridan (1751–1816), one character describes another as *"a practitioner in panegyric, or, to speak more plainly, a professor of the art of* *puffing."* Write a fifty-word panegyric—that is, a puff piece—for a play, film, or television program. Which mediators routinely write such pieces?

Some reviewers have theatrical backgrounds or education. Some do not. Experienced reviewers have trained themselves to recognize their own responses and to turn them into interesting, often witty prose, one of the functions of reviewing being to entertain.

Reviewers develop degrees of power within their communities, the New York reviewers supposedly having life-or-death power over Broadway productions. Their mediation extends beyond the review itself when quotations from the reviews are included in theatrical advertising. Because of this practice, some reviewers come to write quotable reviews, eager, perhaps, to see their names on theatre marquees with those of the actors. When this point is reached, the reviewer, although still a mediator, has crossed over from reviewing into public relations. In this way, a few reviewers become media stars in their own right.

Dramaturgs

A *dramaturg* is a specialist who fuses dramatic literature and dramatic and theatrical history to theatrical production. Dramaturgs need strong grounding in theory and criticism, for they are regularly called on to explain plays and justify decisions made about their productions. Although long active in European theatres, dramaturgs became common in the United States only after World War II. They now work on the staffs of many resident theatre companies. Most gain their training in universities, some of which now offer graduate degrees in dramaturgy.

The tasks of dramaturgs differ from theatre to theatre. Most perform some combination of the following functions:

- Assisting in the selection of plays
- Reading and evaluating new plays
- Providing historical and literary background to directors, designers, and actors
- Assisting directors, sometimes by advising on the production
- Working on plays—adapting, restructuring, translating
- Writing notes for theatre programs
- Preparing materials for use in advertising, public relations, and education

Clearly, dramaturgs influence both productions and audiences directly: productions, through participating in decisions about what plays are produced and how they are produced; audiences, through program notes and public relations materials aimed at preparing audiences to like the production to come. (By shaping plays and productions, dramaturgs influence audiences indirectly as well as directly.)

Specialists in Public Relations, Advertising, Marketing

A specialist in *public relations* strives to position a theatre organization in a favorable relation to its several publics—town, neighborhood, business community, and audience, to name the most usual. The same people may also work to advertise and market individual plays, although the three functions may be separated and undertaken by different staffs. For purposes of discussion, all such people can be considered together because, however different some of their tasks are, they share the goal of persuading people (including audiences) toward a favorable view of the theatre and production.

Theatres differ radically in the funds they can devote to public relations, advertising, and marketing. A student director may well handle all advertising personally, probably by photocopying posters and flyers generated on a home computer. New York producers customarily contract with an advertising firm to promote their productions, and stars often have their own representatives. University theatres often have someone designated to coordinate *front-of-house* activities (all those things that happen on the audience's side of the curtain), including publicity for individual performances. When money is available, advertisements include some combination of radio and television spots, newspaper ads, posters, flyers, photographs, and interviews.

At whatever level, publicity tries to capture the attention of potential audiences and lure them to the production. For each production, publicity people search for an angle, "a hook," that will set this production apart: the actor who goes on even with a broken ankle, the actress whose mother played the same role in the original Broadway production. With the director and, if such a person exists, the producer, the person in charge of advertising will create an image or idea for the production. This image or idea will grow out of the interpretation governing the production and will inform the graphics and text used in advertising the production. (For a play about love, will we emphasize the rose or its thorns? A pink rose or a black one? Will we use the word *love* or the word *passion*?)

A well-conceived advertising campaign will not aim to bring everyone to the theatre but to bring those people likely to appreciate the production. In fact, part of an advertiser's job is to alert people to productions that might be unsuitable for certain groups, most often parents with young children who want to avoid plays whose content or language may be beyond the emotional grasp of youngsters (or at least so the parents hope).

Marketing and advertising are crucial not only in getting audiences—the right audiences—into the theatre but also in preparing them. Successful publicity will raise the proper sort of expectations in an audience. Audiences remain properly skeptical of the claims of advertising ("An all-time laugh riot!!!"), but they also learn how to pick up hints about a production's style, genre, and mood, as well as about subject matter in which they are interested. When audience members arrive at the theatre, if the advertisers have done a proper job, they will know roughly what to expect from the performance.

Agents

An *agent* is a person who links professional theatre artists with the business people who hire them. Most often representing playwrights and actors, a theatrical agent puts her or his clients in touch with the right people, negotiates favorable terms for contracts, helps sort out disputes, and collects and distributes money—for a fee. Agents receive a percentage of their clients' income.

Agents can exert enormous power, for often an artist without an agent cannot get his or her work considered. Theatres, overwhelmed by the volume of plays they receive from aspiring playwrights, may read only those submitted by agents they trust, and producers casting new plays may limit their choices to a list of people previously screened by agents they trust. The situation assumes that agents, or their readers (people employed to read new scripts and report on them), have good artistic judgment. Sometimes they do. Sometimes, a courageous and stubborn agent is the main reason that a great but daring new playwright gets produced, or a young, different actor gets cast.

Agents, by serving as gatekeepers, are very helpful to producers, directors, and casting directors, for agents can eliminate inappropriate plays and people before they overwhelm a system that attracts far more potential employees than it can hire. Agents are likewise sometimes helpful to artists, pointing them toward the most appropriate producers and theatres and freeing them from business details.

The downside of this arrangement is that agents can become a projection of producers' caution. The agent's purpose is to sell—a play, a person, a talent. To do so, the

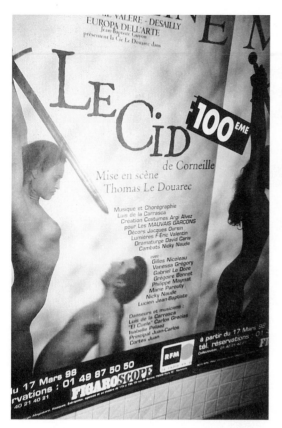

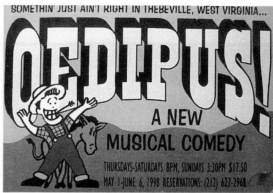

Advertising.

Good mediation shapes an audience's expectations. A tantalizing French poster uses a thoroughly modern image to promote a recent production of a seventeenth-century French classic. An advertising postcard uses both artwork and title to alert the audience that this *Oedipus* isn't Greek tragedy. (Photograph of poster by Michelle Washington; postcard courtesy of Bob Johnson.)

agent has to know the parameters within which a producer or director operates—what is wanted, what is hated, what has worked before. The last is the most burdensome for an adventurous artist. In some cases, an agent will not even offer certain clients to certain producers or directors; more likely, however, is the agent's refusal to take as clients those artists who seem unusual, out of the usual mold, not *what has worked before.* Such an agent comprises a form of prior censorship, closing the gate on some works and some artists before they ever get a chance to enter. In a theatre run on the corporate model, the agent runs the danger of becoming the first line of defense for corporate caution.

Altogether, then, there are a large number of people who try to manipulate in some way what plays and productions are available to audience members and how audience members will relate to those plays and productions. Playwrights set out to tell stories from a certain point of view, making choices about what characters are sympathetic and which events are significant. Theatre artists present one version of the play, however close or far it may be from the script as originally conceived by a playwright. Gatekeepers try to "protect" potential receivers from unsuitable encounters: theorists discourage consideration of plays that fail to meet certain accepted traits; critics and dramaturgs, in different venues, analyze in order to pass judgment on plays and performances; reviewers warn audiences—at least certain audiences—away from some productions. Mediators try to

FIGURE 5.4 **Advertising.**

Theatres themselves often serve as venues for advertising coming
productions, as shown here in Italy and France. Note that the Italian
production is *Some Like It Hot*, obviously based on the American movie,
complete with Italianized images of Marilyn Monroe, Jack Lemmon,
and Tony Curtis. (Photographs from Italy and France courtesy of
Michelle Washington.)

shape what audiences take in: critics shape the ideas of theatre artists, reviewers steer audiences toward plays likely to be congenial to them by describing in general the content
and approach of a performance, and publicity materials try and project excitement for
current offerings. Part of becoming a knowledgeable theatre person means learning how
these influences work and how to use them to enhance the enjoyment of theatre.

KEY TERMS

Check your understanding against this list. Brief definitions are in the Glossary; page references there will direct you to appropriate pages. (Persons are page-referenced in the Index.)

agent	mediator
criticism (dramatic and performance)	modernism
dramaturg	postmodernism
feminist theory (of theatre)	public relations
front of house	reviewer
gatekeeper	semiotics
Marxist theory (of theatre)	theory (dramatic and performance)

Musicals *in* America

1.1 *The Producers* on Broadway with Matthew Broderick. (Photo © Paul Kolnik)

Musicals *in* America, *continued*

AIDA

1.2 *Aida* on Broadway. (Photo © Joan Marcus)

Flower Drum Song

1.3 *Flower Drum Song* at the Mark Taper Forum, Los Angeles. (Craig Schwartz photo)

1.4 *The Lion King* on Broadway, directed by Julie Taymor. (Photo © Joan Marcus)

Musicals *in* America, *continued*

1.5 *A Little Night Music* at the Connecticut Repertory Theatre, directed by Gerry M. English, designed by Michael Franklin-White. (Corporate Scenographics LLC)

1.6 *Ain't Misbehavin'* at Hampton University.

Musicals *in* America, *continued*

Pirates of Penzance

1.7 *The Pirates of Penzance* at Wake Forest University.

Mamma Mia

1.8 *Mamma Mia* on Broadway. (Photo © Joan Marcus)

Into the Woods

1.9 *Into the Woods* at Bowling Green State University.

Musicals *in* **America**, *continued*

1.10 *Rent* on Broadway. (Photo © Joan Marcus)

The *Making* of a *Musical*

2.1 Show Curtain, rendering.

2.2
Costume design, the marching band.

MUSIC MAN

The Music Man at the University of Maryland, directed by Nicholas Olcott, scenery by Dan Conway, costumes by Helen Huang, lighting by Daniel MacLean Wagner, technical direction by David Kriebs. This production opened the University of Maryland's new Center for the Performing Arts in 2001.

2.3 Costume design, Mrs. Shinn.

2.4 Costume in performance. (Stan Barouh photo)

2.5 Costume designs, Harold and Marian.

2.6 *and* **2.7** Costume shop.

2.8 Computer-aided painter's elevation, Pool Hall unit.

2.9 Computer-aided rendering, Pool Hall unit in setting.

2.10 Pool Hall unit in performance. (Stan Barouh photo)

2.12 Scene shop, gazebo under construction.

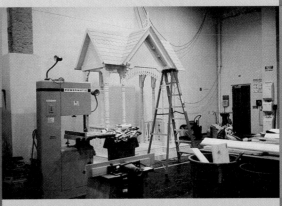

2.11 Computer-aided rendering, gazebo with houses.

2.13 Scene shop, house under construction.

2.14 Scenic house in performance. (Stan Barouh photo)

PLAYS *in* Performance

section 3

3.1
The Vampire, a melodrama from 1827, at DePauw University, directed by Susan Anthony. (Merilyn E. Culler photo)

Plays in Performance, continued

Hay Fever

3.2 *Hay Fever* at the University of South Carolina. Directed by Paul Mullins, setting by Nic Ularu, costumes by Susan Tooker, lighting by Jim Hunter.

A Midsummer Night's Dream

3.3 *A Midsummer Night's Dream* at the Clarence Brown Theatre, designed by Michael Franklin-White, directed and co-designed by Liviu Ciulei.

The Tempest

Antony and Cleopatra

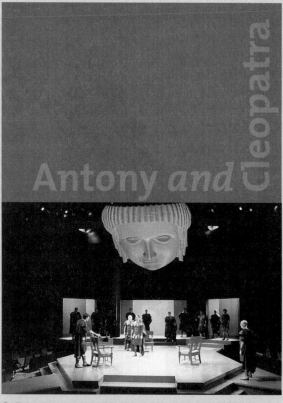

3.4 *The Tempest* at the Public Theatre, New York. (Photo © Michal Daniel)

3.5 *Antony and Cleopatra* at the Guthrie Theatre, Minneapolis. (Photo © T. Charles Erickson)

3.6 *Voodoo Macbeth* at the University of Missouri, Columbia. Direction and costumes by Clyde Ruffin, design by Patrick Atkinson, lighting by R. Dean Packard.

Macbeth

Voodoo

3.7 *Medea* at the *Theatre de la Jeune Lune.* (Photo © Michal Daniel)

Medea

Handke

3.8 *The Hour We Knew Nothing of Each Other* at The Utopian Theatre Asylum. (Courtesy of Natasa and Zeljko Djukic)

Plays in *Performance*, continued

3.9 *Copenhagen* on Broadway. (Photo © Joan Marcus)

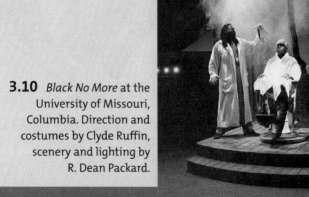

3.10 *Black No More* at the University of Missouri, Columbia. Direction and costumes by Clyde Ruffin, scenery and lighting by R. Dean Packard.

Today's Theatre and Its Makers: Theatre Practice

After briefly introducing the many kinds of theatres that exist today, Part II explores theatre artists—playwrights, actors, directors, designers, and technicians—as they train and as they work. It strives to answer questions such as: What is the nature of the artist's work? What skills do the artists need to practice their craft? Where do they gain such skills? In what venues can they practice their craft? How are they rewarded?

Making Theatre Today: The Context

When you have completed this chapter, you should be able to

- Identify the principal theatre configurations and stage shapes

- Differentiate among the main producing structures in the United States, with an understanding of the strengths of each

- Explain several types of theatre funding

Before studying the people who make theatre happen, we need to examine the contexts in which they work in the United States. In what kinds of spaces can they make their plays? Are some arrangements of actors and audiences better than others for certain sorts of plays? What kinds of producing arrangements are available, and what are their strengths and weaknesses? Finally, how can theatre productions be financed, and what are some implications of the different funding sources?

Theatre Spaces

Given the diversity of theatres around the country, it should not be surprising that they choose different sorts of physical spaces in which to work. With various elaborations, three basic theatre spaces now dominate: proscenium, thrust, and arena stages. In addition to these three, a few less common arrangements can be named and briefly described.

Proscenium Stages

The most popular theatre shape in Western Europe and the United States since the seventeenth century, *proscenium theatres* are marked by a *proscenium arch* that separates the stage and the auditorium.

The stage behind the proscenium arch is typically equipped with a rigging system, which allows scenic pieces to be "flown" (lifted out of sight above the stage floor), and a trap system, which allows objects and people to sink below the stage floor or to rise from it. Some are equipped with wagons or "slip stages" that allow scenery to be moved into place from the *wings,* the spaces on each side of the stage. In most proscenium theatres, there is an area that extends a few feet in front of the arch, an area called the *apron* or *forestage.*

The auditorium is arranged so that almost all seats face the stage. Ground-level seats are *orchestra* seats. Above them are *balconies* (also called *galleries*), which may curve around at least part of the side wall. Older proscenium houses have small, separate balconies, called *boxes,* usually on the side walls of the theatre near the stage. These boxes were at one time the most prized seats in the theatre, but they are now usually avoided because of their bad angle for viewing the stage (bad *sight lines*).

Thrust Stages

Some plays, especially those of Shakespeare and his contemporaries, were not written for production in a proscenium theatre. For this reason, several theatre companies, especially those whose repertory stresses plays from the past, have sought a variation of the theatre used in Shakespeare's day. Such groups have built theatres with *thrust stages* (also called Elizabethan, or Shakespearean, or three-quarter-round stages).

Alley Stage

Proscenium Stage

Thrust Stage

Arena Stage
(Theatre in the Round)

FIGURE 6.1   **Basic Theatre Spaces.**

Actor-audience relationships in four configurations: alley (audience on two sides of the actor); proscenium (audience on one side); thrust (audience on three sides); and arena (audience surrounding actor).

In such theatres, there is no arch separating the actors from the audience. Instead, audience members are placed on three sides of the action, usually on a raked (slanted) floor to improve sight lines, and in balconies. Actors enter the playing area from the back or through *vomitories* (passages that run through and under the audience and open near the stage itself). Because in this theatre elaborate stage machinery cannot be concealed behind a proscenium arch, and because, too, of the close physical relationship between the actors and the audiences, thrust stages tend to rely on acting, costumes, and properties rather than complex scenic effects. Indeed, in such theatres, without a front curtain and proscenium arch to mask them, all scene changes and all actors' entrances must be made in full view of the audience.

Of the many thrust theatres, perhaps the best known are those at the Festival Theatre in Stratford, Ontario, Canada, and at the Guthrie Theatre in Minneapolis, Minnesota, both of whose repertories stress revivals of masterpieces from the past.

Arena Stages

The audience in the *arena theatre* surrounds the playing area, hence its other name: *theatre in the round.* Many people prize the closeness of actors and audiences in arena staging, an intimacy especially well suited to many plays in the modern repertory.

With neither a proscenium arch nor a back wall to mask movements, all property and scenic shifts and all actors' entrances must be done either in blackout or in full view of the audience. Perhaps for this reason, arena stages tend to avoid elaborate scenic effects in favor of close attention to the details of costumes, properties, and acting.

FIGURE 6.2 **Arena Theatre.**
For staging in the round, both actors and scenery need to be visible to audiences on four sides. Compare this photograph with Figure 6.1. *Born Yesterday* at the University of South Carolina. (Directed by Jim Patterson, SSDC.)

Although less common than either proscenium or thrust stages, arena stages exist throughout the country, most notably at the Arena Stage, Washington, D.C., and the original Alley Theatre, Houston, Texas.

Other Configurations

Sometimes from choice and sometimes from necessity, acting companies may take their performances to audiences instead of having audiences come to them. For such performances, a wide assortment of spatial arrangements must be found or created.

The *booth stage* has long been a popular solution. Here, actors erect a curtain before which they play, either on a raised platform or in a cleared area. The result is very much like the thrust stage, with the curtain serving both as a place from which to make entrances and as a background against which to perform. Because it meets the basic needs of performance and can be quickly erected and dismantled, the booth stage has long been the favorite of traveling companies.

Alley stages place the audience on two sides, with the actors performing between them, and often with scenic units at each end. In some countries, such arrangements are found in regular theatres; in the United States, however, they are used mostly by actors who find it necessary to perform in school gymnasiums.

Finally, only the imagination limits the space in which actors perform for audiences. In the United States, we have records of theatre taking place in streets, parks, factories, and even elevators—again, an index of the great diversity of our theatre.

Producing Situations in the United States

Its center is still New York City, but American theatre now touches most cities throughout the country. Although its diversity makes classification difficult, we can divide American theatre first into *professional* and *amateur* (each with several subcategories). Because some theatres resist these categories, we have a third group: *theatres for special audiences.*

Professional Theatre

Broadway

Say the word *theatre* to an American, and he or she will probably think immediately of New York's *Broadway*. The word, in fact, has several different meanings. *Broadway* is, first of all, the name of a street in New York that runs the length of Manhattan. But the word *Broadway* also designates the whole area around Times Square (Broadway and several streets adjacent to it), where most of New York's commercial theatres are located. The word was once used in various union contracts to specify a certain kind of theatre in which only union members could work, and then only for a certain fee or salary. And the word *Broadway* refers to a whole complex of qualities that people associate with the glamorous, glittering world of the legitimate theatre: elaborate settings, rich costumes, distinguished stars, polished performances, and sophisticated musicals and plays.

Although New Yorkers attend the Broadway theatre in large numbers, tourists also make up a sizable part of its audiences. From across the country, people flock into its theatres as part of "seeing New York." They expect to see plays written by the best-known playwrights, performed by the best actors, and designed by the best artists available, for which they are willing to pay—in the early 2000s—about $54 for an *average* ticket. At such prices, Broadway audiences comprise mostly the affluent: a social group that tends to be middle-class or above, white, mature, and somewhat conservative in taste and politics. In 1998, NPR reported theatregoers had an average family income of $91,000.

Broadway is best known for its musicals, where spectacle, rather than idea, is prized. The remaining repertory consists of occasional serious dramas, comedies, mysteries, biographies, and one-person shows. Because of the high costs of producing on Broadway, its theatres seldom offer untried plays; they feature instead revivals of successful plays from past Broadway seasons or recently written plays transferred from successful runs elsewhere, most often London, Off-Broadway, or the regional theatres.

Broadway's reputation today rests in large part on the high quality of its productions. Because many theatre professionals believe that they have not established themselves until they have succeeded on Broadway, Broadway sets the standards of American acting, directing, and design. Broadway artists command among the highest salaries paid in the American theatre, and unions protect them by establishing minimum salaries and controlling working conditions. The major theatrical organizations are the Dramatists Guild (for writers), the Actors Equity Association (for performers), the Society of Stage Directors and Choreographers, United Scenic Artists (for designers), and IATSE (for technicians).

Much of Broadway's appeal, and also many of its problems, stem from money. Its costs of producing continue to climb, for several reasons. As real-estate prices in Manhattan soar, so do the costs of renting theatre space. Personnel costs rise with the demands of the unions. Costs of the goods and services needed to open a show—lumber for scenery, fabrics for costumes, advertising in newspapers and on television—have

Thinking About Today's Theatre

The American actress Tallulah Bankhead (1903–1968) complained that *"it's one of the tragic ironies of the theatre that only one man in it can count on steady work—the night watchman."* From the library or the Internet, discover how many members now belong to the actor's union, Actor's Equity. Then, by consulting the arts and entertainment section of the *New York Times,* find the number of productions currently playing in New York. Based on several familiar plays, estimate an average number of roles in an average play. Calculate how many actors are now working in New York. Evaluate Bankhead's quotation in light of your findings.

become almost prohibitive; and then, there is the money needed to keep the show running once it has opened. Costs are now so high that even a fairly modest show must run months (rather than weeks) in order to recapture its original investment, a situation that has made the *long run* a regular feature of the Broadway theatre.

Huge costs have encouraged a "hit-or-flop" syndrome—a Broadway with no place for the modest success: a hit can make *big* money (*Godspell*, 20,000 percent profit); a flop can lose more than a million dollars. "You can make a killing in the theatre, but you can't make a living."

Another result of high costs has been to limit the potential audience for Broadway shows and to increase the power of certain New York reviewers. As ticket prices rise, the number of people able (or willing) to afford the Broadway theatre declines, as does the willingness of audiences to risk a disappointing evening. Audiences therefore look to a reviewer to steer them toward shows they will like and away from shows they will not like. In so doing, audiences invest certain New York reviewers with enormous power. And this audience affects the repertory in other ways as well, for producers actively seek productions to appeal to its tastes. Thus, the cycle of depending on tried-and-true plays, composers, and artists is reinforced. Simultaneously, opportunities for original plays, untested actors, and unknown directors are further constricted.

FIGURE 6.3   **Broadway.**

The Producers, a Broadway musical taken from a film, epitomizes today's commercial theatre: a Mel Brooks comedy about producing a Broadway musical, it features chorus girls, dancers in top hats, and glitzy costumes. (Photo © Paul Kolnik.)

Broadway has tried to solve some of its money problems. For example, two low-priced ticket sources, the Times Square TKTS booth and the Lower Manhattan Theatre Center, sell tickets at half price on the day of performance for shows not sold to capacity. The computerization of ticket sales allows out-of-towners to compete with New Yorkers for good seats, and credit card payments by phone eliminate the need to write for tickets or to stand in lines to purchase them. The Theatre Development Fund, established in 1967, supports commercial productions of special artistic merit, and New York City offers incentives for the construction of new theatre buildings. The success of these efforts to make Broadway more accessible cannot yet be gauged.

Although detractors of Broadway have long deplored the grip that big business seems to have on it and have predicted its death many times, Broadway continues to be the model of much theatre in the United States. A testament to its authority in theatrical matters is that many other theatres, both amateur and professional, strive to imitate it.

The Road

Many communities regularly import recent Broadway hits by booking the touring theatrical companies (*road shows*) that each year criss-cross the country. They seldom employ the original Broadway cast, but they do use professionals and can even recoup the losses of a Broadway flop. Because road companies travel with complete sets and costumes, they are usually able to offer polished performances of recent hits to audiences outside the major cities, who would otherwise be unable to see them. Business is best for big-name musicals, good for plays with well-known stars, risky for everything else, although certain kinds of shows that may never see Broadway—for example, family-values or gospel plays for black audiences—have found a niche on the road.

Dinner Theatres

Throughout the United States, dinner theatres offer successful Broadway plays of past seasons as the mainstay of their repertories. The quality of such companies varies widely. Some use union personnel, and their quality tends to be higher than those that rely on non-professionals.

Restrictions of space and budget cause almost all dinner theatres to simplify the scenery and costumes of the originals in favor of smaller casts, smaller orchestras, and fewer sets, but, like Broadway, most seek to entertain rather than to elevate or instruct their audiences. In addition to the play itself, they add the sociability of drinks and dinner, so that an evening in the theatre is a festive occasion, not unlike going out for dinner before seeing a show on Broadway.

Off-Broadway

The name *Off-Broadway* derives from the location of its theatres, which lie outside the Times Square theatre district. In addition to location, Off-Broadway houses were once contractually defined by their limited capacity (no more than 299 seats) and by their lower-than-Broadway salaries (as negotiated with the major unions).

Originally (in the 1950s), the goals of Off-Broadway differed from those of Broadway. Off-Broadway sought to serve as a showcase for new talents: Untried artists could work; established artists could experiment with new techniques; new plays could find production. Off-Broadway artists hoped to remain aloof from both threats of censorship and the problems of high-risk commercialism.

Although Off-Broadway continues to offer employment to actors, directors, and playwrights (producing three or more shows for every one of Broadway's by the mid-1980s), its production costs have risen and, with them, its need to succeed at the box office. As risk has become less practical, Off-Broadway has become a rather less expensive version of Broadway, for which it now serves regularly as a tryout space. Shows that succeed Off-Broadway may move to Broadway, often with the same casts, directors, and designers, but with much larger budgets.

Even though Off-Broadway and Broadway overlap in several respects, the lower ticket prices Off-Broadway attract a more diverse audience and thus allow a somewhat more varied repertory. In addition to small musicals and comedies, Off-Broadway produces some serious works and is now home to most new serious plays. For about half of what it costs to see Broadway shows, Off-Broadway audiences can choose among revivals from the classical repertory, recent successes, and original plays. Some of the productions are very good; some are not. But modest risk-taking is part of attending the Off-Broadway theatre and, for those who support it, remains a major part of its attraction.

Off-Off-Broadway

As Off-Broadway moved closer to Broadway—in practice, if not in location—some artists felt the need for an alternative theatre where authors, directors, and actors could work closely together to produce plays in an artistic, rather than a commercial, environment. Thus, *Off-Off-Broadway* grew up in the late 1950s as a place dedicated to the process of creating art and exploring the possibilities of the theatre. It did not want to become a tryout space for Broadway or to succumb to Broadway's or Off-Broadway's commercialism.

Productions feature imaginative, but seldom elaborate, sets and costumes. Although the casts and designers in such spaces are not necessarily union members and are seldom paid even their expenses, they continue to work, exploring the limits of a vision that is often socially, politically, or artistically alien to current American values. Lower ticket prices encourage attendance by people priced out of the Broadway theatre, and the excitement caused by unknown plays and artists draws adventurous patrons to coffeehouses, lofts, cellars, churches, and small theatres tucked away all over Manhattan and even some of the other New York City boroughs, where they watch artists perform plays that stimulate them.

Although sometimes amateurish and often controversial, the offerings of Off-Off-Broadway provide a genuine alternative to the commercialism of both Broadway and Off-Broadway. Off-Off-Broadway remains the focus of what is left of experimental and political theatre in America.

FIGURE 6.4   **Off-Off-Broadway.**
Despite the modest budgets and small spaces, Off-Off-Broadway gives exciting productions of pieces too risky for production on Broadway or Off-Broadway. *You and the Night and the Music* (one of two one-act plays presented under the title *Bridges*), written and directed by Lionel Kranitz, designed by Peter Lach, performed by AEA actors Richard Spring and Ross Haines. (Photograph courtesy of Peter Lach.)

Regional Theatres

The vitality of regional professional theatres is one of the most heartening developments in the American theatre. In major cities throughout the United States and Canada, professional theatres bring art to their audiences. Unlike the Broadway theatre, these groups are usually organized as not-for-profit enterprises and so in theory can be more adventurous with play selection, production style, and personnel decisions. They contribute to theatre throughout America by diversifying and enriching its repertory, developing new audiences, training and revitalizing theatrical artists, and providing employment opportunities. Perhaps for these reasons, regional theatres have been called "the conscience of the American theatre."

Regional theatres offer five major benefits:

1. *A forum where new plays and classics can coexist and provide an alternative to the comedies and musicals that are now the mainstays of Broadway.* Some, like the Arena Stage of Washington, D.C., have earned reputations through the excellence of their classical revivals. Others, like the Actors Theatre of Louisville, have been especially successful in sponsoring new plays. Such theatres have reversed the tradition of plays'

FIGURE 6.5 Regional Theatre.
Minneapolis's Guthrie Theatre, with its thrust stage and heavily classical repertory, is one of the country's most successful regional, not-for-profit operations. Here, their production of Shakespeare's *A Midsummer Night's Dream.* (Photograph by Michal Daniel.)

beginning in New York and then trickling down slowly to the rest of the country. Much new drama now appears first around the country. The best of it moves beyond its local area and throughout the country, often ending in New York.

2. *A source of new audiences for live theatre.* The art of theatre suffers without knowledgeable audiences, because theatre artists become complacent, accepting the ordinary or the mediocre rather than demanding the excellent. With the growth of regional professional companies, audiences across the country have come to appreciate live theatre as an art form and a cultural resource.

3. *A training ground and an energizing center for theatrical artists.* Colleges and universities begin the training of many young artists; the professional regional companies serve to introduce young artists to the profession, allowing them to work intensively with experienced artists. Today, many of our best talents in acting, directing, and designing begin their careers at one of these regional companies—and some elect to stay there throughout their careers.

4. *An important opportunity for the seasoned professional.* Commercial theatre can dull an artist's creativity and vitality because its repertory is restricted and because its productions, when successful, can run for months or years, a numbing experience for an artist. Moreover, the commercial theatre seldom offers those roles from the classical

repertory that stretch the actor's craft. For these reasons, the best actors are often anxious to spend time with a resident theatre, where they can play a wide variety of roles from many of history's best plays. The exchanges between the regional and the New York theatres seem to be raising the standards of the whole profession.

5. *More jobs.* In New York City, job opportunities are dismal. There are many times as many professionals as there are jobs. Regional theatres offer an alternative to New York. For several years, more professional actors have been working outside than inside New York; and designers, few of whom get more than *one* show per season in New York, are now shuttling back and forth across the country, providing scenery, lighting, and costumes for professional productions.

The network of regional professional companies is large and growing. Both in quantity and quality, they are a major force in the American theatre. They may be, when taken together, what so many critics and scholars have long sought: America's National Theatre.

Amateur Theatre

Amateur theatre is theatre performed and produced by people who do not earn their living in the theatre. The two major kinds of amateur theatres in the United States are educational theatres and community theatres.

Educational Theatres

Theatre existed in American colleges and universities even before there were professional theatres here. Theatre and drama were at first extracurricular, performed at special events like commencements. They were later included within the curriculum of departments like classics or English. Drama and theatre became college subjects in their own right only early in the twentieth century, when George Pierce Baker instituted classes in playwriting (and later play production) at Radcliffe College (1903), Harvard (1913), and Yale (1925). By 1914, Carnegie Institute of Technology was offering the first theatre degree. Shortly after World War II, most colleges and universities organized departments of drama (often in combination with speech) and offered, in addition to coursework, both undergraduate and graduate degrees.

Although differing in principal emphases, the functions of *educational theatres* now closely parallel those of the regional professional companies: training future artists, developing new audiences, expanding the theatrical repertory, and providing jobs.

Obviously, the major goal of academic programs is the education and training of students. With the demise of the resident stock companies, training in acting, directing, playwriting, design, and technical production has been largely assumed by the academic institutions. Although many persons complain of the limitations placed on such training because of the basically conservative, even stultifying, atmosphere of many academic organizations, the fact remains that most training for the profession now takes place in this world. Although each program is unique, the general pattern of instruction involves some combination of formal classroom work and public performances of selected plays.

FIGURE 6.6 **Educational Theatre.**
Because they are partially subsidized, university theatres can afford to offer a repertory that goes beyond the latest Broadway hits. Here, Chekhov's *The Seagull* at the University of Missouri, Columbia. (Directed by Cheryl Black; designers—Patrick Atkinson [scenery], Kerri S. Packard [costumes], Charlie Willis [lighting].)

The number of educational theatre programs alone is sufficient to render their influence strong. More than two thousand theatre programs exist in colleges and universities. In small cities without resident professional companies, theatre productions at the college are the best for miles around, and in smaller towns, such productions may be the only opportunity to view a live performance. College and university theatres introduce thousands of students at all levels of education to a variety of plays. For many students, these are the first brush with live theatre.

Happily, because education is a primary goal, such theatres usually display a strong commitment to a wide range of plays and production styles. Alongside standard musicals, comedies, and domestic dramas, collegiate seasons are likely to include significant works from the past and experimental works for the future. Consequently, audiences for university theatre productions often enjoy more variety than in community or dinner theatres.

Too, the number of people required to maintain theatre in an academic setting has given the employment potential of the profession a healthy boost. At the college and university level alone, more than ten thousand productions are mounted each year and more than four thousand teachers are employed. When the growing number of high school drama classes, elementary programs in creative drama, and producing groups devoted to children's theatre are considered, it becomes clear that the academic complex is a major source of jobs. Indeed, educational theatre, considered at all levels, is probably the largest employer of theatre artists and scholars in the United States.

Community Theatres

Community theatres exist throughout the country. Cities with one or two regional professional companies may have a dozen community theatres. In towns with neither professional nor educational theatre (except, perhaps, the annual high school play), a community group may produce plays in a school, a church, or a civic auditorium, providing entertainment and recreation for both participants and audiences.

Community theatres vary enormously. Some pay none of their participants, drawing directors, actors, and office personnel from volunteers in the community; others pay a skeleton staff—a technical director, box-office manager, and an artistic director—who work for a governing board of community volunteers. Almost no community theatres pay their actors or stage crew except under very special circumstances.

In communities without professional companies, community theatres fill the important role of introducing new audiences to the theatre and of keeping live theatre a part of the cultural life of a community. Where professional companies do exist, community theatres serve important recreational needs of people for whom participation in theatre is a greater pleasure than sitting in an audience. In their constant search for volunteers to help with production, such theatres regularly introduce many new people—especially young people—to the world of the theatre. Community theatres are, in fact, the first theatre experience for many people who later enter the profession. Finally, the relatively

FIGURE 6.7 **Community Theatre.**
Amateur theatres within local communities provide both art and recreation. This, the Elden Street Players, is one of more than thirty-five community theatres in the Washington, D.C., area. Jo May and Herbert Rothenberg in *The Night of the Iguana*. (Photograph by Richard Downer.)

modest ticket prices of most community theatres bring into their theatres many who might not at first pay the price of a regional professional company. Some of these new-comers will become lifelong supporters, not only of their local community theatre but also of the regional professional companies and, when in New York, of its commercial theatres.

Theatres for Special Audiences

Some theatres cannot be categorized according to our earlier scheme, for they have both professional and amateur companies. Such theatres define themselves not by their fi-nancial structure but by the specific audiences that they aim to serve.

Children's Theatre

Among the most long-lasting of such groups are the children's theatres. Whether an es-tablished professional company, a university program, or an amateur group composed of community volunteers, whether using adult or child actors, a children's theatre aims to produce plays with special appeal to young audiences in order to instill in such au-diences a love of the theatre.

FIGURE 6.8 **Children's Theatre.**
Imaginative costumes, compelling makeup, and didactic stories about life characterize children's theatre, including this production of *The Tortoise and the Hare* by The Everyman Players. (Directed by Orlin Corey, designed by Irene L. Corey, photograph by Jerry Mitchell, from *An Odyssey of Masquers: the Everyman Players*, Anchorage Press, Louisville, KY.)

The repertory usually consists of plays specially written for youth, using stories and issues of interest to that age group. Their range is great—from imaginative retellings of popular fairy stories, myths, and legends to treatments of contemporary social problems like drugs and divorce. Production styles vary, but most avoid narrow realism. With relatively modest ticket prices (adults often get in at reduced rates when accompanied by a child) and an unusually high commitment to their audiences, children's theatres introduce many young people to the art of the theatre and, from this large group, recruit some as lifelong supporters of all kinds of theatre.

Political Theatres

In another kind of theatre for special audiences, the goals are openly political: black theatre, Chicano theatre, feminist (or women's) theatre, and gay theatre. These groups note (correctly) that theatre through the ages has been controlled by middle- or upper-class white males. Although their individual aims vary, political theatre groups share common assumptions:

- The interests of middle-class white males are not their own.
- Group awareness can be heightened by art. They seek, therefore, a theatre that can display their group's experiences and explore its problems.

These theatres serve their audiences in very different ways. Some favor intense political statements; others avoid polemical works altogether. Many urge a continued separation of their theatres from those of the mainstream; others work to integrate their own art and artists into the commercial theatre as quickly as possible. Some of the theatres produce works with high production values and traditional dramatic texts; others disregard accepted production values and work largely through improvisation. Some seek modest social change; others advocate revolution. Some have budgets of hundreds of thousands of dollars; others have no budget at all. Some charge audiences to attend; others perform in the streets and parks—wherever people congregate—and charge nothing.

Whatever their techniques, these theatres for special audiences strive to offer an alternative to the traditional theatre, which they believe has either demeaned them or ignored them.

Theatre Funding

From its beginnings, American theatre has been organized as a profit-making business. Now businesspeople invest money in a theatre company or a production and hope to recover their investment, with interest, from box-office receipts. This same pattern persists today on Broadway and Off-Broadway, though now the stakes are higher and the sale of film, television, and video rights joins the box office as a likely source of revenue. Broadway funding saw a new development in the late 1990s when a major entertainment corporation (Disney) brought a film-proven property (*The Lion King*) to Broadway at a reported cost of $20 million.

Educational theatres are subsidized. Although the out-of-pocket costs of their productions must often be defrayed by the sale of tickets and program advertisements, the salaries of the faculty (who usually direct, design, manage, and mount the productions) are almost always paid by the university. Because the students who act and crew the productions are seldom paid, the majority of the labor costs associated with producing plays is charged to the university, not to the production. This substantial subsidy allows such theatres to be somewhat adventurous in their selection of plays.

With an occasional exception, government funding for theatre in this country has been conspicuously absent. Thus, one closely watched development was the establishment in 1965 of the National Endowment for the Arts (NEA), whose purpose was to encourage the development of the arts throughout the country. It did so in two major ways: by establishing state arts councils as coordinating and funding units and by subsidizing some existing performance groups. To receive grants, theatres had to be organized as not-for-profit theatres, a radical departure from the Broadway model.

The NEA continues to be controversial. Not all citizens agree that government should fund art when urgent social problems remain unsolved and unfunded. Not all citizens agree that taxpayers should pay for art that some find offensive. The latter issue led to a threatened cutoff of the NEA's funding in 1990 and 1995. Both issues promise to be debated for some time yet.

The precedent set by the NEA may help account for a relatively new phenomenon: Cities and counties, through their parks and recreation departments, are supporting theatre as a form of recreation for citizens who seek an alternative to well-established programs in sports and crafts. Through both advice and money, recreation departments strive to improve the work of local community theatres, which they view as an important resource for the participants and their audiences.

Links to More About Theatre

Marvin Carlson, *Places of Performance: The Semiotics of Theatre Architecture*, 1989.

Margo Jones, *Theatre-in-the-Round*, 1951. Seminal work.

42nd Street. The Myth of Showbiz—instant stardom, your name in lights, true love—or, Theatre as It Never Was.

<www1.playbill.com> Showbiz website. Theatre Central is reachable from here under "Links" or directly at <www.theatre-central.com>. Not exactly rocket science, but hit "Sites" and mess around.

Some people are encouraged that new patterns of funding may be emerging in the United States, patterns that will make it possible to produce theatre freed from the hit-or-flop syndrome, from the drudgery of the long run, and from an unemployment rate of more than 90 percent among Actors Equity members.

KEY TERMS

Check your understanding against this list. Brief definitions are in the Glossary; page references there will direct you to appropriate pages. (Persons are page-referenced in the Index.)

alley stage
apron
arena stage
balcony
booth stage
box
Broadway
educational theatre
forestage
gallery
Off-Broadway

Off-Off-Broadway
orchestra
proscenium (arch and theatre)
regional theatre
road show
sight lines
theatre in the round
thrust stage
vomitory
wings

Playwrights

When you have completed this chapter, you should be able to

- Understand the implications of the words *playwright* and *playwriting*

- Differentiate dramatic dialogue from ordinary language

- Discuss the playwright and the playwright's cultural position

- Explain the playwright's relationships with dramatic and theatrical conventions, with audiences, and with the rehearsal process

The Nature of Playwrights and Playwriting

We must not misunderstand the nature of the playwright's craft. Playwrights create replicas of human action—not records of it (novels) or responses to it (poems). The complexity of playwriting is suggested by the very language that we use to describe it—play*wright* and play*writing*. Plays are both *made* and *written*.

Playwright

Wright means *maker*. Just as a wheelwright is a maker of wheels and a cartwright is a maker of carts, a playwright is a maker of plays. Because playwrights use words on paper to set down their creations, they seem to be "writing." They are in fact, however, creating and organizing actions, using human-like beings (characters) to do so; they are creating replicas of human actions and then setting forth these replicas in language (writing). It is partly accident that what a playwright does looks like what a novelist or poet does—setting down words on paper. If playwrights had a different set of symbols to work with (like a musician's notes or a choreographer's notations) the differences between playwrights and other writers would be clearer.

Playwriting

Although we refer to a play*wright,* we also talk of play*writing* and so acknowledge the importance of *writing* to what a playwright does. Playwrights set forth their replicas of human action in large part by inventing "language" for dramatic "characters" to speak to one another; that is, play*wrights write* dialogue that actors (pretending to be characters) will speak to one another. Dramatic dialogue, however, is not like ordinary language; it must forward plot, reveal character, and express idea, and in a compressed form. The fact that playwrights write words for actors to say and for audiences to hear means that their language must be more active, more intense, and more selective than either everyday speech or other kinds of fictional speech (novels). Playwrights also "write" nonwords: silences, gestures, rhythms, visual images.

Drama and Literature

This dual nature of play*wright* and play*writing* gives a clue to a quality of drama and dramatists that is sometimes misunderstood. Drama is not *primarily* literature, and dramatists are not *primarily* literary artists, although both can be studied *as if* they were. There is a dimension of literary art in drama, of course, but there are other essential dimensions as well. Many highly respected novelists and poets are quite incapable of writing for the stage (the great romantic poets Wordsworth and Shelley are examples); such people were fine literary artists, but they were not good theatrical artists. Conversely, the language of many highly regarded playwrights, when analyzed as literature, seems alternately feeble or overblown (e.g., Eugene O'Neill), but when actors speak the lines in the theatre, the effect is powerful and lasting; such playwrights are fine theatrical artists, but

FIGURE 7.1 **Playwright as Literary Artist.**
Shakespeare managed to be both; many playwrights do not. *Antony and Cleopatra* at the Guthrie Theatre, Minneapolis. (Courtesy of the Guthrie Theatre. Photo by T. Charles Erickson.)

they are not good literary artists. Only the rare person is both literary artist and theatre artist in equal measure, Shakespeare being the premiere example.

Being a Playwright

Playwrights

An idea, an overheard conversation, a need to cry out against an injustice, an urge to break out of self—all these have given rise to plays. This germ may sit in a mind for years before something else urges it into life, or it may bloom at once and become a play written in the heat.

Plays have been written in seven days, and plays have been written in seven years. Plays have been partially written and then put away, often forever.

Plays have most often been written by individuals—playwrights. However, they have also been written by two-person teams, the most famous in America probably having been George S. Kaufman and Moss Hart (*You Can't Take It With You*). They have also been written by collectives, groups of people either dominated by one individual (who, as in the case of Bertolt Brecht, took most or all of the credit) or functioning as a unit, with individual egos submerged in it. Collectives work best when a shared idea unites the individuals: collective playwriting has been, for example, practiced by a number of feminist theatres in which the collective is an externalization of an ideal of sisterhood.

Here, we are concerned mostly with individuals. Generally, they write in isolation for this very public art, theatrical performance. Increasingly, however, playwrights may work with actors, both to try new ideas and new scenes and to improvise around ideas, the improvisations then forming the core of the playwright's next step. Or, playwrights may work with a director or a producer, not quite in a collaboration but certainly in a creative relationship.

Nonetheless, other than in collective situations, it is the playwright's name that goes on the play, and it is the playwright who sits alone with the blank page or the blank computer screen; it is the playwright who listens to demands for changes once production has started; it is the playwright who makes the changes as the first performance comes perilously near; and it is the playwright who takes the heat if the play fails. Or the credit if it succeeds.

Subset: Librettists

Musicals also have playwrights for the non-musical script, called "book-writers" or "librettists," the irony of calling any kind of playwright a book-writer not seeming to matter. (The script is "the book;" actors who haven't yet learned lines are "on book," so such playwrights are not really thought of as writing books, but *the* book.)

The librettist is in a different position from the playwright, far more likely to be working on somebody else's idea than an original one of his or her own. It is not story or character, after all, that drives the musical; it is music. As a result, the book must serve the music's needs, creating cues, setting up situations for kinds of music, driving to climaxes that will be musically expressed.

Before the "integrated musical" (see p. 379) the job was at best mundane, librettos merely providing a framework for the music to rest on. More recent musicals have given more weight to their librettoes and have occasionally drawn established playwrights as their librettists, for example, John Guare for the musical *Two Gentlemen of Verona*.

Subset: The Play Doctor

Once upon a time, there was a unique Broadway professional called the *play doctor*. Not seen so much any more and no longer so called, play doctors were people called in at the last minute (usually out of town) to turn flops into hits. In a sense, play doctors represented the nadir of Broadway's commercialism; in a sense, too, although their goal was audience-pleasing, they represented the opposite of serious playwriting: they were expert not at writing plays, but at rewriting them to meet a commercial need. The most famous was probably the witty Abe Burrows, whose play-doctor reputation took him to TV quiz shows and media fame. Contemporary Broadway, structured on a more corporate model, covers its bets in other ways now—glitz, tie-ins, revivals, adaptations of already proven movies, and so on.

Where Do Playwrights Come From?

From the Theatre

Playwrights frequently come from within the theatre; they are "people of the theatre," who are "theatre-wise." For example, the Roman actor Plautus was a playwright who wrote plays for himself and his actors, and the French actor Molière was a playwright who created vehicles for himself and his troupe. Shakespeare, only a minor actor, wrote many of his most famous roles for other actors in his company, actors whose special strengths and weaknesses he understood and exploited. Such people of the theatre most often work within the dominant theatrical styles of their day, and they probably dominate the theatrical mainstreams.

From Other Fields

Playwrights may start out as something else—not as actors or directors, but as something from outside the theatre altogether. These are not people of the theatre; they are not theatre-wise. Indeed, these people, ignorant of the current conventions of the

FIGURE 7.2   Playwright as Actor.

The seventeenth-century genius Molière was both a playwright and a gifted comic actor, playing many of his own roles, including the protagonist in this play, *The Miser*, seen here in a production by the Old Lyric Repertory Company. (Directed by Linda Linford, scenery by Dennis Hassan, costumes by Nancy Hills, lights by Bruce Duerden. Photo by Donna Barry.)

theatre, may write in new and refreshing ways and so exert a strong appeal to those bored with current practices. Their good plays benefit from the newcomer's gift of ignorance: that is, newcomers may not follow the plays of the mainstream theatre in form, style, length, subject matter, or language. Plays by such newcomers may rarely find commercial production, but they are often welcomed in the avant garde, where they are considered experimental. Then, if their appeal lasts, they may form the basis of a new kind of theatre. Indeed, much of the vitality of *new* movements in theatre of any age comes from the entry of people from entirely outside the theatre who write a play or plays that are unwittingly innovative.

Many Are Called . . .

Lots of people want to be playwrights. The beginning can be difficult:

- Josh is 20 and a college senior. He writes short stories, and he finds his life exciting—new ideas, sex, some drinking, a lot of energy. He has an idea for a play about himself and his life. He writes it quickly; it is full of long, to him amazing discussions among bright college students about life, love, parents, and a future that seems to him deliciously bleak. He sends it to the local nonprofit theatre and it comes back with a curt note, "I'm afraid we found this to be a lot of talk and undramatic." He goes back to short stories.

- Fran is, she believes, trapped in a bad marriage in which she has to hold down a job and cook and clean and mother her two children. When her husband walks out, her rage boils over in the form of a play that she believes strips bare the oppression of women by men. She sends the play to a theatre in town; to her astonishment, they send it back with a note, "This is pretty tame for us." *Tame?* At the fourth theatre she tries, a sympathetic director tells her that she writes pretty well, but her rage is now a cliché. The director gives her a reading list of women authors. A year later, she has the urge to write another play, and it comes out as an up-to-the-minute look at a world that condemns both a husband and a wife to a marriage where love gets driven out by poverty. The first theatre she sends it to produces it.

- Michael writes poetry in iambic pentameter, often with rhyme, supporting himself as a bond broker. He writes five-act verse plays about great men of the past. He sends his plays out, but they always come back. Finally, an agent explains that verse drama died in the nineteenth century; there has been a historical shift that has driven verse from the stage because it no longer carries conviction to most people. "Forget the big heroes and forget verse; write about what you know." Michael thinks the man is a commercial hack and goes on writing his verse plays about great men. The plays pile up in his closet.

Once a playwright gets started and has some productions, however, the way forward isn't necessarily either clear or easy, as some real-life careers show:

- Edward Albee had his first plays produced when he was 20, in Europe and then in the United States. By 24, his short plays dominated Off-Broadway; when he was 26, *Who's Afraid of Virginia Woolf?* had a Broadway production and was an immediate

Thinking About **Playwriting**

Lorraine Hansberry (1930–1965) wrote to an aspiring playwright whose play she had been asked to read: *"I longed for tightness in the writing . . . every single line MUST count."* And indeed, ordinary speech and dramatic dialogue are very different. Take a tape recorder (or a notebook) to a social gathering. Record three or four minutes of conversation. Listen to it carefully to grasp how it differs from dialogue on television or in film. Then convert this ordinary social speech into dramatic dialogue.

success. In the years since, he has been On- or Off-Broadway many times and has been awarded three Pulitzer Prizes, a Kennedy Center Lifetime Achievement Award, and a National Medal of Arts, but he has also had periods of relative neglect. In his seventies he is still writing and still seeing new plays produced.

■ Charles Gordone was a professional actor who had worked on his play *No Place to Be Somebody* for years before it was finally produced Off-Broadway when he was 44. It won the first Pulitzer Prize ever awarded an African-American playwright and made Gordone instantly—but temporarily—famous. The critic Walter Kerr called him "the most astonishing new American playwright to come along since Edward Albee." In the more than two decades that remained of his life, he had other careers as actor, teacher, and cowboy poet, but he never again had a new play produced in a major venue. The reasons are unknowable—personal, psychological, social, cultural—but he is all but forgotten now, his achievement a victim of our culture's tendency to demand, But what have you done *recently*?

■ Megan Terry's first plays were done in a small theatre in Seattle in her early twenties, but at about 30 she began a long-term association with the Open Theatre in New York (see p. 405). *Viet Rock* was both famous and notorious in the 1960s, a rock musical that came from the Open Theatre's collaborative and transformational style. She was hailed as an early feminist playwright for *Calm Down Mother* and *Approaching Simone,* the latter winning an Obie. When she was 43, Terry left New York (the Open Theatre had disbanded) and joined the Omaha Magic Theatre as resident playwright. She has written and co-written many plays produced there as well as working as the theatre's photographer. With more than forty plays published and produced around the world, a recipient of many important awards, Terry in her sixties remains a productive playwright who chose to work outside the commercial theatre.

All three of these playwrights were "successful," but in very different ways and at different ages. None had a straight-line career from first effort to major achievement, or a straight-line career of hits thereafter. All displayed great talent. All received both extravagant praise and harsh rejection. Taken together, they pose a question: what is a successful playwright?

What Helps Playwrights Write Plays?

Although what draws people to theatre and to playwriting remains a mystery, several conditions seem to encourage playwriting.

Other Playwrights

It is not an accident that new playwrights often appear in groups. Whether they are the University Wits of the Elizabethan period or the Off-Off-Broadway playwrights of the early 1960s, they are drawn to playwriting by the same theatrical conditions at the same time—in the case of the University Wits, the explosion of theatrical interest in Oxford and London; in the case of the Off-Off Broadway playwrights, the explosion of theatrical excitement in New York City. Their very number, in turn, increases the excitement, which in turn attracts more new playwrights, so that working playwrights tend to produce other working playwrights.

FIGURE 7.3   The Playwright's Matrix.

Fortunate playwrights belong to a time when several surface at the same time, creating a playwriting "culture" that has a distinctive voice. Shakespeare, although unique in the level of his abilities, was part of such a cluster—the University Wits, the playwrights of rival theatres, the young playwrights who were coming up as he aged. Here, an early play from this rich period, his *Midsummer Night's Dream* at the Clarence Brown Theatre, the University of Tennessee. (Co-designed by Michael Franklin-White and Liviu Ciulei, directed by Mr. Ciulei. Courtesy of the Clarence Brown Theatre, Mr. Franklin-White, and Corporate Scenographics LLC.)

A Vital Theatre

A dying or dead theatre rarely attracts new playwrights; a vital one does—and, para-doxically, a vital commercial theatre attracts new playwrights both to itself and to the avant-garde. A theatre's ability to attract new playwrights is one measure of its own health.

Good Social and Economic Treatment

Playwrights need a theatre that offers them a decent living and an acceptable place in so-ciety. In the United States today, it is said that playwrights can "make a killing but not a living" in the theatre, meaning that one playwright may occasionally hit it really big, earning money to live on for a lifetime, but that most playwrights cannot find enough productions to support themselves. They often turn instead to movies and television. When, on the other hand, a theatre offers large financial rewards, as the American theatre did from the 1920s to the 1950s, many new writers are drawn to it.

Training Playwrights

Unlike actors, directors, and designers, playwrights do not, as a rule, go through structured periods of formal training. To be sure, there are playwriting programs in American uni-versities, but their record of producing playwrights who write plays of recognized qual-ity cannot compare with their records in acting, directing, and design. Courses in playwriting often familiarize theatre students with the problems of the playwright and give an enriching new slant on other areas of theatre work; advanced degrees in playwriting are frequently combined with scholarly work in such a way that playwriting becomes an adjunct of critical study. Playwriting as an academic discipline, however, suffers from the same problems as creative writing in general, and when it seems to produce results it is because the same factors are at work: teachers who are themselves artists and who teach as much by example as by precept; constant encouragement of creativity itself, so that the student is surrounded by other writers and playwrights; and strong professional links with agents, producers, and publishers, so that entry into the mainstream is helped.

To be sure, certain techniques of playwriting can be taught and learned. When a the-atrical style remains in vogue for a long period, playwrights can be "taught" the hall-marks of that style, meaning really that they can be taught how to imitate the plays that have already succeeded in that style. Thus, in the realistic theatre, would-be playwrights could be taught to put exposition into the mouths of characters who had a reason for explaining things; they could be taught to prepare for the third-act resolution by plant-ing information in Act I; they could be taught that taxi drivers and duchesses do not speak in the same way; and so on. Insofar, then, as playwriting is a craft, such teaching was and still can be effective. Its limitations lie in the difference between the craft and the art of writing for the theatre and between the imitation of an existing style and the innovation of a new one. At some point in every age, however, the relevance of an ex-isting theatrical style ends, because styles that have dominated for a long time become increasingly drained of their potential for saying something new.

When imitation of an existing style is not the main object, the teaching of play-writing is far less certain and much less successful. Here is where the gifted newcomer, without experience in the theatre, may suddenly appear to take plays and playwriting in wholly new directions. For a time, critics may cry out that the new works are "not really plays," audiences may be enraged, and teachers of playwriting may be mystified—and lessonless. (The young Tennessee Williams was not thought very good when he tried studying playwriting in a university.)

Rules and Maxims

Many rules have been laid down for playwrights. They have seldom proved to be perma-nent—or to be rules. Rather, playwrights are well advised to follow some old maxims:

- Write what you know
- Write for your own time
- Write action, not speeches
- Write for actors, not readers
- Be passionate, not timid; truthful, not nice

It often helps, too, to be selfish and ruthless. Writers work in solitude and with many ob-stacles; personal relationships sometimes suffer.

If, on the other hand, the playwright is in it only for the money (which is scarcer and scarcer), all bets are off, and he or she is wise to play it safe, aim for the middle, listen to marketing research, and imitate whatever made money most recently.

From Page to Stage: Professional Issues

Writing the Play

Plays begin as a great variety of things: a story overheard, a chance remark, a note jot-ted down on a slip of paper. Plays may set out to retell a legend or myth; they may treat a bit of history or a slice of daily life; they may be adapted from a novel or a ballad; they may be an imagined, onstage symbol or gesture. Moving forward from that genesis is part of the playwright's talent, and it is one of the elements that separates playwrights from wannabees.

Lots of people have *ideas* for plays. The problem is turning them into scripts. For many, the thought of writing a full-length play is a stopper—as formidable as the idea of writing a four-hundred-page book. And, true, full-length plays rarely get written quickly or easily; they demand the commitment of months, at least.

How do you leap from the genesis to the play—to character, dialogue, action—to all those pages? In part, the answer lies in the concepts of dramatic theory (see pp. 73–76), not because most playwrights deliberately apply dramatic theory but because they must work in terms of certain dramatic elements, whether they call them by the same names or not: above all, character, language (*dialogue*), and action. Idea, too, may give the genesis of a play and may dominate conscious thinking during much of the creative process, but "How do I dramatize the idea?" is an unproductive first question for a playwright to ask.

After the Genesis

What happens, then, after the genesis—after the inspiring observation or accident or thought?

The playwright tries to move forward. The urge to make a play is there; it is conscious. It drives the imagination—both conscious and unconscious thought. Certain paths are opened for such thought by the nature of the genesis:

- If the genesis is a story that will also be the play's story (as in Greek tragedy, for example), the next step is character: what kind of people are doing these things?
- If the genesis is a person or the playwright's self (character), then the next step may be language (a burst of statements of character) or action, but, inevitably, action has to come early, because dramatic character is *character in action.*
- If the genesis is an idea—outrage at an injustice, satirical amusement at a subject, a thought (e.g., "Revenge is easy to talk about but hard to do")—then the next step is probably character but may be story, a chain of incidents that embody and illustrate the idea.
- If the genesis is language—an overheard remark, a single great line—then the next step is probably character: who says it and why?
- If the genesis is a situation ("Two guys and a girl are trapped in a stalled elevator, see—"), then the next step may be some dialogue but has to be an action: what do they *do*, not what do they say?
- If the genesis is history and a real person, then the playwright is already bound by some incidents, probably some meaning, and perhaps even some language (famous quotations, letters, and so on); the next step is probably story—trying to make a fictional beginning, middle, and end of a real life.

It is possible to combine two things as genesis—for example, a character and an idea. Let's say that the playwright is struck by a real-life character who is the head of the Central Intelligence Agency; at the same time, the playwright is troubled by America's foreign policy. Character and idea interplay here and produce at least a situation and probably a story: is the CIA head a victim of internal betrayal? Or is he a dangerous ideologue pushing an agenda? Or is he a dying man trying to pursue an ideal? Or perhaps a different question occurs to the playwright: what is the head of the CIA like at home? Does this play *have* to be set in government offices?

Moving On

Playwriting is an act of the imagination. It is neither entirely rational nor entirely conscious.

FIGURE 7.4   **Genesis of the Play.**

Plays come from all sorts of beginnings—personal experience, memory, an overheard conversation, a famous event. Here, a play about an affliction, Michael Medoff's *Children of a Lesser God,* directed by Michael O'Hara at Ball State University. (Courtesy of Ball State University.)

If two or more playwrights are collaborating, however, the post-genesis process may *seem* conscious, because they talk it through: verbalizing forces an appearance of consciousness but probably hides both conscious and unconscious work by the individuals. Collaboration is different from individual work in this way—more dependent on language (so they can communicate), often more dependent on decisions that demonstrate that people are working together. ("Okay, we agree that this couple is isolated in a VIP airport lounge and their flight is cancelled, and then—") The individual working alone may not put many thoughts into language and may not recognize decisions as such. However, as the individual or the pair or the group now move forward, certain things take shape

- Situation—rough ideas of setting, social level, relationships, important aspects of the play's world—politics, religion, conditions of threat
- Tone—comic or serious or satirical or mixed
- Plot—not merely the story, but the ordering of the incidents as they relate to character, action, and idea
- Form—whether the play is to be long or short, in quick scenes or long acts, in a single piece or three or five

Other matters include rhythm, pace, rising and falling action, and climax, as well as, in certain kinds of drama, "big moments" and sure-fire act endings. The seasoned playwright, who has worked a lot with actors and may have certain actors already in mind, may also write consciously to give actable depth to character and dialogue for those actors.

Dialogue

Much of this work will be externalized as dialogue. Playwrights must try to become masters of spoken language, both by hearing it and by creating it. The language of a play carries a huge burden: not only the meaning of the words, but also character and tempo and the externalization of much of the action. As well, each character should have unique speech patterns and vocabulary, and ideally each character could be recognized by language alone.

Dialogue can take on a life of its own and lead away from what the playwright sets out to do in a scene. Character may lead this digression, but so may idea, or the interplay of characters-in-action may simply be too tempting. Playwrights can welcome a certain amount of such digression, but they have to cut it off if it threatens the progression of the play itself. Other theatrical concepts are useful here, whether the playwright uses the same terms or not: through-line, motivation, objective (pp. 142ff.). Working with actors on such a scene will help: seasoned actors show unease or confusion when motivations go off on a tangent. This can be particularly true where the playwright has let dialogue, especially dialogue about idea, go off on its own.

Finishing a Draft

As plays take shape, playwrights may show them to other people—lovers, acquaintances, theatre professionals. When a draft is finished, some playwrights set to work again with a director or a producer or with actors. However it goes, the play is not finished until it is on a stage in front of an audience.

A playwriting teacher who became a New York theatre critic once said that the playwright was the complete theatrical artist; directors were three-quarters artists, actors half. The suggestion is probably unfair, but it tries to get at the playwright's unique situation—creating something (and something important) from nothing. Actors and directors have the play itself to base their work on; like musicians, they are playing somebody else's score. Playwrights, like composers, play what is in their heads.

Conventions

Playwrights always have to strike a balance between their own imaginations and the realities of the theatres in which they work. Plays must, among other things, provide a framework for other theatrical arts, especially acting and design, and so plays are circumscribed by both theatrical and dramatic conventions. These matters, and the technical means of accomplishing them, are things that playwriting courses can teach or the playwright can learn in the theatre itself as apprentice or actor.

In the modern realistic theatre, for example, playwrights have had to strike a balance between their own impulse to expand meaning and the stage's impulse to limit meaning to the same role that it plays in real life. For earlier playwrights, language was a primary means of theatrical communication, and early realistic plays about upper-class life could be heavily verbal because the people that the plays were about were (or so it was believed) articulate and literate (e.g., the plays of Shaw). However, as the theatre focused more on inarticulate protagonists in a democratized theatre, verbalism became a less useful tool, and playwrights found themselves trying to find a compromise between their own impulse to "say" things and their characters' inability to do so.

Other times have required playwrights to strike different sorts of balances. The Greek theatre, for example, limited the playwright to only three actors and thus affected the number and flow of characters within plays; Shakespeare's theatre used men to portray women's roles, a practice that surely affected the nature of female characters in drama. Playwrights in seventeenth-century France were expected to use language and portray morality appropriate to aristocrats; playwrights of the early nineteenth century were expected to enable displays of acting and feats of spectacle. Whatever the age, no playwright escapes the compromise required between the creative impulse and the conditions of the theatre.

Audiences

"The drama's laws/The drama's patrons give," wrote Samuel Johnson in the eighteenth century. He meant, of course, that audiences—by their attendance and their responses—decide what traits plays ought to have and which plays are good or bad. Audiences, rather than critics or theorists, establish the "laws" of drama.

The remark illustrates the uneasy relationship between the playwright and the audience, for, to the playwright, the audience is a fickle monster that can make the artist either rich and loved or humiliated and poor. Between playwright and audience exists a relationship that is often ambivalent in the extreme.

Audiences do not care for "the laws of drama" so often promoted by critics, theorists, and scholars. Audiences care about their own responses. They are, however, often conservative and cautious. When they go to a theatre, especially a mainstream, commercial theatre, they want to be entertained, to get their money's worth. They seldom want to be lectured at, shocked, offended, frightened, or bored. As a result, they look with enthusiasm on any novelty—so long as it resembles what they are already familiar with.

The audience's desire for something that is new enough to be interesting but familiar enough to be comfortable often leaves playwrights in a quandary. They may be torn between their own wish to innovate and the audience's insistence that they imitate features of earlier works. And playwrights must find their audience if they are to work as playwrights. What to do?

Playwrights and Their Culture

To speak to a culture, playwrights must see and understand the culture's center. Socially, they may be outsiders, but they must be in touch with their world. Outsiders or insiders, playwrights must understand their own time and their own place:

- They must know the culture's language, the vocabulary and the rhythms of these people at this moment.

- They must know behaviors—how people gesture, how people move, how people talk to each other; they must know manners or the lack of manners; they must know how people interact—how they probe and get to know each other, how they fight, how they avoid fighting, how they show love, how they show the dying of love.

- They must know what people believe: what they want, what they shun; what they fear, what they desire; what hangs over them, what lures them on. It is not enough to have read in *Time* that ours is a consumer culture; the playwright must have lived that consumerism, engaged in it, watched it, understood it, objectified it. The same is true of gay culture, youth culture, Latino culture—you can't make it up.

- They must know the issues of the time, both personal and public—private and public desire, private and public fear, private and public attitude—whether their world is melancholy or buoyant, the Jazz Age or the Mauve Decade.

This acute sense of the present is just as important if playwrights write historical plays. It is impossible to recover the past in all its density and detail; therefore, what playwrights reveal is their own time in terms of the past, insofar as it can be known or insofar as the past is useful to them (e.g., Arthur Miller's *The Crucible*). Historical plays may use elevated language or heroic character, but they remain primarily of their own time, their own culture. You can write a modern play about Shakespeare, using language that sounds to a modern ear "Elizabethan," but you cannot write a truly Shakespearean play about anything.

The Playwright as Outsider

Successful outsiders have included *Molière,* the great French playwright of the seventeenth century, who was the son of a commoner and spent years fighting his way up through traveling theatre companies. He became the preeminent theatrical observer of the French court and a protégé of the autocratic and snobbish Louis XIV. *Oscar Wilde* was also a commoner, an Irishman, and a bisexual, but he wrote brilliant and successful comedies about Victorian England's upper crust. *Tennessee Williams* was an American southerner, a homosexual, and a boozer, and he wrote mostly about victims and losers, yet he became one of the greatest theatrical illuminators of American culture, his position so central that at least one line has come into American speech, "I have always depended on the kindness of strangers."

All three both observed and expressed their cultures, but none of the three ever rose to the top of their *societies.* Molière was denied Christian burial because he was an actor; Wilde was abandoned by the Victorian upper class he had celebrated when he was tried for homosexuality; Williams made a lot of money but lived outside the mainstream. For the outsider, then, playwriting can be socially dangerous: acute knowledge and observation, coupled with success, can cause deep resentment among the powerful.

The Insider Playwright

Social insiders also make successful playwrights, but usually when they write about a limited or minority culture instead of the mainstream. Black, gay, and feminist play-

FIGURE 7.5   **The Outsider Playwright.**

For all his success, Molière was a social outsider whose observations of his society sometimes got him into trouble. Here, his *The Miser* at the University of Vermont. (Costumes by Martin A. Thaler. Bill DeLillo photo.)

wrights, for example, have written from a position (perhaps constructed) as insiders in the black, gay, and feminist cultures, outsiders in the social mainstream. As mainstream culture has seemed to fragment since about 1950—more an appearance than a reality, perhaps, and partly the result of giving attention to formerly marginalized cultures—this kind of insider playwright has become more common in the United States. Since the 1960s, we have seen many such playwrights in "political" theatre (pp. 404ff.), the tendency being for the minority-culture playwright to dramatize the problems of that minority in opposition to the mainstream, and thus to make it visible to the mainstream.

A playwright who is an insider in mainstream culture *and* its center of power would be much rarer, although in seventeenth-century England, a number of the "Restoration" playwrights were aristocrats and politicians who wrote for and about a very small world of culture-makers and power-wielders. Such playwrights are probably atypical, however. No simple reason can be given, but we would point out that playwriting is hard work, and people who already have power and money perhaps don't see the point of it. After all, whether insider or outsider, playwrights are never content to chill out and be cultural consumers: their eyes are always looking, their brains always clicking, everything they see and hear being filed away for future use.

A Case in Point

Tony Kushner's *Angels in America* opened on Broadway in the early 1990s after earlier productions in Los Angeles. One of the outstanding dramas of the late twentieth century, it was an outsider's play that located itself in the heart of the culture. Its principal subjects included homosexual life, only recently real to most Americans; AIDS, an epidemic little more than a decade old when the play was written; love and personal loyalty; and, through the real historical figure Roy Cohn, political and moral corruption. Cohn, a homosexual homophobe and an assistant to the notorious Senator McCarthy, opened the play to resonances far beyond what it would otherwise have achieved; so, too, did the brilliant concept of the angels of the title. They, and their lair in heaven, gave the play religious dimension and a level of spectacle that lifted it far above most dramas of the nineties.

Written in a contemporary idiom, the play was the resonant, meaningful work of a playwright who "wrote what he knew" but metamorphosed it into a penetrating look at America at the end of the twentieth century, and at the situation of some ordinary Americans at the turn of the twenty-first—powerless, alienated from government and God alike, comforted by personal relationships, getting along on grit and humor and

FIGURE 7.6 *Angels in America.*
Actually two plays, it made dazzling theatre of a mosaic of a real-life figure, AIDS, and angels. Ellen McLaughlin in "Millennium Approaches," the first of the plays, directed by Oskar Eustis with Tony Taccone at the Mark Taper Forum. (Courtesy of the Mark Taper Forum. Photo by Schwartz/Thompson.)

luck. It was funny and unsettling and startling and visually splendid, and it put the theatre itself back at the center of the culture, at least for a little while.

Getting the Play Produced

In recent years, the number of theatres in which new plays can be produced in the United States and Canada has increased. Many plays now begin their lives in regional theatres; in addition, such organizations as the National Playwright's Conference of the O'Neill Theatre Center give first productions to a wide spectrum of scripts, many of which are later produced elsewhere. New York, however, remains the goal of most playwrights. There are two reasons: money and status. Broadway royalties are far higher than anywhere else, and Broadway production is subject to the best reviewing and is the most prestigious.

Plays are not produced at any of these theatres by accident. Nor are many new plays that attract widespread attention (except at an institution such as the O'Neill Center) scripts that come out of nowhere. Most are submitted to regional theatres or Broadway or Off-Broadway producers by agents. Far less often, a play may reach a producer by way of an actor or a director. In any case, the playwright's first high hurdle is finding that first production, whatever the medium used to reach a producing organization.

After an initial success, the playwright may move toward the mainstream; an audience may be moving toward the playwright at the same time, both being the product of historical change. Sometimes, audiences accept new language, new ideas, and new forms with a speed that is startling.

If the moment is not right, however, the playwright may not find an audience, may not even find production, and then will stop writing or go to television or films.

Working with the Play in Rehearsal

Producers have readers who read scripts and make comments. When a script is accepted for production, it already has an accompanying list of such comments as well as the producer's own views; added to these will be the ideas of the director when one is chosen. Each principal actor will add ideas, and each of these people—producer, director, actors—may have still other ideas that have come from friends, spouses, lovers, and relatives. The playwright having a first play done is tempted to try to please everybody. By the time several plays have been done, however, the playwright may be downright rude about suggestions coming from any source at all. Between these two extremes lies the kernel of the playwright's work during the production period: accepting ideas for changes that are wisely based in the unique circumstances of the production.

Perhaps regrettably, in the modern American theatre the director is assumed to have considerable critical skill and to be an expert in everything from dramatic structure to dialogue. Changes in a script, however, are rarely simple; a Broadway playwright said some years ago that altering a play is like taking bricks out of a wall: for every one that is taken out, half a dozen others have to be put back. At times, the playwright wonders what it was about the play that ever caused people to want to do it, because they have asked for so many changes that nothing seems to be left of the original.

FIGURE 7.7   **New Plays.**

New York is no longer the principal venue for new scripts; now, they find production all over the country—even all over the world. (A recent Irish play got its first production in Moscow.) This is Hershell Norwood's *Billie's Blues* at the University of Louisville African-American Program's Fifth Annual Juneteenth Festival of New Works. (Courtesy of Hershell Norwood. Directed by Nefertiti Burton, photo by Aukram Burton, Aukram@Ramimages.com.)

Paying the Playwright

A few playwrights do make livings, especially as the number of regional theatres has multiplied, but the hit-or-flop life of Broadway still prevails; the playwright can still make only a killing, rarely a living. Standard Broadway contracts, under the aegis of the Dramatists Guild, give the playwright a percentage of the theatre's weekly gross, a percentage that climbs as the gross climbs past certain plateaus. On a hit, these figures can be impressive—thousands of dollars a week. On a modest success, they can be a thousand a week or less. On a flop, nothing. Considering that few playwrights have a successful play every year, we can easily see that the income from even a hit must be spread over several years, and that after an agent's commission and professional expenses and taxes are taken out, the prorated remainder may be less than many businesspeople take home. There is, of course, the significant additional income of film and television sales—and perhaps most importantly, there is the secondary income of amateur and stock production.

Amateur rights are handled mostly by two organizations, the Dramatists Play Service and Samuel French, Incorporated. They collect royalties on productions by amateurs (community, school, and university theatres) for the life of the play's copyright—since the Copyright Law of 1977, the author's life plus fifty years. Although the royalty on a single performance of a play is small, the collective royalty per year on a play that is popular with the nation's several thousand community and college theatres can be large, and even plays that fail on Broadway can become staples of amateur theatre and go on providing income for decades.

Yet, with all this, relatively few people make a living as playwrights. It is a difficult craft that requires special talent, and it is made far more difficult by the conditions under which plays must find production. Many potential playwrights now move to television and film, and there is some question whether—despite grants, theatres, and organizations that encourage new plays—playwrights may continue to decline in number until the theatre itself recovers its vigor.

Establishing a Career

Once established, the American playwright enjoys one or more years of acceptance and then, more often than not, begins to lose the audience. Yesterday's innovator becomes tomorrow's has-been. Rare is the contemporary playwright who is a lifelong success, even a lifelong presence in the theatre; most reach a plateau and then seem to imitate themselves or to decline. One American playwright estimated that an Off-Broadway or Broadway career lasts ten years. Significant exceptions appeared, however, in the 1990s: three playwrights who had had first successes in the 1960s and 1970s (Edward Albee, Terence McNally, and John Guare) were major prizewinners.

Links to More About Theatre

George S. Kaufman and Moss Hart, *Light Up the Sky.* A play about a playwright.

Toby Cole and Helen Krich Chinoy, *Playwrights on Playwriting,* 1960.

Robert Nemiroff, *To Be Young, Gifted, and Black,* 1969. Lorraine Hansberry.

<www.artslynx.org> Go to Artslynx International Theatre Resources and click on "Playwrights" and "Playwrighting Resources" [sic].

What Is Good Playwriting?

Good playwriting is playwriting that produces good theatre. Exactly what makes a play good is the subject of continuing dispute, even among theatre scholars, but some of the traits of such plays have already been suggested in Chapters 3 and 4. The questions at the ends of these chapters can offer a beginning glimpse of what makes for good playwriting.

The great German theorist Goethe suggested another set of questions to help assess the worth of a play and playwright: 1. What did the author set out to do? 2. Did he or she do it? 3. Was it worth doing? These questions are useful inasmuch as they remind us that a playwright may exhibit great technical skill (he or she set out to do something and did it quite well), yet still produce an inconsequential play (it wasn't worth doing). Great plays, finally, must do more than entertain, although they must do that at a minimum.

KEY TERMS

Check your understanding against this list. Brief definitions are in the Glossary; page references there will direct you to appropriate pages. (Persons are page-referenced in the Index.)

copyright   royalty
dialogue   wright

Actors

When you have completed this chapter, you should be able to

- Explain the paradox of the actor

- Explain the relationship between actor and character and between character and real person

- Explain the goals of rehearsal

- Understand the actor's vocabulary

- Explain how an actor creates a role

- Discuss the possibilities of acting as a profession

The Nature of Acting

The actor stands at the center of the theatre. Without him or her, there is nothing—an empty building, a hollow space. Directors cannot direct or designers design without actors; the playwright can create only works to be read like novels.

The actor alone *can* make theatre without the help of other artists. The actor can make costumes, can build a theatre, and can provide at least crude scenery for it. Out of such an actor-intensive theatre may occasionally grow a sophisticated one, such as the *commedia dell'arte* of Renaissance Italy (pp. 300ff.). More often, however, such an actors' theatre changes in the direction of the theatre that we know, adding playwright, designer, and director. No matter how far this theatre develops, however, it remains the descendant of that primal theatre—actor-centered.

The Actor and the Performer

Acting must not be thought of merely as an ability to entertain—to clown at parties or to tell jokes. The latter are parts of a talent for *performing*—that is, for reaching and de-

FIGURE 8.1 **The Heart of the Theatre.** Only the actor can make theatre without other support. This is from a performance of *She Stoops to Conquer* at Trinity University. (Bob Brevard photo.)

lighting an audience without regard to character or theatrical action. As we have already tried to suggest, there is more to acting than this. A good actor is also a good performer; a good performer, however, may not be a very good actor.

Some kinds of theatre or related arts put a higher premium on performing than on acting; circus high-wire work, for example, requires great performers and has no use for actors. Musical comedy, on the other hand, requires both acting and performing, for the ability to "sell" a song requires performing of a high level.

The performer plays *to* the audience; the actor plays the character *for* the audience.

The Paradox of the Actor

The French theorist Denis Diderot (1713–1784) used the expression "the paradox of the actor" as the title for an essay on acting in which he tried to capture what seems to be an essential contradiction in the art: *In order to appear natural, the actor must be artificial.*

Natural versus Artificial

Throughout the history of acting, almost every change in acting for the mainstream theatre has been seen as a move toward the "natural" or the "real." Partly, changes in philosophy are at work: When an age's idea of "what it is to be human" changes, the manner of depicting human beings on the stage changes as well, and the older concept of "real" or "natural" is viewed as outdated and artificial.

Hearty Welcome.   *Sublime Adoration.*   *Painful recollection.*   *Terror.*

FIGURE 8.2   **The Paradox of the Actor.**
Every age has its own idea of what seems "natural" or "real," including these Romantic illustrations that look decidedly unreal to us. Yet actors using these gestures were, just like modern actors, experiencing the paradox of the actor—to find images of the natural and the real through a process that is unnatural and unreal.

However, there is a distinction to be made between the idea of what humanity *is* and the idea of what humans *might* or *should be*. Certain ages and certain forms of theatre have set up many "proprieties"—rules based on the ideal. On the stage, we find such extremes of stage propriety as the outdated "rule" that the left hand must never be used for an important gesture. Such acting will seem "artificial" to anybody who believes that the stage must imitate life explicitly.

Inspiration versus Technique

Our own age is one whose theatrical heritage is primarily a "natural" one, at least in the realistic theatre. Modern American actors sometimes speak disparagingly of an actor who is "technical," meaning one who builds character out of careful, conscious use of body and voice—rehearsed inflections and carefully chosen poses and gestures. Their belief is that "technical" actors work mechanically and so fail to bring imagination and life to their work. The technical actor is seen as "full of tricks."

At the far extreme from the technical actor is the "inspirational" one, whose work, although carefully rehearsed, is not assembled from external behaviors but is created through application of mental and emotional techniques that supposedly work to reach the actor's emotional and mental center and then somehow push outward into onstage movement and vocalization. In theory, the character created by the inspirational actor

FIGURE 8.3 **Inspiration and Technique.** Seeing only the finished performance by a gifted actor, it is usually impossible to tell which route was taken to the final product. This is Sarah Bernhardt, one of the greatest of international stars in the late 1800s; she may often have been "technical" because of constantly repeated performances, but her impact on audiences was phenomenal—that is, she seemed inspired.

will be more "natural" because it rises from inner sources that also give us music and poetry. To the inspirational actor, her approach is fresh and her creation original.

Inner and Outer

Technical and inspirational acting have their direct counterparts in "outer" and "inner" acting. As one actor put it, "I like to build my house first—then I start to live in it." She meant that she liked to create the "outer" part of the role; then, comfortable with that— voice, posture, costume, gesture—she could move inward toward emotional intensity and conviction, believably "living in" the shell she had created.

Other actors work from the inside out. All of their early work will be devoted to mental, emotional, and spiritual exploration. Only when that work is completed do they feel that an outer structure can be built. In the cases of both the "inner" and the "outer" actor, truth to the character is being sought, and the difference is really a difference of emphasis and of sequence. The "inner–outer" distinction is not quite the same as the "technical–inspirational" one; the "technical" actor's work begins and ends with externals, whereas the "outer" actor's work finally leads inward, and the "inner" actor's work leads toward externals in a way that the "inspirational" actor's does not. Inspiration supposedly gives rise to externals through a nonintellectual leap, and, as Diderot suggested, those externals can vary from performance to performance and may supply only an occasional "sublime moment."

Being and Pretending

To reach emotional truth, it has been said, the actor must *be* the character; on the contrary, another point of view insists, the actor must always stand aloof from the character and *pretend.* Here is precisely the paradox that Diderot observed. If an actor were really to *be* the character, how would he control onstage behavior? What would keep the actor from becoming inaudible at times? What would keep the actor, as Othello, from actually killing the actor who plays Desdemona? What would cause the actor to modulate the voice, control the tempo of a performance, listen to other actors? And, contrarily, if the actor always pretends, what will he be but a lifeless imitation of humanity? How will the actor keep the speeches from sounding like empty nonsense? How will gestures be anything but graceful hand-waving?

Because the actor is at the center of the theatre, this paradox is the paradox of the theatre itself: In order to be convincing, one must lie. The actor both "is" *and* "pretends," exploiting both inner and outer, both technique and inspiration. It is never enough for the *actor* to be satisfied that a sigh or a smile is perfectly truthful; the sigh or smile must also have the carrying power and the communicative value to be perfectly truthful *to the audience.*

The Actor and the Character

Understanding Character

It should now be clear that actors neither create real human beings, on the one hand, nor somehow transform themselves and erase their own personalities on the other. Instead they engage in a creative act whose end product is a construct, that is, an entity made by human agency for a particular purpose. Both the actor and the audience must remember this—even though actors and audiences may speak of the construct by its name, "Hamlet," it is not a real person named Hamlet. The construct remains an invention, and one actor's construct may be quite different from another's construct of the same name—Laurence Olivier's from Kevin Kline's Hamlet, for example.

In the literary sense, character is a construct that represents human personality and that expresses itself through *action*. In the sense of the word used by Aristotle, the effectiveness of a character depends on how well it fits into and affects plot. This idea has an important implication for the actor: We define character on the basis of the function within the artistic whole and *not merely on the basis of how well it imitates a human being.* Therefore, a dramatic construct may be a convincing imitation of a human being in its superficial attributes—it may talk like one and may have preferences in clothes and food and entertainment like one—and yet it may be a "bad" character in that it makes no important contribution to the artistic whole and the action. An actor who concentrates on mannerisms of the character and fails to grasp the character's function as contributor to the action will fail and will be guilty of what the Russian actor and theorist Stanislavski called "tendencies."

For the actor, character means something like "the imitation of a human being as it expresses itself through the words and the decisions created by the author, *in relation to the other characters in the play and their decisions and words.*" The actor's character exists on the stage (only) and has no life off the stage; the actor's character exists in an artificial time scheme that is quite different from the time scheme of real life. It may be helpful for the actor to figure out where the character is coming from when it walks on the stage, what it has been doing, and so on, but such analysis has to be limited strictly to conclusions relevant to onstage action and onstage time or it will lead to sideshows and tendencies, or even to the creation of a play that the author never wrote (and one that, regrettably for the audience, takes place offstage).

The actor is a person; the character is a construct. In order for the character to *seem* to be a person during the two or three hours of performance, actors use their *consciousness*, their *instruments*, and their *imaginations*.

Constructing Character

Consciousness.   Consciousness refers to matters that are under the conscious control of the actor. Discipline, for example, is essential because actors cannot create character unless they can control themselves and their work. Concentration is crucial, as the expression "the show must go on" suggests. Although a cliché, the expression captures well the actor's tenacious ability to continue when his or her own physical or emotional self is hurt or threatened. Without proper discipline and concentration, no other work of the actor can succeed.

Analyzing text is also important, for actors must be able to break a dramatic text into acting units and understand the complex relationships among parts of the play and its characters. Understanding the play and the character's place in it, however, is not enough. Actors must then discover ways of communicating their understanding to audiences. In this regard, making good choices is an essential task of an actor, who must discriminate among possible solutions to each acting problem. Choices may be as simple as selecting between two qualities of voice for a word or as complex as identifying a memory among many memories from which an emotion springs. In today's theatre, actors are aided in this phase of work by directors.

Instrument.   By *instrument* we mean the entire physical self (body and voice) that the actor uses in playing a character. The instrument is the medium through which the consciousness and the imagination express themselves.

The instrument is given to the actor at birth; that is, the size and shape of bones, the delicate tuning of vocal mechanisms, and the size and shape of the body. The instrument can be developed, however, through training.

Imagination.   Imagination is the wellspring of creativity, the mysterious force that impels all art. Sometimes the imagination works while the conscious mind is asleep. Imagination opens the door to memory, processes nonrational data, and offers new ideas for performance.

Talent: A Synthesis

Successful actors use consciousness, instrument, and imagination in balance. The complexity of the process is beyond description. Talent, we may be able to say, is the ability of the consciousness to inspire in the imagination a set of actions and sounds that the instrument can express to an audience as theatrical character.

Training Actors

Although there are supposedly actors who are "born," and although there have been young children who were talented actors, it is a fact of theatrical life that all actors must train long and hard and must refresh that training throughout their careers. There was a time when would-be actors "came up" as apprentices, moving from small roles in minor companies to larger roles and more important theatres. They learned by imitation and by taking hints from experienced actors. Nowadays, most professional actors have formal training, either in a college or in one or more private studios.

Actor training does not refer to a specific kind of study or to a set period of time. There are a number of actor-training systems. The most influential in the United States and Canada are those based on the ideas of Konstantin Stanislavski. Other systems have very different foundations, such as the psychological theory of transactional analysis or the theory of games and improvisations. Different as these are, they are helpful in varying degrees to different actors. No one system is best for everybody. The important thing about these systems is that they organize the work of the actor's consciousness, instrument, and imagination. Without a workable system, the would-be actor makes progress only randomly, repeating mistakes and often making bad habits worse.

Preliminary Training

Most systems require some kind of preliminary training, a process of *un*learning mistaken notions and bad habits. It is also a process of training mind and body to adapt to the conditions of the theatre instead of the conditions of life (by learning, for example, that behavior that is considered ridiculous in life is sometimes essential in rehearsal and performance).

It is usually thought to be unwise for beginning actors to go directly into the rehearsal and performance of plays or parts of plays—"scene work." Instead they are given preliminary training in the following areas.

Relaxation

Many people who want to learn to act are so tense that they are quite literally unable to act. Physical tension causes sudden, random, or pathological movement (shaking, trembling) and dangerous misuse of the vocal mechanism. Tense actors may think of themselves as *in*tense and not tense; they see themselves as "really into" a role, when the teacher or the audience sees nervous, confusing, and uncontrolled movement.

Relaxation exercises cover a broad range from disciplines as different as modern dance and yoga. All are intended to cause the consciousness to let go of the body, to re-

FIGURE 8.4   Training: Relaxation.
Actors have to learn to release tension, in part because performance itself creates tension. All acting teachers use exercises that help actors learn to relax. Here, master New York acting teacher Walt Witcover and students.

turn it to its natural state of receptiveness and awareness, and to make the body itself supple and loose.

Contact or Awareness

The relaxed body, freed from the tyranny of tension, becomes aware of itself and its environment. The consciousness no longer hurries it along toward some rigid goal; it has time, as it were, to stop and enjoy the scenery (including its own internal scenery). The coming and going of the breath, the comfortable positions of the body in standing, sitting, kneeling, and lying, the sense of the nearness and farness of objects and people—these things and many more can be explored. Sensory awareness is raised, and exercises are given that can be repeated (throughout the actor's life, if necessary) to maintain or renew that awareness.

Contact with others can also be taught so that the beginning actor learns to relate to other people, to help them, and to accept the help that they offer. The accepting of such help is, perhaps surprisingly, difficult for many beginners. Taking and giving are the bases of good performance.

Centering

Many disciplines, among them Eastern meditative religions and some schools of modern dance, emphasize exercises that focus on a bodily center—that is, a core of balance and physical alignment, a place from which all movement and energy seem to spring. This idea of a center concerns both the body (balance, weight, and placement) and the voice (breathing and sound making). In yoga, the abdomen below the diaphragm is such a center; in the dance of Martha Graham, the center is slightly above the pelvis.

Centering leads the beginning actor away from the mistaken idea that the physical self is located in the head and the face, that the voice is located in the mouth and the throat, and that the physical relationship to the rest of the world is located, through gravity, in the feet; rather, the actor finds the center somewhere near the crossing point of an X of arms and legs—a center of gravity, a center of balance, a center of diaphragmatic breathing.

Play

Dramas are "plays"; actors are "players." Yet beginners are often anything but playful. A terrible seriousness rules the work. To counter this tendency, they learn how to play, both to play games and to approach the creative act joyously. Many theatre games are versions of children's games or of adult "parlor" games that are noncompetitive fun.

Training the Consciousness

Certain areas of the actor's conscious work can be taught through example and through guided participation in production work. These include discipline, concentration, theatrical analysis, observation, and script analysis.

- *Discipline.* Actors are taught to be prompt, alert, and ready to work. Actors prepare: They bring to rehearsals whatever homework on the play has been requested. Actors are *constructive,* not destructive: They don't make comments about other actors, don't break out of character while another actor is working, and don't indicate in any way that another actor's experiment with a character is dumb. Actors are respectful: They talk to the director about problems, not to other actors or to the costume designer or to the playwright.

- *Concentration.* It is only through remarkable efforts of concentration that progress is made. An actor who cannot attain such concentration may need to return to exercises in relaxation and contact to find out what is distracting the mind.

- *Observation.* Observation can be taught through devices that require attention to detail, such as talking through or writing highly detailed descriptions of objects (a specific chair, a dead fish). It can be encouraged by requiring the keeping of a notebook or diary. The goal is to cause actors to build a "library" on which they can draw in building character.

Theatrical Analysis

It should be a goal of actors' training to make them aware of their place in the theatre in each production. This does not mean merely that actors must understand their roles;

FIGURE 8.5 Concentration.
Peter Handke's *The Hour We Knew Nothing of Each Other* at The Utopian Theatre Asylum. Directed by Zeljko Djukic, costumes by Natasa Djukic. (Photo by Jason Holmes.)

it means that actors must grasp how they relate to the entire complex of the performance, including:

- *Spatial understanding,* which includes an awareness of each setting in which the actor appears, its shapes and proportions, as well as an understanding of the relationship of the setting to the size and shape of the theatre and its audience. To reach this goal, actors in many theatre training programs are required to study design, lighting, and costume and to work on productions in nonacting jobs.

- *Research resources,* for which the best preparation is usually a study of the history of the theatre. Knowledge becomes a resource, and formal study in this discipline will include a working knowledge of resources in the field.

- *Dramatic appreciation,* for which the best preparation is usually a study of dramatic literature and a broad reading in the field. Every actor is expected to know the classics of each period.

Script Analysis

The dramatic script is the foundation of the actor's work. Imagination and instrument are the means through which the script is embodied. Training in script analysis has three principal goals:

- *An understanding of the entire drama.* On the first reading, the actor will be making judgments and sorting out impressions. Trained in the theatre, the actor will read the script as a "notation" for a performance: The potential for production will be grasped, at least in general. An awareness of the play's *totality* will take shape. Of particular importance to the actor on first reading will be the *style* of the play, its main *impact* on its audience, and its overall *shape.* Under *style,* the actor will understand the degree of abstraction of the script; the kind of language, whether poetic or mundane; and the historical period. The *impact* will be comic or serious and will be expressed most importantly through language or action, idea or spectacle. The *shape* will describe the play's gross structure and its overall rhythms, whether it builds slowly or quickly to crises, whether it relaxes gradually from them or drops abruptly. This first contact with the totality of the play will also indicate what demands it will put on its actors—the size of the cast, special requirements of their instruments, the size of the major roles, and the relative degree of intensity of the emotions to be embodied.

Thinking About *Acting*

According to American actor Denzel Washington (1954–present), *"Acting is like investigative reporting. [In both fields] you search out your character."* List the information about character that an actor searches out in the script. In addition to the script, list other tools that an actor can use to investigate character, and describe how each can be helpful.

- *An understanding of the place of the character in the whole drama.* The actor is trained to resist one question—*What makes my character stand out?*—and to ask another one instead—*How does my character contribute to the whole?*

  Dramatic action means change; when a character is offstage, changes are taking place, and when the character returns, those changes must be noted. The actor balances two lines of development: the character's and the play's.

- *An understanding of the details that make up the character.* A deeper understanding of the play and the character's part in it emerges from repeated readings, as does a detailed sense of just what the character is. The actor may keep a notebook about the character, including those things discussed under "Character" in "How to Read a Play," especially action and decision, with character traits as they appear in the stage directions, the character's own speeches, and the speeches of others. All must be evaluated in terms of the production and should be discussed with the director and the other actors. For example, one character says to another that she shows "facial contortions" and her voice goes up "two octaves." The actor playing the character described must know whether these things are true (that is, whether the other character's description is accurate) and then work out when and where to use these traits.

It is essential for actors, as for all theatre makers, to look at the play in terms of its theatricality, that is, of those things discussed in Chapters 3 and 4. Such a breakdown gives them a grasp of the play's entirety and of its theatrical potential. It should not, however, dictate character. Grasping a play's idea, for example, must never suggest to the actor the reason for the character's existence, nor should the actor worry about how to "play the idea," or, worse yet, how to *be* the idea. The actor who says something like "In this play, I represent goodness" simply has not done the proper homework. Except in pure allegory, characters do not represent abstract ideas; they represent persons (who may embody or apply certain ideas).

In the same way, script analysis should help the actor to avoid moral value judgments. Characters in a play are not "good" or "bad" *to themselves.* Few real persons say, "I am a villain." The actor does not, then, play a villain; the actor plays the representation of a person whose actions may be judged, after the fact, as villainous—by others.

Put most simply, training in script analysis is training to read. It is training to understand what is on the page—not what might have been put on the page but was not, and not what the actor might prefer to find on the page. Script analysis deals with a very limited amount of information and tries to squeeze every drop from it; it neither invents nor guesses. Most of all, it requires that the actor read *every* word and understand it in clear detail; from that clarity and that detail will come an understanding of the script that can be returned to again and again when acting problems arise.

Training the Instrument

"Stage movement" and "voice production for the stage" sound like (and are) titles of academic courses. They suggest that the subject matter can be learned and that then, like familiarity with Shakespeare's plays or a knowledge of the calculus, they can be forgotten or assimilated. In actuality, the training of the instrument is a lifelong process.

The actor's body need not be heavily muscled, but it should be flexible, strong, and responsive. The actor does not train as an athlete does (one set of muscles would be developed at the expense of others); instead, the goal is resistance to fatigue, quick responsiveness, and adaptive ability (that is, the ability to imitate other kinds of posture and movement or to adapt movement to, for example, aged posture and movement or the posture and movement of a body much heavier). The actor also learns the following:

- *Body language and nonverbal communication.* We all express our emotional states and our basic psychic orientations through body language. The actor learns to "move" the physical center to match that of the character. The actor also learns how all of us communicate without words, through such simple gestures as the waving of a hand ("hello" or "come here" or "no thank you") to complex "statements" of posture and gesture that say things completely different from the words that pass our lips. Such training takes two forms: study of the subject (much of it still in the fields of psychology and anthropology) and application to the actor's body.

- *Rhythmic movement.* Ballroom dancing, simple modern dance, disco dancing, and the like help the actor to move to an external rhythm.

- *Period movement and use of properties.* Historically accurate, and theatrically effective, use of fans, canes, swords, shawls—the list is endless.

FIGURE 8.6 **Movement Training.**
A class in clown techniques at the Beijing Opera Institute. (Courtesy of the People's Republic of China.)

- *Movement in costume.* Theatrically effective movement and gesture in wigs, capes, hoop-skirts, boots—again, the list is a long one.

- *Movement onstage.* Traditional interior settings do not have walls that meet at the same angles as rooms, and so stage furniture in such settings is rarely angled as real furniture is. As a result, "crosses" (movements from one point onstage to another) take unreal routes. On thrust and arena stages, the actor learns to play to all of the audience, to adapt posture and movement so that each section of the audience is treated fairly. Too, there are ways of bending, sitting, and standing that are appropriate to the stage in that they are not awkward or comical, although training in these "correct" ways of doing things is becoming more appropriate to training in period movement.

Voice Production

The human voice is a product of controlled muscular work and chamber resonance (head and chest). Its shaping and control are not simple. Nonetheless, we make sounds and shape them all the time—only to find that our everyday sounds are inadequate for the theatre because they cannot be heard, they cannot be understood, and they are unpleasant. Unlearning and relearning are necessary for most actors.

The human voice is produced when air is forced over the vocal folds or cords, causing them to vibrate and to set a column of air vibrating, producing sound. This sound induces vibrations in cavities in the head and in bones in the head and chest. The sound is shaped in the throat and mouth, primarily with the jaws and tongue, and is further shaped into the sounds we call words by initiation of sound; interruption of sound by

FIGURE 8.7   **Voice Training.**
Vocal exercises in a class with Adrianne Moore at Utah State University. (Courtesy of Utah State University.)

Links to More About Theatre

The Entertainer. The late Laurence Olivier in a film about the theatre.

Toby Cole and Helen Krich Chinoy, *Actors on Acting,* 1949.

Uta Hagen, *Challenge for the Actor,* 1991.

George S. Kaufman, *The Royal Family.* Based on the Barrymores, ham on wry.

<www.actorsequity.org> Actors Equity (U.S.) website.

the interaction of lips, tongue, and teeth; and placement of sound through action of the lower jaw and of the tongue.

The actor trains the vocal mechanism for maximum control of every word that is uttered, as well as for the production of sounds that are not words. He or she also seeks training and does exercises in breath control, relaxation of the vocal apparatus, dexterity, resonance, and such technical matters as dialects and accents.

Training the Imagination

The word *training* may be inaccurate. Actors go through a process in a training atmosphere and are encouraged to discover their imaginations. Whether or not the imagination itself can be "trained" remains open to question, and many psychological data suggest that what we have called imagination is a capacity of the brain and the mental-emotional self that is always at work but that rarely surfaces. Still, if one can teach the rational brain mathematics, perhaps one can teach the nonrational brain imagination. Most certainly, one can try to encourage the nonrational brain to speak up and make itself heard.

Creative Exercise

In the belief that all people have imaginations and are "creative," teachers devise exercises to free actors from both embarrassment and inhibition. Writing down dreams as

FIGURE 8.8   **Training into Performance.**
At the focus of training is the role, sometimes far down the line from beginning exercises.
Shaw's *Heartbreak House* at the University of South Carolina, directed by Jim Patterson, SSDC.
(Courtesy of The Department of Theatre, Speech, and Dance, the University of South Carolina.)

a regular part of daily preparation can help many, especially those who insist that they "never dream" or "dream nothing interesting." The fact of causing themselves to remember and write down dreams leads to an acceptance of the idea of dreaming and hence to a greater willingness to "listen to" their dreams, which demonstrate imaginative elements—images, metaphors, and puns. Dreams are often playful in their structure and their language, and they have both content and form that our rational minds would never think of.

Childhood memory can be turned to good account in the same way. An exercise in memory becomes an exercise in imagination as the actor finds how much detail the mind is capable of holding and of using.

Other exercises in sensitivity or creativity use group participation in building a story or a moment. Each actor in turn builds on the story.

Image Exercises

The creative mind probably works, at least a good deal of the time, in images rather than in words (although many words are themselves images). Image exercises encourage the actor to grasp the mental pictures that the brain offers. For example, simple character creation around pictures, objects, or sounds can be beneficial. An actor is given an object and told to perform a related character for the group: a knife is set out; the actor bends forward, walks with difficulty, the body held to protect its center greedily. From "knife," the actor went to "sharp," sharp in business, a miser, then added the element of "a cutting wind."

Visualization

Group exercises build a scene, each member contributing details and working to *see* the scene. Such an exercise is useful in touching the actor's sense of creativity, in sharpening concentration and sense of detail, and in preparing for those times in rehearsal and performance when the actor must "see" for the audience:

> HORATIO: But look, the morn in russet mantel clad
> Walks o'er the dew of yon high eastward hill.
>
> *Hamlet*

Sense Memory

Like group storytelling, individual recounting of the "picture" around a memory encourages a sense of detail and of *sense memory*. As many senses as possible are incorporated. Such memories need not come from childhood; they may come from the day before, even moments before. The purpose is to cause actors to capture a sensory moment in all its fullness and, through both remembering it *and* recounting it, to cause them to be able to create such sensory reality around moments that come not from memory but from the theatre.

Improvisation

No single word and no single tool has been more used and misused in the last several decades than *improvisation*. Improvisation—the creation of quasi-theatrical characters or scenes or plays without the givens of drama—has been used to create theatre (without a playwright), to enlighten an actor about a character (the so-called *étude*, or improvisation based on material in a dramatic script), to structure theatre games, and to teach many aspects of acting. As a tool for training the imagination, it is an application of the techniques already mastered. In a sense, it is the basis of some of the other techniques; having an actor create a character around an image is such a use of improvisation. It can be used to apply the imagination, to stimulate it, or to supply raw materials not within the actor's experience. (That is, an improvisation focused on a frightening event may help the actor who has never experienced fear.)

In order to work, improvisation is kept simple and is carefully focused by the instructor. Improvisations can quickly develop along unwanted lines, especially with actors who want to "tell stories" (create theatrically interesting situations); when that happens, there are often so many processes going on that student actors do not understand what they are doing. For the purposes of the imagination, it may be enough to create, for example, a scene of the sort discussed under "Visualization" and then to have the group improvise their participation in the scene—feeling the air, wading into the water, and setting up a picnic on the beach.

Training in Acting Systems

Ideas originated or articulated by Konstantin Stanislavski, modified by the American Method and subsequent theories, continue to dominate the work of most American actors.

The American Stanislavski System

In this system, the actor is trained to analyze character for:

1. *Given circumstances.* These are the undeniable givens that the actor must accept: age, sex, state of health, social status, educational level, and so on. Often they are contained within the script, either in stage directions or in dialogue; sometimes they must be deduced or even invented. (How old is Hamlet? Was he a good scholar at the university? Is he physically strong or weak?)

2. *Motivation.* Realistic theatre believes in a world of connectedness and cause. All human actions in such a world are caused or motivated. To play a character in such a world, the actor looks for the *motivation* behind each action.

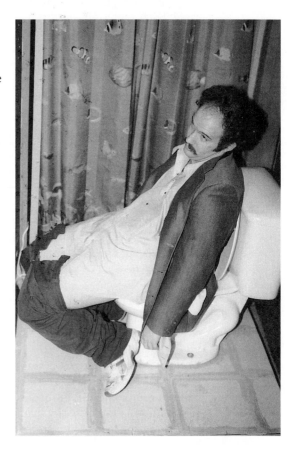

FIGURE 8.9 **Given Circumstances and Situation.**
Actors are called on to do all sorts of things and to make everything believable within the context of the play. Michael Kass in George F. Walker's *Suburban Motel: Criminal Genius* at the Ulysses Theatre Company, Chicago, directed by Zeljko Djukic, costumes and setting by Natasa Djukic. (Courtesy of the Ulysses Theatre Company. Photo by Nesho Dimov.)

Some teachers have their students make notebooks for each character with a column in which a motivation can be noted after each line or each gesture. It is important that the student actor understand that, in this system, *all* behavior is motivated—every word, every movement, every inflection. All action results from choice.

3. *Objective.* Like motivation, the *objective* is part of a system of causality. It is the goal toward which an action strives. Motivation leads to action; action tries to lead to objective.

4. *Superobjective.* "Life goal" might be an equivalent of the superobjective if a dramatic character were a real person. The *superobjective* includes all objectives pursued by a character and excludes all improperly defined objectives. For example, we might say that Hamlet's superobjective is "to set the world right again"; his objective in the first scene with his father's ghost might be "to listen to this creature from Hell and put it to rest" (thus setting the world right by quieting the ghosts in it). In this case, the objective and the superobjective agree. If, however, the superobjective was defined as "to take my father's place in the world," and the objective in the ghost scene was defined as "to listen to the ghost out of love for my father," the two would have to be brought into sympathy. By defining the superobjective, the actor is able to check on the validity of all the character's objectives.

Both the objective and the superobjective must be active. We have expressed them here as infinitives—"to set," "to listen"—but the actor does better to express them in active terms beginning with "I want," so that their strength and vitality are clearly visible. This "I want" is sometimes called the *through line* of the role.

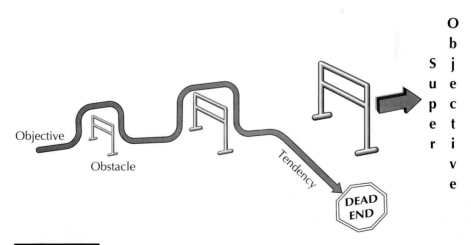

FIGURE 8.10   **Objective and Superobjective.**

Every properly defined objective leads toward the superobjective; objectives that deviate from this line are "tendencies" that go nowhere. Obstacles to achievement of objectives— other characters, events—provide much of the drama. Obviously conflict is the result of mutually blocking objectives by two characters.

Beyond Stanislavski: Acting in a Postmodern Theatre

Although Stanislavski's system still dominates actor training in the United States, it may be under challenge, especially outside the commercial theatre. Plays different from those associated with modern realism often require quite different approaches by the actor. Today's new plays and new views of theatre—especially those that are highly experimental—may lead to a different sort of training system for the actor as well. What will characterize this new system of acting, if one emerges, is unclear, but some of the following trends may become important in its formation.

Many postmodern plays are not organized by cause and effect; they do not assume a world of causality or connectedness, achieving their unity through ideas, perhaps, or mood or visual images. Actors in such plays might, therefore, be expected to place less emphasis on issues like motivation, superobjective, and through line and more, perhaps, on matters of vocal and physical flexibility, symbolism, and aesthetics.

Many postmodern plays stress multiple levels of reality, with irony and parody often important. Actors preparing for such plays may be asked (and indeed have been asked by the German theorist Bertolt Brecht) not only to play the role but also to comment on the role at the same time. Such a request seems to mean that actors must engage the audience in the role while, at the same time, requiring the audience always to recollect that they are watching a role being acted and not a life being lived. One technique for accomplishing this dual focus has been costume manipulation and cross-gender casting: The audience watches a female actor cast in a male role put on and take off her costume (and so her role); in this way, the actor can both play and comment on the role—and at the same time reveal the social construction of gender within a play and a society. Separating the voice and body of the actor is another such technique: The audience hears an actor's pre-recorded voice over loudspeakers while seeing the actor moving and, perhaps, speaking.

Many postmodern plays deny the actor a single role or a stable character, the plays' point often being that human beings themselves lack stable identities. In such plays, actors play multiple roles (including those of animals or inanimate objects) or many characters, and they do so without the changes in costume or makeup that have historically suggested such changes. Called *transformations,* such rapidly shifting roles would seem to place a greater premium on vocal and physical dexterity and imagination than on truthful inner work or a strong through line.

Although it is far from certain, it does seem that such requirements, if they come to occupy a major place in the mainstream theatre, may effect major changes in the ways we now think about and train our actors.

Audition, Rehearsal, and Performance

Actor training goes on long after actors get on the stage. Most actors continue to work on their instruments throughout their careers, and many return to professional workshops to refresh and sharpen their inner work. After the initial period of actor training, however—college, sometimes graduate school, an independent studio or teacher—the actor begins to look for roles and, having found one, begins the work of building and performing a character. Each step in the process has its special conditions, and for the professional actor, these steps will be repeated over and over throughout his or her life.

Audition

Most actors get roles through *auditions* ("tryouts"). Stars are the exception; sometimes productions are built around them.

Most auditions are done for the director. Usually, the stage manager is there as well, along with someone representing the producer, if there is one. Somebody is there, as well, to read with the actor if a scene with another character is being read. (Usually, the stage manager does this.) At many auditions, actors are expected to bring prepared monologues.

The most important things an actor can show in an audition are basic abilities and the capacity to work creatively with the director and other actors. One of the director's problems in auditions is to try to sort out the creative actors from the "radio actors"— those who have the knack of reading well on sight but who lack the ability to create. Therefore, actors are often asked to improvise as part of auditions and to work with other people. Cleverness in a first reading is not necessarily an advantage. What may count more is the capacity to work creatively and interpersonally.

Rehearsal

The actor will undoubtedly arrive at the first rehearsal with many questions. One of the functions of rehearsal is to answer those questions and to turn the answers into performance.

Actors often work very slowly in rehearsal. An outsider coming into a rehearsal after, let us say, two weeks of work might well be dismayed by the apparent lack of progress. Actors may still be reading some lines in flat voices, and, except for bursts of excitement, the play may seem dull and lifeless. This situation is, in part, intentional. Many actors "hold back" until they are sure that things are right. They do not want to waste energy on a temporary solution to a character problem. Temporary solutions have a way of becoming permanent: Other actors become accustomed to hearing certain lines delivered in certain ways and to seeing certain movements and gestures; they begin to adapt their own characters to them. Instead, many find it productive to withhold commitment for a good part of the rehearsal period.

The actor experiments. Some of this experimenting is done away from the rehearsals; homework takes up a lot of the actor's time. Much of it takes place in rehearsals. Again and again, an actor will say, "May I try something?" Or the director will say, "Try it my way." *Try* is the important word—experiment, test. The good actor has to be willing to try things that may seem wrong, absurd, or embarrassing.

Most important, the rehearsal period is a time for building with other actors. Actors use the word *give* a lot: "You're not giving me enough to react to," or "Will it help you if I give you more to play against?" Such giving (and taking) symbolizes the group creation of most performance.

FIGURE 8.11 Rehearsal.

In a room with the ground plan marked with masking tape on the floor, actors and directors rehearse, often using the plainest of furniture and "dummy" props. (Courtesy of Anne Fliotsos and the University of Missouri, Columbia.)

At some point during rehearsals, the creative and lucky actor may have a "breakthrough." This is the moment when the character snaps into focus. Motivations and actions that have been talked about and worked on for weeks may suddenly become clear and coherent. The breakthrough may be partly a psychological trick, but its reality for the actor is very important: The creative imagination has made the necessary connections and has given usable instructions to the instrument. The character is formed.

The rehearsal period, then, is not merely a time of learning lines and repeating movement. It is a time of creative problem-solving, one in which the solving of one problem often results in the discovery of a new one. It is a time that requires give and take, patience, physical stamina, and determination. It frays nerves and wearies bodies. The intensity of the work may cause personal problems. Nonetheless, many professional actors love rehearsal more than performance because of its creativity.

Performance

Performance causes emotional and physical changes associated with stress. Some change, of course, is helpful; it gets the actor "up" so that energy is at a peak, ready for the concentrated expenditure that rehearsal has made possible. Too much stress, however, cripples the actor. "Stage fright" and psychosomatic voice loss are very real problems for some. Ideally, good training and effective rehearsal will have turned the actor away from the root cause of stress (dependence on outside approval of the performance); where this does not happen, the actor may have to return to relaxation work or find therapeutic help.

Opening nights raise energy levels because of stress and excitement. As a result, second nights are often dispirited and dull. The wise actor expects this pattern. Again, preparation is a help—complete understanding of the role and the total performance, creative rehearsal work, open lines between consciousness and imagination. Before the second and subsequent performances, the prepared actor reviews all character work, goes over notes, reaffirms motivations and objectives. The good actor does not say, "Well, we got through the opening; the rest will take care of itself."

Once in performance in an extended run, actors continue to be aware of a three-pronged responsibility: to themselves, to the other actors, and to the audience. Those responsibilities cannot end with the reading of the reviews.

In developing his system of acting, Stanislavski was interested both in actor training and in the problems of performance. His work cannot be viewed as merely a study of how the actor prepares; rather, it is also a prescription for the continuing refreshment of the performing actor. His system allows the actor to create what has been called the "illusion of the first time" again and again. Put most simply, this means that the actor is able to capture the freshness and immediacy of the "first time" (both for the character and for the audience) by going back each time to the mental and emotional roots of the truthfulness of the performance. This process is possible only if performance is grounded in truth discovered during rehearsal—or, in some cases, during performance itself.

Continued performance for the trained actor, then, is not merely a matter of repeating rehearsed sounds and gestures night after night; it is a matter of returning to or discovering internally satisfying truths (motivations and objectives) and satisfyingly effective externalizations of them. Such a system may not be perfect, but it is far better than the repeated performance that grows tired with repetition and that leaves the actor disliking both the performance and the audience because of boredom.

Audience response to performance sometimes suggests where a performance is effective or poor, and the actor works at correcting errors as the performance period continues. Thus the creation of a character must seem completed by opening night, and yet it is never truly finished.

The Personality of the Actor

The personality of men and women who act has been a source of fascination for centuries. Actors have long been seen as special sorts of people because of their ability to interpret human psychology and because of their apparent ability to balance both halves of the "paradox of the actor." Too, a number of traditions have come to surround the acting profession, and, if they were not always accurate, they have come to seem accurate as actors themselves believed them: "all actors have to be crazy"; "all actors are immoral"; "the theatre attracts misfits and oddballs"; "actors like to show off"; and so on.

FIGURE 8.12 **The Professional Actor.**
Resumés, professionally made photos, and photocopied reviews of the actor Ruth Ann Phimister. These are part of the professional's expenses, along with clothes, travel, continuing training, and union dues in a competitive, chancy profession. (Courtesy of Ruth Ann Phimister. Her photos by © Elizabeth Lehmann, New York City.)

Such ideas are no better than gossip until they are proved by objective standards, and, for every immoral actor and show-off, there is an opposite to disprove the stereotype. Nonetheless, some of these old ideas persist.

Because of a lack of hard data and the persistence of stereotypes, we cannot describe accurately the "personality of the actor." We might note the following, however.

The actor's profession puts him or her outside the mainstream of most lives, because actors work odd hours, work at a very high level of energy and concentration, and live a life of extreme professional and financial peril.

Part of the actor's reward is applause and other forms of audience approval, and a personality geared toward applause may be an insecure one; yet, to face tryout after tryout, opening after opening, show after show takes stamina and a courage unknown to men and women in secure careers.

The actor's personal relationships are easily threatened by unusual hours, job insecurity, and the need to be able to move geographically on short notice.

Because theirs is a high-stress life, actors are as subject to the allure of drugs and alcohol as the rest of the population, and perhaps more so.

The ability and desire to act, like all creative work, is "different," and the committed actor may be judged an outsider by the rest of society.

The qualities that make a good actor—creativity, concentration, determination, stamina, access to the imagination, playfulness, the ability to cope with rejection, nonrational thinking, and detailed emotional memory—should be kept separate from qualities that may appear because of the profession of acting and its stresses; in other words, the nature of the profession in our society may bring out behavior that is not typical of the art of acting but of our society's use of it. Thus, the "personality of the actor" has to be a composite of those qualities that make up talent and those qualities that appear in response to the environment in which talent is used.

What Is Good Acting?

Understanding the art of the actor depends, first, on the ability to separate the actor from the role. An attractive or well-written role can obscure the actor's lack of imagination; a poorly written role can hide the actor's excellence; an unsympathetic role can make the actor seem unsympathetic. By learning to read and see plays, we learn to distinguish the character from the actor, then to see what kind of material the actor had to cope with. For example:

Good acting has detail and "texture" (variety and human truth), but it is not merely a collection of details; it has what one artist calls a "center," another a "through line"— a common bond tying all details together and making the whole greater than the sum of its parts.

Good acting has the capacity to surprise. Its truth is recognizable, but it goes beyond imitation to revelation.

Good acting, then, has technical proficiency, truth, a through line, and creativity; bad acting calls attention to itself, lacks technical control, dissolves into mere details because of its lack of a through line, and never surprises with its creation.

KEY TERMS

Check your understanding against this list. Brief definitions are in the Glossary; page references there will direct you to appropriate pages. (Persons are page-referenced in the Index.)

audition	objective
given circumstances (of characters)	sense memory
improvisation	superobjective
instrument	through line
motivation	transformation

Directors

When you have completed this chapter, you should be able to

- Describe the major tasks of a director, noting which are mostly artistic and which mostly managerial

- Differentiate the worshipful from the heretical director and discuss strengths and weaknesses of both approaches

- Describe the purpose and process of production meetings

- Describe the director's work with actors

- Explain the director's use of space

- Define the art of the director

There have always been theatre people who exercised a strong, central influence on productions, but in the sense that the word is now used, directing is a phenomenon of the nineteenth and twentieth centuries. Despite the relatively late appearance of directors, they are now the dominant figures in theatrical production.

The Nature of Directing

Before the emergence of directors, leading actors mostly interpreted their own roles, decided what they would wear, and decided where to stand and when to move on stage, often without regard to what other actors were doing or wearing. Designers, when there were any, built and painted backgrounds for the actors, intending that the same settings would be used over and over again for different plays. Towns or organizations or groups decided what plays to produce, and sometimes they would even write the plays to produce. Older performances, then, had a multiplicity of effects, a relatively uncoordinated production.

FIGURE 9.1 **Before Directing.**
Until the mid-1800s, directing as we know it hardly existed. Early play scripts sometimes showed "tableaux" arrangements for curtains or big moments—lesser actors in an arc upstage with the principals down center. Modern ideas of focus and composition were not, we think, practiced; leading actors made sure that they were the center of attention.

A Director's Goals

When directors came into being, the responsibility for many tasks formerly done by several people or not done at all were vested in one person—the director. Apparently the previous multiplicity of effects began to seem undesirable, and some closer coordination and unification of effects was sought. Thus, directors came into being to *unify*, to bind all elements of a performance together into a unity—of both interpretation and presentation. *Interpretation* here means not only that the actors and designers all understand the play in the same way but also that they all understand and agree on the nature of the intended audience and the limitations of talent and circumstance under which they will be working together. *Presentation* here means all the elements that the audience will see and hear: the text, actors, scenery, properties, costumes, lighting, and sound all must "fit together," be appropriate for the intended audience, and be developed with due regard for the particular circumstances of the production.

We can deduce something more about directing by recognizing that, in the nineteenth century when it appeared, illusionistic detail was becoming important in the arts, and industrialism was becoming important in Western society. Inasmuch as the era of the director is the era of the pictorial illusionist and of the industrial manager, then, directors are involved in *unifying*, making pictures and illusion, and organizing and managing. They are products of industrial culture, which prizes organization, order, and materialism.

To be sure, the degree to which directors unify, make pictures and illusion, and organize and manage depends in part on their situation. For example, in commercial theatres like Broadway's, overall artistic vision may rest with the producer rather than with the director, and many routine details of rehearsal and performance may devolve to a stage manager instead of remaining with the director. On the other hand, in high schools and small community theatres, more and more tasks fall to the director, so that he or she may personally supervise (or even execute) almost every aspect of a production.

A Director's Responsibilities

The following comprise the director's usual responsibilities:

- Selecting or approving the play (including work with a playwright on an original script)
- Interpreting the play
- Approving and coordinating the designs (scenery, costumes, lighting, sound)
- Casting and coaching actors
- Staging (including "blocking," orchestrating voices, and setting tempos)
- Planning and coordinating the production
- Scheduling and conducting the rehearsals
- Serving as liaison among all members of the production team

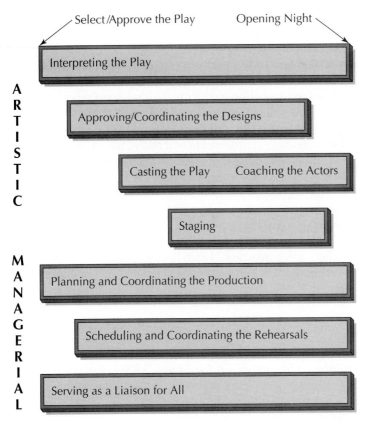

Select/Approve the Play   Opening Night

Interpreting the Play

Approving/Coordinating the Designs

Casting the Play   Coaching the Actors

Staging

Planning and Coordinating the Production

Scheduling and Coordinating the Rehearsals

Serving as a Liaison for All

A
R
T
I
S
T
I
C

M
A
N
A
G
E
R
I
A
L

FIGURE 9.2   **The Director's Responsibilities.**
The modern director is both artist and executive. The work begins at play selection and ends after (sometimes long after) the first performance. Many tasks go forward simultaneously, ending and beginning at different times.

This list suggests that a director's responsibilities are not only artistic (the first five items on the list) but are also managerial (the last three). However, these responsibilities are not discrete and separable. For example, the artistic responsibilities are listed in roughly the order in which the director undertakes them, but in fact they overlap: Some occur simultaneously (coaching actors and staging, for example); others, like interpreting the play, continue throughout the process of production. The managerial responsibilities are also listed roughly in order, but again there is overlap; for example, a director serves as liaison throughout the production process. Also, the managerial and artistic functions overlap: planning, coordinating, and scheduling take place mostly *before* rehearsals begin, as do selecting plays, coordinating designs, and casting actors. As a part of conducting rehearsals, the director is coaching actors and staging.

A Director's Traits

This wide range of responsibilities requires a person of many abilities. Directors need skills in organization in order to plan, coordinate, and schedule. Such skills include an ability to put ideas in order and to combine them with the ideas of other people, as well as the ability to order rehearsals, schedules, and budgets. Directors also need abilities in making decisions, including the clearheadedness to define problems and see the conditions under which they must be solved (including limitations of time, budget, and available talent). Directors need sensitive interpersonal skills to coax performances from actors and to work effectively with all other members of the production team, inspiring each whenever possible, working creatively with them on group solutions to complicated problems, and imposing solutions only when absolutely necessary. Directors must have artistic vision and talent, which, although hard to define, are absolutely essential for successful productions. Finally, directors need both stamina and concentration if they are to exercise their talent and carry out their many responsibilities.

Directors have to be both artists and managers in almost all of their work, and they are unique among professionals precisely because of this unusual combination of traits: on the one hand, the often solitary consciousness of the artist, and on the other, the gregarious organizational intellect of the manager. Within the same person, then, the artist proposes and the manager disposes, sometimes at widely different times and sometimes simultaneously.

A Director's View of Text

What is the director's responsibility to the dramatic text? Is it the director's job to put the play on the stage with utmost fidelity, or is it the director's job to create a theatrical event to which the script is merely a contributing part? Can the director cut lines or scenes, transpose scenes, alter characters? Can the director "improve" the play, or must it be treated as a sacred object?

Directors vary widely in the way they answer such questions. Their views range from veneration of the text to near indifference; the play is seen as a holy object on the one hand, as a merely useful artifact on the other.

The Worshipful Director's Approach

A director who venerates the text might say: "The play is the only permanent art object in performance; it is a work of art in its own right, to be treated with respect and love. Because it has stood the test of time, it has intrinsic value. By examining it, we can know its creator's intentions—what meanings the playwright meant to convey, what experiences the audience was meant to have, what theatrical values were being celebrated. The playwright is a literary artist and a thinker, and the playwright's work is the foundation of theatrical art. It is the director's job to mount the playwright's work as faithfully and correctly as is humanly possible.

"Historical research and literary criticism are useful tools for the director; they illuminate the classic play. Quirky modern interpretations are suspect, however: To show Hamlet as a homosexual in love with Rosencrantz and/or Guildenstern would be absurd and wrong because we know that such a relationship would never have been included in the tragic view that Shakespeare held.

Worshipful and Heretical Directors.

André Antoine's production of Racine's *Andromaque* (*above*), was an attempt early in the twentieth century to re-create the conditions of the original performance, down to candle footlights and onstage audience. (Paradoxically, the actors still look like early-twentieth-century people.) By contrast (*below*), Jim Patterson's production of *As You Like It* at the University of South Carolina ignores the conditions of original performance and suggests an anti-heroism not to be found in a worshipful production. (*AYLI* setting by Dennis C. Maulden, lighting by Ann Courtney, costumes by Rebecca Dosen.)

"The director's job is not primarily to create theatre; it is to cause the play to create theatre. The difference is crucial. The director says quite properly, 'I must allow the play to speak for itself and not get in the way.' To do otherwise is to betray the play, and I will not do it *even if the 'betrayal' is great theatre*."

The worshipful director views a different approach with something like horror; at best, such productions cause regret. Most often, a single word is used by the worshipful director to describe non-worshipful productions: *wrong*. Because they are not faithful to their classic originals, they are *wrong*.

The Heretical Director's Approach

A director who does not venerate the text might say, "*Interpreting the text* means *making a theatrical entity of it for an audience*. Not making *the* theatrical entity of it, and not 'finding its meaning' or 'doing it correctly.' There is no single interpretation of a play that is correct. There are only interpretations that are right for a given set of performers under a given set of conditions for a given audience.

"How, then, can a director judge the rightness of the production? The director does not, any more than a painter judges the rightness of a painting. The director's final criterion is the satisfaction of an overall goal: Is it good theatre?

"It is foolish to think that the director's task is to stage the play according to some other standard. Fidelity to some 'authorized' or time-honored view of the play is not, simply in and of itself, a good thing. It is foolish to say that the director did the play wrong unless what the director did was to make bad or dull theatre. The director has to be faithful to a vision, not to tradition or academic scholarship or propriety; only when that vision fails can the director be said to be wrong.

"Does this mean, then, that the director has no responsibility to the 'meaning' of the play? Yes, in the sense that the director's responsibility is to the meaning of the performance, of which the play is only a part. Are we, then, to have homosexual Hamlets? Yes, if such interpretations are necessary to make the plays into effective theatre and if they are entirely consistent within their productions. Are we, then, to have productions of classics that are directly opposite to their creators' intentions? Yes, because it is finally impossible to know what somebody else's intentions were and because an intention that was dynamite in 1600 may be as dull as dishwater in 2005; and anyway, theatre people have always altered classics to suit themselves. *Macbeth* was turned into an 'opera' as early as 1670, and *King Lear* had a happy ending in the eighteenth century."

The extremes of the heretical director's views can lead to results that many people find offensive or meaningless; on the other hand, those views can also lead to innovative and exciting productions.

A Best Approach

Generally both sorts of directors take a risk: the heretical director takes the chance of being ridiculous, the worshipful director of being vapid. At their best, however, both can create productions that thrill audiences, the one with revelations of familiar material, the other with a brilliant rendition of the strong points of the classic.

The Director at Work

Selecting the Play

Directors in community, school, and university theatres most often select the plays they direct; in professional theatre, directors at least approve the scripts (if they are staff directors) or find themselves "matched" to a new play by a producer. Never, however, should a director take on a play he or she does not like. The demands are too great, the depth of involvement too extreme; the dislike would ruin the production.

Directors choose to do plays because the plays excite them; idea and spectacle are probably the most common elements to prompt directorial interest. However, if theatrical elements conflict, directors sometimes find that they have made a bad choice; that is, they may love the idea of the play but may not know how to make the music of the language exciting or how to compensate for a lack of spectacle. As directors gain self-knowledge through experience, they learn what they do well or badly, and they learn to make wise script choices. Most important, perhaps, is the acquired knowledge of learning to study the script in great depth—not to be led astray by enthusiasm for a single element, only to find to one's sorrow later that serious problems were overlooked.

Interpreting the Play

The work of interpretation is an open-ended process, and, like the actor's, it never really finishes; it merely stops. A director who does more than one production of the same play may create quite a different production the second time: The process of interpretation has gone on and has changed as the director and the world have changed.

Finding a Springboard

With the script chosen, the director begins to translate that early enthusiasm into the stuff of performance. To do so, the director needs a "springboard," a taking-off place from which to make a creative leap. The terms *concept* and *directorial image* are also used, but *concept* implies rational thought, and *image* implies picture making, and the director's process at this stage may be neither rational nor pictorial. Certainly, very few directors begin their creative work with a reasoned, easily stated idea, and those who are drawn to a script because of (for example) its music or because of the opportunity it gives to display the artistry of an actor will probably not begin with images. On the contrary, what many directors begin with is a seemingly random, sometimes conflicting medley of ideas, impressions, and half-formed thoughts whose connections may still be hidden. It is then the director's task—and the exercise of a special talent—to sort all these out and to find their connections and to see which can be given theatrical life and which cannot. Thus, much of the director's early work is not the definition and application of a "concept," but the establishment of a jumping-off place, the sorting out of raw materials from a whirlwind of impressions.

FIGURE 9.4 Springboard.

Like the playwright's idea for the play, the director's idea for the production may come from any of many sources, some irrational. Here, the stained-glass windows of churches were clearly the springboard. (*The Book of Job,* produced by the Everyman Players. Photo by Orlin Corey, from *An Odyssey of Masquers: The Everyman Players,* Anchorage Press, Louisville, KY.)

Seldom—perhaps never, except in the most perfunctory sort of work—is the springboard merely "to do the play." A director who sets out merely "to do the play" is like the actor who sets out to learn the lines and not bump into the furniture—going through the motions without ever confronting the real task. This is as true of a classic play as of the most avant-garde script. It might seem that classic plays would be an exception because, supposedly, so much is known about them and so many other productions can be drawn on—the director would simply stage the play's established greatness. Such an approach is a guarantee of dullness, at best. A play will not be exciting in performance simply because other audiences have found other productions exciting; it must be made exciting all over again every time it is staged.

Assessing Strengths and Weaknesses

In early readings, the director usually has both positive and negative thoughts about the play and its audience impact. Two lists could be made, one of strengths and one of weaknesses. These two lists taken together would show how the director's ideas were forming. It is important to remember that weaknesses as well as strengths are included. Just as artists in any form are inspired by obstacles, so the director is inspired by script problems (as, for example, poets used to find inspiration in the problem of rhyme).

Let us suppose that the director is considering Ibsen's *A Doll's House,* a realistic nineteenth-century play. The play is a classic of its kind and so has established merit; on the other hand, it is also old enough to seem dated to a modern audience in language and some plot devices. Thus, after early readings, the director could list some strengths and weaknesses:

Strengths	Weaknesses
Strong subject matter	Creaky structure—melodramatic
Excellent central character	Dated language
Great third-act climax	Some "serious" stuff now "funny"
Good potential for probing Victorian attitudes	Soliloquies, set speeches very hard to make convincing today

To the director who is excited by the play and is setting out to do it, these two columns might better be titled "Potentials" and "Challenges." From the realization of the one and the solution of the other will come the director's best work.

Analyzing the Text

No matter what the orientation toward the text, the director must now work to analyze it: take it apart, reduce it to its smallest components, "understand" it. (To *understand* does not mean to "turn the script into a rational description of itself"; it means, rather, to make the director's consciousness capable of staging it.) The job of interpretation has many aspects, which are often explored simultaneously, both before and during rehearsals.

As a beginning, the director will want to ask and answer the kinds of questions suggested in Chapters 3 and 4. But the director's analysis will be much more detailed. Each decision about the play must be measured against an idea of how the anticipated audience will react (with the qualification that every good director knows that mere reaction is not in itself a good thing; the *proper* reaction is what is wanted). In thinking about audience, the director will explore many of the issues raised in Chapter 2, but again in considerably more detail. To see the differences between a director's analysis and the more general analyses offered elsewhere, we can look briefly at five representative areas.

Tone, Mood, and Key. Funny/serious, cheerful/sad, light/heavy—the possibilities are many and must be identified for each act, each scene, and each line, as well as for the entire play. Neither laughter nor powerful emotion belongs unchangeably to every line of a script. Even when the proper tone is found for the play, the lines alone will not deliver that tone to an audience. Laugh lines must be carefully set up and "pointed," with both "business" (small activities performed by actors) and timing; moments that have a wonderful potential for powerful emotion can easily be lost without careful, intense study and work by the director.

Of particular interest in this aspect of interpretation is mood—the emotional "feel" that determines tempo and pictorial composition—and key—(as in "high key" and "low key"), the degree to which effects are played against each other or against a norm for contrast. High-key scenes may even go to chiaroscuro ("light/dark") effects that use the darkest darks and the lightest lights, as in dramatic painting.

FIGURE 9.5 **Mood.**
Color, lighting, costume, and flute music set mood for this play-within-the-play scene from Anton Chekhov's *The Seagull* at the University of Missouri, Columbia. (Directed by Cheryl Black, scenery by Patrick Atkinson, costumes by Kerri S. Packard, lighting by Charles Willis. Courtesy of the University of Missouri, Columbia.)

The Six Parts. The director must study the play to find which parts are most important and which can be used most creatively to serve the play. Spectacle (including lighting, costume, the pictures created by the actors' movement, and scenery) and sound (including music, sound effects, and language) are often parts that the director can manipulate and can bring to the play as "extras" that the playwright has not included. Character, idea, and story, on the other hand, are usually integral to the script itself, although subject to considerable interpretation and "bending" by director and actors. Many directors annotate their scripts in great detail for these three parts, some marking every line of dialogue for its contribution to character, idea, or story. Such annotations give the director both an overall sense of the play's thrust and specific instances of that thrust at work.

This area of interpretation is critical. A part misunderstood at this stage can mean a moment lost in performance, or even an important thread through the whole play; to miss a major emphasis can mean a failed production. For example, a play that depends heavily on the beauty and intricacy of its language (sound) will usually suffer if directed to emphasize story or character, with the language overlooked or ignored (a not infrequent problem in productions of Shakespeare's plays); a play of character, if directed for its story, often has incomprehensible spots and long stretches where nothing seems to happen. Thus, the director must not only pick the part or parts that can be given theatrical life, but must also pick the part or parts that the script gives theatrical life. This means knowing which part(s) is most important; where in the play each has its heights and depths; and how the director will give theatrical excitement to each.

Action and Progression. Performance is active and most plays have progressive actions; that is, they occur through time (audience time and their own time), and they must seem to increase in intensity as time passes (as, that is, the audience is led from preparation through complication to crisis and resolution).

There is a trap here for every director, however, in that it is the very nature of audience perception to need greater stimulation as time passes—a familiar enough situation to all of us, who can become bored after a time with something that entertained us at the beginning. Thus, it is part of the director's problem to counter the apparent drop in intensity that occurs as time passes by using every device possible to increase intensity, that is, to support theatrically the progressive intensity of the script. When it enjoys a performance, an audience's responses may be compared to a parabola: they start at a low point, rise higher and higher as time passes, and usually fall off after the climax. The

FIGURE 9.6 Action.

This moment of intensity has been set along a line of progressive intensities that makes the performance work over time. Sujin Park's *A Hired Soldier* by the Company Michu, directed by Daehong Kang, Seoul, Korea, 2000. (Courtesy of Seoul Performing Arts Festival, Seoul, Korea.)

director wisely structures the performance to serve this perceptual structure (or another equally satisfying one). The director cannot allow a performance to become static, or it will seem to fall off rather than to remain still.

It is not enough, then, to find the important elements and to know where the script emphasizes them. The director must now find how each element grows in interest as the performance progresses. The word *progression* must be used again and again: What is this character's progression? What is the progression of the story? Is there progression in the spectacle?

If the progression is missed, the audience will become confused or bored. They may say things such as "It went downhill," or "It got dull after the first act," or "It went nowhere." Theatre people seeing such a performance often say that "they played the last act first," which is a way of saying that the climactic points or the important parts were so much in the director's mind that the entire play was directed to emphasize them, and the progression was thus destroyed.

The reverse of the question "What is the progression?" is "What can I save for the climax?" In other words, how can the director emphasize the highest point of the performance (usually toward the end, coincident with the story's climax) by contrast or by saving effects for that moment? Preparation and contrast are important; equally important is saving something—the final high pitch of emotion, the most exciting tempo, the loveliest visual effect.

Idea. As we have pointed out earlier, idea is the part of theatre that gets the most attention after the audience has left the theatre and the least while it is enjoying the performance. Idea is also an important reason that some directors select a play, many directors being committed to plays because of enthusiasm for their subject or approach. It is therefore important to remind ourselves that idea does not always express itself in individual speeches or literal statements that can be neatly extracted from the play. Instead it is woven into the other parts of the play, the texture of the performance, the actors' creation of their roles.

Idea can become a trap for an unwary director. A director must NOT direct a play so that it is "about the idea." The other parts determine the shape of the production; idea inheres in all of them but must be blatant in none. Even an impassioned "idea" speech at the most thrilling moment of the play must spring from action and character and must exist because of action and character. If the speech exists only because the playwright or the director wants to "make a statement," the speech will leap out of the performance, and the performance will suffer. Inasmuch as the play's ideas emerge from individual moments and meanings, individual actions and characters, a director carefully directs the moments and meanings, the actions and characters, NOT "the idea." Where meanings excite the director, they become something embedded in the entire performance.

Environment. As the actor determines "given circumstances," the director determines *environment*: place, time of day, historical period. Much is given in the script, although if it is given only in the stage directions, the director may choose to ignore it. Some directors cross out the stage directions before ever reading them, believing that they were

FIGURE 9.7   Environment.

The director has two criteria for his choices of environment: good acting spaces for the cast and communication of his idea of the play. Here, Arthur Miller's *All My Sons* at South Carolina State University. (Directed by Frank Mundy, designed by Robert A. Osei-Wusu. Courtesy of South Carolina State University.)

written either for some other director's production (e.g., for Broadway) or for readability for armchair theatregoers. Classic plays often have no stage directions at all.

Questions of tone, mood, and key also influence the director's thinking about environment. There are excellent reasons for putting a murder mystery in a country house on a stormy night, just as there are excellent reasons for putting a brittle comedy in a bright, handsome city apartment. It is not only the rightness of the environment for the characters that the director thinks of (i.e., if they are rich they should have a rich environment, if Russians they should have something Russian, and so on) but the rightness for the indefinable subtleties of mood: the laziness of a warm day, the tension of an electric storm, the depressing gloom of an ancient palace.

Through these early attempts at assessment and analysis, the director develops strong ideas about the production of the play. These will probably change as the director works with the play, but it is the director's springboard and interpretation that shape the whole, guiding the rehearsals and the work of both designers and actors.

Approving and Coordinating the Designs

The director is rarely a designer, but he or she knows the practical needs and the aesthetic values of both play and production. Communicating feelings and ideas about play and production to designers is an important directorial skill, especially when it can be done without insisting on restrictions of budget or personnel.

Communication is best started early. When feasible, meetings between the director and designers begin months before rehearsals; practicality may dictate, however, that they come only weeks or days before casting.

Agreeing on Interpretation

At early meetings between director and designers, matters of budgets, schedules, and working methods are discussed, but most importantly the director begins to explain his or her interpretation of the play and approach to the production. Based on the director's ideas and images, the designers begin to form their own ideas about the production, which may be somewhat different from the director's. The director weighs all the ideas, accepting some, rejecting or modifying others. Because the goal is for the direction and the designs to work in harmony, unifying the several interpretations is one of the director's first tasks.

Out of these early meetings grows a regular series of production meetings attended by the director and designers and perhaps others (the producer, technical director, and stage manager, for example). These regular meetings aim to facilitate communication, to improve efficiency, and to assure artistic coordination.

Agreeing on Presentation

Having developed a shared interpretation of the play, the director and designers next work together to translate that interpretation into the presentation—the stuff of theatre. Using the results of the director's initial analysis as the starting point, they now collaborate to realize the play's potential on the stage.

For example, they will work to provide the actors with a suitable *environment,* deciding how best to convey to the audience a proper sense of place and time. They will come to share a vision of mood and decide how best to express it through the visual potency of lighting, set, and costume; they know that inconsistency of mood leads to a severe weakening of the performance. They will work to assure that all elements of the production fit together. The director must be careful at this stage not to be so rigid or so narrow as to cause the designs to make a single statement over and over. In other words, both unity and variety (or variety within unity) are wanted in the designs. The director also works with the designers to achieve progression in the designs just as in the overall production.

Satisfying the Practical and Aesthetic

In all of the design areas, both the practical and the aesthetic must be considered. The kind and amount of movement wanted by the director influences costume design; the costume designer's work influences movement (as when, for example, the tight corset of the late nineteenth century or the very broad skirts of the eighteenth century are used). So, too, with colors: Bright pastels may be suitable for a comedy; dull colors and heavy fabrics under gloomy light may match a serious interpretation. Practical considerations influence other decisions: Certain areas will have to be brightly lighted so that the action can be seen; certain actors will have to be in strong colors or outstanding costumes so that they will gain focus. Lighting colors must be carefully coordinated with the colors of sets and costumes so that lights do not wash out or change other colors; the location of lighting instruments has to be coordinated with the location of set pieces and rigging to avoid casting shadows or creating physical interference.

Developing a Ground Plan

The *ground plan* is a "map" of the playing area for a scene, with doors, furniture, walls, and other details indicated to scale. In a realistic interior, the director may almost design the entire acting space simply by setting down directorial needs in detail. The number and location of entrances, the number and location of seating elements, the number and location of objects that will motivate behavior and movement (for example, stoves and refrigerators, fireplaces, closets, and bookcases) are important to the way many directors think about realistic plays and may be determined by such directors even before they meet with their designers. Some directors even give their set designer a ground plan, complete except for small matters of dimension. Others may remain open until the designer has created a ground plan around a more general statement of needs.

In the nonrealistic play, or sometimes in the realistic play with exterior scenes, directors may have less rigorous requirements. Still, for variety, mood, and emphasis, the director will probably specify differences in level, separation of playing areas, the location of seating elements, and so on.

As well, other design elements may be suggested or required by the director; for example, the size and shape of the space where a crowd is used, or where a sense of the isolation of a single figure is wanted, or where a feeling of cramped oppression is sought. Special effects may require special space.

Once ground plans are established, they become the basis for all staging. Drawn to scale, they can be used with scale cutouts of furniture and actors to plan staging. They are also the basis for the three-dimensional model that the designer usually provides.

Communicating Decisions

As the production meetings continue and rehearsals near, these and many other matters will have been considered: budget, shifting of scenery, time for costume changes, location of offstage storage space. As decisions are made final, each designer provides the director with a detailed plan in the most appropriate form: color renderings and fabric swatches for costumes; ground plans, scale drawings, renderings, and models for sets; light plots with gel colors for lights. The sound designer (where one exists) may work with an annotated script and lists of sound materials (music, sound effects). These renderings, plans, and other materials represent the culmination of the designers' work with the director: detailed, readable plans for a total production, all in harmony with each other and with the director's interpretation of the text.

Casting and Coaching Actors

Casting

"Style is casting," the late director Alan Schneider said. The remark underlines the enormous importance of casting; its success or failure indelibly stamps the production.

The producer or director puts out a *casting call* and schedules auditions or tryouts. In New York, much casting is done through agents and private contacts. In university and community theatres, almost the opposite situation holds true, because maximum participation is wanted and closed or private auditions are educationally suspect. In repertory theatres, of course, where the company members are under contract, the director must work rather differently to make the company and the plays mesh, and casting and play selection influence each other.

The director's conduct of a casting session is a trial of tact, patience, and humanity. Auditions exist for the director, but would-be actors often believe that the sessions exist for them, and directors disabuse them of this error as gently as possible. Both good and bad actors try out, including good actors who are wrong for the play and poor actors who may have a quality that seems right. The director wants to hear and see each one but wants to see and hear only enough of each one to know what each can do. Directors learn to make sound preliminary judgments on the basis of less than a minute's audition. It remains the director's task, however, to be considerate, positive, and polite and to remain open to rethinking these preliminary judgments. The goal is to relax tense actors, to help rid them of nerves that obscure talent by strangling good voices and tensing flexible bodies.

The director or an assistant keeps notes, often in the form of a checklist with headings for physical characteristics, voice, and so on. "Type" may also be indicated—the range of given circumstances that the individual's voice and body would suggest in the realistic theatre.

The director is looking for potential. Script readings, performance of prepared materials, and improvisation and theatre games may be used. Some actors will be called back one or more times because the director feels that they have more potential than was shown the first time or because more information is needed; and, as a final decision nears, the director will want to compare the "finalists" very carefully.

The actual selection of a cast is complicated and, finally, irrational. It is a creative act—the creation of the artistic unit that will bring life to the play. Feelings and hunches are important; so, unfortunately, are personal prejudices. Above all, the director wants to be sure, for replacing an actor after rehearsals have started upsets the creative process.

After the director chooses the cast, actors are notified. In university theatres, a cast list is posted. In other situations, the director notifies actors personally or has them notified through their agents. Once the casting is complete and the designs have been approved, the director is locked into some decisions that are all but irreversible. He or she has decided what the production is to be, settled on designs, assembled a cast, prepared a rehearsal script (including cuts, changes, and notes), and found a dependable assistant. Throughout rehearsals, the director will continue to analyze and interpret—changing this image, shifting that idea, experimenting, remaining open to fresh insights. In rehearsal, creative actors will bring new ideas, to such a degree that some directors believe they never fully understand a play until it is performed.

Coaching

Most modern directors involve themselves closely in their actors' creation of their roles. The influence of Stanislavski, in particular, has led to a collaboration between actor and director that has developed, in some cases, into a great dependency on the director, a de-

FIGURE 9.8   Rehearsal.

Actor coaching goes on both during rehearsal and outside of rehearsal; it is only part of the rehearsal process. (Courtesy of Saint Mary-of-the-Woods College. Photo by Sharon Ammen.)

pendency that is sometimes fostered by the teacher–student relationship at universities. Just as there are now playwrights who expect to have their plays "fixed" by the director (a relationship that grew primarily from the Broadway playwright–director collaborations of the twentieth century), so there are actors who expect to have their interpretations "fixed" or even given to them whole by their directors. Particularly in educational and community theatres, great trust is put in the director by the actors, and many interpretations are virtually handed down entire from director to actor.

When the actor and director work in a productive collaboration, however, the director functions as a coach who advises, inspires, and encourages the actor. Significantly, the director works in such a relationship with questions rather than with statements ("Why do you think the character says it just that way?" instead of "What the character means is. . . ."). The director will have mastered the actor's vocabulary and, using it, can ask those questions that the actor may not yet be able to phrase. The director is the sounding board and the artistic conscience of the actor—mentor and interpreter, bringing to the actor's work another dimension, another voice, another view of the whole play and all the characters.

The Director and the Actor.   The director and the actor have had to learn to need each other, for there is no reason to suppose that early directors were warmly welcomed by actors, who, until then, had been independent. There is still much in the relationship to make it difficult for both. The actor is worried about one role, the director about the entire performance; the actor works from a narrow slice through the play, the director from the whole thing; the actor risks everything in front of an audience, the director does not; the actor naturally resents commands, and the director sometimes has to give them. Add to these differences the natural indifference or apathy of people brought into a working situation by professional accident rather than affinity, plus the stressful atmosphere of rehearsals, and the relationship can be strained.

Perhaps surprisingly, then, most directors and actors work quite well together. Credit for much of this goes to the director's human skills, although some of it must go to the patience and determination of the actor. The most potent factor may be, in the end, the knowledge that both are engaged in a creative enterprise whose success benefits both.

Actors depend on their director. Therefore, the more precise and sure the director can be, the better. Precision and sureness come from *preparation,* and so the basis of the most productive actor–director relationships is the director's own work in advance of rehearsals.

The Director and the Characters.   Many directors are themselves actors and/or acting teachers. They understand actors' approaches and vocabularies. Only rarely do they try to impose a new system on their actors, and then only if they are director-teachers. Thus, their work on character will be adapted to the system used by the actor playing the role.

Basically, the director does the same character homework as the actor, keeping a notebook, with pages or columns for each character. The director focuses, however, not on the objectives and motivations of a single character (except when working with the actor playing that character) but on shifting patterns of objectives that conflict, part, run parallel, and conflict again. It is not merely that the director maintains an overview of the terrain that the actors travel; it is that the director finds the heart of the play in the coexistence and conflict of character lines.

Too, the director is profoundly concerned with the "outside" of the performance. The director is a master communicator, interested almost obsessively in *things that signal to the audience.* The actor devotes time and energy to the inner reasons for giving signals; the director works on those inner reasons only to help the actor, saving creative energy for the signals themselves.

As the director plans the schedule, attention is given to how each actor will build character. Some actors make great progress early, but one or two may never do so. Still, the director knows that by a certain date, "inner" work must be well under way. By some later date, the director must let go and "sit farther back," working more externally and more comprehensively. The closer the date of the first performance, the less attention the director will be able to give to detailed actor-coaching, which is only one aspect of the modern director's total job.

Staging

"*Blocking*," "staging," or "traffic direction," as some people wryly call it, is one of the director's inescapable responsibilities. No matter how much the actors and even the director are devoted to inner truth and to characterization, the time must come when the director must shape the actors' moves and timing and must give careful attention to movement, picture making, and rhythm. It is in the very nature of theatre that the visual details of the stage have significance, and the director must make that significance jibe with interpretation.

Significance is the crux of the matter. We live in a world where movement and visual arrangement signify: They give signals. In the realistic theatre, the same things signify that do in life; in the nonrealistic theatre, these things can be kept from signifying or can be made to signify differently.

Before the appearance of the director, audiences seemingly found less significance in stage movement, gesture, and picture—or, more accurately, they found a *theatrical* significance in them: The star took center stage, facing front, with other actors flanking and balancing; a hero's movement pattern and posture were heroic; the heroine moved so as to show herself off and to divide or punctuate her speeches. Modern staging, with its meticulous attention to visual symbolism (sometimes called *picturization*), beauty (*composition*), and movement was probably not seen before the nineteenth century, except in special cases.

Much of what is taught about directing today is devoted to these matters. By and large, what is taught has been established by tradition and extended by popular theory, little of it having been tested objectively. Much of the theory of picturization, for example, the supposed "meanings" of various stage areas, derives from the traditional use of the proscenium stage and probably has less relevance to thrust and arena staging. As realistic plays exert less influence on the theatre, and as new theories of theatre evolve, many of these traditional theories of directing will probably fade.

Movement.   As actors are aware of and exploit "body language," so the director is aware of and uses "movement language." Stage movement is often more abundant than real-life movement. In a real situation, people often sit for a very long time to talk, for example, whereas on a stage characters in the same situation will be seen to stand, walk, change chairs, and move a good deal. Partly, this abundance of movement results from the physical distance of the audience—small movements of eyes and facial muscles do not carry the length of a theatre. Partly, it results from the director's need for variety, for punctuation of action and lines, for the symbolic values of movement itself, and for the changing symbolic values of picturization.

Stage movement is based partly on the received wisdom of the movement implied by such statements as "Face up to it," "She turned her back on it," "He rose to the occasion." Too, it serves to get characters into positions with which we have similar associations—"at the center of things," "way off in the blue," "out in left field."

The director is concerned with direction, speed, and amount of movement. Direction reveals both motivation and human interaction; speed shows strength of desire or strength of involvement (impassioned haste, for example, or ambling indifference); amount is perhaps most useful for contrast (a character making a very long movement after several short ones or in contrast with the small moves of several other characters).

Movement also punctuates the lines. It introduces speech: The character moves, catches our attention, stops and speaks. It breaks up speech: The character speaks, moves, speaks again, or moves while speaking and breaks the lines with turns or about-faces. (Pacing is frequently used for this reason. In life, we associate pacing with thought, and so a pacing character may seem thoughtful, but the turns are carefully timed by the director to mark changes in the speech itself.)

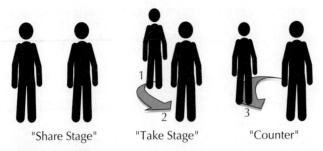

"Share Stage"   "Take Stage"   "Counter"

FIGURE 9.9   **Blocking Shorthand.**
Directors of proscenium productions sometimes rely on a
tradition of movement that is given in a kind of shorthand:
actors "share stage" when they turn one-quarter toward each
other; an actor "takes stage" by making a small movement
downstage and out; an actor "counters" by making a small
move away and a turn back to balance other movement. These
unmotivated movements are now dated, and may in fact date
to the era before directing.

Movement patterns have a symbolic value much like that of individual movements
and can be derived from the same figures of speech: "twisting him around her finger,"
"winding her in," "going in circles," "following like sheep," "on patrol," and many others
suggest patterns for characters or groups. They are used, of course, to underscore a pattern already perceived in the play or the scene.

Visual Symbolism

The exploitation of the stage's potential for displaying pictures is not entirely limited to
the proscenium theatre but has its greatest use there. From the late nineteenth century
through the middle of the twentieth, the proscenium was seen literally as a picture frame,
and the audience sat in locations that allowed it to look through the frame at its contents.
With the return of thrust and round stages, however, this "framing" became impossible,
and audiences were located on three or all four sides of the stage, so that each segment
of the audience saw a different picture. Thus, only certain aspects of picture making have
universal application, and of these the most important by far is visual symbolism.

Stage Areas.   On the proscenium stage, there is said to be symbolic value of stage areas. These areas are Down Center, Right, and Left (*Down* meaning toward the audience,
Right meaning to the actor's right and thus the audience's left) and Up Center, Right, and
Left. Down Center is unquestionably the most important (or "strongest") area, followed by Down Right and Down Left. Traditional wisdom has it that Down Right is
more important than Down Left and that it has a "warmth" that Down Left lacks. The
Upper areas are weaker, and Up Left is supposed to be the "coldest." The real value of
identifying the stage areas is in creating variety and identification, variety because it is

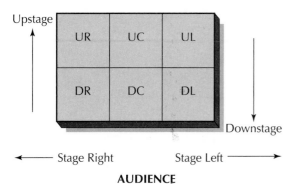

Upstage

| UR | UC | UL |
| DR | DC | DL |

Downstage

←——— Stage Right   Stage Left ———→

AUDIENCE

FIGURE 9.10 **Proscenium Stage Areas.**
"Up" and "Down" are away from or toward the front of the stage, dating from the era when the stage sloped from back to front; "Left" and "Right" are from the actor's point of view when facing the audience.

tedious if the audience has to watch scene after scene played in the same area, and identification because the association of an area with a character or a feeling is an important tool for conveying emotional meaning to the audience. And, unquestionably, the matter of strength does have some importance, if only because common sense tells us that the downstage areas are stronger because we can see and hear the actors more clearly there—and, as a result, we want to play the most important (but not all) scenes there.

Stage Relationships.   Puns and traditional sayings give us a clue to how another kind of visual symbolism works—and also suggest to us how the mind of the director works as it creates visual images of the sort that communicate to us in dreams. "Caught in the middle," "one up on him," and "odd man out" all suggest arrangements of actors. When a director combines them with area identification, for example, they become richer and more complex. The additional use of symbolic properties or set pieces—a fireplace, associated with the idea of home ("hearth and family"), for example—gives still greater force to the picture. Thus, a character who "moves in" on the hearth of a setting while also moving physically between a husband and wife ("coming between them") and sitting in the husband's armchair ("taking his place") has told the audience a complicated story without saying a word.

Sometimes, the playwright's own symbolism creates a rich texture of both picture and movement. Take, for example, this scene from Shakespeare's *Richard II* (Act III, Scene iii):

["King Richard appeareth on the walls" (First Quarto); "Enter on the walls" (First Folio)]:

NORTH: My lord, in the base court he doth attend
                To speak with you; may it please you to come down?

RICHARD: Down, down I come, like glist'ring Phaeton . . . ,
                Wanting the manage of unruly jades.
                Is this the base court? Base court, where kings grow base.

[Richard comes down to stage level; the usurper Bolingbroke kneels to him, as is evident from omitted material]

BOLINGBROKE: Stand all apart,
              And show fair duty to his Majesty.

["He kneels downe." First Quarto.]
              My gracious lord.

RICHARD: Fair cousin, you debase your princely knee
              To make the base earth proud with kissing it . . .
              Up, cousin, up; your heart is up, I know,
              Thus high at least, although your knee be low.

The scene begins with Richard "on high" while his enemies are in the "base court" at stage level. (A base court was a part of a castle, but *base* means "common" or "unworthy," as well as "low" in both the physical and the social sense.) Richard says he will

FIGURE 9.11   **Visual Symbols.**
Metaphors are often the basis for movement. Here, for example, "He came between them" (*above*); "Odd man out" (*middle*); "She ran circles around him" (*below*).

come "down, like glist'ring Phaeton," that is, like the young man who drove the chariot of the sun too near the earth because he could not control the horses that pulled it ("wanting the manage of unruly jades"). But the audience already knows (from earlier reference) that the sun is Richard's emblem, and the director has probably made sure that it is visible on Richard's costume and may even be suggested by the shape of his crown, so the sun is being *debased,* brought down, even as Richard physically moves down to stage level. There, the usurper tells everyone else to "stand apart," that is, to give them room, but the word *stand* may be ironic and the director may use it to make an ironic picture, because they should kneel to the king. Bolingbroke himself does kneel (stage direction, First Quarto), but the gesture is a mockery, as Richard notes, "You debase your princely knee/To make the base earth proud . . . /Up, cousin, up . . . ," reminding the audience that Richard himself was, only moments ago, "up" on the higher level. And Richard goes on: Touching his crown (a traditional bit of business), he says, "Up, cousin, up/Thus high at least. . . ." That is, he will raise himself high enough in the presence of his king (though he should be kneeling) to seize the crown.

Thus, in a quick sequence of moves and gestures, the symbolic flow of the scene is given to the audience. With a scene of this richness and detail, the director need only follow its lead; few modern scenes are this explicitly symbolic, however, and directors usually have to create their own visual symbols to match the interpretation.

Mood. Mood is established most readily with lighting and sound and with the behavior of the characters. However, certain visual effects of character arrangement contribute, as well: horizontals, perhaps, for a quiet, resigned scene; looming verticals and skewed lines for a suspense melodrama. Mood values are subjective and irrational, however, and hard to describe. In reality, what the director remains watchful for are clashes of mood, where movement and visual symbols conflict with other mood establishers.

Focus. A stage is a visually busy place, with many things to look at; therefore, the audience's eyes must be directed to the important point at each moment. A number of devices achieve *focus: framing* (in a doorway, between other actors, and so on); *isolating* (one character against a crowd, one character on a higher or lower level); *elevating* (standing while others sit, or the reverse, or getting on a higher level); *enlarging* (with costume, properties, or the mass of a piece of furniture); *illuminating* (in a pool of light or with a brighter costume); and *indicating* (putting the focal character at the intersection of "pointers"—pointing arms, swords, eyes, and so on).

Focus is largely a mechanical matter, but it is an important one that affects both movement and picture making.

Visual Aesthetics

Most stage pictures are rather well composed, or good to look at, but directors are often careful to study the production with an eye to improving the aesthetic quality of the scenes. What is *not* wanted is easier to say than what is: straight lines, lines parallel to the

| **FIGURE 9.12** | Focus. |

In the schematic (*above*), only two of the figures have focus—the seated one, because of mass and unique position; and the nearest standing one, a weaker emphasis deriving from the first. In the engraving (*below*), the figure in the doorway has focus: he is isolated, framed by the doorway, illuminated uniquely by moonlight, indicated by the arms and eyes of the others, and facing the audience while the others have their backs turned.

stage front, evenly spaced figures like bottles on a supermarket shelf. *Balance* is sought so that the stage does not seem heavy with characters on one side, light on the other. Composition is, finally, an irrational matter and a highly subjective one; directors who concern themselves with it in depth learn much from the other visual arts, especially traditional painting.

FIGURE 9.13 **Composition and Balance.**
In the schematics, a realistic director would reject the top and middle because one is too balanced, the other not balanced enough. The bottom looks realistically uncontrived but is balanced. A nonrealistic director might prefer the top or middle. The old photograph (*below*) shows the kind of over-direction used in melodrama. The pointing arms and the mass of the crowd are too contrived; a good realistic director would bleed the crowd out the door and break up the postures and levels. A nonrealistic director, on the other hand, might make it look even more contrived.

Rhythm

Rhythm is repetition at regular intervals. The elements of rhythm in the theatre are those things that regularly mark the passage of time: scenes, movements, speeches, words. For the director, rhythm includes tempo and timing, as well as one aspect of progression. The director is concerned, then, not only with the interpretation of character and the visual signals of interpretation but also with the rate(s) at which things happen.

We have seen that speed of movement is important to movement's meaning. Now we may say that it is also important to intensity and rhythm. We associate quickness with urgency, slowness with relaxation; change in speed is most important of all. We may compare this phenomenon with the beating of a heart: Once the normal heartbeat (base rhythm) is established, any change becomes significant.

The director establishes the base rhythm with the opening scenes of the play and then creates variations on it, and the shortening of the time between moves, between lines, and between entrances and exits becomes a rhythmic acceleration that gives the audience the same feeling of increased intensity as would a quickening of the pulse.

Pace is the professional's term for "tempo," but it is not a matter of mechanical tempo. Much of what is meant by *pace* is, in fact, emotional intensity and energy, and the director who tries to create a feeling of intensity by telling the actors merely to "pick up the pace" or "move it along" will probably succeed only in getting the actors to speak so fast that they cannot be understood. Tempo has to grow naturally out of understanding and rehearsal of a scene, not out of a decision to force things along. Indeed, the scornful dismissal of such an attempt as "forcing the pace" and "pumping it up" suggests how futile it is.

Timing is complicated and difficult, something felt rather than thought out. Comic timing is the delivery of the laugh-getter—a line or a piece of business—after exactly the right preparation and at just that moment when it will most satisfy the tension created by a pause before it; it also describes the actor's awareness of the timing that has produced previous laughs and of how each builds on those before. The timing of serious plays is rather different and depends far more on the setting of (usually) slow rhythms from which either a quickening tempo will increase tension or a slowing will enhance a feeling of doom. For example, at the end of *Hamlet,* Fortinbras has the following speech (Act V, Scene ii):

> Let four captains
> Bear Hamlet, like a soldier to the stage;
> For he was likely, had he been put on,
> To have prov'd most royally; and, for his passage,
> The soldier's music and the rights of war
> Speak loudly for him.
> Take up the bodies: such a sight as this
> Becomes the field, but here shows much amiss.
> Go, bid th' soldiers shoot.
>
> [A dead march. Exeunt, bearing off the bodies; after which a peal of ordnance is shot off.]

FIGURE 9.14 Timing.

Some moments must be timed by the director for effect. Here, as the woman behind the screen pops her head up, the tall man turns the shorter one's head away at precisely the right moment so that he will not see her. If the moment is not timed exactly right, it will not be funny. (*The School for Scandal*, directed by Jim Patterson, SSDC, at the University of South Carolina; setting by Dennis C. Maulden, lighting by Ed Intemann, costumes by Lisa Martin-Stuart.)

This follows an active scene of dueling, argument, and violence, and a short, less active scene of Hamlet's and Horatio's final words to each other, with the arrivals of ambassadors and Fortinbras. Fortinbras' speech is jumpy and uneven, effective because it lacks regular rhythm, but it finally settles down into the firm, regular rhymed couplet, "Take up the bodies . . ." that sets the final rhythm of the play. The rest could be timed on a metronome, taking the base rate (the pulse) from the couplet. *Go* is a long sound, followed (in one director's view) by a pause of two beats. The words that remain have but a single stress among them, on *shoot*. After this one-beat word, there is another pause of as long as three beats (in the major rhythm of which *Go* and *shoot* are major units). Then, the drum ("a dead march") starts its slow beating on the same tempo; a measured number of beats later comes the cannon sound ("a peal of ordnance"); another measured number of beats later, the lights begin to dim or the curtain to close, still on units of the original rhythm.

This control of a scene may seem unnecessarily rigid, and controlled rhythm of this kind works only when it is carefully planned and rehearsed, because there is no such thing as a timing that is "almost rhythmic." The rhythm is either exact or it is nonexistent, and it is in such stage effects as the drum and the cannon that the director can most carefully control it. (It was partly because of the desire for control of such effects, in fact, that the director came into being.)

Planning and Coordinating the Production

In a Broadway production, many managerial functions are performed by the producer or the producer's office. In community and school theatres, the director performs most or all of them: scheduling, budgeting, personnel selection, research, and some aspects of public relations all fall to the director's lot.

Scheduling includes the overall flow of production work from inception to performance, including production meetings, rehearsals, and the coordination of design and technical schedules, at least for purposes of information (including costume fittings for actors, clearing of the stage for construction work, and so on). These schedules are kept by the director or the stage manager on some easily read form like an oversized calendar.

Budgets are rarely initiated by a director, who does not hold the purse strings of the theatre, but the director must be able to keep a staff budget and to understand and honor costume, setting, and other budgets. In many college and university theatres, the director functions as producer and has budget control over the design areas (that is, the production money is budgeted as a single figure, which can be carved up as the director wishes).

Personnel selection (not including that of the actors) covers the director's own staff, most particularly the stage manager and assistants. In many situations, it will extend to the choreographer and the music director, with whom the director must work closely; it may include selection or at least approval of designers.

Research is carried out by a director on virtually any aspect of the production. Designers do their own research, to be sure, but such matters as the actors' accents, social mores, manners and mannerisms, the traditions surrounding the staging of a classic, the historical conventions associated with it, critical comments on it, and the work of other actors and directors in other productions of it concern many directors. In some theatres, directors have the help of a dramaturg in this task.

Public relations is not usually a directorial responsibility, but as a matter of taste and even of self-protection, the director often wants at least advisory approval of graphic and written material. Staging publicity photos, providing historical material from research, and doing interviews to publicize the production are only a few of the things that a director may also do.

Thinking About Directing

"For a stage set to be original, striking, and authentic, it should first be built in accordance with something seen.... If it is an interior, it should be built with its four sides, its four walls, without worrying about the fourth wall, which will later disappear so as to enable the audience to see what is going on."

—André Antoine, French director, 1858–1943

Follow Antoine's procedure and make a ground plan of a familiar room. Next, decide which wall to remove. Do the actors have good entrances and exits? Can they move easily from place to place inside the room? Does any furniture need to be adjusted to aid the actors' movements or the audience's view? Repeat the exercise but remove a different wall. Which arrangement is better? Why?

Scheduling and Conducting the Rehearsals

Every director has a rehearsal pattern, and every pattern has to be adaptable to the special needs of each cast and each play. In general, however, a structure like the following is used:

First Rehearsal

The cast gathers, a trifle nervous and unsure. Many are strangers to each other. The director plays the role of host—making introductions, breaking the ice, moving these individuals toward cohesion. The play will probably be discussed at some length, the director explaining general ideas and the overall direction; the designers may be asked to show and discuss models and sketches. Certain practical matters are got out of the way by the director or the stage manager (the signing of necessary forms, the resolving of individual schedule conflicts, and so on).

Then the play is read, either by the entire cast or by the director or the playwright. Some directors interrupt this first reading often, even on every line, to explain and define; others like to proceed without interruption so that the actors may hear each other. Either way, once the books are open and the lines are read, the rehearsal period is truly under way.

Rehearsal by Units

Rehearsing entire acts is often not the way to do detailed work, and so the acts are further broken down into *French scenes* (between the entrance and exit of a major character) or *scenes* (between curtains or blackouts), and then further into *beats* or *units* (between the initiation and end of an objective). These short elements are numbered in such a way that, for example, all the appearances of a major character can be called by listing a series of numbers, for example, 12, 13, 15, 17, meaning scenes 2, 3, 5, and 7 of the first act. By scheduling detailed rehearsals this way, the director often avoids keeping actors waiting. This same number system can be used to call scenes that need extra rehearsal.

As a general pattern, it can be said that many directors move from the general rehearsal of early readings into increasingly detailed rehearsals of smaller and smaller units, and then into rehearsals of much longer sections when the units are put back together.

Run-Throughs

A *run-through* is a rehearsal of an entire act or an entire play; it gives the director (and the actors) insight into the large movements and progressions of the play. After run-throughs, the director will probably return to rehearsal of certain small units, but, as performance nears, more and more run-throughs are held.

Technical and Dress Rehearsals

As production coordinator, the director cannot forget the integration of lights, costumes, sound, and scenery into the performance. *Technical rehearsals* are devoted to any or all of these elements, normally done with the actors but sometimes without them (when "cue-to-cue" or "dry-run" technical rehearsals are held). In either case, the stage manager usually takes over the management of the script and the cues in preparation for running the show during performance; the director makes the decisions affecting the look and sound of the production and conveys them to the stage manager.

Dress rehearsals incorporate costumes into the other technical elements, and final dress rehearsals are virtually performances. Nothing is now left to chance: Actors must be in place for every entrance well in advance of their cues; properties must be in place, with no rehearsal substitutes tolerated; costumes must seem as natural to the actors as their own clothes (achieved by giving them, weeks earlier, rehearsal costumes of cheap materials); every scene shift and light cue must be smooth, timed as the director wants it.

And then, for the director, it is over. To be sure, polishing rehearsals may be called even after opening night, or full rehearsals if the play is a new one that has gone into *previews* (full performances with audiences in advance of the official opening) and needs fixing; but, as a rule, when the play opens, it belongs to the actors and the stage manager, and the director is a vestige of another era in its life. The director may continue to check the production regularly, even for months or years if it is a Broadway success, but, in effect, after opening night, the director is a fifth wheel.

More than one director has compared directing to being a parent, the child being the production. The director rears it from birth to maturity and then pushes it out into the world. It is a paradox of the craft—as it is, perhaps, of parenting—that the proof of one's success is the loss of one's function.

Links to More About Theatre

 In the Bleak Midwinter, directed by and starring Kenneth Branagh. A comic look at the director's craft.

 Ellen Donkin and Susan Clement, *Upstaging Big Daddy,* 1993. Directing meets feminism.

Charles Marowitz, *Prospero's Staff,* 1986.

 Michael Frayne, *Noises Off.* Great theatrical farce.

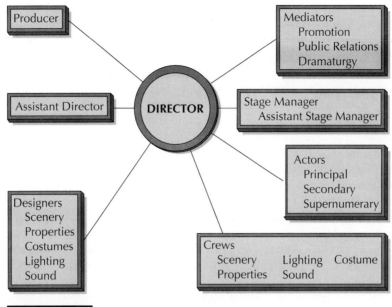

Producer	Mediators Promotion Public Relations Dramaturgy
Assistant Director	Stage Manager Assistant Stage Manager
	Actors Principal Secondary Supernumerary
Designers Scenery Properties Costumes Lighting Sound	Crews Scenery Lighting Costume Properties Sound

FIGURE 9.15   **The Director as Liaison.**

The director is at the center of a network of people working for the success of the production.

Serving as Liaison among All Members of the Production Team

Throughout the work of the production, the director is the person who ensures that all members of the production team are pulling in the same direction, working together to assure a successful production. He or she makes sure that the actors know what the designers are doing, and vice versa. The director makes certain that actors go promptly when the costumers call them for fittings, and that the designers provide needed drawings to technical staff, and on and on. He or she mediates disagreements and serves as final arbiter on differences of opinion. In short, the director is that crucial person who bridges the gap between the theatre's potential and the audience's enjoyment; the director is the person who is most responsible for realizing that potential.

Training Directors

There is no one pathway that leads to becoming a director. Many of today's directors began as actors, choreographers, stage managers, or even designers. Some of today's directors have come from fields entirely outside theatre; others have pursued graduate work in theatre, specifically as directors. Probably today's directors in the professional and commercial theatres have somewhat more varied backgrounds than those within the educational theatre, most of whom have a graduate degree in theatre. Most professional directors (but not most academic directors) belong to the Society of Stage Directors and Choreographers.

Directors of whatever background and formal training, however, are expected to have a body of knowledge and skills. For this reason, theatre accrediting programs do not recognize undergraduate majors or degrees in directing, only graduate ones. For persons who want to pursue graduate work in directing, there are two usual pathways: a Master of Fine Arts (MFA) degree in directing or a Ph.D. in theatre's history, criticism, or literature, with supervised opportunities in directing.

Because of the complexity of the director's responsibilities, it is difficult to know exactly how to train someone to be a director. Directing, like any artistic practice, has changed since its beginnings. Directing will doubtless change again in the future, but we cannot say with certainty in what directions. We can note that a few theatres now function without directors, most notably theatres organized around cooperative or communal practices. We can also note, by contrast, that a few theatres now function with directors who exert complete control over all aspects of production, taking over responsibilities usually assumed by actors and designers. In the absence of a clear direction for the future, the director's training must remain wide-ranging and flexible.

Given the complexity of the task and the training needed, directors might be thought to be in short supply. In fact, however, the market for directors, both in educational and professional venues, is glutted. Unemployment rates are at least as high for directors as for actors. Perhaps this situation is less surprising when we remember that for every one director there are many actors, designers, and technicians required: It takes a rather large pyramid of people to support the one directing figure at its top.

What Is Good Directing?

To understand directing, we must be able to assess what the director has brought to the play and what the play presented to the director as strengths and weaknesses. Our evaluation of the direction will then depend on answers to questions like:

- How well did the director analyze and interpret the script?
- How well did the director solve the problems presented?

It is important to separate the production being studied from the play being studied. The production is not necessarily bad because it fails to stage the "playwright's intentions," nor is it necessarily good because it either stages the "playwright's intentions" precisely or turns them upside down. As we have seen, different kinds of directors take different approaches; we must try to understand the approach and then evaluate it for what it is.

Good directing is seen in an internally consistent, exciting production. It deals with the play's problems and exploits the play's strengths in terms of the director's approach.

Good directing shows most of all in the work of the actors. If the actors are good and are working in a theatrically compelling whole, the director has laid a good foundation. If the actors have not been unified, if they seem to hang in space when not speaking, if they perform mechanically, if they lack motivation at any point, if they do not perform with each other, they have been poorly directed.

Good directing has technical polish—smooth cues, precise timing, and a perfect blending of all elements—that radiates "authority," the artists' confidence in their work.

Good directing creates compelling pictures and movement, but only when they expand the work of actors and playwright, never when they contradict—and never when they exist for their own sake.

Good directing gives the performance tempo without giving it mechanical speed; there is no sense of too-fast or too-slow, but the organic tempo of a living entity.

Good directing combines all elements into a whole; there is no sense of good ideas left over or of things unfinished. Everything belongs; everything is carried to its proper full development; nothing is overdone.

The good director, then, understands the play and takes a consistent approach to it, bringing the actors to life in a complete production; the bad director does not fully understand the play, often failing to ask detailed questions; does not coach the actors or coaches them only incompletely, or directs them mechanically in postures and positions and movements dictated by a mechanical notion of visual symbolism and visual beauty; achieves not tempo but clockwork timing; and leaves ideas undeveloped and elements unassimilated.

KEY TERMS

Check your understanding against this list. Brief definitions are in the Glossary; page references there will direct you to appropriate pages. (Persons are page-referenced in the Index.)

balance	French scene
beat (unit)	ground plan
blocking	pace
casting call	picturization
composition	preview
dress rehearsal	rhythm
environment (of the play)	run-through
focus	technical rehearsal

Designers and Technicians

When you have completed this chapter, you should be able to

■ Explain how mood, abstraction, historical period, and socioeconomic circumstances affect design

■ Enumerate the major responsibilities of each designer—scenery, lights, sound, costumes—and of the technical director

Sitting in the modern theatre, we sometimes take the presence of scenery so much for granted that it is easy to forget that theatre does not have its roots in either spectacular effects or localizing settings. We have become acculturated to the presence of physical environments that so closely suit the mood and meanings of each play that we may lose sight of the fact that the theatre for a very long period used little more than the theatre space itself as environment, and that for centuries after that it was satisfied with stock settings that could do for many plays: a room in a palace, a garden, a forest. We live in a period of magnificent settings and superb designers; however, stage design has not always been considered fundamental to theatre or its performance.

Much the same thing is true of costume designers, although it seems likely that their art (extended to include the making of masks) is a very, very old one, whereas the sound designer is a recent innovation. Creators of lighting effects may be said to go back to the Renaissance, but the art of stage lighting came into its own when a controllable means of illumination was invented: gaslight (about 1830).

Actors, directors, and playwrights work with life as their material. Theatre designers, however, work with the environment of human life, and their materials are the materials of our world: light and shadow, fabric and color, wood and canvas, plastic and metal and paint. Because of their materials, designers are far more influenced by technology than are actors, playwrights, or directors. This dependence explains the role of another theatre professional, the technical director. Advances in technology inevitably change the way in which theatre designers practice their art, and, in the case of both light

FIGURE 10.1   **Before Designers.**
This French theatre from the 1600s shows a stage with a stock setting of houses in perspective. Carpenters and painters were undoubtedly used; however, that the setting was designed is questionable.

and sound, technology virtually created those arts. Recently, computers have changed the way in which designers make their designs. Thus, theatre designers stand in both the world of the artist and the world of the technician, and they must be expert in both.

The Nature of Design

Because the designers derive their materials and their subjects from the real world, their art is the creation of worlds on the stage. These worlds are sometimes imitations of the real world, sometimes not; in either case, they use familiar materials, but often in unfamiliar ways. The scenic and costume designers know that their products will be seen under colored light and so will look different on the stage from the way they look in sunlight; the lighting designer knows that the audience must see the actors, no matter what the demands of mood, color, and emphasis, and that the surfaces being lit are different from the things they imitate; the sound designer may be asked to create sounds that never existed in life or to amplify and distort real sounds to match the needs of an unreal world.

The world that the designers create is the world of the play, which is not at all the same thing as a literal copy of the real world. Each designer goes about his or her task differently in creating that world, but they all share a common goal: to create an environment within which the actors can create convincing life. This goal means that the designers must work as a team and that they must work in concert with the director so that a compatible world is created by all of them.

This environment begins with the play. Contemporary design is tied inescapably to the dramatic text. The world that it creates has its roots deep within that text—not merely in the stage directions, but in the lives of the characters.

Several factors, all to be found in the play, govern how the designers create their world.

Tone and Mood

Designers pay close attention to the differences between comic and serious drama, but these two categories are simply not enough. Every play is its own category and must be approached through the range of tones that it contains: lightheartedness in several early scenes and great seriousness in a last act; both the romantic quality of a protagonist and the fragility of another major character, both funny gags and the real sadness of a central character's dilemma. And they must express these subtleties in the settings, costumes, lights, and sounds that are required by the scripts.

Level of Abstraction

The designers are faced with a wide spectrum of possibilities, from literal realism to fantasy to almost pure abstraction. At one extreme, for example, could be the setting for an

FIGURE 10.2   Tone and Mood.

Comedy, warmth, and our own nostalgia for a bygone era inform the design for the production of Kaufman and Hart's *You Can't Take It with You* at Wake Forest University.

American tragedy, where the decision might be made to create a literal replica of a house in New England down to the last detail of the patterns in the wallpaper. At the other extreme might be one of the "space stage" settings of the 1920s—abstract constructions of stairs, ramps, and levels. In costuming, we might find real clothes, purchased in stores and dyed to look sweaty and dirty; at the other extreme, we might find costumes that use elastic fabric, extensions of limbs, and various kinds of padding to change the outline of the human body.

In part, the decision about how abstract the designs will be comes from the designers' and director's interpretation of the script; in part, it comes from a decision about how

FIGURE 10.3   Production Style—Abstraction and Realism.

The right picture shows a realistic setting from early in the twentieth century; the left one shows a setting by Emil Pirchan from the 1920s that is deliberately nonrealistic and eliminates virtually all detail. Yet both settings are offices; style makes them different.

much the abstraction or literalism of the play itself will be emphasized. In a realistic play, for example, the decision to create literal settings and costumes is not an inevitable one; with equal justification, the designers might decide to create a mere suggestion of a house. In the same way, the designers of a play of Shakespeare's may decide that an abstract setting is inappropriate and may go to quite literal, realistic settings.

Historical Period

The shifting of classical plays from one period to another has become common. Designers are confronted constantly with plays that do not have contemporary settings, costumes, and sound. The look and the "feel" of other periods become important aspects of design.

The lighting designer is also affected by historical period, when, for example, ideas about the direction and quantity of light and the quality of shadow come from paintings and engravings of another period. In setting and costume, some of the implications of historical period are obvious; the kinds of problems that they raise are most often handled by careful research by the designers. Sound, too, may be affected if period music is used or if certain kinds of sounds are called for—a trumpet flourish or the sound of *Hamlet's* "peal of ordnance."

Historical period contains a trap for the designers in the perceptions and knowledge of the audience: The designers must consider not only what things looked like in the period but what the audience *thinks* they looked like. What we know of the 1920s, for example, is conditioned by what we have seen in cartoons, old movies, and magazines—but did all women really bob their hair, and did all men really wear knickers and high collars? In the Elizabethan period, did all houses have plaster-and-timber fronts, and did all men wear puffed-out breeches and hose? Did warriors in the tenth century wear plate armor? Or, to reverse the calendar, will all people in the distant future wear tight-fitting clothes of unisex design?

And there is still another trap: contemporary fashion. Audiences are greatly influenced by their own ideas of beauty. As a result, a hairstyle that is supposed to be of 1600 and that was designed in 1930 will often look more like a 1930 hairstyle than a 1600 one; or to take a familiar example from the movies, cowboys' hats in the movies of the 1940s looked far more like 1940s' ideas of what was becoming to men than they ever looked like the actual headgear of westerners of the frontier period.

So designers must think of several things at once when confronted with historical period. It is not enough to go to a book and copy literally what is there.

Geographical Place

Like historical period, geography greatly influences design, unless the decision is made to abandon it altogether (that is, to be abstract instead of literal). The whitewashed houses of the Greek islands are different in color, texture, and scale from the adobes of Mexico or the balconied houses of New Orleans; the traditional clothes of Scotland, Morocco, and Scandinavia are distinct; the light in Alaska and Texas is very different. Sound and light are quite different outdoors from in. Even at considerable levels of abstraction, differences in geography inform some design decisions.

Socioeconomic Circumstances

Wealth and social class influence clothes, furniture, and environment in many places and periods, and, therefore, their imitation on the stage. As with the other considerations, a decision may be made to ignore such matters, but a decision must be made. The matter itself cannot be ignored. And the more realistic the level, the more important these considerations become.

Historical period greatly complicates social and economic matters. As with other historical elements, audiences may have general or inaccurate ideas about what constituted the look of wealth or position or power or poverty in a distant era. What, for example, did a wealthy merchant wear in the seventeenth century that a noble did not? What furniture did the noble own that the merchant did not? What separated serf from artisan in the Middle Ages?

Aesthetic Effect

Put most simply, every designer hopes that the designs will have beauty. That beauty is a variable should be clear—the romantic loveliness of a magic forest cannot be compared with a construction of gleaming metal bars and white plastic plates—but that every designer aims at a goal of aesthetic pleasure seems true. Intentional ugliness may occasionally be aimed at, but even then we are tempted to say that the result is beautiful *because* its ugliness is artfully arrived at.

Composition and balance enter into aesthetic consideration, just as they enter into the considerations of the director. Teamwork is again essential, as setting, costumes, and lights are inevitably seen by the audience as a whole. Thus, unity is also an aesthetic aim, one achieved through a constant sharing of ideas by all the designers.

Designers at Work

Although many of their decisions are reached together at production meetings, the designers do most of their work in solitude or with the technicians who execute their designs—the scene designer with the technical director and builders and painters, the costume designer with cutters and sewers, and so on. At this stage of their work, each specializes and proceeds separately.

The Scene Designer

It is the scene designer's job to create a performing space for the actors and a physical environment for the play's action. The result is the setting, which normally has the added function of supplying the audience with clues about the play's locale.

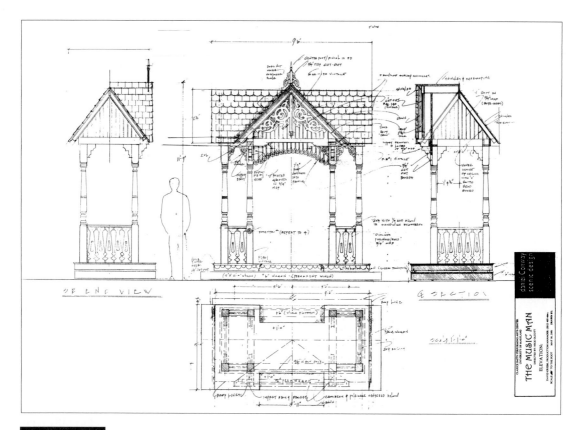

FIGURE 10.4 Elevation.

A detailed elevation from which a scenic piece can be built, designed by Dan Conway for *The Music Man* at the University of Maryland. The production required 27 plates of drafted scenery, including 15 scene plans, and more than a dozen hand-painted elevations.

Other important questions are:

- *The number of settings* (Can the entire play be played in one set, or must different sets be designed and changed for each scene, or can some sort of *unit set* serve for all scenes?)

- *The shape and size of the stage* (Will the audience surround it or look at it through a proscenium arch? If it is small, how can it be kept from seeming cramped? Will the actors play within the setting or in front of it?)

- *The sight lines* of the theatre (What peculiarities of the theatre's architecture demand that the settings be built in special shapes so that every member of the audience can see?)

- *The means of shifting the scenery* (Is there overhead *rigging* so that scenery can be "flown," or is there an elevator stage or a turntable stage for bringing new settings in mechanically?)

- *The materials from which the scenery will be built* (Is it better to use traditional *flats* of wood and canvas, or will built-up details of wood or plastic be better, or will such special materials as poured polyurethane foam or corrugated cardboard or metal pipe be better?)
- *Any special effects* that make special scenic demands (Are there vast outdoor scenes in a proscenium theatre that require large painted *drops,* or will such unusual events in the play as earthquakes or explosions require special solutions?)
- *Any decision to imitate historical scenery* that creates special requirements (That is, if a seventeenth-century play is to be done with Italianate scenery [pp. 296ff.], what will the effects be?)
- The demands of *budget* and *schedule*

These matters may influence the designer before any designs are made, although preliminary doodles and sketches may attempt to catch the "feel" of the play before any practical matters are dealt with. These early impressions will spring from early readings of the play, and they will eventually be incorporated in some form into the *rendering* of the settings that the designer gives the director. Together, they will have worked out the *ground plan* of each setting, and the ground plan will form the basis of both renderings and three-dimensional models. If the renderings are acceptable, the designer will proceed to elevations and scale drawings of all scenic pieces, and these, with all instructions for building and painting, will go to the production's technical director.

In addition, the scene designer is normally in charge of the design or selection of all *properties,* the things used by the actors that are not part of the scenery (furniture, flags, hangings, and so on), as well as such "hand props" as swords, cigarette cases, guns, and letters. Where such things must be designed, as in a period play, the designer creates, and the technical staff executes; where they are acquired from outside sources, the designer haunts stores and antique shops and pores over catalogs of all sorts. In plays done with minimal scenery, as in arena staging, the properties take on added importance, and their design and selection must be carried out with the greatest care. A festival such as the one in Stratford, Ontario, has special shops devoted to property making.

Computer-Aided Design (CAD)

The computer has changed the ways in which many designers work, replacing the pencil with a mouse, and paper with a screen. Everything from sketching to coloring is possible with new, powerful programs that cut through such time-consuming jobs as lettering.

Computer-aided design (CAD), as this process is known, has familiar applications for home use that can be seen at any software store: programs for planning rooms or whole houses, gardens or small buildings. Architectural CAD programs used in theatre work in the same way; with such a program networked by a whole design staff, the saving in time and work more than makes up the expense (see Figure 10.5). Lighting designers also use theatre-specific programs like Light Write.

CAD has pretty well made older drafting tools—compasses, T-squares, triangles—obsolete. It allows the designer to sketch in a simulation of pencil, if that's what is wanted, and then to turn that sketch into an elevation or a three-dimensional picture. Directors

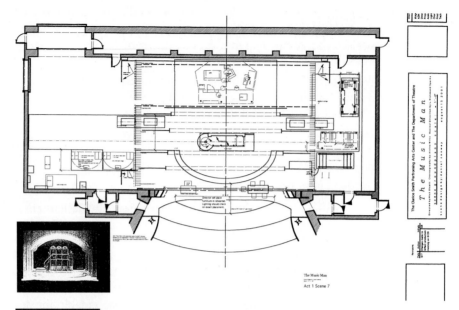

FIGURE 10.5 **Ground Plan.**
The "map" of the setting for one scene from *The Music Man* at the University of Maryland, designed by Dan Conway. Computer-generated plates for this production were sent electronically to the scene shop, where a digitally controlled router table cut scenic components directly from the designer's elevations.

can be "walked through" computer mockups of several design ideas. (See color Figures 5.19–5.22.) Set designers can then use the computer to take the agreed-upon idea to a rendering in any of several styles, from simulated watercolor to bright photo-realism, and from there to scale elevations, detailed plans with dimensions, and final renderings from which full-size scenic painting can be done. Directors can be shown simulations of a setting from many points of view. (See Figure 10.6).

CAD is not magic, however. "The computer is a remarkable tool. It is changing the way we design, draft, and render. But you still have to draw in order to visualize your ideas. Learn when to use the computer, and also when not to" (Michael Franklin-White). Like pencil and paper, CAD is a tool, a great saver of time and tedium but no replacement for creativity.

The Technical Director

Broadway productions have large technical staffs, and they contract out such jobs as scene construction and painting. Small community theatres may have only a single technician to do almost everything. In all kinds of theatres, however, a person exists to oversee the execution of designs and to organize and manage the technical production and its relationship with the theatre. This person is the technical director.

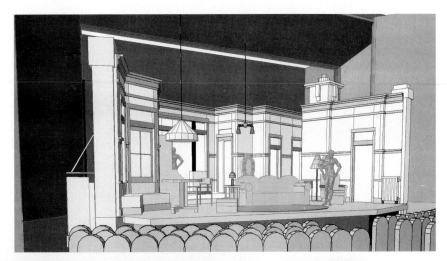

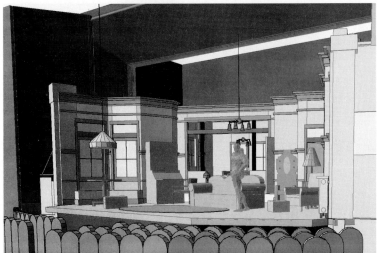

FIGURE 10.6 CAD.

Three computer-aided designs for *Lost in Yonkers,* designed by Jim Hunter at the University of South Carolina. Note how the computer allows the designer to show the director and others three views of the same setting, two of them along the side sight-lines and one from above the stage. Such visuals help both designer and director to have a sense of perspective, of sight lines, of blocking of part of the set by furniture or walls, and so on.

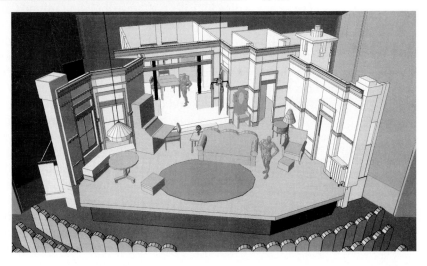

FIGURE 10.7 Tech Work On and Offstage.

Above, the master carpenter works in the scene shop; *below,* a large scenic piece is secured so it will fly over the stage. (Courtesy of Montgomery College.)

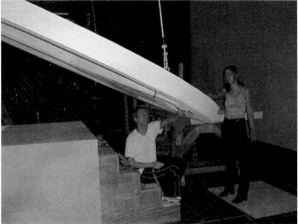

The technical director rules the theatre building around the playing area and behind whatever barrier separates audience from backstage. The job is a tangle of details and responsibilities: he or she knows the theatre building thoroughly and coordinates its maintenance with the building's owner; he or she sees that an ample stock of cables, nails, paint, and a thousand other things are kept on hand; he or she sees to the upkeep of tools, from pencils to table saws; he or she has oversight of backstage scheduling; he or she knows what scenery and properties are in storage and maintains their inventories. In short, the technical director has a huge responsibility and a day-to-day schedule that can be crushing without the most careful planning (and an even temper).

In university theatres, the technical director usually attends meetings at which plays are first selected; even at this earliest stage, his or her advice will be needed to determine if a potential play is too demanding for the theatre's physical capabilities. Later, the technical director takes part in all production meetings, advising director and designer on the practicability of ideas and the likelihood of deadlines. Throughout, the technical director is responsible for setting and meeting scenic and property schedules. (Lighting may fall within his or her responsibility, as well; costumes generally do not.) On top of all this, in educational theatre the technical director does a great deal of the actual work of construction and painting, as well as instructing students working on the production.

Many technical directors are capable designers in their own right. When not executing their own designs, however, they must work objectively, remembering Lee Simonson's dictum that "technology is the tail to the poet's kite." It is the technical director who causes the poet's kite to fly—but not to fly away.

The Costume Designer

The costume designer clothes both the character and the actor, creating dress in which the character is "right" and the actor is both physically comfortable and artistically pleased. This double responsibility makes the costumer's a difficult job. It is never enough to sew up something that copies a historically accurate garment; that garment must be made for a character, and it must be made for an actor. The actor must be able to move and speak and should also feel led or pushed by the costume to a closer affinity with the character and the world of the play. Generally, actors want costumes to be

FIGURE 10.8 **Costume Design.**
Costume designers have to think of both the actor and the character. This costume began with a pencil sketch (*left*), moved through a color rendering to which swatches of fabric were attached (*center*), and became a costume fitted to the actor (*right*). A design for the character of Arnolphe in Molière's *School for Wives,* played by Mitchell Hébert. (Designed by Helen Huang, USAA.)

becoming to them personally, and costumers need tact in dealing with people who feel that their legs or their noses or their bosoms are not being flattered.

In designing for the character, the costumer must keep firmly in mind the given circumstances of the character, such as age, sex, state of health, and social class, as well as the focal importance of the character in key scenes (Should it form part of a crowd or stand out?), and most important of all, those elements of character that would express themselves through clothes. Is the character cheerful or somber? Simple or complex? Showy or timid? Majestic or mousy?

Other important matters are

- *Silhouette* (the mass and outline of the costume as worn)
- *The costume in motion* (Does it have potential for swirl or billow or drape or curve as it moves? Does it change with movement? Will it encourage, even inspire, the actor to move more dynamically? What aspects of it—fringe, a scarf, coattails, a cape, a shawl—can be added or augmented to enhance motion?)
- *Fabric texture and draping* (Does the play suggest the roughness of burlap and canvas or the smoothness of silk? What is wanted—fabrics that will drape in beautiful folds, like velour, silk, or jersey, or fabrics that will hang straight and heavily?)
- *Fabric pattern* (All-over, small, repeated patterns as opposed to very large designs on the fabric, or none at all?)
- *Enhancement or suppression of body lines* (The pelvic V of the Elizabethan waist, or the pushed-up bosom of the French Empire, the pronounced sexuality of the medieval codpiece, or the body-disguising toga; and, for the individual actor, are there individual characteristics like narrow shoulders, skinny calves, or long necks that must be disguised?)
- *Special effects* (such as animal or bird costumes or fantasy creatures), where necessary

In addition, the costumer must consult with both scene and lighting designer to make sure that the costumes will look as they are designed to look under stage light and against the settings. Practical considerations like budget and deadlines are, of course, always important.

The costumer's designs are usually presented as color renderings, normally with swatches of the actual materials attached, and with detailed notations indicated for the costume shop supervisor. From these, patterns are made, where needed; the costumer selects the fabrics and usually oversees their cutting and the construction of the costumes themselves. Most theatre companies of any size keep a stock of costumes from which some pieces can be "pulled" for certain productions, thus saving time and money. Costume support areas of any size usually include, besides the stock, fitting rooms, cutting tables, sewing machines and sewing spaces, and tubs for washing and dyeing.

The Lighting Designer

When stages were lit by candles, attempts to control the light were very crude and seldom very successful. In those days, the lighting designer's work was largely confined to special effects, such as fire. With the introduction of a controllable light source, however,

section 4

MASKS and FACES

4.2 Double makeup in *Quartet*, costume, lights, and makeup by Natasa, directed by Zeljko Djukic, at the Open Theatre/T.U.T.A.

4.1 Painted mask, Korea. (Courtesy of Elbin Cleveland)

Masks and *Faces*, continued

4.3 Mask, India. (Courtesy of Farley Richmond)

4.4 Ceremonial mask, Mexico.

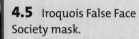

4.5 Iroquois False Face Society mask.

4.6 Masked chorus, *The Oresteia*, University of South Carolina. Directed by Robert Richmond, designed by David Coleman. Jim O'Connor, artistic director.

4.7 Masks by James R. Adams for Roman comedy: *The Pot of Gold* at Manchester College. Directed by Scott K. Strode, designed by Stephen A. Baraka.

4.8 Mask for modern *commedia dell'arte*. Interlocken European Commedia Troupe. (Photo by and courtesy of Peter Avery)

Masks *and* **Faces**, continued

4.9 *and* **4.10** Creating a Makeup, and the Makeup Completed: Rat in *The Tortoise and the Hare*, Everyman Players. (From *An Odyssey of Maskers*, Anchorage Press, Louisville; courtesy of Orlin Corey)

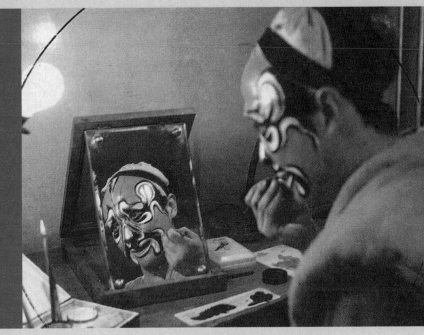

4.11 Makeup, China: a *Jing* actor makes up. (Courtesy of the People's Republic of China)

4.12 Makeup, India. (Courtesy of Farley Richmond)

4.13 Makeup, Beijing Opera. (Courtesy of Yi-Hui Lee)

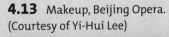

Masks *and* Faces, continued

4.14 Makeup, America. The actor Walt Witcover in makeup and costume for a one-man show. (Courtesy of Walt Witcover)

4.15 Makeup, America. *The Colored Museum* at Hampton University.

DESIGNER'S
World

5.1 Computer design for *Romeo and Juliet* by Michael Franklin-White. (Corporate Scenographics LLC)

Designer's World, continued

5.2 Less Is More: a minimalist scene from *Flower Drum Song* at the Mark Taper Forum, Los Angeles; light and three lengths of iron pipe create the scene. Lea Salonga, *center*. Robert Longbottom, director and choreographer. (Craig Schwartz photo, courtesy of the Mark Taper Forum)

5.3 Design for Tragedy. *The Oresteia* at the University of South Carolina, designed by David Coleman. Directed by Robert Richmond; Jim O'Connor, artistic director.

5.4 Design for Realism. *A Streetcar Named Desire* at South Carolina State University, designed by George Epting, directed by Frank Mundy.

Designer's World, continued

5.5 Design for Comedy. *Misalliance* at Dartmouth Summer Repertory.

5.6 Design for a New Interpretation. Molière's play of the 1600s, *The Misanthrope*, at Wake Forest University.

5.7 Design for Postmodernism. Molière's *Tartuffe* at the University of Missouri, Columbia. Directed by Suzanne Burgoyne, scenic design by R. Dean Packard, costume design by James Miller, lighting design by Sandy Harned.

5.8 *and* 5.9 Design at a Small College. *The Wiz* and
A Woman's Worth at the Saint Mary-of-the-Woods College.

Designer's World, continued

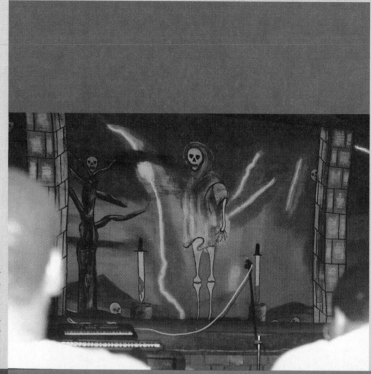

5.10 Design in Africa. Limited resources create different solutions. Courtesy of Jessica Kaahwa, director and photographer.

5.11 *Getting Out* at the University of Vermont.

A New Direction: Corporation Design

5.12 Computer-aided rendering, Parke-Davis meeting design.

Corporation theater is a relatively new application of theatrical design to corporate meetings once called *industrials* but now described as "a form of advertising, but with a distinctly theatrical flair. . . . In the past twenty years, this industry has grown from two-screens-and-a-podium to elaborate productions rivaling anything in New York."

Corporate Scenographics is a design firm that works in this field. Their work has been described in this way:

> In a typical week, the staff of four makes drawings and sketches of ideas for sets and sends them off to the producer . . . using faxes or scanned images attached to e-mails. Then they make elaborate renderings showing various looks at specific moments in the show, using 3D computer-aided drawings. These are converted into photographic realism using additional software, and, finally, color is applied using Adobe Photoshop, making an airbrush-enhanced, photo-realistic rendering. At the same time, the staff drafts the set idea into a scaled architectural drawing using AutoCAD and then adds color and tones using Adobe Illustrator.
>
> This work is sent to the producer. . . . When [we] are awarded a show, we draft all the parts of the setting, make a detailed model in scale, and provide color specifications, samples, and "painter's elevations" so that scenery shops can build and paint the sets at full size.

Michael Franklin-White

5.13 *and* **5.14** Parke-Davis meeting designs.

5.15 McDonald's Tour, 1996.

5.16 McDonald's Tour, 2001.

5.17 Pfizer meeting, 1998.

5.18 Pfizer meeting, 2002.

Computer-Aided Design

1

Alternative designs for a production of *The Baltimore Waltz* at the University of South Carolina. Designs by Jim Hunter. "Working together at the computer, the director's or designer's ideas and rearrangements were instantly visualized. The 3D "walk-through" capabilities of VectorWorks allowed the team to explore the scenery from audience and performer viewpoints." Jim Hunter.

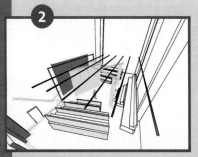

2

5.19 "A very early possibility, the above view is as if from [the auditorium] looking up into the stage house. [Performance and audience were on a proscenium stage.] The yellow "S-shaped" scrim/curtain winds through the performance area surrounded by a thrust seating arrangement. Note the light blue outline of the [proscenium] stage apron and the black outline of the proscenium arch." Jim Hunter.

5.20 "In this later view, taken as if from behind the [proscenium] stage house looking out toward the auditorium, the three-sided seating arrangement has been rotated.... The yellow curtain is now on two tracks, allowing for added flexibility...." Jim Hunter.

5.21 "Still later, the column and window elements have been included but the curtain effect is now in a square... This view is taken as if in the upstage left corner of the [proscenium] stage house." Jim Hunter.

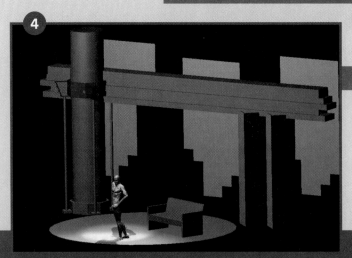

3

4

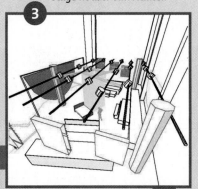

5.22 "The final arrangement evolved into the small show portal seen. The curtain track element is now hidden behind the header of the portal." Jim Hunter.

FIGURE 10.9 Costumes and Makeup Backstage.

Above, the costume shop, with costume designer Peter Zakutansky; *below*, his work with student actors in the dressing room. (Courtesy of Montgomery College.)

and with the demand in the nineteenth century for more and more realistic imitations of phenomena like sunrise and moonlight, the designer's task became more challenging. The possibilities of stage lighting expanded from simple imitation of natural effects, and lighting became a design element as important and as potent as scenery itself.

The possible uses of theatre light are enormous. Through manipulation of intensity and direction, for example, a designer can change the apparent shape of an onstage object. Through manipulation of intensity and color, the lighting designer can influence the audience's sense of mood and tone. Through manipulation of direction and color, the designer can create a world utterly unlike the one in which the audience lives, with light coming from fantastic angles and falling in colors never seen in nature.

Modern equipment has made theatre lighting more flexible than early designers ever dreamed. Small, easily aimed instruments (lighting units) and complex electronic controls, often with computerized memories, have made possible a subtlety in stage lighting that was unknown even thirty years ago.

The lighting designer works with three fundamentals: color, direction, and intensity of light. These are partly interdependent because of the nature of the light source, usually an incandescent filament. Color is changed physically by the placement of a transparent colored medium (usually called a *gel*) in the beam of light; this is not usually changed during a performance. Direction is a function of the location of the lighting instruments, of which hundreds may be used in a contemporary production. Each instrument is plugged into an electric circuit either individually or with a few others to illuminate the same scene. The location of instruments is rarely changed during performance, and so designers are limited by the number of instruments and the number of electrical circuits available to them. Light *intensity* is controlled by changes in the electrical current supplied to the instrument; this process is called *dimming* and is done by manipulating the levers on *dimmers,* of which several kinds are in use. All have the same goal of changing the amount of light coming from the instrument from zero to full intensity, with the capability of stopping at any point in between.

The lighting designer's plan is called a *light plot.* It shows the location and direction of each instrument, as well as what kind of instrument is to be set at each location—usually either a *floodlight* (soft-edged and wide-beamed) or a *spotlight* (hard-edged and narrow-beamed). The locations chosen are over and around the playing area, so that light falls on the actors and the acting space at an angle, both vertically and horizontally. (Light that falls straight down or comes in parallel to the stage floor gives unusual effects, although both have their uses.) In addition, such subsidiary instruments as *light borders* or *strip lights* (rows of simple lights without lenses, suspended overhead for general illumination), *footlights* (at floor level along the front of many proscenium stages), and *follow spots* (very powerful spotlights that swivel so that their bright beam can constantly illuminate a moving performer) are sometimes used.

The lighting designer is usually responsible for projected scenery or projected shadows, clouds, and similar effects.

The lighting designer has the special responsibility of making everyone else's work accessible to the audience. Light determines what the audience will see. Light creates depth, for one thing, and it can make an actor's eyes seem to sink into deep sockets or vanish in a bland, flat mask. Light gives or takes color, and it can make costume colors

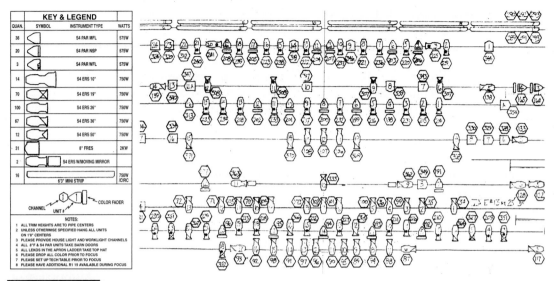

FIGURE 10.10 Light Plot.

This small section of a plot for *The Music Man* shows the planning for a show that used 365 instruments and had 230 light cues. Lighting designed by Daniel MacLean Wagner. (Courtesy of the University of Maryland.)

glow with vibrancy or fade into dirty gray. Light is selective, and it can show the audience precisely what is to be seen.

In making the other artists' work accessible to the audience, the lighting designer has to consider all three elements: intensity, direction, and color. There are no hard-and-fast rules here; rather, there is need for a manipulation and an experimentation that is like putting paint on canvas. Although much of the lighting designer's work is done in production meetings and at the drawing board, much more of it is done in technical rehearsals, when, with the director, the designer experiments with colors and intensities and, frequently, makes decisions to change the locations and the plugging of instruments. Because of this experimental work that comes very late in the production period (often only days before opening), the lighting designer's work is crammed into a short time, and he or she works then at great intensity.

The Sound Designer

Sound became a theatre art with good stereo equipment and related amplification, blending, and tuning equipment. To be sure, sound was used in theatres before that time, and as long ago as Shakespeare's Globe, someone had to be responsible for rolling the cannonballs that simulated thunder, but a sound that could be shaped dimensionally and controlled in pure, correct tones was not possible until very recently. To the regret of many, the sound designer's job has been expanded in many theatres to the "miking" of performers, so that today many actors are heard through speakers rather than directly.

As good as modern equipment is, it is not yet good enough to imitate in range, vibrancy, and direction the natural voice of the actor. It has proved a benefit, however, to actors who lack sufficient voice to be heard in large theatres.

As equipment becomes still more sophisticated and as expertise increases, the work of the sound designer may become as important and creative as that of the lighting designer. Limited at present to concepts of "sound effects" and "background music," the sound designer may one day be able to wrap the audience in sound as the lighting designer wraps the stage in light, and to play as flexibly with sound as the other plays with light. Rock concerts and sound-and-light shows are already pointing the way.

Training Designers

Because theatre designers create environments and use materials of the real world in order to make their art, they must be trained not only as artists but also as artisans. Theatre designers therefore study at least two different sorts of subjects, the artistic and the technical; some designers also need another sort of information, the historical, in order to prepare for their role as theatre designers.

Although some theatre designers (especially in Eastern Europe) customarily design all aspects of a production, most in the United States specialize in one area: scenery, properties, costumes, lighting, or sound. All need certain kinds of basic information. For example, all need proficiency in dramatic analysis. Most need to learn about color, line,

FIGURE 10.11 **What Is Good Design?**
A costume by Martin A. Thaler for *Vinegar Tom* at the University of Vermont.

mass, composition, balance, and other such basic elements of design, and most need to master basic techniques of drawing and rendering and use of CAD programs. They require some understanding of visual communication (that is, how people are likely to interpret certain colors, shapes, lines, and proportions). Finally, because every play presents a unique problem in design, all designers need skills in basic research methods that will allow them to pursue the design of any play independently.

Beyond such basic, shared areas of study are others specific to each area, because the technical skills needed by each designer vary considerably. For example, scenic designers and technical directors often study basic construction and (occasionally) carpentry; scene designers will usually take courses in scene painting as well. With the arrival of new metals and plastics came a need for training in welding and form-making. These designers will also often study engineering in order to discover how the aesthetic requirements of a design can be safely built and safely used. Costume designers usually study basic sewing, pattern-making, drafting, and draping as well as some specialized areas like millinery. Lighting and sound designers take courses in electricity, electronics, and instrumentation. Most designers now are expected to be proficient in computers.

Because of the importance of plays from the past, training in scenery, property, and costume design (less often in lighting and sound design) usually includes quite a bit of history. Scenic designers, for example, need to know the history of architecture and furniture. Costume designers need to know the history of fashion, textiles, and accessories (jewelry, wigs, etc.). The history of visual painting often suggests not only the techniques of painters in each age that designers might want to use in order to capture the "look" of the age but also the telling details of design—fabrics, jewelry, upholstery, and so on. Sound designers, especially, often want courses in the history of music.

In other periods, training in design came primarily through an apprentice system where a beginner worked with a more experienced artist until attaining an acceptable level of craft. Now, however, proficiency in design and technical theatre usually comes from pursuing a graduate degree (especially the Master of Fine Arts—MFA) in theatre at a university. The job market in design and technical theatre remains strong (unlike that in acting, playwriting, or directing), in part because the need for such people far exceeds

Links to More About Theatre

Irene Corey, *The Mask of Reality,* 1968.

Robert Edmond Jones, *The Dramatic Imagination,* 1941. Theory and inspiration by America's exponent of the New Stagecraft.

<www.siue.edu/COSTUMES/> A USITT site.

<www.inch.com/~kteneyck/> Site of the New York studio of Karen Ten Eyck. Photos, designs, and more. Can be slow to load, depending on your PC, but worth every second.

Thinking About **Design**

> *"To surround a play with foreign bodies of scenery . . . [that] obscure its meaning while they pretend to illustrate it . . . [is] an artistic crime."*
> —Harley Granville-Barker, director, 1877–1946.

Study the illustrations in Chapters 10 and 19 and evaluate their scenic designs in terms of Granville-Barker's criterion.

the number of them well trained in these fields; university training usually leads to steady work either in the professional or educational theatre.

What Is Good Design?

Good design is good art. It is created in terms of the production, however, and it is created within the context of other artists' decisions. Knowing what is the product of a designer and what of a director can often be difficult, however, and, especially in our director-dominated theatre, assessing each designer's work is sometimes challenging.

Good design, above all, serves the actor—giving the actor good spaces in which to act, clothing the actor, illuminating the actor.

Good design serves the production. It does not necessarily serve the "playwright's intentions"; interpretation may have greatly changed this production from those intentions. Obvious changes may have been made—in historical period, geographical location, social class—along with less obvious ones (genre, mood, style); the play may even

FIGURE 10.12 **Model and Finished Set.**
Designer Michael Franklin-White's model for *K-2* (*left*) and a photograph of the set in performance (*right*). (Courtesy of Michael Franklin-White and Corporate Scenographics LLC.)

have become the framework, in this production, for an idea the very opposite of the "intention." In serving the production, good design meshes with other elements and does not call attention to itself.

Good design, where possible, is dynamic, not static: It has the capacity to change as the performance progresses. Such change is clearest in costumes and lighting, less so in scenery, where the number of sets is limited. A set that makes a powerful statement right off the bat and never goes beyond it for the entire performance may be a bad set.

Good design is not redundant. It does not merely "state the theme." It has its own complexity.

Good design has detail and texture (variety within the whole): Light is not merely a bland wash of light; a costume is not merely a wide stretch of draped and sewn fabric; a setting is not merely a painted surface.

Good design has technical finish. Designers must design within the technical limitations of their theatres, so that everything the audience sees is technically well done. Often, designers oversee the technical work or approve it; nothing second-rate should pass their eyes.

Good design is daring: It tries new technologies, avoids old solutions, and chances failure.

The good designer, then, is one who creates effective works of visual art that serve the actor, that are right for the performance, that are richly textured and dynamic, and that can be perfectly finished by the technical capabilities of the theatre. The bad designer is one who ignores the actor; who creates ugly or uninteresting things; who designs for a predetermined idea of the play, not for this production; who creates statically; who ignores the capabilities of the technical facilities and allows shoddy work to go on the stage.

KEY TERMS

Check your understanding against this list. Brief definitions are in the Glossary; page references there will direct you to appropriate pages. (Persons are page-referenced in the Index.)

CAD	light plot
dimmer	properties
floodlight	rendering
follow spot	silhouette
gel	spotlight
ground plan	strip light (light border)

Theatre of Other Times and Places: Theatre History

Theatre: Present and Past

We study theatre's past in part to understand how theatre relates to the larger culture—how forces for change work in theatre and beyond it. We also study theatre's history to discover how we differ from (and how we resemble) the peoples and practices of other times and places. Finally, we study theatre's history to enhance our experiences of today's theatre, both as audience members and as theatre practitioners.

Theatre history, however, is no more free of fads, hidden agendas, and unstated assumptions than any other kind of history. In the United States, it has been heavily tilted toward American subjects, then toward British and European ones; it has remained fairly indifferent to those of Asia and Africa.

The growing globalism at the beginning of the twenty-first century, however, argues for widening our vision to include other cultures. This book continues to emphasize western traditions, because they have dominated North American culture, but we have treated major theatres and dramas of Africa and the East as well, pointing to interconnections where they exist and explaining conventions that differ from those with which we are most familiar. We have tried to suggest that such culture has a tradition of theatre that is as rich in its own way as our own.

As you read what follows, then, you should notice where emphases have been put and where omissions have been made. You should ask yourself why these are as they are—remembering that in history of all sorts, a lack of evidence in one area and an over-supply in another greatly affects how much appears on the page. The modern period, for example—especially since the invention of photography and cheap printing—has so much information about itself that we have a hard time limiting it. Remember, too, that time is a quirky editor—through accident, war, intentional erasure, and neglect, it drops masses of information that would be thought vital if we could have it. Remember, too, the old adage of historians: it is the winners who write history. And remember, finally, that until quite recently, most people went unrepresented in history, including theatre history, which took as its subject people very like the ones who wrote the history: educated, male, close to the center of power, white, often affluent.

It has been said that art validates the center of power. No more important understanding can come from the study of theatre's past than to learn how theatre art and socio-political power come together and drift apart, validating and then becoming invisible to one another. To understand that relationship is to understand how theatre history is history.

The Sweep of Theatre History

"Looking into history is like shining a flashlight into a cave. You can't see the whole cave, but as you play the flashlight around, a hidden shape is revealed."

Our light shines mostly on western Europe and the United States, the cultures most directly relevant to us. We will from time to time, however, flick the beam to the east long

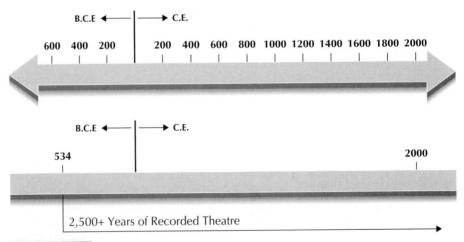

FIGURE III.1 Timelines.

As the timelines make clear, the institution of theatre has a history of more than 2,500 years, compared with film's one hundred or so and television's even shorter one.

Façade Stage

enough to illuminate major theatrical traditions unfolding there, showing that other sophisticated traditions existed—and still exist—alongside our own. Within the western tradition, three major shapes can be seen, and we have organized our history around them.

The earliest confirmed records of theatre are those of Athens, Greece, in the fifth century before the Common era (B.C.E.). Greece was then at the western edge of several highly developed civilizations, most notably those in China, Persia, and Egypt. Athens created a rich theatrical tradition—two kinds of formal drama: tragedy and comedy; actors playing in front of neutral backgrounds in outdoor spaces with audiences curved in front of them; a performance style that included music, dancing, and masks; and the world's first and still-important work of dramatic theory, Aristotle's *Poetics*. When Alexander the Great unified Greece and took his armies eastward in the 330s B.C.E., he carried this theatre as far as modern Afghanistan and northern India. Although no direct connection can be proved, India developed its own Sanskrit drama and dramatic theory soon thereafter.

At about the same time, both political and cultural power in the Mediterranean moved westward from Greece to Rome. The Romans built unified theatre structures as far north as Britain and around most of the Mediterranean fringe, including North Africa. Rome had an important written comedy and a less important tragedy, both based on Greek models. But after the first century B.C.E. its dominant form was mime, which left no dramatic theory or scripts of any quality but was hugely popular. When the Roman Empire split in two in the fourth century of the Common era (C.E.), the eastern part, centered at Constantinople (modern Istanbul), flourished; the western empire declined and after the sixth century C.E. existed only in name. Theatre continued in the east, with mime a popular form throughout the vast eastern empire, stretching even to southern Russia. But theatre seems to have almost disappeared in the west. The first part of our history ends here.

Found Spaces

Theatre—or at least records of theatre—did not surface again in western Europe until the late tenth century C.E. Then, "Latin music drama," a sung drama with highly stylized staging, performed in Benedictine monastic churches as a part of the liturgy, appeared in England; a Christianized version of Roman comedies, perhaps staged, perhaps not, appeared in Germany. These two kinds of drama were soon joined by other religious and secular theatres throughout Europe. In whatever venue, the medieval plays shared a staging that put the performance in pre-existing spaces, with

Thrust Stage

symbolic distance, acting, and costumes. By the fourteenth century, secular plays and professional actors began to appear; by the sixteenth, they had overwhelmed the earlier religious dramas. In Japan during the same period, an entirely unrelated form, *Noh,* was appearing; based in Zen Buddhism, it was mystical, symbolic, and austere.

In the late sixteenth century, a professional, secular theatre replaced the religious theatre. In England and Spain, medieval theatrical conventions (generalized playing area and symbolic structures) persisted, but they now appeared in free-standing theatres rather than found spaces. Spanish and English public theatres, including Shakespeare's Globe, were partly open overhead, and both featured an elevated stage that thrust into the audience and, through doors at its back, opened to a part of the structure that housed dressing rooms and stage machinery. Theatres of great spectacle rose in the east about the same time—in Japan, *Kabuki,* which used the world's first rotating stage; in China, early precursors of Beijing opera. Both used stunning costumes, makeup, masks, and movement. With the end of England's and Spain's Golden Ages, the second part ends.

When machinery and scenery became important, indoor theatres with a stage at one end became more common, and a new set of staging conventions developed in Italy, conventions that moved theatre away from emblem and toward illusion. In Europe, an age of great scenic display and great scenic designers and inventors lasted from the middle of the seventeenth century (earlier in Italy) through the middle of the nineteenth. It was matched by great, sometimes pyrotechnic acting. Theatres got bigger as cities grew, and performances attracted new audiences drawn by the spectacle.

With the coming of railroads in the mid-1800s, whole productions could travel, multiplying the potential audience and making theatre for a time the most popular entertainment in European and American cultures.

After 1850, forward-looking artists moved the style of acting, scenery, and plays toward Realism, the literal mirroring of surface reality (and the opposite of the magical and the spectacular). Such plays demanded, and such audiences seemed to want, smaller theatres again, with both acting and scenic area entirely behind a proscenium, through which the audience looked at the performance as through a picture frame. Realism spawned immediate reactions, all of which changed but failed to replace it. Some of the most popular theatres, however, continued to produce spectaculars with only hints of realism and the several styles that followed it.

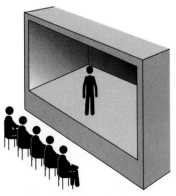

Proscenium Stage

The increasing westernization of the world, which reached its height during the nineteenth and early twentieth centuries, had profound effects on world theatre. As European colonialism swept through Africa and Asia, Western drama and theatre came along with it, with major effects: Realistic dramas and illusionistic staging of the sort popular in the colonizers' countries began to be produced in their colonies, the dramatic and theatrical conventions of their own traditional dramas adapted to fit a Western aesthetic more closely, and dramas such as Noh and Kabuki came to be viewed and treated as museum pieces. Part three of our history ends here.

Façade Stages (534 B.C.E.–c. 550 C.E.)

The first phase of theatrical and dramatic history for which we have records began in the sixth century B.C.E. and ended around 550 C.E., a period of about one thousand years. These thousand years are studied together because they share certain major conventions of performance:

1. *A façade stage,* where actors performed in front of a neutral background
2. *A relationship with religion,* in which plays were presented as a part of larger, religious celebrations
3. *A sense of occasion,* because performances were offered only on special occasions and never often enough to be taken for granted
4. *A noncommercial environment,* in which wealthy citizens or the state itself bore the costs as part of the obligations of citizenship
5. *A male-only theatre,* in which women participated only as audience

This theatre appeared first in Greece and later, in modified form, in Rome. Roughly contemporary with Roman theatre was a theatre and drama in India, which may or may not be related to those of the west.

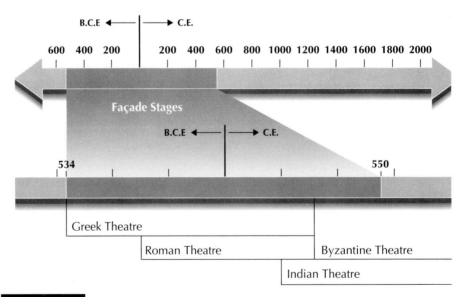

FIGURE IIIa.1 Timeline.

Façade stages dominated theatre for its first thousand years. Beginning in Greece in 534 B.C.E., drama and theatre appeared in Rome by 240 B.C.E. and in India somewhat later.

11

The Theatre of Greece

When you have completed this chapter, you should be able to

- Explain why there are different theories of the origins of theatre and what some of those theories are

- Discuss the relationship between theatre and religion in Greece

- Discuss the role of competition in Greek theatre festivals

- Trace the development of the Greek physical theatres and their plays and playwrights

- Identify the major periods of Greek theatres, with approximate dates

- Explain how a Greek performance would have looked in the principal periods—what masks and costumes were used, what a chorus did, what acting space was used

- Explain important differences between tragic and comic performances and occasions

The very first records of drama and theatre come from Athens, Greece, and date from the sixth century B.C.E. Within a hundred years, Athenian drama had reached a peak of excellence seldom equaled since. The result is that, when people speak of Greek theatre today, they are almost certainly referring to the plays and productions of the fifth century B.C.E. in Athens.

Why drama and theatre should arise there and not in other civilizations of the time remains a mystery, but Athens' position in the ancient world offered some advantages.

Greece, a peninsula about half the size of New York state with its numerous bays, harbors, inlets, and adjacent islands has one of the longest coastlines in the world. Its geography made it, during the sixth century B.C.E., the leading merchant of the Mediterranean, a role it took over from the Phoenicians. Exporting pottery, olive oil, wine, and slaves, Greece brought in a variety of items from North Africa and the East, where advanced civilizations were already flourishing in Egypt, China, India, and Persia (today's Iran). In fact, Greece formed the western edge of the then-civilized world and served as a crossroads for trade.

To speak of "Greece," however, is misleading, for there was no unified nation. Rather, on the peninsula were organized individual city states, each called a *polis* (pl. *poleis*) and each consisting of a town and its surrounding countryside. Each *polis* issued its own coin, raised its own armies, and so on. Although several were important (e.g., Corinth, Sparta, Thebes), by the fifth century B.C.E. (400s), Athens had emerged as both cultural leader and trading giant, with its own outposts in Italy, Sicily, France, and Spain. As the word *outposts* suggests, western Europe was at the time a cultural backwater. And Athens itself was a small city by modern standards—100,000 people, about the size of Utica, New York.

By the fifth century B.C.E., the golden age of Athenian theatre and drama, Athens had already established the world's first democracy, providing a model for the participation of citizens in the decisions and policies of government. The *polis* had become so central in their lives that a later philosopher defined man as "a political animal," that is, as one who lives in a *polis.* Part of being political was being social—people who could, lived in the town, even though they might have a farm in outlying lands. Under Pericles, its great fifth-century B.C.E. ruler, Athens created statues and buildings, arts and philosophies whose excellence made them dominant in European culture for more than two thousand years. By then as well, Athens had developed an alphabet that included both vowels and consonants, becoming the first in history to represent speech both systematically and consistently.

Athenians took great pride in their civic accomplishments. To celebrate its culture, facilitate the exchange of goods, and pay tribute to various gods, Athens sponsored a number of public festivals each year. At three of these festivals, each devoted to the god Dionysus, the earliest recorded theatre and drama appeared. Why did this new art arise? Why did it take the form it did? Why was Athens rather than Egypt, Persia, China, or India the birthplace of drama?

Theories of the Origins of Theatre

There is almost no written evidence from which to draw information about the origins of Greek drama. The earliest account is Aristotle's *Poetics,* written about two hundred years

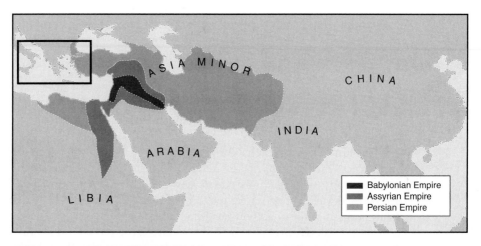

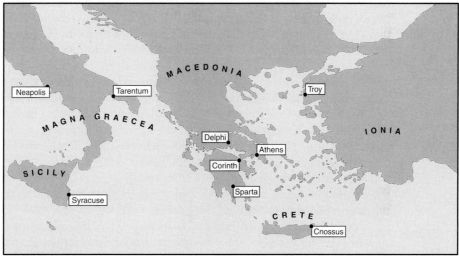

FIGURE 11.1 **The Civilized World.**

By the fifth century B.C.E. (400s), Greek city-states (*below*) influenced much of the Mediterranean, including some outposts on the Italian peninsula. But Greece was at the far western reaches of the civilized world, with older cultures well established in China, India, and much of today's Middle East (*above*).

after the fact. He claimed, in Chapter 4, that "tragedy was produced by the authors of the dithyrambs, and comedy from [the authors] of the phallic songs." Dithyrambs were choral odes (poems performed by a chorus). During certain periods, dithyrambs were devoted to the god Dionysus (whom Aristotle never mentions), but at other times they praised various heroes (who were the subjects of many tragedies). Phallic songs were rites celebrating male sexual potency, but their precise nature is unknown. Although tantalizing, then, Aristotle's account is not very helpful, for we cannot tell from his account which kind of dithyrambs or phallic songs he had in mind, nor can we discern *how* or *why* the authors changed the one to tragedy and the other to comedy. Moreover, Aristotle was writing about two hundred years after the first recorded theatre performance, and we have no idea where he got his information.

In the absence of certainty, several theories have arisen to explain how and why drama came into being. These theories have relied on evidence drawn from fields such as anthropology and linguistics and from contemporaneous art works, especially vase paintings.

The Ritual Theory. Probably the most fashionable, but not necessarily the most correct, view of the origin of theatre is the ritual theory, which proposes that Greek drama evolved from early religious rituals devoted to the god Dionysus. The theory has strengths: drama first appeared in Greece only at great religious festivals and only at festivals devoted to the god Dionysus, who in Greece was associated with wine and sexuality. But it also has weaknesses: no extant Greek tragedy features Dionysus as a central figure or displays the sort of orgiastic worship associated with Dionysus. (On the contrary, Greek tragedy is serious and stately.) Few reputable scholars still accept the idea that drama "evolved" in some organic, necessary way from religious ritual, although most acknowledge that ritual elements can often be found in tragedy, as in daily life.

The Great Man Theory. Some scholars propose that the appearance of tragedy and comedy arose as creative acts of human genius. Arguing that art neither evolves like a biological organism nor happens by chance, such scholars search for the birth of drama in a revolutionary invention of a gifted human being. According to this view, an artist purposefully synthesized elements that already existed in Athenian society into a new form, the drama. The theory has strengths: it isn't bothered by Dionysus' absence or the absence of orgiastic ecstasy from extant tragedies. More important, storytelling, music, and dance *did* already exist in Greek society and so were readily available for use. But this theory also has weaknesses: human genius is itself mysterious, and so the theory leaves much unexplained.

The Storytelling Theory. Some scholars propose that Greek drama developed from storytelling. The idea here is that storytellers would naturally tend to elaborate parts of the telling by impersonating the various characters, using appropriate voice and movement. From here, it seems a short step to having several people become involved in telling the story; from this telling, it is thought, drama and theatre arose. This theory, which clearly emphasizes the role of actors and acting in drama, has strengths: Athens had a rich and long tradition of epic singers—storytellers who gave public performances of works such as Homer's *Iliad* and *Odyssey,* for example. The theory has a major weakness, however: it fails to account for the prominent position played by the chorus in Greek drama.

The Dance Theory. Other theorists suggest that movement rather than speech was at the core of the drama. The idea here is that dancers first imitated the physical behavior of animals and humans. When dancers costumed themselves in appropriate skins and garments, they came to impersonate the animals and humans. When several dancers joined together in impersonation and then embroidered this performance with sounds and words, drama was born (the argument goes). Again, this theory has strengths: it accounts well for the dancing chorus present in all Greek drama, and it explains the animal choruses of several comedies (e.g., *The Birds, The Frogs*). But it too has weaknesses: it suggests a primacy of chorus that most Greek drama does not display, and it fails to account for the separation between actor and chorus that began with the first Greek drama that we know anything about.

In fact, no one knows the origin of Greek drama. The argument over origins is often an argument over the nature of theatre itself. To anthropologists, who look upon theatre as a kind of performance closely related to impersonations as different as the Mandan Buffalo Dance, the Iroquois False Face Society, and the Egyptian "Passion Play," the essence of theatre is ritual, and so they tend to favor the ritual theory. To artists who look at world theatre and see a form rich in human meaning and almost indescribable in complexity, only an artist's creation can explain its beginnings, and so they favor the "Great Man" theory. For those who believe drama began with the actor, the storyteller theory works best; for those who find the essence of Greek drama in its chorus, the dance theory seems better.

The theory that is accepted often has real-world consequences. A director who prefers the ritual theory, for example, might choose to insert ritual elements such as incense burning and incantation into a tragedy, whereas one who prefers the great man theory may stress instead the individuality of character. A director who prefers the dance theory may emphasize the centrality of the chorus, extending its opportunities for singing and dancing, while a director who follows the storytelling theory might shrink the choral odes and even the size of the chorus, throwing added weight to the actors.

FIGURE 11.2 Chorus.

All Greek drama used a chorus, one piece of evidence pointing toward the dance theory of origins for drama. Shown here, a detail from a vase painting that seems to show a chorus. Notice, too, the masks and tails, and the musicians.

From that question and its attempted answers have already come some insights into the nature of Greek drama. We have, during the preceding discussion, encountered three important traits of Greek theatre, traits that may seem odd next to current theatrical conventions.

Traits of Greek Theatre

Greek theatre was closely associated with Greek religion. A form of polytheism, ("many gods"), Greek religion was both private (a part of daily life and centered in the home) and public, expressing itself at a number of major festivals, each devoted to a specific god. During its golden age, drama appeared only in Athens and at only three festivals of Dionysus: the City (or Great) Dionysia, the Rural Dionysia, and the Lenaia. An altar was a permanent fixture of the performance space.

Even after the golden age, drama and theatre continued their close association with Greek religion, with seats of honor for the priests of Dionysus set aside in the audience area. Still later, when an actors' union formed, it called itself the "Artists of Dionysus" and drew its officers from the ranks of Dionysian priests.

Greek theatre was performed only on special occasions—the festivals. Held only three times a year, the festivals that produced drama were religious but far from solemn— Mardi Gras and Halloween are, after all, rooted in religious practices. The festivals were filled with activities: parades, contests, choral dances, markets, so that even without drama and theatre, the festivals drew large crowds. Both the celebratory nature and the relative rarity of the festivals may have made attending theatre more like celebrating an anniversary or going to Mardi Gras than like attending theatre or movies today.

Greek theatre was choral. In addition to actors, the performance of Greek drama required a *chorus*, a group of men who dressed alike, who were masked alike, and who moved, sang, and spoke together most of the time. Chorus members (probably fifteen for tragedy and twenty-four for comedy) looked upon participation as both an honor and a civic duty; they were not paid to participate.

The chorus affected Greek drama in important ways. Its costumes, songs, and dances added much spectacle to the performance. Because the chorus danced as it spoke, chanted, and sang, its rhythms indicated, both visually and orally, the changing moods within the play. By focusing attention on certain characters and events and avoiding others, by supporting some actions and denouncing others, the playwright used the chorus to provide a point of view for the audience; that is (according to some) the chorus serves as an "ideal audience." In this way, too, the playwright helped establish the ethical system operating in the play and indicated the moral universe of the characters. Finally, and perhaps most important of all, the chorus—like the actors— participated directly in the action, providing information, making discoveries, deciding, and doing.

The chorus also influenced a number of theatrical practices. Because the chorus usually came into the performing space soon after the play opened and remained there until the end, its presence had to be considered in both the physical layout of the

Links to More About Theatre

H. D. F. Kitto, *Greek Tragedy,* 1939. Brilliant and profound.

<www.theatron.co.uk> Now a commercial site, but still interesting—classical theatre meets the computer.

<http://didaskalia.berkeley.edu> Computer simulation of the Theatre of Dionysus, among other things.

<www.didaskalia.net> A different *Didaskalia;* click on "agora" for discussion groups.

<www.georama.gr/eng/history/oz.html> Click-on map of Greek sites that brings up images.

theatre and the action of the drama. It required a space large enough to move about in. Its presence had to be justified and its loyalties made clear whenever characters shared secrets. Because the vocal and visual power of the chorus was great, the actors undoubtedly adjusted their style of performance so as not to be overwhelmed by the impact of the chorus.

To these three traits, we need to add one other, and it also differs markedly from contemporary practice:

Greek theatre was competitive, like so many other activities in Greek culture. Dramatists competed for awards in writing, and actors competed for awards in performing. To assure fairness in the competition, various rules and regulations governed who competed, who judged, and who won.

Plays were produced by the city-state in cooperation with selected wealthy citizens. (Women were not considered citizens.) At the Great Dionysia, three tragic writers (always male) competed each year for the prize. To compete, each submitted three tragedies and one *satyr play* (a short comic piece that followed the tragedies and occasionally burlesqued them). One day was set aside for the work of each tragic author; therefore, each year nine tragedies and three satyr plays were presented at the Great Dionysia. At the Lenaia, only four tragedies competed each year, each by a different playwright. At both festivals, five comic playwrights (always male) competed for a prize, and a single day was set aside for this competition.

How the competitors were selected is unknown, but, once chosen, each author was matched with a wealthy citizen-sponsor, who was then responsible for meeting the costs incurred by the chorus. These citizen-sponsors could have a major effect on the

FIGURE 11.3 **Oedipus the King.**

Considered by many the greatest tragedy ever written, *Oedipus the King* did not win its competition, presumably because the sponsor was too stingy to give the play an exciting visual presentation. Shown here in a 1955 production at the Stratford Shakespearean Festival, Ontario (Canada). (Directed by Tyrone Guthrie and designed by Tanya Moiseiwitsch. Courtesy of Stratford Festival Archives.)

outcome of the contests. Legends tell us that *Oedipus Rex* lost its competition because of a sponsor too stingy to fund a suitable production, but that Aeschylus's *Euminides* had costumes and masks so spectacular and frightening that pregnant women miscarried when they first saw the chorus, the result of the lavish support of its sponsor.

Most sponsors took their responsibilities seriously, although there were both carrots and sticks to encourage them to do so. Carrot: Support of a chorus was one of the civic duties of a wealthy citizen: those not tapped to fund dramas might be asked to outfit a warship or fund some other equally important project. Considerable acclaim flowed to those who mounted successful productions. Stick: Any wealthy citizen pleading insufficient funds to sponsor a chorus could be challenged by any other citizen. Should the challenger win, he and the would-be sponsor exchanged assets.

The method of selecting judges was ingenious and complicated, devised to assure that all major units of the polis were represented and that the gods had some say in the final decision. First, the names of all eligible citizens were collected within each political unit, and one name drawn from each of the ten units. The votes of only five of these ten citizens actually counted, however, allowing the gods to determine which five votes determined the winner. To serve as judge was both a civic duty and an honor.

Audience members who attended performances, then, not only heard and saw the plays, they also learned who won the contests. For this reason, attending Greek theatre probably had some of the elements of a long-standing football rivalry, as well as those elements now associated with theatre and drama.

Plays and Playwrights

Of the thousands of plays written for the Greek theatre, only forty-six survive complete, although many fragments have also come down to us. Most plays come from fifth century B.C.E. Athens and from four authors: Aeschylus (seven), Sophocles (seven), Euripides (eighteen), and Aristophanes (eleven). From these four authors came some of the world's greatest plays—plays that are still performed for their powerful effects on audiences, plays that have provided other playwrights (from William Shakespeare and Jean Racine to Eugene O'Neill and Wole Soyinka) with stories, and plays that have given their names to underlying patterns of human behavior ("Oedipus complex," "Promethean struggle"). A fifth name—Thespis—is important, although such a person may never have existed.

Thespis.   The semilegendary Thespis supposedly wrote tragedies using only one actor and a chorus. Although none of Thespis' works survived, they probably were based on the intensification of a single event rather than the development of a story, because stories require that changes occur. With only one actor and a chorus, the opportunity to introduce new information into a scene (and thus to introduce change into a situation) was severely limited. The continual disappearance of either the actor or the chorus to fetch new information would obviously have been awkward and was thus necessarily curtailed.

Aeschylus.   Aeschylus probably introduced a second actor, thereby permitting change to occur within the play. Although a second actor would also allow conflict between two characters, Aeschylus still tended to depict a solitary hero, one isolated and facing a cosmic horror brought about by forces beyond his control. With such a grand tragic conception, Aeschylus required great scope, and so he often wrote *trilogies,* three plays on a single subject that were intended for performance on the same day. One of his trilogies, the *Oresteia* (458 B.C.E.) (comprising the *Agamemnon,* the *Choëphoroe,* and the *Eumenides*), has survived intact along with several single plays. All display characteristics for which Aeschylus is admired: heroic and austere characters, simple but powerful plots, lofty diction. His general tone is well summarized by an ancient commentator: "While one finds many different types of artistic treatment in Aeschylus, one looks in vain for those sentiments that draw tears."

FIGURE 11.4   **Oedipus the King.**
The scene where Oedipus blinds himself, from a recent production of the play at the University of the Pacific, directed by Jeffrey Ingman and designed by Peter Lach. Compare the style of this production with the style in Figure 11.3.

Sophocles.   Sophocles was credited with adding the third actor and with changing practices in scenic painting and costuming. Less interested than Aeschylus in portraying solitary heroes confronting the universal order, Sophocles wrote plays that explored the place of humans within that order. The tragedy of Sophocles' heroes typically erupts from decisions made and actions taken based on imperfect knowledge or conflicting claims. Various aspects of the hero's character combine with unusual circumstances to bring about a disaster caused not by wickedness or foolishness but merely by humanness. For Sophocles, to be human was to be potentially a hero of tragedy.

The role of the chorus in Sophocles' plays remained important but not so central as in Aeschylus'. Conversely, the individual characters in Sophocles tend to be more complex, to display more individual traits, and to make more decisions. The result is that in Sophoclean tragedy, the actors, not the chorus, control the rhythm of the plays. Unlike Aeschylus, Sophocles did not need a trilogy to contain his tragedies; his plays stood alone. Of the more than one hundred attributed to him, seven have survived. Of these, *Oedipus Rex* (c. 427 B.C.E.) is recognized by most critics as among the finest tragedies ever written.

Euripides.   Euripides was never very popular during his lifetime but came to be highly regarded after his death. Growing up at a time when Athens was embarking on policies

FIGURE 11.5 Oedipus the King.

Yet another style dominated this production of the play at South Carolina State University. (Adapted and directed by Frank Mundy, scenery by Robert A. Osei-Wusu, costumes by Vivian C. Brooks, lighting by Douglas Johnson. Compare with Figures 11.3 and 11.4.)

of imperialism and expansionism, Euripides became a pacifist and a political gadfly. Although the populace viewed him with considerable distrust, the intellectual elite apparently admired him. It is reported, for example, that Socrates, one of the wisest men of the age, came to the theatre only to see the tragedies of Euripides and that Sophocles dressed his chorus in black on learning of the death of Euripides.

In comparison with the plays of Aeschylus and Sophocles, those of Euripides are less exalted and more realistic. His characters seem less grand and more human; their problems are less cosmic and more mundane. Euripides tended to examine human relationships and to question the wisdom of social actions: the purpose of war, the status of women, the reasons for human cruelty. *Medea* (431 B.C.E.) is an example.

In keeping with Euripides' changed outlook came changes in dramatic technique. Replacing the philosophical probings common in the plays of Aeschylus and Sophocles, Euripides substituted rapid reversals, intrigues, chase scenes, and romantic and sentimental incidents of the sort later associated with plays called *melodramas.* (Euripides is said by some to be the father of melodrama.) He further reduced the role of the chorus, until sometimes it was little more than an interruption of the play's action. As the role of the chorus declined and the subjects became more personal, the language became less poetic and more conversational. Many of the changes that Euripides introduced into

The **Story** of the **Play**

Sophocles, *Oedipus the King*, 427 B.C.E.

Oedipus, king of Thebes, is appealed to by the people (the chorus) to save them from the plague that grips the city. Oedipus has already sent his brother-in-law, Creon, to the oracle at Delphi for a solution; Creon returns and announces that the oracle says that the city must banish the murderer of the former king, Laius. Oedipus vows to "reveal the truth" and save the city.

He calls the blind seer Teiresias to him and asks his advice. Teiresias is evasive, then, pressured, says, "It is you." Angered, Oedipus turns on Teiresias, says that he and Creon are plotting against him. The old seer warns Oedipus of one who is "his children's brother and father, his wife's son, his mother's husband."

Oedipus rages again against Creon. His wife, Jocasta, widow of the former king, Laius, tells him of another old prophecy: Laius would be murdered by his own child. When she describes Laius, Oedipus is shaken and demands to see the one survivor of the killing of Laius. He tells of his own long-ago visit to Delphi and a prophecy that he would kill his father and sleep with his mother, which caused him to flee Corinth, his childhood home. He recounts the later killing of a stranger at a crossroads.

A messenger from Corinth comes with news that Polybus, the king of Corinth and Oedipus' supposed father, is dead. Oedipus is not to grieve, however—Polybus was not, the messenger says, Oedipus' real father; rather, the messenger as a young man got the infant Oedipus from a shepherd; the baby's ankles were pierced—hence the name Oedipus, "swollenfoot."

Jocasta, suddenly frightened, begs Oedipus to give up his quest for the truth.

An old man, the survivor of the attack on Laius, is dragged in. He was the shepherd who gave the infant Oedipus to the messenger; now, hounded by Oedipus, he says that the infant was to have been abandoned in the wild because he was the child of Laius and Jocasta, and there was a prophecy that he would kill his own father, but the shepherd gave him to the messenger to take away, instead.

Oedipus sees the truth: he is the source of the plague, the murderer of his father, the husband of his mother.

Jocasta kills herself.

Oedipus blinds himself with the pins in Jocasta's jewels. He begs to be driven from the city.

Greek tragedy, although denounced in his own time, became standard dramatic practice during the Hellenistic Age.

Aristophanes and Old Comedy. Comedy was introduced into the Great Dionysia in 486 B.C.E., fifty years after tragedy. It seems never to have been comfortable there, perhaps

FIGURE 11.6 **Oedipus the Myth.**
The Greek myth and play of Oedipus have inspired others to adapt the story to their own culture. Here, a production of *Oedipus, That's Human,* written by Myunghwa Kim and directed by Kwangbo Kim of Chungwoo Theatre Company. (Photo courtesy of Seoul Performing Arts Festival, Seoul, Korea. See also Figure 5.3b.)

because the festival was an international showcase for Athenian culture and thus often visited by foreign dignitaries. The real home of comedy was the winter festival, the Lenaia, where a contest for comedy was established in 442 B.C.E. At both festivals, an entire day was set aside for competition among the comic playwrights, five of whom competed.

Of the twelve extant Greek comedies, all but one are by Aristophanes; therefore, information about comedy during the Classical Age necessarily comes from these plays. It is possible, of course, that Aristophanes was atypical, and so the conclusions drawn from his works may be incorrect.

Although no two are exactly alike, surviving examples suggest a set structure for *old comedy:*

■ Division into two parts separated by a direct address by the chorus or choral leader to the audience, breaking the dramatic illusion

- A first part consisting of a prologue, during which an outrageous idea is introduced, and then a debate as to whether the idea should be adopted, ending with a decision to put this "happy idea" into action (In Aristophanes' *The Birds*, for example, the happy idea is to build a city in the sky.)
- A second part made up of funny episodes and choral songs showing the happy idea at work

The happy idea is the heart of old comedy: it is outrageous and usually fantastic, and it contains social or political satire. In *The Birds* (414 B.C.E.) building the city in the sky is an attempt to get away from the mess on earth. The happy idea also enables the spectacular costuming and behavior of the chorus, which often gives the play its name (the birds found in the sky).

FIGURE 11.7 **Greek Old Comedy.**

Political satire and exuberant spectacle marked most Aristophanic comedy. The political bite of *The Birds* came from its happy idea: to establish a sky kingdom to escape the mess on earth. Shown here in production at the University of South Carolina. (Directed by Jim Patterson, SSDC.)

Theatre Buildings and Practices

Although almost all extant Greek plays date from the fifth century B.C.E., most of the extant Greek theatre buildings date from later periods—sometimes much later periods. The result is unsettling: For the time when we know about theatre buildings and production practices, we know almost nothing about plays; conversely, for the time when we know the plays, we know almost nothing about the theatre buildings.

In Greek, *theatre* meant "seeing-place" or "spectacle-place." Athens' first theatre was apparently in the market, but it soon moved to the outskirts of town. There, the Theatre of Dionysus, Athens' first important theatre was situated on a hillside, where the audience sat, with a circular playing area (the *orchestra*) at its base; a path or road separated audience and playing area and provided entrances (*parodoi*). This arrangement—hillside, orchestra, parodoi—was fundamental to all Greek theatres. In many theatres of the time, however, the orchestra was rectangular rather than circular, an arrangement that would make sense inasmuch as tragic choruses (unlike the dithyrambic chorus) displayed themselves in ranks and files rather than in circles.

By the middle of the fifth century, a scene house (*skene,* "tent" or "booth") had been added at the edge of the orchestra opposite the audience. Its original layout is unknown, but it probably had two or three openings and was first needed as a changing room for the actors, only later becoming a kind of setting. It may first have been cloth (a tent) but was certainly wood in short order, becoming stone only centuries later. Whether wood or stone, it provided background and acoustical support and allows us to call the Athenian theatre a *façade stage*—a conventional form in which actors perform in front of a neutral façade, with the audience arcing to three sides or less. Reminder: Because the fifth-century theatre was wood (rather than stone) it was impermanent, and so architectural examples of this theatre have not come down to us. The stone theatres whose pictures appear in many books are from later years, the periods for which we have no plays.

Audience

The outdoor theatre put the audience at the mercy of the weather; certainly, individuals must have used cushions, sunshades, umbrellas, etc. The hillside, with its wooden benches, could hold about fourteen thousand, and the audience was as visible as the actors in the natural sunlight. Theatre was apparently open to all, including women and slaves, but the exact social makeup of the audience is unknown. Records suggest that it could be unruly.

Acting

The first victor in the Athenian tragic contest was supposed to be Thespis, who also acted in his play (c. 534 B.C.E.)—hence *thespian* for actor. Acting, like playwriting, remained a competitive activity during the Classical Age, and rules governed its practice.

FIGURE 11.8 **Theatre Buildings during the 400s B.C.E.**
A conjectural reconstruction of the early Theatre of Dionysus, showing audience area, orchestra, rock outcropping, and temple, and the same theatre after the appearance of the scene house, probably around mid-century.

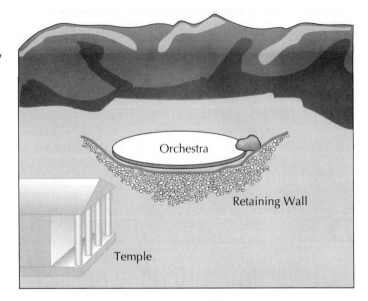

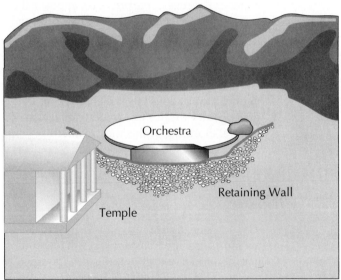

For example, all actors were male. Apparently no more than three *speaking* actors were allowed in the tragedies and five in the comedies, although any number of extras might be used. Because the leading actor, or *protagonist,* was the only one competing for the prize, he was assigned to the playwright by lot, so that chance rather than politics decided who got the best roles. The second actor and the third actor were probably chosen by the playwright and the protagonist in consultation. With only three actors, doubling of roles was required, for the plays themselves often had eight or more characters. If the protagonist had an exceedingly demanding role, like the title role in *Oedipus Rex,* he might play only one character, but the second and third actors were expected to play two or more secondary roles. Doubling, the use of masks, and the use of only male actors suggest that the style of Greek acting was more formal than realistic; that is, although the acting was true and believable *in its own terms,* its resemblance to real life was of considerably less importance than its fidelity to the dramatic action. Given the size of the audience, the physical arrangement of the theatre, and the style of acting, it should be no surprise that vocal power and agility were the actor's most prized assets. Actors, like sponsors and chorus members, performed as part of their civic duties. They were not paid professionals.

Settings and Machinery

The essential setting was the *skene.* We do not know whether its appearance was changed to suggest different locations; that is, we don't know whether there was scenery in our sense of that word. We do know that some sort of *flat* (two-dimensional surface for painting) existed, but we do not know how it was used—or where.

We do know that two machines provided special effects:

■ The *eccyclema* was a movable platform capable of being rolled or rotated out of the skene to reveal the result of an offstage action. In Aeschylus' *Agamemnon,* for example, the body of the murdered Agamemnon is "revealed" (rolled out?), and in the *Eumenides,* the Furies (avenging goddesses) seem to have entered first while asleep (rolled into view?).

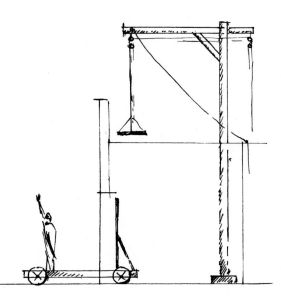

FIGURE 11.9 Skene, Eccyclema, Mechane.
By the middle of the fifth century B.C.E., the Athenian theatre had a wooden *skene* with roof and doors (number uncertain) and two pieces of stage machinery—the *eccyclema,* a movable platform, shown here in the center doorway, and the *mechane,* a crane to fly actors and properties in and out of the playing area.

■ The *mechane* was some sort of crane that allowed people and things to "fly" in and out. In Aristophanes' *The Clouds,* the character Socrates hangs over the performing space during some of his dialogue, and in Euripides' *Medea,* Medea flies away in the mechane to escape her pursuers. In fact, Euripides so often has gods fly down to sort out the characters' problems at the end of his tragedies that a too-obviously-contrived ending of a play came to be called (in Latin) a *deus ex machina* (god from the machine).

Properties were numerous, and we hear of altars, tombs, biers, chariots, staffs, and swords in tragedy. Comedies often required furniture, food, clubs, and so on.

Costumes and Masks

Because in Greek theatre one actor played several roles, costumes and masks were exceedingly important—they enabled audiences to identify quickly and certainly which character in the play the actor was impersonating. The mask and costume, in a sense, were the signs of character. A different principle governed the chorus, where the goal was to make its individual members appear to be a group, and so choral costumes and

FIGURE 11.10 **Greek Tragic Masks.**
During the fifth century B.C.E., tragic masks covered the whole head and looked rather natural, as is clear from this archeological find. (Photographs courtesy of American School of Classical Studies at Athens: Agora Excavations, and reproduced with permission.)

masks were similar. Although historians once argued for "a tragic costume" for tragic characters, most now agree that some version of normal Athenian dress seems likelier. In tragedy, such dress was perhaps more elegant than normal, and in comedy it was certainly altered to make it laughable—ill-fitting, exaggerated, and so on—but the basic look was recognizable.

From references in plays, we know that a costume's appearance allowed audience members to know a character's *ethnicity* (references are made to some dressed as Greeks and to others dressed as foreigners), *gender* (males and females are identified as such at a distance), and *social role* (military heroes, servants, shepherds, and so on were visually identifiable). In the case of comedy, the costume for certain male characters featured a stuffed, oversized penis (phallus). The color of costumes was also a sign: reference is made to black for characters in mourning and yellow for an especially effeminate male character, to cite only two examples.

All performers, both actors and chorus members, wore masks. They were full-face, and they carried their own hair style and, of course, their own set facial expression. During the fifth century B.C.E., the masks looked natural in tragedy, although in comedy they could distort features to provoke laughter. Again, masks for actors aimed for individuality and quick recognition of character, while choral masks stressed resemblance, membership in a group. Occasionally, comic masks resembled the faces of living people, a fact we glean from an account of Socrates, who, from his seat in the audience, stood up and turned so that others could see that the mask worn by the actor in a comedy mimicked his own face.

The End of Athens' Golden Age

At the end of the fifth century B.C.E., Athens lost its premiere position among the Greek *poleis*. First it was defeated by Sparta, a militaristic state with few aspirations to high culture. With Spartan influence came some sort of censorship, which had the immediate effect of toning down the political satire of Greek old comedies and substituting comedy with a more benign tone (called *middle comedy*). Then, near the end of the fourth century B.C.E. (300s), Alexander the Great overran all the Greek *poleis* and folded them into a single, centralized government. He then conquered many of the advanced civilizations that abutted him, lands south through Egypt and east as far as India and modern Afghanistan and Pakistan. Founding Alexandria (Egypt) as his capital, he ruled one of the world's great empires in a brief age now called *Hellenistic*. As Alexander and his armies conquered lands, they exported Greek culture to them.

The culture of Hellenistic Greece, however, differed from that of Athens. The individuality of the various *poleis* declined, replaced by a cosmopolitan culture centered in Egypt. Gone were Athenian democracy, its great drama, and the centrality of its gods. The trend was toward a common government, common civilization, and common religion. The empire's center of gravity shifted away from the Greek peninsula, which now rested on the westernmost edge of Alexander's holdings, and toward the

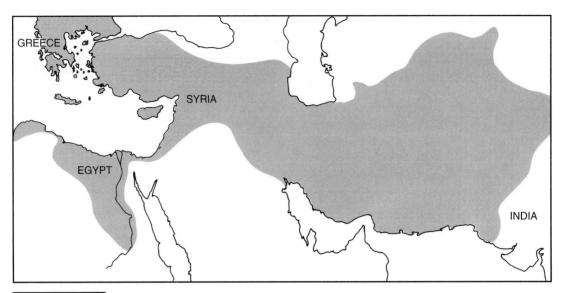

FIGURE 11.11 Hellenistic Period in Greece.

The conquests of Alexander the Great in the 300s B.C.E. extended Greek influence but led to
a shift of power away from Athens. Theatres began to be built throughout Greek lands, and
acting became professionalized.

east, where different religious and philosophical systems were already highly developed. Towns and then cities grew up, as trade competed with agriculture for attention. Within a hundred years, the Hellenistic world had more than four hundred cities with populations over 200,000, that is, twice the size of Athens during its golden age (fifth century B.C.E.).

Greek drama changed. Plays began to be performed throughout Greek lands, not merely at Athens, and they were now performed on special military and civic occasions as well as at Dionysian festivals. Satyr plays disappeared. Tragedy declined in popularity; such tragedies as were written apparently modeled themselves on Euripides' plays, with a reduced emphasis on the chorus and an increased emphasis on sensation, realism, and melodrama. (Only fragments of such tragedies exist today.) Tragedies from the fifth century B.C.E. continued to be revived, however, attesting to their power to move audiences. Comedy remained popular, but it abandoned both its political bite and its formal structure. *New comedy,* as Hellenistic comedy is now called, told domestic tales of middle-class life structured as a series of episodes interrupted by incidental choral songs. New comedies took as their subjects such things as love, money, and family, often including intrigues involving long-lost children and happy re-unitings. Although there are many fragments, only one complete new comedy remains, *The Grumbler* by Menander.

Thinking About Greek Theatre

The Greek word for idiot, *literally translated, means one who does not participate in politics. That sums up my conviction on the subject.*
— Gladys Pyle

Athenian politics and Athenian theatre of the Classical Age interacted in ways that few later theatres have. Cite examples of this interconnection in the plays, the layout of the theatre buildings, the arrangements for production, and the role of various sorts of theatrical participants. Do these data suggest other conclusions about the nature of Greek theatre of the Classical Age? About the nature of our own?

Although actors remained exclusively male, they became professionalized, organizing themselves into a performing guild called the Artists of Dionysus. From changes in the plays (and also in theatre buildings, costuming conventions, and masks), we can infer that acting style changed, becoming grander, showier, and more formal in tragedy, and probably less boisterous, more restrained, and more representational in comedy.

Of far greater consequence than the drama itself during these years was Aristotle's theory of drama, written very early in this period, probably in response to the philosopher Plato's condemnation of theatre. Providing a theoretical definition of the form tragedy (his theory treated neither comedy nor mixed forms), Aristotle set the boundaries for the next two thousand years of dramatic theory. His major points included "tragedy . . . is an imitation of an action that is serious, complete, and of a certain magnitude . . . in the form of action, not narrative . . . producing pity and fear and the catharsis of such emotions." The meaning of the definition has been endlessly debated, especially the phrase about catharsis, which some scholars believe refers to the response of audiences (though elsewhere Aristotle said he did not intend to talk about audiences) and other scholars think refers to emotions embedded within the episodes of the play itself.

He then defined and discussed the six parts of a play (see Chapter 3). Of the six parts, plot was the most important to Aristotle. He therefore discussed it in the most detail, considering its *wholeness* (having a beginning, a middle, and an end, connected by causality); its *unity* (so that if any part is removed, the whole is disturbed); its *materials* (suffering, discovery, and reversal); and its *form* (complication and dénouement).

He argued that the best tragic protagonist is one who causes his own downfall through some great tragic error (*hamartia*), that the play's language should be both clear and interesting, and that spectacle is the business of the stage machinist rather than the poet.

Because *The Poetics* is so packed with ideas and its translation so difficult, its meaning has been debated for two thousand years. Certainly, it remains the base from which most discussions of dramatic theory must proceed, through either acceptance or rejection of its primary tenets.

Theatre buildings also changed. Great stone theatres sprang up both on the Greek peninsula and on conquered lands (especially modern Turkey), and they tended to share common features:

- A two-storied *skene*
- A long, narrow, high stage attached to the *skene,* usually with steps or ramps at the ends but sometimes with entrances and exits only through the *skene.* Its use is unclear.
- An orchestra, as before, but now of uncertain use.

Unfortunately, we do not know how plays were staged in Hellenistic theatres. Were actors on stage? in the orchestra? some combination of the two? Where was the chorus?

Costumes and masks also changed, and they changed in similar directions. Those in tragedy tended toward greater size and grandeur. Unlike masks of the golden age, the masks of tragedy during the Hellenistic Age are the familiar masks of cliché, having a high headdress (*onkos*) as well as exaggerated, often distorted, eyes and mouths. Footwear for tragedy may have featured a high platform boot, called a *cothurnus,* rather than the soft slipper of former days. Such changes enlarged the physical appearance of the actor and brought him greater focus, suggesting an altered acting style. Comic masks ranged from somewhat lifelike to quite outrageous, matching the types of characters that began to repeat in comedies of the period.

FIGURE 11.12　**Hellenistic Theatre Buildings.**
Stone remains of several Hellenistic theatres have led scholars to speculate that a typical Hellenistic theatre looked something like the reconstruction shown here.

FIGURE 11.13 Hellenistic Masks and Costumes.

By the 300s B.C.E., tragic masks and costumes had become more exaggerated, with high headdresses and enlarged eyes and mouths on the masks and perhaps elevated shoes on the actors, all of which served to enlarge the actors' physical presence. Comedic masks and costumes, on the other hand, seem to have moved in the opposite direction, becoming more natural-looking.

Truth be told, drama and theatre from the Hellenistic period would not be important except for three things:

- The promulgation of Aristotelian theory
- The mistaken assumption that these buildings and practices represented the buildings and practices of fifth-century B.C.E. Athens
- The strong influences of these plays, buildings, and practices on Roman theatre and possibly on Indian theatre as well

Before leaving Greece, we should note that there existed alongside these state-supported festival theatres another kind of performance, the *mime*. Very little is known about it, except that it seems to have been popular and perhaps slightly disreputable. Its troupes included women, its actors apparently often played barefoot, and mime troupes were not allowed to perform as part of the festivals (probably explaining why so little evidence about them has come down to us).

FIGURE 11.14   **Greek Mime.**

This detail from a vase (*right*) may show a dramatic scene from mime as played in Greek outposts on the Italian peninsula. The appearance of comic nudity, including the oversized phalloi of many male comic figures, may have been achieved through costume tights and padding.

Indian Theatre

The multilingual culture of India was already old and advanced when Alexander the Great reached it in the fourth century B.C.E. (300s). Its earliest theatre and drama developed at roughly the same time as that of Rome. It is therefore tempting to suppose that Indian practices, like Roman ones, owed much to Hellenistic Greece. Indeed, there are anecdotes of theatrical productions given by Alexander's military men in India, and some Indian artifacts suggest familiarity with Greek dramatic texts. Still, no direct borrowing is yet certain.

The Indian subcontinent, stretching from the Himalayas to the Indian Ocean coast, was broken politically into many units. Its social system depended heavily on a caste system that slotted each person at birth into a specific position within the society. Hinduism was its major religion, an infinitely flexible set of gods and practices that insisted on little except the importance of doing one's duty in order to improve one's status in the next incarnation. Sanskrit was its spoken and written language, and later the language of its ruling and intellectual classes. It was in Sanskrit that the first extant records of an Indian theatre appeared.

The earliest record was the *Natyasastra*, a long treatise on theatre and drama, somewhat analogous to Aristotle's *Poetics*. Probably derived from oral tradition and ascribed to the mythical authority Bharata, it was probably written down sometime between 200 B.C.E. and 200 C.E. Its basic assumptions were those of Hinduism: a universe of unity expressed through multiplicity, therefore aesthetically an art of multiple forms—dance, song, and poetry—unified through total performance into a form that would induce in the receptive audience a state of understanding—*rasa*. The *Natyasastra* is a valuable source of theatrical evidence, for it not only offers detailed analyses of Sanskrit dramas, it also reveals an India of

- Professional acting companies that included both men and women and that toured
- Performances that included both song and dance, accompanied by onstage musicians
- Permanent indoor theatres built of wood and stone, seating two to five hundred spectators, with elevated stages and close connections to temples
- Rigid caste limits, restricting this kind of theatre to the elite Brahmin (priestly) caste

Sanskrit drama included at least a thousand plays in the period 200–800 C.E. Of these, the plays of Kalidasa are best known in the West, and his *Sakuntala,* which reached Europe in the early nineteenth century, is the most often seen. In seven "acts," it follows a highly romantic love action between a king and the modest Sakuntala and includes the intercession of gods, a curse, and a ring that is lost and then found in the belly of a fish.

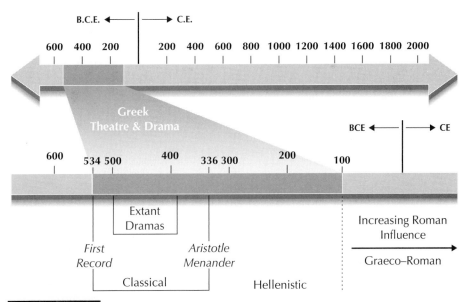

FIGURE 11.15 Timeline.

Although Greek theatre began in the sixth century (534) B.C.E. and continued thereafter, its golden age was the fifth century (400s) B.C.E. The Hellenistic period saw the building of stone theatres and the theorizing of Aristotle but the decline of drama. After 100 B.C.E., influence shifted increasingly to Rome.

Sakuntala is a play of many scenes, places, and moods, unified not by action but by *rasa*, the state of perception and emotion (in this case, love) induced in the audience. Like much of Sanskrit drama, it took as its source the *Mahabharata,* which, with the *Ramayana,* is the great source work of Hindu culture.

After Alexander died, his empire soon collapsed, with various pieces of it drifting into other rising centers of power. By a hundred years before the Common Era, Greece had fallen within the sphere of a spreading Roman influence as the center of civilization shifted west. From this time, Hellenistic theatrical trends continued but were altered to bring them more in line with Roman practice. Not only were Roman theatres built on Greek lands, but Hellenistic theatres also began to be remodeled to make them look more like Roman theatres, producing hybrids that we now call Graeco-Roman theatres (the age itself is sometimes referred to as the *Graeco-Roman period*). Although records show that theatre performances persisted in Greece, the center of influence—and with it the theatre—had clearly shifted west, to Rome itself.

KEY TERMS

Check your understanding against this list. Brief definitions are in the Glossary; page references there will direct you to appropriate pages. (Persons are page-referenced in the Index.)

chorus	middle comedy
City Dionysia	mime
cothurnus	new comedy
eccyclema	old comedy
façade stage	onkos
flat	orchestra
Graeco-Roman period	protagonist
Hellenistic Age	Sanskrit drama
mechane	skene

The Theatre of Rome

When you have completed this chapter, you should be able to

- Discuss the relationship between theatre and religion in Rome

- Trace the development of Roman physical theatres and their plays and playwrights

- Identify the major periods of Roman theatres, with approximate dates

- Explain how a Roman performance would have looked in the principal periods—what masks and costumes were used, what acting space was used

- Explain the important differences between the plays of Plautus and Terence and those of Seneca

- Explain the importance of Vitruvius and Horace

Greek culture had penetrated parts of the Italian peninsula even before the golden age of Athenian drama, when Rome was only one small town among many. The people of the Italian peninsula were mostly self-sufficient herders and farmers, who early established a republican form of government. Having relatively little interest in arts, literature, and philosophy, they excelled instead in practical activities, becoming superb agriculturalists, soldiers, engineers, builders, and rhetoricians. Their religion was polytheistic, with most Roman gods having clear Greek equivalents. (Bacchus corresponded to Dionysus, for example.) They also had a gift for adapting useful ideas from other cultures, whose practices they modified to suit Roman tastes and needs.

While Alexander the Great was building his Greek empire, a distinctly Roman culture began to coalesce. First, Rome unified much of the Italian peninsula, and then, having built a navy, began to expand to other lands around the Mediterranean Sea, which was soon thought of as the "Roman Lake." By the third century B.C.E., Rome was a leading Mediterranean power. When Alexander's empire began to break apart, Rome moved to fill the void left in the west.

It was in this republican Rome that theatre and drama appeared in 240 B.C.E. Regrettably, the same major problem haunts the study of Roman theatre as of Greek: For the periods when we know most about plays (B.C.E.), we know least about theatres be-

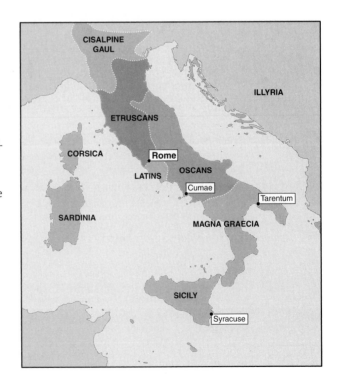

FIGURE 12.1 Map. During Athens' golden age (400s B.C.E.), Rome was simply one small city among many on Italy's peninsula, less important than the Etruscans to the north and the Greeks to the south. During Greece's Hellenistic period, a distinctly Roman culture emerged; it overtook the Greek by the time of Christ.

cause they were built of wood and have not lasted; conversely, when we know most about theatres (C.E.), we know almost nothing about plays.

Roman Festivals and Theatre

Roman dramatic and theatrical practices mostly reproduced those of Hellenistic Greece (see pp. 229–234) but modified by earlier Italian traditions of performance. Roman festivals, called *ludi*, differed from Greek festivals mostly by having activities such as acrobatics and rope-dancing compete directly with plays for public attention. At first, there was a single play, but the number of plays grew steadily over time.

Roman Drama

No Roman tragedy survives, but fragments suggest that they resembled Hellenistic tragedy (see p. 230). Some presented upper-class Greeks (in which actors wore Greek costume); others told of upper-class Romans (in Roman attire). Tragedy was never very popular in Rome, perhaps because as a people the Romans lacked deep interest in philosophy and ethics, the usual emphasis in Athenian tragedy.

Comedy was far more popular and, like tragedy, divided into two types: that written about Greeks (this time middle- or lower-class, and so costumed) and that about Romans (ditto). In addition to many titles and fragments, twenty-seven complete comedies survive, all by two authors: Plautus and Terence, both of whom wrote during the second century B.C.E. (100s) and about the Athenian middle class. Both drew heavily from Greek new comedy for their stories and approach. *Neither used a chorus.* Despite these strong similarities, the two authors are very different in other ways and so suggest quite a range within Roman comedy.

Plautus, the older of the two, was an actor as well as a playwright. Of the more than one hundred works credited to him, twenty-one have survived, a tribute to his popularity. Probably his experiences as an actor accounted for the theatrical (as opposed to literary) qualities of his comedies. Plautine comedies are noted for their loosely linked episodes, which are filled with visual gags, verbal wordplay, and characters who are ludicrous in appearance as well as behavior. Plautus often broke the dramatic illusion and addressed his audience directly. Among his many plays, *The Braggart Warrior, The Menaechmi, Pot of Gold,* and *Amphitryon* have been copied by Shakespeare, Molière, and others.

Terence wrote more refined comedies. His plots, although based on those of the Greek Menander and his contemporaries, often combined two or more of the Greek comedies into a single, highly complicated dramatic action. He avoided the episodic quality of Plautus's plots in favor of more carefully contrived actions that proceeded by means of seeming cause and effect. His characters, too, appeared more normal and

FIGURE 12.2 **Plautus's Comedy.**

Plautus's *Menaechmi,* a comic romp featuring separated twins and mistaken identity, is still performed—and it was the basis of Shakespeare's *Comedy of Errors.* Notice how Martin A. Thaler's costume designs for the doctor and the cook in the *Menaechmi* capture their comic qualities.

human, and thus more sympathetic. The result was, of course, comedies that were more elegant and refined but less robust and free, more thoughtful but less fun than Plautus's. Finally, Terence's use of prologues was unusual; in them he argued matters of dramatic theory, encouraged audiences to behave politely, and defended himself from the attacks of critics. In a prologue that is as revealing of republican audiences as of Terence's playwriting, for example, he complained that the first performance of the play had been spoiled because the audience got more interested in a nearby troupe of acrobats. It may help to distinguish Terence from Plautus to know that, although Plautus is occasionally performed even today, Terence almost never is. And Terence, not Plautus, was used in schools during the Middle Ages as a way to teach the Latin language and proper Latin usage.

Links to More About Theatre

 James H. Butler, *Theatre and Drama of Greece and Rome,* 1972.

 Satiricon. Directed by Federico Fellini. Some theatre, much decadence.

 <www.classics.ox.ac.uk/apgrd/> The Archive of Performances of Greek and Roman Drama. Scholarly but interesting; click on "Images."

<didaskalia.berkeley.edu/stagecraft/roman.html> Good discussion with images and bibliography.

Although comedy had always been more popular than tragedy in Rome, its popularity waned within fifty years of Terence's death. Thus, by the time the first stone theatre was built (55 B.C.E.), the great period of Roman tragedy and comedy was over.

Theatre Buildings, Scenery, Costumes, and Masks

Roman theatres, like Greek, were façade stages. As far as we can tell, their basic arrangement remained scene house, aisleways, and orchestra. Assuming that Rome's early wooden theatres resembled its later stone ones, Roman theatres differed from Hellenistic theatres in several ways:

- They stood on level ground (rather than hillsides), with built-up, stadium-style seating.
- Their orchestras were half-circles, rather than full circles or rectangles.
- Their long, deep stages were closed at both ends by the building itself, which jutted out.
- They used a front curtain, the first to do so.

As in Greece, the façade of Roman theatres served as background. In tragedy, the doors of the façade represented separate entrances to a palace or other public building, with the stage floor representing the ground in front of the building. In comedy, the doors were entrances to separate houses, with the stage representing a street running in

FIGURE 12.3 Roman Tragic Actor.
Interpreting evidence is often difficult. This statue, once
thought to be a Greek actor, is now believed to be Roman.
The large blocks under the feet, once thought to be parts
of platformed boots, are now interpreted as the means
by which the statue was attached to its pedestal.

front of them. There were *periaktoi,* machines that could be rotated to reveal one of three
scenes: tragic (e.g., columns and statues), comic (e.g., balconies and windows), and
satyric (e.g., trees, caves, and "other rustic objects"). Records tell of two *periaktoi,* one
near each end of the stage. Because they could not possibly have hidden the whole
façade, they must have served simply to inform the audience of location, not to portray
any place in a realistic way. Although temporary, these wooden theatres could be quite
spectacular, according to ancient accounts.

As in Greece, all actors of comedy and tragedy wore masks, and the masks resembled those of Hellenistic Greece, with high *onkos* and distorted eyes and mouth, for
tragedy, and a range from somewhat realistic to comically distorted for comedy. The
conventions of costuming were also rooted in Hellenistic conventions (see p. 230), with
actors wearing a version of either Greek or Roman dress (depending on the kind of
tragedy or comedy).

Audiences

Theatres of the *ludi* were free and open to all, and probably somewhere between ten and
fifteen thousand people attended. Great care was taken to assure the comfort of audiences, with wide and numerous aisles allowing for ease of entering and exiting the space.

The Empire and the End of Roman Drama

About a hundred years before the beginning of the Common Era, Rome's republican government gave way to an imperial one, and soon thereafter it confronted the growing challenge of a new religion, Christianity, that had arisen in one of its own territories. Whereas Rome was perfectly happy to accommodate this new god (it had routinely adopted the gods of any culture with which it came into contact), Christians refused to allow their god to be assimilated into the Roman pantheon. Indeed, they insisted that their god alone should be worshipped, a rigidity unwelcome in a culture whose religion depended more on traditions than passions.

Within three hundred years, the Roman Empire had spread as far north as England, through parts of Africa and the Middle East, and as far east as Syria. Christianity had spread with it. This expanding empire traded widely, importing luxury items from the east and exporting mass-produced, useful articles. The sprawling empire encouraged more roads, better water management, a strong civil service, and a permanent military class. Travel, encouraged by both war and trade, promoted a kind of cosmopolitanism.

FIGURE 12.4 **Roman Comedy.**
Although a few comedies of Plautus are still produced, Roman comedy is most popular today as adapted by Molière, Shakespeare, and America's musical theatre. Shown here, the American musical A *Funny Thing Happened on the Way to the Forum*, a pastiche of Roman comic stories and conventions. (Produced at Western Michigan University, directed by D. Terry Williams, photograph by Mary Whalen.)

Despite their growth, Romans still did not define themselves through their art, literature, or philosophy. Instead they concentrated on increasing personal comforts (through elegant homes, public baths, entertainments) and continued to demonstrate their superiority in practical matters. For example, they wrote how-to manuals.

Three Important Texts

Two how-to manuals, both written near the turn into the Common Era, are of special importance to theatre and drama, because, when they were re-discovered at the Renaissance (c. 1400s), their advice on how to build theatres and write plays was put into practice.

The Roman architect Vitruvius wrote a ten-volume work on how to lay out a city. As a part of this larger work, he set down guidelines for building both theatres and the scenery to go in them. Without illustrations and with often ambiguous descriptions, the books were easily—and badly—misinterpreted by Renaissance designers, but their influence was enormous.

The Roman poet Horace described how to write good plays in his *Ars Poetica*, a work that was to exert even more influence during the Renaissance than did Aristotle's *Poetics*, which it superficially resembled. Unlike Aristotle's work, a philosophical inquiry into the nature of the form tragedy, Horace's is a practical guidebook aimed at people who want to write plays. As such, it is considerably more prescriptive than Aristotle's work, suggesting such things as

- The importance of keeping comedy and tragedy separate
- The need to have a unity of time and of place as a way of achieving unity of action
- The need for drama to teach as well as please

Ars Poetica had no immediate influence on Roman practice. Its importance, like Vitruvius's, comes from its powerful influence much later on Renaissance theory and drama.

The third important text is really a set of texts. Although Roman tragedy and comedy were not played in public theatres by the 100s, dramatic readings were apparently given at banquets in private homes. Ten such literary tragedies have come down to us, nine by Seneca, who wrote them just after the turn of the Common Era. The importance of Seneca's tragedies rests neither on their literary excellence nor on their position among contemporary Roman audiences but on their monumental effect on later writers, who discovered, translated, and copied them (see p. 294), probably because they were both linguistically and physically more accessible than the earlier Greek tragedies.

Seneca's plays display characteristics assumed to be typical of Greek Hellenistic tragedy. The chorus is not well integrated into the action, and so the (usually four) choral odes (songs) serve to divide the plays into five parts. His protagonists are often driven by a single dominant passion that causes their downfall. His minor characters include messengers, confidants, and ghosts. His language emphasizes rhetorical and stylistic figures, including extended descriptive and declamatory passages, pithy statements about the human condition (*sententiae*), and elaborately balanced exchanges of dialogue. Many of his plays feature spectacular scenes of violence and gore. Although Seneca's plays are now rarely done, they are important, like the writings of Vitruvius and

Horace, because of their influence on Renaissance writers, who re-discovered tragedy through Seneca and tried to follow what he did in making their own tragedies.

Theatre Buildings

In spite of these three important written sources, theatre buildings rather than texts dominated the empire. In the Common Era, Rome built great stone theatres, first on the Italian peninsula and then throughout its empire (remains are still visible in Libya and Turkey, for example). Although the basic pattern of scene house, aisleways, and orchestra remained, stone theatres were probably more ornate than earlier wooden ones. Now used by audiences rather than choruses, the aisles separating the scene house from the orchestra were covered over, causing the buildings to form a single architectural unit, rather than two (as in Greek theatres). The façades were decorated with details such as statuary, niches, and columns. A roof extended over part of the stage, both protecting the elaborate façades and improving acoustics. Audience comfort remained a high priority, with awnings sometimes protecting audiences from sun and rain and, in at least one theatre, a primitive air conditioning system consisting of large fans blowing over ice brought down from mountaintops.

Theatrical Entertainments

Into these theatres came new theatrical entertainments that replaced comedy and tragedy. An indigenous rural Italian farce featuring four grotesquely masked characters was popular for a while. *Pantomime*, a solo dance performed by a non-speaking performer (wearing a mask with a closed mouth) could be comic but was more often serious. It filled the void left by tragedy.

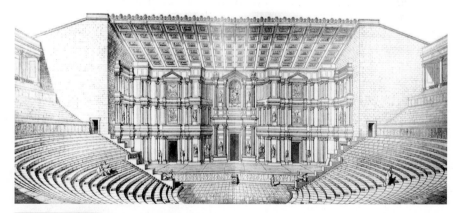

FIGURE 12.5   **Roman Stone Theatres.**
Most extant Roman theatres date from the empire, because they were then built in stone. Imaginatively reconstructed from ruins, this imperial Roman theatre shows a half circle (orchestra), elaborate façade, deep and roofed stage, and architectural connection between stage house and auditorium, all features different from Greek theatres.

Most popular of all, however, was *mime,* which may have come from Greece, for Greek mime (the word refers both to the form and the performers) had a long history, although it was never performed at Greek festivals. In Greece, mime was unimportant, but Roman mime became so popular during the empire that it drove all other forms of theatre from the stage.

Several traits of mime make it important:

- Mime included women among its performers, the only theatrical entertainment in Greece or Rome to do so.

- Performers in the mime did not usually wear masks, so their faces were both noticeable and important. Indeed, mime performers were often successful because of their looks: the very handsome or beautiful and the extraordinarily grotesque or ugly.

Mimes could be either comic or serious, simple or spectacular, but, whatever their form, they usually dealt with contemporary life. They became both Rome's most popular and its most notorious theatrical entertainment during the empire (both East and West). Some mime actresses set fashions in clothes and behavior; one (Theodora) married an emperor; some became the equivalent of movie stars. Despite this popularity, no complete mime scripts have been passed down to us; the assumption is that they, perhaps like sitcom scripts, were thought (by those who kept libraries) to have no lasting value.

Christian Opposition to Theatre

Christianity's opposition to theatre was not to Roman comedies or tragedies, which it had not seen and did not know. The opposition was to mime. Because some mimes included real sex and violence as part of the performance, and because many of them mocked Christianity, Christian writers and believers demanded—unsuccessfully—the outlawing of theatre. Mime was not alone in its excesses; equally popular were chariot

FIGURE 12.6 **Roman Paratheatrical Entertainments.** Animal fights, chariot races, and sea battles all appealed to Roman audiences and, during the empire, managed to crowd theatre out of the cultural centrality it had held in Greece.

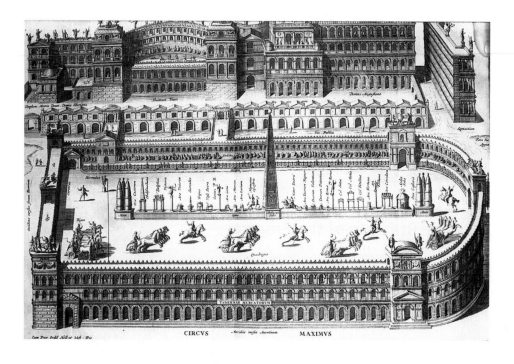

racing, gladiatorial contests, animal fights, and sea battles in which violence and death were also expected and applauded. Although these entertainments took place in special buildings such as *amphitheatres* (e.g., Rome's Colosseum) and *circuses* (the Circus Maximus), theatres were occasionally appropriated for such events, reinforcing the arguments of those who wanted to ban theatre. That mime had to compete directly with these other kinds of performance probably explains its occasional rawness. That mime replaced comedy and tragedy in Rome's public theatres surely offers hints about Romans and their culture. The antipathy between theatre and the Church, which dates from the early Roman Empire, finds echoes still today.

The Breakup of the Empire

By the early 300s C.E., the Roman Empire had become too large and unwieldy to rule effectively. It was therefore broken into two administrative units, with the western unit claiming Rome as its capital and the eastern unit being ruled from Constantinople, a new city built by the Emperor Constantine. Constantine moved to this new capital, taking much of the population of Rome with him, thus tilting the empire's center of gravity far to the east. The result was a shift in power and cultural influence. Constantinople grew more powerful and turned eastward. Rome, now a much smaller city, once again found itself on the western fringe of the civilized world.

By the middle of the sixth century (500s), the western empire was disintegrating, its system of roads and waterways crumbling, its trade sporadic, and its security destroyed. Whatever unity remained in western Europe came mostly from the Christian church through a network of churches and religious houses bound through the Pope in Rome, but the center of the empire had fallen.

The Byzantine Empire: Its Rise and Fall

Constantinople and the eastern empire, on the other hand, flourished. Considering themselves Romans, for a time they continued to speak Latin, to enjoy chariot races and theatre, and to trade with such Italian satellites as Ravenna but increasingly with countries to the east. They soon adopted Greek for official documents, however, established a Christianity (now called Orthodox) that was tied more closely to the government than to the Pope, and gradually easternized, some say "Orientalized," their culture. Later called *Byzantine* (after the early town of Byzantium, which Constantinople had replaced), this empire had a thriving trade, successful military, and highly developed culture, including theatre.

Constantinople never entirely lost contact with the west; it continued to send gifts, receive envoys, and marry its leading families with those of the west. Still, its major interests lay increasingly in the east. This rich Byzantine culture persisted for almost another thousand years. Weakened by one of the western Crusades in the thirteenth century (1200s), the eastern Roman Empire was finally overwhelmed by Muslim Turks in the fifteenth century (1400s), just as the western empire was beginning to recuperate and enter its great Renaissance.

Byzantine Theatre

Byzantine theatre is not well known in today's western world, for a couple of reasons. The language in which its records appear are not those in which most western scholars are competent, and many of the records were, until the late 1980s, inaccessible because they were held behind the so-called Iron Curtain. With the fall of the Soviet Union and the political realignment of Russia and the United States, more information should soon become available. As of now, however, the available scholarship suggests that Byzantine theatre included

- The continuation of mime
- An interest in Greek tragedy (which may have been literary only)
- The exportation of performances and an idea of performance to Asia Minor and what is now Ukraine (The cathedral at Kiev, Ukraine, has frescoes of mime.)

Just as Roman theatre of the west left a legacy for the Renaissance in western Europe, so, too, may have Byzantine theatre. There are tantalizing hints that Byzantine theatre may

FIGURE 12.7 **Mime Performers.**
This wall painting from a cathedral in Kiev shows a variety of musicians and performers, including one featuring an animal. Dating from the early Middle Ages, the painting strongly suggests continuing Byzantine influence as far north as today's Ukraine. (Painting redrawn and published in Allardyce Nicoll, *Masks, Mimes, and Miracles,* 1931.)

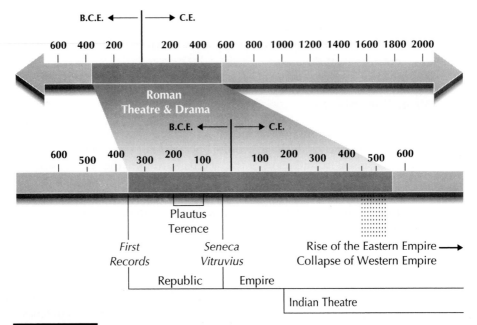

FIGURE 12.8 Timeline.

Plautus and Terence date from the Republic; Seneca and Vitruvius from about the time of Christ; extant Roman theatre buildings from the empire, a time when Indian theatre also flourished. The collapse of the empire in the West left flourishing civilizations far to the east, in Byzantium, India, and China.

have influenced both Italian popular theatre (see p. 301) and the medieval theatre of Europe (see p. 255).

The Roman Empire—east and west—was thus unparalleled among great civilizations because it remained intact so long, although its final iterations would scarcely have been recognized by the Italians who first created it.

Thinking About Roman Theatre

Knowledge of [another] culture should sharpen our ability to scrutinize more steadily, to appreciate more lovingly, our own.

—Margaret Mead

Several people have compared U.S. culture to Roman culture, both its republican and its imperial periods. Theatre is, of course, an important part of culture. What points of similarity can you cite between American and Roman theatres? Points of difference? Does American theatre more resemble Greek or Roman theatre?

KEY TERMS

Check your understanding against this list. Brief definitions are in the Glossary; page references there will direct you to appropriate pages. (Persons are page-referenced in the Index.)

amphitheatre
Byzantine
ludi

mime
pantomime
periaktoi

Emblem, Environment, and Simultaneity (c. 950–c. 1650)

The second phase of theatrical and dramatic history began in the tenth century and ended about 1650 (approximately two hundred years earlier in Italy). Theatres during these six hundred years shared several important theatrical conventions and so can be usefully studied together. Their major shared traits are:

- The communication of meaning through *emblems*, shorthand embodiments of richer content (a flag standing for a country, a crown for a king)
- The use of existing environments for performance
- A staging convention of simultaneous settings where several locations are presented simultaneously to the audience
- Complicated plays with numerous characters, many lines of action, and elastic time and place
- A mostly male theatre, in which women participated only as audience

Over the last two centuries of this period, rapid change led to overlap between this period and a new one then coming into being. This overlap was possible because of social and economic stratification into a court theatre, a popular theatre, and an embryonic professional and commercial theatre.

During this period, too, came a new form of dance drama in India, the first records of a Chinese theatre, as well as "the oldest major theatre art . . . still regularly performed": Japanese *Noh*.

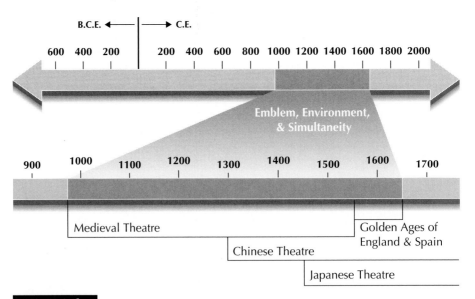

FIGURE IIIb.1   After the fall of the Western Roman Empire (c. 550 c.e.), organized theatre disappeared from Europe until the end of the tenth century, when it reappeared using different conventions. These conventions were, in turn, replaced after about 1650.

13

Theatre in the Middle Ages

When you have completed this chapter, you should be able to

- Explain how and when a new kind of theatre came into being several hundred years after the fall of Rome in the West

- Discuss how the medieval theatre was part of its culture

- Trace the changes in medieval theatre from its beginnings to its end

- Describe the physical types of medieval theatres, and discuss how the various theatres were funded and organized

Even after the 500s, Constantinople continued as a center of trade and civilization. Increasingly "Orientalized" and bureaucratized, the Byzantine Empire had a highly developed culture, one focused on luxury and one that looked east rather than west for its markets and goods. Arts and entertainments, including theatre, flourished there through most of the period, not ending until the 1450s.

China, too, was flourishing. An ancient culture, China had developed in a region of diverse geography and languages. Nonetheless, while Europe was struggling to create order after the collapse of Rome, China was already a stable empire whose central administration effectively governed a vast area. A series of invaders changed the governors of China but not the institutions of Chinese government, and so Chinese society and Chinese culture existed self-sufficiently, exerting influence on Japan and Southeast Asia. The first records of theatre in China appear in the early ninth (or maybe tenth) century C.E., when a palace theatre school, the Pear Garden, was established.

Western Europe, on the other hand, was in increasing disarray after the fourth century, and, after its collapse in the sixth century, Rome had no political successor. Some city states of the Italian peninsula avoided the general decline by maintaining strong trading connections with Constantinople or other cultures. Western Europe, however, continued to crumble as various forces that had before served to unify Europe weakened or disintegrated. The Roman system of roads and waterways fell into disrepair, and transportation and communication became at first troubled and at last almost impossible. Laws were ignored and order broke down, replaced by the rule of force: bands of

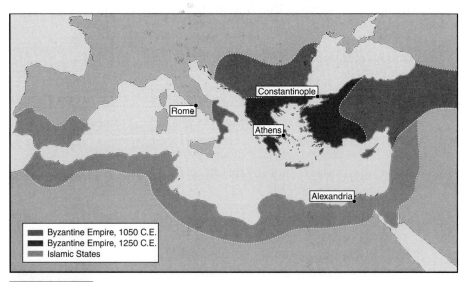

FIGURE 13.1   The Byzantine Empire.

While western Europe was in disarray, the Eastern Empire, centered in Constantinople, flourished and regularly traded with the Far East. Meanwhile, the influence of Islamic states of the Middle East and North Africa grew, spilling over into Spain.

pirates and brigands grew wealthy and influential enough to challenge rulers. Without the support of a government, the monetary system failed, and barter, with all its cumbersome trappings, became the basis of trade. Out of this disarray emerged a different kind of Europe, one with different languages, traditions, and cultures—one that was fragmented and local, lacking a center of the sort Rome had provided.

The prevailing social organization was feudal, where the social base was not the town but the manor, a self-contained agricultural unit that could offer security to those within it. On the manor, each serf owed absolute allegiance to the lord. Serfs worked the land and maintained the manor in return for protection from the lord, who would fight to maintain safety for those within. Just as serfs owed allegiance to their lord, lesser lords owed allegiance to more powerful ones, who could call on them to raise armies. Travel among manors was irregular, a fact that worked against unity within Europe.

The Christian church, on the other hand, was a weak unifying force because its services were conducted in Latin, its pope led the whole church, and its priests and especially its monks occasionally traveled. Like social organization, church organization was hierarchichal, with priests reporting to bishops and bishops to archbishops, to cardinals, and finally to the pope. This hierarchy ensured an orderly governance in an otherwise chaotic world, and its teachings gave it a substantial base of power.

The power hierarchies of both feudalism and Christianity were essentially pyramidal, with one (male) person at the top, relatively few (male) persons immediately under him, and so on until, at the base of each pyramid, were the peasants, that great mass of people who tilled the land and provided all those above them with the necessities and amenities of life. The two pyramids interlocked when Church leaders were drawn from the noble classes; the peasants provided goods and services for both Church lords and secular lords.

The life of the medieval peasant was one of work, ignorance, and want; that of people above the peasant varied. Because earlier historians saw this extended period as a lower one between two higher ones (Rome and the Renaissance—the "rebirth"), they called this the *Middle Ages* or the *medieval* (middle) period.

Early Medieval Drama and Theatre

For many years, historians believed that no theatre or drama outlived the collapse of Rome, but it is now certain that theatre continued in the Byzantine Empire and that remnants of professional performers traveled about in Italy, France, and Germany. Scattered references to *mimi, histriones,* and *ioculatores* (all words to describe actors) surfaced periodically in western medieval accounts, but the degree to which such performers performed actual plays, as distinct from such variety entertainments as juggling, tumbling, dancing, and rope tricks is not known. As well, there were various sorts of performance based in pagan worship, some of which may have been dramatic. But it is clear that, if traditional dramas were performed in the West between the collapse of Rome and the tenth century, their scale was much reduced and that, if theatre (as distinct from performance) existed at all, it was feeble.

Two almost simultaneous events toward the end of the tenth century marked the reentry of theatre into western Europe. The first, the plays of Hroswitha, offer incontrovertible evidence of continuity with Roman drama; the second, the liturgical manual of Ethelwold, shows the Christian church staging a small play as part of a worship service.

Hroswitha, a religious leader (and noblewoman) was attached to the Benedictine monastery near Gandersheim (in modern Germany) and linked to a court that had ties to Constantinople. She wrote seven plays (c. 950), the first still-extant dramas since the early days of the Roman Empire. Based on the comedies of Terence, Hroswitha's plays sought to celebrate "the laudable chastity of holy maidens" and *may* have been performed at court and at the monastery. Hroswitha is important on three counts: as the first known female playwright, as the first known post-Roman playwright, and as proof of an intellectual continuity from Rome to the Middle Ages. For reasons not entirely clear (but perhaps related to the fact that men have written most histories), Hroswitha's contributions have been largely overshadowed by a different strand of theatre, one that also emerged in the tenth century and also at a Benedictine monastery.

Ethelwold, Bishop of Winchester, England, issued in 975 the *Regularis Concordia*, a monastic guidebook, which, among other things, described in detail how one part of an Easter service was to be performed. For about a hundred years before Ethelwold, the Church had been decorating and elaborating various of its practices. Music, calendar, vestments, art, architecture, and *liturgy* (rites, public worship)—all had changed in the direction of greater embellishment. One sort of liturgical embellishment was the *trope* (any interpolation into an existing text). One Easter trope was sung by the choir antiphonally and began, *"Quem quaeritis in sepulchro, o christocole."* Translated into English, the trope read in its entirety:

Whom seek ye in the tomb, O Christians?
Jesus of Nazareth, the crucified, O heavenly beings.
He is not here, he is risen as he foretold;
Go and announce that he is risen from the tomb.

It was this trope to which staging directions were added in Ethelwold's *Regularis Concordia:*

While the third lesson is being read, four of the brethren shall vest, one of whom, wearing an alb as though for some different purpose, shall enter and go stealthily to the place of the "sepulchre" and sit there quietly, holding a palm in his hand. Then, while the third response is being sung, the other three brethren, vested in copes and holding thuribles in their hands, shall enter in their turn and go to the place of the "sepulchred," step by step, as though searching for something. Now these things are done in imitation of the angel seated on the tomb and of the women coming with perfumes to anoint the body of Jesus. When, therefore, he that is seated shall see these three draw nigh, wandering about as it were and seeking something, he shall begin to sing softly and sweetly, *Quem quaeritis.*

TRANSLATED BY THOMAS SYMONS

Ethelwold's text (less so Hroswitha's) reveals three conventions that operated in medieval theatre. Medieval staging was

- *Simultaneous*—that is, several different locations were present in the performing space at the same time. Such an arrangement meant conceptualizing two different kinds of space: small scenic structures that served to locate the specific places (called *mansions*), and a neutral, generalized playing space (called *platea*).

- *Emblematic*—that is, meanings from the performance reached the audience through costumes and properties that were signs or symbols whose meanings communicated easily with the audience. Among mansions, for example, an animal mouth signified hell and a revolving globe stood for heaven.

- *Environmental*—that is, performed in available spaces rather than in structures specially built and set aside for the purpose.

Hroswitha's plays had no immediate successors, but from the tenth through much of the sixteenth century, many dramas such as *Quem Quaeritis* were performed inside monastic and later cathedral churches as a part of the liturgy (and so are also called *liturgical drama*). Such plays were chanted or sung (rather than spoken) and were given in the

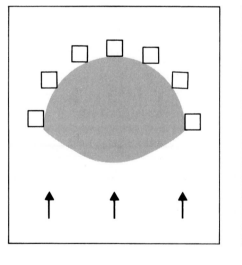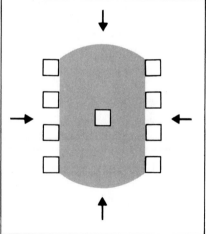

→ audience

platea

mansion

FIGURE 13.2 **Simultaneous Staging.**

Medieval staging used two kinds of spaces: generalized playing space (called a *platea*) and specific locations (called *mansions*), which appeared simultaneously adjacent to the platea.

language of the Church (Latin), and so are called Latin music drama. They were acted by clergy, choirboys, monks, and occasionally traveling scholars and schoolboys (and, occasionally, nuns); the actors, then, were almost always male (except in convents).

From the very short *Quem Quaeritis,* Latin music drama blossomed into many plays of varying lengths and varying degrees of complexity. The subjects of most such plays were Biblical, usually drawn from events surrounding Christmas and Easter: the visit of the three Marys to the tomb, the travel of the Magi, Herod's wrath. Other Latin music dramas, however, depicted such diverse stories as the life of the Virgin Mary, the raising of Lazarus, and Daniel in the lion's den. Almost all were serious, but at festivals like the Feast of Fools and the Feast of the Boy Bishops, the usual dignity was abandoned and in its place was substituted considerable tomfoolery. Latin music dramas continued to be performed in churches well into the sixteenth century, overlapping other types by hundreds of years.

Plays performed in the church were produced by the church. Actors were churchmen (except in convents, where churchwomen performed). Costumes were based on church vestments, rich with meaning. A key identified Saint Peter; hoods signified women; wings meant angels; wallets and staffs identified travelers, and so on. Staging depended on existing church architecture. For example, the choir loft might represent heaven, the crypt hell, and the altar the tomb of Christ. For elaborate plays, special mansions might be constructed, some small but others large enough for several persons to be hidden in. Special effects required machinery capable of flying objects and actors in and out of the playing area. For example, angels and doves flew about, Christ rose to heaven, and the three kings followed a moving star that led them to the stable of the Christ child and there stopped to mark the spot.

Although early audiences consisted only of those residing in the monasteries or convents, when the plays began to be performed in cathedral churches as well as monastic ones, general audiences attended.

Medieval Culture and Theatre, c. 1200–1550

Several shifts within medieval culture began to coalesce by 1200. Population increased rapidly. Towns grew up around monasteries and manors to provide goods and services, serving as centers of trade. Increased trade encouraged the development of still more towns, many now located where goods that had been shipped by water (the preferred method) were transferred to land (roads were still terrible). The names Ox*ford* and Cam*bridge* reflect this origin. Trade expanded again when a series of crusades against Muslims and others (including Constantinople) prompted new shipbuilding, opened new sea routes, and established new trading ports and new markets, an expansion aided by improved sea manuals and the discovery of the compass.

Commercial theory changed. Early medieval theory was grounded in theology: usury was condemned, merchants were supposed to work for the benefit of society, and profit was considered a kind of parasitism. No more. Merchants began to form monopolies, and maximum profit rather than just price became the goal. Modern commercial structures (e.g., banking, partnerships) emerged. Because merchants and tradesmen lived outside the feudal system, they gradually undermined it by providing refuge for serfs seeking to escape their lords. Towns sponsored fairs to bring people from great distances and so facilitate trade. Thus, towns and commerce competed directly with manors and agriculture for social leadership.

At about the same time, the domination of the Church and its monopoly on matters of faith began to erode, with Martin Luther later posing the most direct threat (1521). The separation of religion from everyday life was underway.

With the decline of feudalism and the authority of the Church, and with the emergence of towns and nationalism, the era was metamorphosing into a new kind of culture: that is, after about 1200 western Europe was in a transition between medieval culture and a new one that would coalesce by 1550 (one hundred or so years earlier in Italy)—the Renaissance.

Religious Drama Outside the Church

After about 1200, medieval drama reflected these cultural shifts in several ways. In addition to Latin music drama, which continued to be performed in churches, new kinds of religious drama appeared. These dramas differed from *Latin music drama* in several ways:

- They were performed outdoors rather than inside churches.
- They were spoken rather than chanted or sung.
- They were in the vernacular (e.g., French, English, German) rather than in Latin.
- Laymen, rather than priests and clerics, served as actors.
- The stories and themes, no longer limited to liturgical sources, became more far-ranging.
- The performances tended to cluster in the spring and summer months, especially around the new Feast of Corpus Christi, rather than spreading throughout the church year, as before. They became known as *Corpus Christi plays*.

Of these changes, the most significant was the shift from a universal language (Latin) to the various national tongues, for with this shift came an end to an international drama and the beginning of several national dramas, a trend important to the future of both theatre and drama.

The plays remained decidedly religious, if not always scriptural. In general, they dealt with:

- Events in the life of Christ (*The Second Shepherd's Play*) and stories from the Old Testament (*Noah*)—plays often called *mysteries* or *mystery plays*
- The lives of saints, both historical and legendary, called *miracles* or *miracle plays*
- Didactic allegories, often about the struggle for salvation (*Everyman*)—so-called *moralities* or *morality plays*

FIGURE 13.3   **Medieval Plays in Modern Production.**

Two Noah plays; *left,* from the N-town cycle, produced at Grantham (UK). (Photograph by Chris Windows.) *Right,* produced by the Department of Theatre Arts, Towson University, for the York Cycle in Toronto, Canada, 1998. (Directed by Ralph Blasting, photograph by Megan Lloyd, scenic design by Daniel Ettinger, costume design by Cheryl Partridge.)

Although the plays differed in subject matter and form, they shared several characteristics. First, they aimed to teach or to reinforce belief in Church doctrine. Second, they were formulated as melodramas or divine comedies; that is, the ethical system of the play was clear, and good was rewarded, evil punished. Third, the driving force for the action was God and His plan rather than the decisions or actions of the dramatic agents. To a modern reader, the plays often appear episodic, with their actions unmotivated, their sequences of time and place inexplicable, and their mixture of the comic and the serious unnerving.

In fact, their traits expressed the medieval view. The plays presented the lure and strength of sin, the power and compassion of God, and the punishment awaiting the unrepentant sinner. They called for all people to repent, to confess, and to atone for their sins.

The Story of the Play

Anonymous, *Everyman*, c. 1490

God sends Death to summon Everyman, who must bring a "sure reckoning." When Death gives the message to Everyman, saying he must "go a long journey," Everyman cries that he is not ready; he begs for time; he tries to bribe Death, who tells him he *must* make the journey and should find what friends will go with him.

Everyman asks various friends—Fellowship, Kindred and Cousin, Goods—to go with him, and they agree until they learn what the destination is; then they depart.

Good Deeds speaks "from the ground." He cannot go because he is too weak to walk, but he calls his sister, Knowledge, who says, "Everyman, I will go with thee and be thy guide."

Knowledge takes him to Confession; after confessing, he whips himself as a penance, and Good Deeds is able to rise and walk.

Knowledge gives Everyman a "garment of sorrow" to wear instead of his worldly clothes. She tells him to call his Five Wits, his Beauty, his Strength, and his Discretion. Everyman receives the sacrament and then journeys to his grave, where Beauty refuses to enter with him; then Strength, then Discretion, then Five Wits desert him, but Good Deeds remains at the graveside. They pray, and then Everyman goes into his grave alone.

An angel appears, saying his reckoning is "crystal-clear," and a Doctor (learned man) gives a short speech to explain the play.

Because history was God's great lesson to humankind, the drama that expressed His plan was nothing less than the entirety of human history, from Creation to Doomsday. Any combination of events, any juxtaposition of characters, and any elasticity of time or place that would illuminate God's plan and make it more accessible and compelling was suitable drama. The great dramas of the 1400s and 1500s that showed this history are called *cycles*, or *cosmic dramas*, and some took days, even weeks, to play from end to end.

Why such dramas came to be done outside the Church building has been endlessly debated. Some thought that they had been forced out of the church because of abuses such as those at the Feast of Fools. Others argued that the appearance of drama outdoors merely reflected the changing needs of the plays and their audiences for more space and freedom. More likely is the increasing power of towns, which fastened on plays and other public shows as expressions of their new status. Whatever the reason for the development, records of religious plays given outside of churches appear by 1200 and are common by 1350, when relatively abundant accounts describe a civic and religious theatre of magnificent proportions throughout most of western Europe.

Staging Religious Plays Outside the Church

Although churches continued to produce Latin music dramas throughout the period, other religious plays had different producing arrangements. Sometimes, town officials took charge; sometimes, special committees did the job. Sometimes labor and religious organizations (*guilds* or *confraternities*) assumed responsibility, often under the town's protection.

Guilds were frequently called on to produce a single play in a group, sometimes on the basis of particular skills or association with the play's subject: Noah plays, which required a real (perhaps half-size) ship, went well with shipbuilding, for example. Because of both financial investment and tradition, plays tended to stay with the same guild for many years. As the plays and processions showed the wealth of the town, so the play and its properties showed the wealth of the guild.

Roles in the plays were open to all male members of the community (in France, occasionally, women might perform) and were generally performed without compensation. As in any primarily amateur operation, the quality of the performances varied considerably, and it was probably in an attempt to upgrade the general level of acting that many cities hired professional "property players" to take the leading roles (after c. 1450) and to instruct the others. Although these few actors were paid, they were not looked down on as socially undesirable, as were professional actors in secular plays.

We have no textbooks of medieval acting. We believe that it was, like the costumes, emblematic. It probably depended on reducing character to large, symbolic strokes, without "inner" work or "psychology." We do not know how amateurs handled the problem of being heard and understood outdoors. Some pictures of the period show prompters or directors, book in hand, standing among the actors; this professional may literally have been cueing gestures and turns of voice.

Some plays and some roles suggest a tradition of satirical or comic playing, with caricature an established technique. The traveling actors of the countryside probably emphasized low comedy and certainly passed on techniques and traditions that would flourish later with Shakespeare's clowns.

The staging of religious plays outside the church took two major forms, still within the conventions of emblem, environment, and simultaneity:

- *Fixed staging*, which occurred throughout Europe, except in parts of Spain and England
- *Movable staging*, which was used most importantly in parts of Spain and England

In fixed staging, mansions (or *scaffolds*) were set up, usually outdoors, in whatever spaces were available (e.g., courtyards of noble houses, town squares, the remains of Roman amphitheatres). Depending on the space, the mansions were arranged in circles, straight lines, or rectangles, and the platea and the audience area were established accordingly. Although the individual arrangements varied, heaven and hell (ordinarily the most ornate mansions) were customarily set at opposite poles.

In movable staging, *pageants* (pageant wagons) allowed the audience to scatter along a processional route while the plays were brought to them and performed in sequence,

FIGURE 13.4   **Medieval Plays in Modern Production.**
Cycles often depicted Biblical scenes from the beginning of the world to the last judgment. Above, *The Creation,* performed by the Department of Drama and Theater Arts, University of Birmingham (UK). (Directed by Joel Kaplan, at the York Plays at Toronto Festival.)
Below, *The Last Judgment* from the N-Town cycle, produced at Grantham (UK). (Photograph
by Chris Windows.)

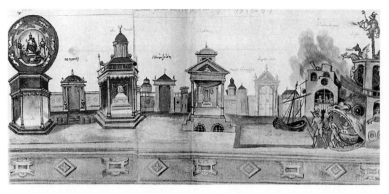

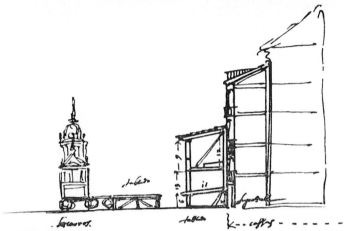

FIGURE 13.5 **Fixed and Movable Staging.**
Most places on the continent set up mansions in some already existing space (a village square, a private home), and the mansions remained fixed throughout the performance (*above*). In parts of England and Spain, on the other hand, mansions were set on wagons that traveled from place to place, moving the plays to the audiences. (*Below,* courtesy of the Ayunta-Miento de Madrid.)

much like a parade with floats. Each play, then, was performed several times. A likely pattern was for the first play (e.g., Creation) to be presented at dawn at the first station; when it moved to the second station to perform, the second play (e.g., the Fall of Man) was presented at the first station. For most of the day, several plays were performing at once. The word *pageant* is important in a discussion of movable staging because it was used to describe the play itself, the spectacle of the plays in performance, and also the vehicle on which the presentation was staged.

The appearance of pageant wagons has been much discussed, but, as available evidence is scant, few firm conclusions are possible. Only one English description, dating from slightly before 1600, has survived, and its reliability is suspect:

Every company had his pagiant, or parte, which pagiants weare a high scafolde with two rowmes, a higher and a lower, upon four wheeles. In the lower they apparelled themselves, and in the higher rowme they played, beinge all open on the tope, that all behoulders mighte heare and see them. The places where they played them was in every streete.

An obvious problem with the description, and one of the reasons its accuracy has been questioned, is that the wagons as described would need to be more than twelve feet tall to allow for the wheels and the two levels, yet narrow enough to be pulled by horses through the medieval streets. The resulting structure would be highly unstable and perhaps unable to turn corners as required in its trek from station to station.

The enormous complexity of some late medieval dramas also required specialists to oversee the production and to serve as the medieval counterpart of the modern producer. Although responsibilities differed with circumstances, the tasks of one medieval producer in France included:

- Overseeing the building of a stage and the use of the scenery and machines
- Overseeing the building and painting of scenery and the construction of seating for the audience
- Checking all deliveries to ensure accuracy
- Disciplining the actors
- Acting in the plays whenever necessary
- Addressing audiences at the beginning of the play and at each intermission, giving a summary of what had happened and promising greater marvels to come

Because special effects in the dramas were so extraordinary, some men, called *masters of secrets,* became specialists in their construction and workings, which included:

- Flying: angels flew about; Lucifer raised Christ; souls rose from limbo into heaven on Doomsday; devils and fire-spitting monsters sallied forth from hell and back again; platforms made to resemble clouds (*glories*) bore choruses of heavenly beings aloft
- Traps: appearances, disappearances, and substitutions, as when Lot's wife was turned into a pillar of salt and tigers were transformed into sheep
- Fire: hell belched smoke and flames (in 1496 at Seurre, an actor playing Satan was severely burned when his costume caught fire), and buildings ignited on cue

Costumes were primary carriers of meaning within the convention we have called emblematic: They indicated, symbolically and clearly, the nature of the wearers. At its most sophisticated, this convention became a rich source of both meaning and spectacle: In a parade of the seven deadly sins, Pride was dressed entirely in peacock feathers (the feather's "eye" symbolizing the love of display and self-admiration); a costume recorded for a late morality had symbols of coinage embroidered all over it. In the guild-produced plays, large sums were spent on such costumes, which were then used year after year. Masks were rare, probably being restricted to devils.

Audiences for these great outdoor performances of the towns comprised a broad spectrum, from local religious figures to town officials to ordinary citizens. The audience was not universal, however, because a fee was usually charged, and so some of the population was most likely excluded. The well-to-do paid extra to sit in stands or special scaffolds or, when pageant wagons were used, in the windows of selected houses. Those who paid the least stood to watch the plays. Those who paid nothing may have been able to see the processions, if not the plays.

Audiences were subject to the weather, and they saw the plays against a backdrop of their fellow citizens and their own town. Food and drink were probably available. Toilet facilities were provided in at least some sets of stands erected for the gentry.

Secular Drama

At about the same time that religious dramas appeared outside the Church, the first records of secular dramas appear. Secular drama may have been an outgrowth of outdoor religious drama, or it may have developed quite independently, growing out of traditions from early pagan performances. When the great religious plays were at their zenith, this secular tradition was moving tentatively toward maturity. Several principal venues of secular drama existed.

At court and in the homes of the very wealthy, performances were given at tournaments and on holidays (especially Christmas and Mardi Gras). There, theatre pieces might be presented within another activity—for example, between the courses of a formal banquet; such a short dramatic entertainment was called an *interlude*. Short plays might also be given in connection with gift-giving by costumed revelers, as in entertainments called *mummings* and *disguisings*. The most spectacular of the noble and court entertainments, however, was the *masque*, in which allegorical compliments to the guests of honor were framed by intricate dances involving the courtiers themselves.

FIGURE 13.6 **Secular Theatre.**
At about the same time that religious performances appeared outside the churches, some non-religious (secular) plays also appeared. Here, a dance of fools.

PHORMIO
PARASITVS

THRASO
MILES

FIGURE 13.7 Secular Theatre.
Plays from Rome, especially the tragedies of Seneca and the comedies of Terence, were regularly performed in schools and universities. Here, redrawn from a medieval manuscript, two stock characters of Roman comedy, the parasite and the soldier.

Towns staged *street pageants* and *entries* in connection with various special occasions, often during the visit of an important dignitary. As a part of these events, plays were combined with elaborate processions. The plays were given for the instruction and entertainment of the visiting dignitaries, whose procession through the town constituted the major entertainment for the townspeople who watched it.

In schools and colleges, *Roman comedies and tragedies* were studied, copied, translated, and emulated during much of the fifteenth century.

For ordinary people in the towns and countryside, *farces* poked fun at all manner of domestic tribulations, particularly infidelity and cuckoldry.

In many instances, secular *morality plays* featured classical gods and heroes rather than Christian virtues and vices, and occasionally morality plays were drawn into the religious battles of the Reformation: For example, anti-Catholic moralities costumed devils as Catholic prelates and Christian figures as Protestant ministers; anti-Protestant moralities did just the reverse.

Toward the end of the period (after c. 1450), a class of professionals appeared to put on such shows, including writing and staging them; they were often attached to courts or noble houses but, despite their skills and success, were servants.

Producing arrangements for secular dramas varied enormously. Towns produced some (e.g., street pageants), courts produced others (e.g., masques), and schools produced their own. Audiences varied with venue: audiences at royal banquets were very limited (courtiers), as were those of rural villages (peasants). But, like audiences of the great religious dramas, most comprised men and women of different social classes. The degree of spectacle also varied widely with the venue, with those produced by towns and courts being most spectacular because they were considered an index of the power and prosperity of the producer. In fact, theatre became a vehicle for displaying power, its opulence a sign of the importance of the town or court producing it. On the other hand, popular farces acted by tiny troupes, often families, were performed wherever the actors could get permission—no easy thing in the tight medieval world. They have left little record.

Thinking About **Medieval Theatre**

Medieval theatres were not simple, as this account from Valenciennes (1547) makes clear. *"Truth, the angels, and other characters descended from very high. . . . Lucifer was raised from Hell on a dragon without our being able to see how. . . . Devils carried the souls of Herod and Judas through the air. . . . The fig tree, cursed by Our Lord, appeared to dry up, its leaves withering in an instant. The eclipse, the earthquake, the splitting of the rocks, and the other miracles at the death of Our Lord were shown with new marvels."* Explain how such effects could be achieved. In addition to information in this and earlier chapters, books explaining magic tricks may be helpful.

Medieval secular theatre, although never as grand as the religious, was nonetheless important because from it came the major thrust toward developing a theatre that was both professional (people could earn their living at it) and commercial (audiences provided the money to support it). Community and amateurism thus dissolved. Theatre became a kind of commodity that some people (audiences) paid to see other people (artists) do.

The End of Medieval Religious Theatre: The Transformation of Medieval Secular Theatre

By the sixteenth century, a series of factions splintered away from the Roman Church; this religious Reformation quickly became political as rulers and nations found reasons to break from Rome or stay with it. The religious theatre was a visible annoyance to both Protestant and Catholic authorities, offending the one with doctrines already rejected, offending the other with doctrines better kept in church, at least until things quieted down. Worse, zealots on both sides were writing morality plays that cast their opponents as devils. In place after place, religious plays were therefore outlawed by both Protestants and Catholics: Paris, 1548; England, 1558; the Council of Trent, 1545–1563.

Controlling production of these religious plays, when outlawed, was made much easier because printing presses were not yet generally available. In the absence of mechanical printing, which could quickly duplicate an original, copies of scripts were rare. Sometimes only a single handwritten copy, with production notes, was maintained. This master copy, or *register*, was held by a responsible person or office. In preparation for a production, all acting parts had to be copied from it. Obviously, anyone who could get the register could stop production. In the sixteenth century, when religious dramas were being censored and then banned, central governments began to "call in" registers for "correction"—from which the registers never reappeared. The end of medieval religious drama was thus very quick. It had reached its height only shortly before it was banned. (Much of the best and most elaborate medieval religious theatre came between 1500 and 1550.)

Medieval theatre in the West, however, left important legacies: its conventions of acting, staging, and playwriting and its highly developed technology of special effects. These practices grounded a newly emerging northern Renaissance theatre, whose flowering in England and Spain produced their Golden Ages. The early professionals who had worked in the late medieval theatre were the forebears of a great upsurge of professionalism visible after about 1550. And most significant of all, when churches and towns ceased to produce theatre, theatre became a commercial venture. Regular performances in capital cities replaced occasional performances in small cities and towns; permanent theatre structures replaced the streets or town commons; and professional actors replaced amateurs. Commercial theatre replaced communal theatre just as surely as towns and trading replaced manors and feudalism.

Theatres in the East

In China during the Yuan dynasty (1300s), hundreds of plays were written, including some of China's most important dramas, notably Gao Ming's *The Lute Song* (c. 1360). Yuan drama relied on classical Chinese novels and history for their stories and characters. Each play divided major characters into four types—man, woman, and two types of clowns—and each unfolded in several acts in which each had a major song. Traveling troupes of actors (both women and men) performed these plays in temporary theatres throughout southern China. Such conventions probably resemble those of Byzantine theatre more closely than those of western Europe at the time.

Long developing under Chinese (and to a lesser extent, Indian) influence, Japan by the 1300s was beginning to break away from China, turn its back on the outside world (except for minor trading contacts), and form a distinct culture of its own, one marked by a feudal society with an emperor nominally at its top; a warrior ethic that made the samurai warrior a model; and a system of religion that included native Shinto ("the way of the gods"), Chinese Confucianism, and, above all, a form of Indian Buddhism, Zen. It was at this time of transition that Japan's first major theatre developed.

Noh has been called "the oldest major theatre art . . . still regularly performed." Poetic and austere, it is a theatrical expression of Zen Buddhism. Its originators were a father and son, Kanami (1333–1384) and Zeami (1363–1444), both professional actors attached to a temple. They wrote most of the more than two hundred extant Noh plays, creating a body of work with certain rigid characteristics. Each had a three-part structure (*jo, ha,* and *kyu*) that depended on the interaction of two characters: the protagonist (*shite*) and an accidental confidant (*waki*). Each play dealt with one of five subjects—god, man, woman, insanity, and demon—and a Noh performance included five plays, one on each of these subjects and in that order.

Noh's basic traits persist to the present. Its plots are simple; their abundant exposition seems natural to a form that is concerned not with events but with the effects of past events. The protagonists are usually tormented figures—dishonored warriors, crazed

FIGURE 13.8 **Japanese Noh.**
"The oldest major theatrical art . . . still regularly performed," Noh is typified by compressed, poetic drama and symbolic, nonrealistic staging with close ties to Zen Buddhism. (Courtesy of the Japan Information and Culture Center, the Embassy of Japan, Washington, D.C.)

Links to More About Theatre

 William Tydeman, *The Theatre in the Middle Ages*, 1978.

 Hildegarde of Bingen, *The Ordo Virtutum*. (several versions)

 <www.uwec.edu/jerzdg/psim/> Wonderful simulation of the York processional cycle in action.

<http://collectorspost.com> Go to "Medieval Drama Links." Pages of medieval drama links, including discussion groups.

women, guilty priests—whose appearance in the *kyu* section in a different form is, to a Westerner, a kind of exorcism. Profoundly influenced by Zen Buddhism, however, Noh's ideology is intuitive, not rational, and its goal is an understanding reached by a mental leap from appearance to reality. Indeed, the resolution of the plays comes from the protagonist's confrontation with hidden reality.

The shape of each plot is roughly the same: In the first part (*jo*), the confidant introduces himself and travels to a destination symbolized by a pillar on the stage; the protagonist enters and the two characters exchange questions and answers until the protagonist's concern and his reason for being at that place is clear. In the second part (*ha*), the protagonist performs a dance that is related to the concern, either by expression or narrative or symbol. In the third part (*kyu*), the protagonist appears as a new self, one called forth by the first two sections, thus resolving the play.

Staging is emblematic and highly conventional. Performances unfold on a small, raised stage, with all entrances made along a raised passage (*hashigakari*) at one side; at the rear is a wall with a pine tree painted on it. Onstage are musicians (three percussionists and a flute) and a chorus, soberly dressed and not masked, both of whom help establish the very deliberate tempo of the performance. Costumes are elaborate and include masks for some characters, but there is no scenery and very few symbolic properties. All performers are male, with the male voice undisguised even for female roles.

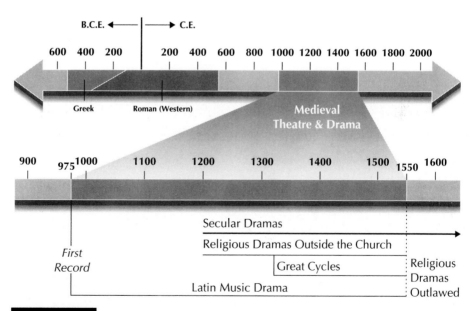

FIGURE 13.9 Timeline.

Medieval theatre and drama began in the late 900s in England with a sung Latin playlet and in Germany with an adaptation of Terence suitable for cloistered Christian women. By the end of the period in the mid-1550s, such plays had been joined by great civic cycles, moralities, and miracles, and a range of secular performances.

Dance was fundamental to Noh (and other) Japanese drama, a trait it shared with Indian but not Chinese plays. Indeed, Japan's dramatic theatre apparently developed from or alongside dance, incorporating intricate forms of movement that demanded special training.

KEY TERMS

Check your understanding against this list. Brief definitions are in the Glossary; page references there will direct you to appropriate pages. (Persons are page-referenced in the Index.)

confraternity	miracle play
Corpus Christi play	morality play
cosmic drama	Noh
cycle play	pageant
emblem	Pageant wagon
guild	*Quem Quaeritis*
interlude	register
Latin music drama	scaffold
liturgy	simultaneous staging
mansion	trope

The Golden Ages of England and Spain

o   b   j   e   c   t   i   v   e   s

When you have completed this chapter, you should be able to

- Discuss major traits associated with the Renaissance

- List the principal kinds of drama, important playwrights, and plays from the age of Shakespeare and the Spanish Golden Age

- Distinguish between public and private theatres

- Describe the major staging conventions of Shakespeare's theatre and compare them (that is, note similarities and differences) with medieval conventions

- Compare the physical theatres of Shakespeare and the Spanish Golden Age

- Compare the role of women in the theatres of Shakespeare and Spain

- Explain the importance of masques in English theatre history

Italy, perhaps because still weakly tied to Constantinople by tradition and trade or perhaps because once the heart of an empire, made the transition from a feudal society to a modern, commercial one earlier than the rest of western Europe. Indeed, by 1300 in Italy, new ideas, social organizations, attitudes, and discoveries had begun to peek through the medieval order. For the next two hundred years, these new ideas gradually took hold and spread throughout western Europe, heralding the arrival of the *Renaissance* ("rebirth"). (See Chapter 15.)

Once underway, the Renaissance unfolded throughout western Europe, but it did so at different rates and with different effects. Italy and southern Europe embraced Renaissance ideas earlier and developed somewhat differently from England, Spain, and northern Europe, at least for a while. But even within the Renaissance of northern Europe stark differences were visible. Spain and England, both strong naval powers and vigorous traders, were early rivals. Spain, importing gold from its Central and South American colonies, pulled money to its profligate central government and clung to Roman Catholicism and absolute monarchy. England, on the other hand, developed a strong merchant class, broke with Rome, and moved toward constitutional monarchy.

By c. 1550 (when medieval religious drama ended), the Renaissance had already revolutionized many former attitudes and practices throughout western Europe, though it had done so on different timetables and with different effects. Regardless of date or location, however, several traits distinguish this new Renaissance culture from the medieval culture preceding it.

People of the early Middle Ages had supposed that the temporal world would be destroyed, that the unrighteous would be purged, and that the righteous would be transported to a world of bliss. In the Renaissance, however, new secular and temporal interests joined earlier divine and eternal ones. A love of God and His ways, long the basis of human behavior, was joined by a newfound admiration for humankind, whose worth, intelligence, and beauty began to be celebrated. This new concern for people and their earthly lives was called *humanism*.

At about the same time, the older theology, a complete system based on divine revelation, gave way to competing philosophical systems that stressed *secularism* (that is, they advocated ethical conduct as an end in itself rather than as a prerequisite to heaven, and they argued for logical systems of thought independent of divine revelation). In science, an earth-centered astronomy was challenged by a sun-centered universe in which human beings were relegated to life on a relatively minor planet, no longer at the center of creation.

Within the Church, demands for reform led to breaks with Rome: some Christians (such as Martin Luther) protested against the Church at Rome and launched what came to be called the *Reformation*.

In sum, although God, His Church, and His theology remained a central fact of human life in the Renaissance, they were no longer absolute and unquestioned. Humanism and secularism were competing with them for acceptance. But the emergence of new ideas and attitudes was only part of the phenomenon. Vital, too, were factors that encouraged the widespread dissemination of the new spirit, factors such as the growth of trade and the arrival of the printing press.

FIGURE 14.1 **Renaissance World.**
Among the many re-discoveries of the Renaissance was the proposal by Copernicus that the earth moved around the sun—instead of the other way around, as Ptolemy had long taught. The Church opposed Copernican ideas because they seemed to displace people from the center of the universe, relegating them to a peripheral planet.

By the Renaissance, exploration and discovery had increased commercial areas far beyond the Mediterranean and close-in Atlantic. Marco Polo had opened Asia, Columbus had opened the Americas, and a series of West African ports hop-scotching to the Cape of Good Hope opened a feasible sea route to India. Improved navigation aids and some road improvements joined with new postal systems to improve both transportation and communication. (For example, a trip of seventy-five miles that took eight days in 1500 took only six by 1600.) New organizations arose for raising capital (e.g., joint stock companies) and insuring against catastrophic loss (e.g., associations among merchants). Wholesalers and middle-men transformed the nature of trade and took their share of the growing profits.

Along with goods, trade also led to the exchange of ideas. At the center of most of the various trade routes of the fourteenth century were the city-states of Italy, which soon became centers of a commerce in ideas, skills, and products. When Constantinople fell to the Turks in 1453, many scholars and artists came to Italy and with them came plays and treatises from ancient Greece and Rome, rescued from endangered libraries. Their study and interpretation began almost at once.

The introduction of the Gutenberg printing press to Italy at about the same time allowed the rapid reproduction of documents arriving from the East as well as of the interpretations and imitations of these documents. Certainly, the printing press allowed a veritable explosion of accessible information, so much so that, by 1500, numerous academies in the city-states of Italy were devoted to the study and production of Roman plays. Shortly thereafter, Italians began writing their own plays in imitation of the Roman models.

Patronage of the arts during the Renaissance was a major and acknowledged source of prestige, and, because the nobles' courts engaged in rivalries over which was to become the cultural center, painters, musicians, sculptors, architects, and writers flourished.

Such changes in viewpoint and technology predictably brought changes in theatre and drama. Theatres in both England and Spain, although influenced by Renaissance ideas, also built on secular staging conventions of the late Middle Ages. Both produced glorious dramas and robust public theatres soon after the end of medieval religious drama (c. 1550). By 1600, both were enjoying their Golden Ages of theatre and drama, with new free-standing theatres, professional players, paying audiences, and expansive plays of great complexity.

The Renaissance in the North: The Age of Shakespeare

The reign of Elizabeth I (1558–1603) brought greatness to England. With her ascent to the throne, the nation achieved the political and religious stability that permitted its arts and literature to thrive. When, in an attempt to mute religious controversies, the government outlawed religious drama, it opened the way for the rapid development of a secular tradition of plays and playgoing. When the queen finally agreed to the execution of Mary Stuart, her chief rival for the throne and the center of Catholic assaults on the church and throne, Elizabeth's political situation was secured, and the domination of Anglican Protestants within the Church of England was affirmed. The English navy defeated the Spanish Armada in 1588 and established itself as ruler of the seas and leader among the trading nations. England, for the first time in generations, was at peace at home and abroad and was filled with a national confidence and a lust for life seldom paralleled in history.

About twenty years after Elizabeth outlawed religious drama, commercial theatres began to open in London. They replayed some medieval conventions, but with one great difference: for the first time since the Romans built theatres in England, the English were building special structures and setting them aside for use as theatres—the age of staging in found environments was at an end.

Physical Theatre

In 1576, two commercial theatres opened in London, one an outdoor (or "public") theatre and the other an indoor (or "private") theatre. Thus, when Shakespeare arrived in London about fifteen years later, these two sorts of theatre were well established, and he wrote for and acted in both. Although their precise appearance cannot be known, their general features are well established.

Outdoor, *public theatres* (of which nine were built between 1576 and 1642) consisted of a round or polygonal, roofed, multileveled auditorium that surrounded an open *yard,* into which jutted a platform raised to a height of four to six feet. The entire yard (or *pit*) and part of the stage platform were unroofed. The audience, probably numbering as many as 2,500, surrounded the playing area on three sides, some standing in the pit and others seated in the *galleries* or the still more exclusive *lords' rooms.*

The actors worked on a raised stage and apparently awaited cues and changed costumes in a *tiring house,* located at the rear of the platform. Covering part of the stage was a roof (the *heavens*) supported by columns resting on the stage and apparently decorated on its underside with pictures of stars, planets, and signs of the zodiac. Gods and properties flew in from the heavens.

The stage floor was pierced with *traps,* through which characters could appear and disappear. Connecting the tiring house with the stage were at least two doors, which often represented widely divergent locations (as, for example, when one led to the fields of France and the other to the shores of England). Atop the tiring house, a flag flew on days of performance, and at a level just below, in an area called the *hut,* were probably housed the various pieces of equipment and machinery needed for special effects. A

FIGURE 14.2 **Public Theatre.**
The Swan drawing is the only visual evidence for the interior of an Elizabethan public theatre: outdoors, a roofed structure pierced by doors and an audience on three sides of a raised stage, thrust out from the structure. Problems with the drawing cause some to discount its evidentiary value.

musicians' gallery was apparently located just below the hut, at the third level above the stage.

Other points are less certain. The plays clearly required two playing levels, an upper and a lower, and some sort of *discovery space*, a place where objects and characters could be hidden from view and discovered at the appropriate time. Most scholars agree that the discovery space was located between the two doors, but some conceive of it as a permanent architectural part of the theatre, whereas others conceive of it as a portable unit to be added or deleted as required; some picture the discovery space as a recessed alcove (a kind of miniproscenium theatre), whereas others see it as a pavilion that jutted out into the stage. Obviously, any decision about the conformation of the space at stage level had implications for the upper level as well. Obviously, too, the degree of permanence of the discovery space would radically affect the general appearance of the theatre. The whole problem has been made thornier by the absence of such a space in the one extant sketch of a public theatre and by the appalling problems with sight lines that any sort of discovery space seemed likely to introduce. Because the available evidence will not permit the issues to be resolved, ideas about the appearance of Shakespeare's playhouse must remain tentative.

About the indoor *private theatres* even less is known. They were roofed, smaller, and therefore more expensive to attend than the public playhouses. Despite their name, they were open to anyone caring to pay. Initially, the private theatres attracted the most fashionable audiences of London, who came to see erudite plays performed by troupes of boy actors. As the popularity of children's troupes waned, the adult troupes that performed in the public theatres in the summer took over the private houses for their winter performances. The fact is significant because it indicates that the arrangement of the stage spaces in the theatres was probably similar.

Audience

Audience for the public theatres was like medieval ones, but more urbanized and probably more sophisticated. It did not include the poor or the very rich. It was sometimes rowdy, easily distracted. It was probably heavily male. A good part of it was educated enough to get jokes and learned allusions; most of it was fascinated by language, and so sat rapt through long soliloquies and much lyric poetry.

Private theatres supposedly attracted a more discerning and probably a more affluent audience. They sat indoors, were warmer in winter, less bothered by rain and slush. Probably mostly male, they were self-aware as embodiments of the new.

Production Practices

Both the physical arrangement of Elizabethan theatres and the medieval features of the plays argue against the use of elaborate scenery. In the theatre there were few places to hide scenery and no way of moving it on and off stage readily, and the plays moved from place to place quickly, with little or no break in the action. Small properties were therefore important, and we find stage directions for the use of ladders, chairs and tables, tapestries, a free-standing arbor, etc. The underlying conventions were clearly medieval,

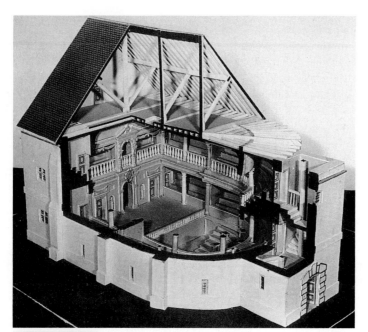

FIGURE 14.3   **Private Theatre.**
Indoors, with fewer seats, private theatres cost more to attend and so probably drew a somewhat more elite audience. Although their exact appearance is uncertain, this reconstruction by Richard Leacroft probably shows the major features of such a theatre. (From Richard Leacroft, *Theatre and Playhouse,* Methuen Publishing Limited.)

with a chair representing a throne room, for example, and an arbor, a garden. The onstage columns and the two doors also sometimes represented specific locations, thus resembling medieval mansions. On the other hand, such things as "a view of Rome" appeared on lists of properties, and so perhaps some locations were illustrated in paintings. Most of the stage platform worked like a medieval platea, serving alternately as a bedroom, a throne room, and a rampart in quick succession.

Costuming was probably more important to spectacle than scenery. Contemporary accounts mention rich fabrics in many colors. Again, the basic convention was medieval, undoubtedly emblematic, with real Elizabethan dress the basic look. Nonetheless, other periods, countries, and races were signified by individual costume pieces—a turban, a Roman breastplate—but historical accuracy was unknown.

Most actors wore contemporary dress, some of it the castoffs of patrons or wealthy friends. Actors mostly supplied their own costumes, and building up a stock would have been important to an actor; however, unusual characters—devils, angels, allegorical figures, Turks, savages—would have called for help from the theatre company. This was a society emerging from medieval ignorance of the great world, and the theatre was one place where sophisticated London saw its new knowledge in three living dimensions.

FIGURE 14.4 **Elizabethan Tragedy.**
Actors (all male) here perform *The Spanish Tragedy,* a popular revenge tragedy by Thomas Kyd. The dialogue (in balloons from the characters' mouths) suggests the story: "Alas, it is my son, Horatio;" "Murder helpe Hieronomo," "Stop her mouth."

Masks were used rarely, and then only for specific reasons—masks were no longer a major convention of theatre.

Actors and Acting

A royal official, the Master of the Revels, licensed acting companies. The license protected actors from harsh medieval laws against players ("rogues and vagabonds"). Actors in the London troupes were further protected by nominal servant status in noble households: servants "belonged" to a household and found a medieval (feudal) shelter there. Despite this status, a few actors became wealthy: Shakespeare was able to retire as a gentleman.

The troupes themselves were organized as self-governing units—*sharing companies*—whose members shared expenses, profits, and responsibilities for production. A very few members owned a part of the theatre building itself; these were called *householders.* The most valuable members of the company held a whole share in the costumes, properties, and other company possessions; lesser members owned only half or quarter shares, with their influence and income reduced accordingly. In addition, each company hired some actors and stagehands (*hirelings*), who worked for a salary rather than for a share of the profits.

The precise style of acting is unclear, but vocal power and flexibility were prized. Plays of the period offered ample opportunity to display breath control and verbal dexterity in the monologues, soliloquies, complicated figures of speech, and symmetrical and extended phrases. On the other hand, oratorical and rhetorical techniques did not seem to overpower the actors' search for naturalness. Contemporary accounts, including lines from Shakespeare's *Hamlet,* spoke of an acting style capable of moving actors and audiences alike. The goal was apparently a convincing representation of a character in action performed by an actor with a well-tuned vocal instrument.

Because all members were male, the roles of women were taken by men or young boys, many of whom were apprenticed to leading actors in the troupe. Among the actors, most specialized in certain kinds of roles (e.g., clowns, women, or heroes), and

FIGURE 14.5 Shakespearean Comedy.

A man of the theatre as well as a poet, Shakespeare offered comedies with complicated plots of love and disguise, such as *Twelfth Night*, in production here at Wake Forest University Theatre. (Directed by John Gulley; designers—Darwin Reid Payne [scenery], Mary Wayne-Thomas [costumes], and Jonathan Christman [lighting]. Photo by Bill Ray III.)

some were widely admired in Shakespeare's day: Richard Tarleton as a clown, Richard Burbage as a tragedian.

By the time that Shakespeare arrived in London about 1590, then, his was a proud and growing nation whose power wanted to be celebrated. In place in the capital was an English secular theatre with permanent buildings, professional actors, and a legitimacy based on its own identification with capital and court.

Plays and Playwrights

Added to the general well-being of the nation was the vigor of the court, the schools, and the universities, where scholars were remaking Italian humanism and classical documents with an eye to English needs and preferences. In particular, university students (the *University Wits*) were applying classical scholarship to the English public stage and laying the foundations for the vigorous theatre to come. These University Wits brought the erudition of humanistic scholarship to the English stage.

Thomas Kyd and Christopher Marlowe, in particular, broke new ground in tragedy. Both adapted techniques from Seneca. Marlowe created a "mighty line" of sonorous blank verse, the tragedy *Doctor Faustus*, and the history play *Edward the Second*. Kyd is remembered for his revenge tragedy *The Spanish Tragedy*.

Thinking About Elizabethan Theatre

To be or not to be. That is the question.
—William Shakespeare

Hamlet's famous soliloquy, from which these lines come, was traditionally staged in the theatre with the actor playing Hamlet alone on stage, delivering the lines. When fidelity to the real world became a goal of theatre, dramatic characters talking to themselves went out of fashion and so soliloquies disappeared from dramas. But a problem remains: how can soliloquies found in older plays like Shakespeare's be staged in ways that are appealing to modern audiences? Movies solve the problem of revealing inner thoughts in several ways, only some of which are possible on stage. What stage-worthy techniques can you suggest for presenting soliloquies for modern audiences?

Shakespeare (1564–1616)

Born in provincial Stratford-Upon-Avon, a day's journey from London, in 1564, Shakespeare was a middle-class boy who grew up as the nation moved from medieval to Renaissance. Not university-educated, Shakespeare nonetheless had the solid basics of village schools: Latin, the classics, the foundation of writing style. His early life appears to have included acquaintance with powerful local families; his father, although a tradesman, was a man of position in the town.

Shakespeare married a local woman but did not stay long in his hometown. By his mid-twenties, he had gone to London to take up the perilous profession of acting, putting his father's trade behind him. He took with him, however, the rural England and the English characters of his youth, which would inform his plays and his poetry for his entire life.

When, rich and famous, he retired about 1612, it was to Stratford that he returned, there to purchase a handsome house and display the gentleman's coat-of-arms his success justified.

William Shakespeare was the greatest playwright of the English-speaking world and one of the greatest dramatists of Western civilization. Between 1590 and 1613, a period now acknowledged as the greatest age of English drama, Shakespeare wrote thirty-eight plays, which for convenience are customarily divided into three types:

- History plays (those treating English history), such as *Henry IV* (Parts 1 and 2), *Henry V, Henry VI* (Parts 1, 2, and 3), *Henry VIII, Richard II,* and *Richard III*

- Tragedies, such as *Romeo and Juliet, Julius Caesar, Hamlet, King Lear, Othello, Macbeth,* and *Antony and Cleopatra*

- Comedies, ranging from popular romantic works such as *Love's Labor's Lost, As You Like It, Twelfth Night, Much Ado About Nothing,* and *A Midsummer Night's Dream* to the darker tragicomedies such as *All's Well That Ends Well* and *Measure for Measure*

Shakespeare's plays and those of his contemporaries in England (and Spain) shared more ideas and techniques of playwriting with the Middle Ages than with Greece and Rome. Important traits of Golden Age plays (including those of Shakespeare) include

- *An early point of attack.* Plays began near the beginning of the story, with the result that the audience sees the story develop onstage rather than learning about it secondhand through messengers or reporters.

- *Several lines of action (subplots).* Early in the plays, the various lines appear to be separate and independent, but as the play moves toward its resolution, the several lines gradually merge so that, by the play's end, the unity of the various lines is evident.

- *A large number and variety of incidents.* The mixing of tears and laughter is not uncommon, nor is the close juxtaposition of tender scenes of love with brawling scenes of confrontation.

- *Free use of time and place.* Action unfolds across several months or years and in several locales.

- *An unusually large number and range of characters.* Casts of thirty are common, and among the characters can be found kings and gravediggers, pedants and clowns, old people and youths, city dwellers and rustics, rich people and poor ones.

- *A language in the plays that is infinitely varied.* Within the same play are found lyric passages, elegant figures of speech, ribald slang, witty aphorisms, and pedestrian prose, all carefully chosen to enhance the play's dramatic action.

In sum, the art of Shakespeare and his contemporaries was an expansive one that filled a very large dramatic canvas with portraits of a wide cross-section of humanity engaged in acts ranging from the heroic to the mundane. The texture of the plays is rich, detailed, and allusive. Whereas classical plays such as *Oedipus Rex* had late points of attack, unity of action, and relatively few characters, locations, and incidents, Shakespeare's plays told their stories from the beginning and included many rich details in several developing lines of action, each with its own characters. Whereas classical plays adopted rather restricted patterns of time, place, and language, Shakespeare ranged freely. Whereas the power of classical tragedy rested on intensity achieved through concentration and sparseness, Shakespeare's power emerged through the wealth of detail, the range of emotion, the sweep of his vision.

With Shakespeare's death in 1616 came a decline in the quality, if not the quantity, of drama. Although many playwrights were esteemed in their own day, none has achieved the modern admiration accorded Shakespeare. Thus, the golden age of English theatre was already in decline after 1616.

Court Masques and New Conventions: Inigo Jones

Not all theatre was done in public and private playhouses. By invitation only, some individuals formed a courtly audience for plays and spectacles staged in royal and noble houses. Although both Henry VIII (Elizabeth's father) and Elizabeth had supported

FIGURE 14.6 The New Globe Theatre.

Completed in the late 1990s, the structure seeks to replicate Shakespeare's outdoor theatre. Shown here is the New Globe, exterior and interior. (Photograph of Globe interior courtesy of F. J. Hildy.)

theatrical entertainments, it was the Stuart kings who followed them, James I and Charles I, who perfected splendid court *masques.*

Stuart masques were allegorical stories designed to compliment a particular individual or occasion. Their texts were little more than pretexts for elaborate scenic displays and lavish costumes. Although the major roles and all of the comic or villainous characters were played by professionals, the courtiers themselves performed the heart of the masques, three spectacular dances. Great sums of money ensured the splendor of the entertainments; one such masque cost a staggering 21,000 pounds at a time when the average *annual* wage for a skilled worker was about 25 pounds.

Although many leading dramatists wrote masques, Ben Jonson was the most significant. Annoyed that the text assumed such a clearly secondary position to the scenery, Jonson stopped writing masques in 1631.

The star of the masques was not the playwright but the scenic designer, Inigo Jones. An Englishman by birth, Jones studied in Italy, where he learned the newest techniques of stage painting, rigging, and design. He introduced many of these into the English court when, in 1605, he staged his first masque for James I. *By the end of his career, Jones had introduced into the English courts* (but *not* into the theatres) *all the major elements of Italianate staging then developed* (see pp. 296ff.).

Stuart masques, then, have a significance that exceeds the number of persons who saw them:

- First, they were using Italianate systems of staging during the first half of the seventeenth century, at a time when the English public and private theatres still relied on scenic practices that were essentially medieval.

- Second, the close association of the masques with the monarchy, added to their expense, were major factors in the closing of theatres when a shift in power occurred.

The Closing of English Theatres

In 1642, a civil war broke out. It pitted those in favor of monarchy, courtiers, and an Anglican Church that echoed Roman Catholicism against (to oversimplify the many contentious issues to the point of caricature) those who favored Parliament, merchants, and a much simplified Anglicanism. The parliamentarians under Oliver Cromwell won, deposed the king, seized power, and closed the theatres (in part because they had been so closely associated with the monarchy). Music, however, was not banned, and so a writer of masques named William Davenant produced operas, staging them using the Italianate system. Thus were Italianate conventions of staging introduced to the English public, having by then been used at court for almost forty years.

With the closing of the theatres in 1642, an English secular theatre based loosely on medieval conventions closed as well. When English theatres reopened in 1660, England adopted the Italianate conventions already in use on the continent.

The Spanish Golden Age

During the Middle Ages, Spain's theatre had paralleled England's in important ways. Its medieval dramas had included Latin music drama, religious plays, comedies and farces, school and university plays, and even court interludes. Their staging conventions were similar; both used movable more often than fixed staging. During the transitional period from Middle to Golden Ages, small troupes of professional players toured until permanent theatres were built in Madrid in the early 1580s.

The public theatres of Spain, like the English, remained essentially medieval. The earliest permanent public theatres, The Corral del Cruz and the Corral del Principe, were both outdoor theatres with thrust stages. Audiences stood in a central yard or sat in galleries and boxes on three sides of the stage. The stages, whose backgrounds were pierced with entrances, were partially roofed (held up by two columns), were served by traps and flying machines, and featured both a discovery space and a secondary acting area above the stage. Conventions of scenery, costume, and playwriting also resembled those of England. As in England, the Spanish *court* theatres used the newer, Italian conventions. (See pp. 296ff.)

Spanish theatre differed from the English, however, in its treatment of women. Women worked as actors in the Spanish theatre, suggesting a more public role for Span-

FIGURE 14.7   Spanish Theatre.

Here, the stage of the Corral de Comedias (1628), the last remaining theatre of Spain's Golden Age. (Photograph courtesy of F. J. Hildy.)

ish women than for English. On the other hand, Spanish women who attended plays were physically segregated from men: the women sat in a special gallery opposite the stage, and that gallery had a separate entrance that was guarded, suggesting a more protected role for them. This seeming contradiction in the treatment of women in theatre probably derived at least in part from the longtime occupation of Spain by Muslims, whose cultural and religious practices distanced Spain from English (and continental) culture.

A less striking but still important difference was the location of Spanish theatres, each of which was typically set up in the yard at the center of a block of houses. An awning stretched over a part of the yard as protection against the elements. Audiences not only stood or sat in covered benches along the side of this yard or in galleries or boxes opposite the stage, but they also could rent spaces in the windows of adjoining houses.

Spain's Golden Age, however, was noted not for its theatrical practice but for its plays. During this one hundred years, Spanish playwrights wrote thousands of plays. Like medieval and contemporaneous English plays, they featured a welter of characters and events, spanned many times and places, and mixed laughter and tears. Secular tragicomedies, plays on religious subjects, cloak-and-sword plays, and farces were all popular. The earliest important playwright, Lope de Rueda, specialized in farces and religious plays. Another, Lope de Vega, may have originated the cape-and-sword plays, swashbucklers that subsequently influenced both English and French dramatists. The author of more than five hundred works, Lope de Vega is now best known for his play *Fuenteovejuna*.

The best-respected Spanish playwright of the Golden Age, however, was Pedro Calderon de la Barca, whose *Life is a Dream* epitomized the poetry and intellect of his best works. Calderon stopped writing for the stage about 1640; the theatres were closed shortly thereafter for royal mourning (1644–1649). When they reopened, the Golden Age had passed, although the public theatres remained in use into the eighteenth century.

The Golden Age theatres of England and Spain mixed medieval traditions with ones that were quite new. Far from Italy, where the Renaissance had already peaked, England and Spain maintained essentially medieval conventions of both drama and theatre (except at their courts, where Italian conventions prevailed). But there was one important difference: both could now boast a sophisticated secular drama performed by professional actors in theatres built specifically to house them. In a major departure from medieval theatrical practice, theatre was commercial rather than communal. This shift was to have far-reaching consequences.

Theatres in the East

India's Sanskrit, already the language of a small elite, had become archaic at the time of the West's middle ages; several popular languages superceded it. In many places in

India, therefore, Sanskrit theatre absorbed or was absorbed by other forms, with highly variable results. Among the most important (because still done today in southern India) is Kuttiyatam.

An integration of dance, poetry, music, story, and impersonation, Kuttiyatam performances unfold over several days and include part or all of a traditional Sanskrit play. A popular, stock figure, the Vidusaka, interprets and comments on the Sanskrit, using satire, comedy, and parody and so violates its purity that its clowning has been called obscene. Actors, family troupes of the Chakyar lineage (traceable to the tenth century), train rigorously for many years before appearing. Performances unfold in an indigenous theatre building called a *kuttambalam,* which has a square raised stage with a pillar-supported roof, a rear wall with two doors and two copper drums (for rhythmic accompaniment), and an audience that surrounds the stage on three sides. Because the *kuttambalam* is built close to a temple, the actors perform facing the deity.

Although aesthetically based on the *Natyasastra,* Kuttiyatam offers the possibility of change and adaptation, which pure Sanskrit theatre did not.

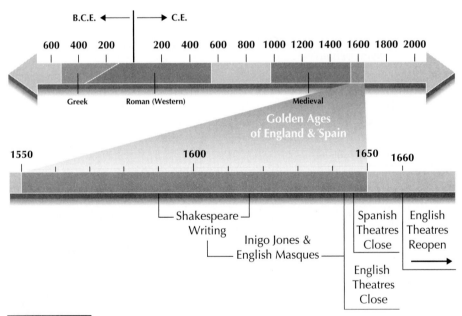

FIGURE 14.8 Timeline.

The Golden Ages of England and Spain overlapped the final years of medieval theatre, beginning roughly 1550 (when religious drama was outlawed) and ending roughly 1650, when both theatres were closed for political reasons. When English theatres re-opened in 1660, they used very different conventions.

Links to More About Theatre

Andrew Gurr, *The Shakespearean Stage, 1574–1642*, 1970.

N. D. Shergold, *A History of the Spanish Stage*, 1967.

Shakespeare in Love. Funny—with a script by a noted British playwright.

<http://web.uvic.ca/shakespeare/Library/SLTnoframes/intro/introsubj.html>
Vast amount of material on Shakespeare and his theatre. For scholarly editions and data, use only http://web.uvic.ca/shakespeare.

<www.rdg.ac.uk/globe/home.htm> Great site on The New Globe.

KEY TERMS

Check your understanding against this list. Brief definitions are in the Glossary; page references there will direct you to the appropriate pages. (Persons are page-referenced in the Index.)

discovery space	pit
galleries	private theatre
Golden Age (England, Spain)	public theatre
heavens	Renaissance
householder	sharing company
Kuttiyatam	tiring house
lords' rooms	trap
masque	yard
musicians' gallery	

Illusionism (c. 1550–1960)

The third phase of theatre's history dates from about 1550 through about 1960. Theatres during these four hundred years shared several important theatrical conventions and so can be grouped for study. Their major shared traits are

- Theatre buildings with a proscenium arch, which frames the action on stage
- Scenery and costumes that seek to create the illusion of fidelity to life outside the theatre
- A mostly commercial environment
- A mix of men and women
- A stratification of theatre

These new conventions took hold first in Italy and then spread through western Europe and its colonies, where they dominated theatre practice through much of the twentieth century. During these same four hundred years, Turkey developed an improvisational theatre, perhaps based on Byzantine mime or Italian *commedia,* and somewhat later in this period, two great forms of Eastern theatre arose: *Beijing opera* in China and *Kabuki* in Japan.

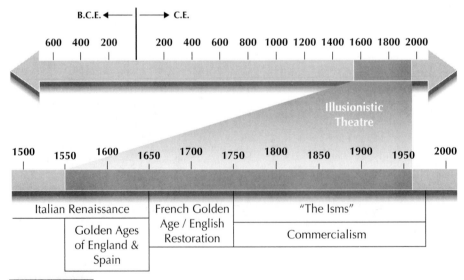

FIGURE IIIc.1

A new set of dramatic and theatrical conventions arose during Italy's Renaissance, soon spreading throughout western Europe.

The Italian Renaissance

When you have completed this chapter, you should be able to

- Define and discuss Neoclassicism, Italianate staging, and *commedia dell'arte*

- Explain how Neoclassicism departed so radically from medieval theatre

- Trace Italianate staging from Vitruvius through Serlio to Torelli

- Discuss the importance of Roman ideas and their interpretation to Renaissance theatres

Theatre in Italy

The Renaissance in Italy, unlike the same years in England and Spain, revolutionized theatre and drama. In their efforts to recapture the practices of Greece and Rome, Italian artists set theatres in Europe on a new path—a path toward *illusionism*. Theatre was thereafter to seek an illusion of real life.

Three contributions of the Italians were to have far-reaching effects:

1. The Neoclassical ideal in playwriting and criticism
2. The Italianate system of staging and architecture
3. A popular theatre known as *commedia dell'arte*

Mainstream Theatre

Theory: Neoclassicism

Neoclassicism literally means "new classicism," but in fact it was based far more heavily on Rome than on Greece. Neoclassicism, as first developed by the Italians and later adopted throughout most of western Europe, rested on five major points:

1. Verisimilitude, and the related decorum
2. Purity of genres
3. The "three unities"
4. The five-act form
5. A twofold purpose: to teach and to please

Verisimilitude. Central to Neoclassical doctrine was a complex concept called *verisimilitude*—literally, "truth seeming." But the meaning of *verisimilitude* is more involved than its facile definition might suggest, for artists have always aimed to tell the "truth." Thus, the critical problem for a student of Neoclassicism is to understand what "truth" meant to the Neoclassicist.

Truth for the Neoclassicist resided in the essential, the general, the typical, and the class rather than in the particular, the individual, and the unique. To get at truth, a Neoclassical artist had to cut away all that was temporary or accidental in favor of those qualities that were fundamental and unchanging. To be "true" meant to be usually true, generally accurate, typically the case. The humanness of one person, for example, rested in those essential qualities that he or she shared with all other people, regardless of place, century, or ethnicity. Individual differences were not important, because they were not essential to humanness. Such a view of truth placed a premium on classification and categorization, and *verisimilitude* had a meaning very different from that ascribed to it by our own age's view of the importance of individuality and uniqueness: fidelity to essences.

Neoclassical truth implied other matters as well. Verisimilitude in drama required the elimination of events that could not reasonably be expected to happen in real life.

FIGURE 15.1 Renaissance Life.
Medieval life changed as Europe moved into the Renaissance. Trading rivaled agriculture; cities rivaled manors; science challenged religion; gunpower and canons eclipsed the mounted knight. Here, a knight on horseback falls before the cannon.

Although an exception was made when ancient stories or myths incorporating supernatural events were dramatized, even then the dramatist was expected to minimize the importance of such events, perhaps by putting them offstage. Because in real life people generally talk to one another rather than to themselves, monologues and soliloquies were customarily abandoned in favor of dialogue between major characters and their *confidants* (see p. 44).

The tendency of people to behave in certain ways because of age, social rank, occupation, gender, and so forth could be observed; therefore, characters in drama were also expected to behave with the same *decorum* (that is, they were to embody the traits normally held by members of their group) or, if they did not, they would suffer ridicule or punishment for their deviations.

Finally, because it was believed that God ruled the world in accord with a divine plan and that He was a good God, verisimilitude required that dramatic actions be organized according to moral principles—so that good was rewarded and evil punished. Although in daily life good occasionally went unrewarded and evil unpunished, such observable events were believed to be aberrational and therefore unsuitable subjects for drama.

Purity of Genres.   Verisimilitude also inspired *purity of genres,* meaning that the two major forms, tragedy and comedy, must not be mixed. The injunction against mixing did not mean merely that funny scenes were improper for tragedy or that unhappy endings were inappropriate for comedy. Both tragedy and comedy were far more rigidly defined than today, and the rule against mixing the forms meant that no element belonging to the one should appear in the other. For example, *tragedy* was supposed to

FIGURE 15.2   **Italianate Staging.**
This illustration from a collection of Terence's plays not only suggests the renewed interest in Roman drama but also shows clearly the new conventions of staging that soon dominated western Europe: single-point perspective within a framed space, with an audience on only one side—the proscenium theatre. (Courtesy of Rare Books Division, New York Public Library Astor, Lenox, and Tilden Foundations.)

depict people of high station involved in affairs of state; its language was to be elevated and poetic; its endings were to be unhappy. *Comedy,* on the other hand, was supposed to display persons of the lower and middle classes embroiled in domestic difficulties and intrigues. Its language was always to be less elevated, often prosaic, and its endings were to be happy. Purity of genres meant, then, that a prose tragedy or a domestic tragedy could not exist—both were a contradiction in terms. It also meant that kings and queens could not appear in comedies, and affairs of state were not suitable subjects for comedy.

The Three Unities.   Verisimilitude and interpretations of classical examples created the Neoclassical notion of "the *three unities*"—time, place, and action. Although Aristotle had argued cogently for plays with a unified action, Neoclassical theorists were more concerned that their plays unfold within a reasonable time and a limited place, so that verisimilitude would not be strained. No audience would believe, the Neoclassical argument went, that months had passed or oceans had been crossed while the audience sat in the same place for a few hours. Theorists varied in the strictness of their requirements for unity (some argued for a single room, others for a single town; some required that the playing time of the drama equal the actual time elapsed, others that no more than twenty-four hours elapse). Most Italian theorists accepted some version of the three unities after about 1570.

Five-Act Play.   By then, as well, Neoclassicists had adopted the five-act play as standard for drama, a norm probably derived from the theories of Horace and the practices of Seneca (five sections separated by choruses), although neither had used the "act" as a dramatic unit.

Purposes of Drama.   The Neoclassicists found a justification for drama and theatre in their ability to teach morality while entertaining an audience. To teach and to please were defined as the dual purposes of drama, and playwrights took care that their plays did both. The idea of a drama's existing only for its own sake or as an expression of an individual artist was not accepted.

By 1600, Neoclassical ideals were being accepted in other parts of Europe. They remained dominant for the next two hundred years among educated and courtly audiences. Neoclassicism's propriety and concentration may account for its lack of appeal to many people, who sought more spectacle than the three unities permitted. Thus, despite the acceptance of Neoclassicism as an ideal, its tenets were undercut in a variety of ways—by spectacle, for example.

Physical Theatre: Illusionism

The Italianate theatre and its system of staging, like Neoclassicism itself, developed as a mixture of ideas and techniques from ancient Greece, Rome, and contemporary Italy. Most important from the ancients was the work of Vitruvius (see p. 244).

Vitruvius in the Renaissance. Early in Italy's Renaissance, Vitruvius's Roman work on architecture, which had existed only in manuscripts, was printed. By 1500, it was the acknowledged authority in the field, and interpretations and commentaries in Italian followed. Although he had written about architecture and scenery, Vitruvius had provided no illustrations. As a result, the Italians translated him and provided illustrations in terms of their practices, most notably a fascination with *linear perspective*— a means of representing spatial depth (three dimensions) on a two-dimensional surface. On the stage, perspective became a means of representing greater depth than in fact existed.

Perspective. Although known to the Romans, *perspective*, when re-discovered by Italian painters, caused an artistic revolution. Artists worked to master the "new" technique, and spectators hailed its ability to trick the senses. The "vanishing point," to which objects receded away from the viewer, became, in stage design, the key to false, or forced, perspective, through which a stage depth of thirty feet could be made to seem three hundred. On the stage, achieving this sense of depth often meant actually constructing three-dimensional objects (usually buildings) in false perspective. An actor—whose real size could not be changed—would dwarf the upstage buildings if he appeared up there, and so acting took place in front of the scenery.

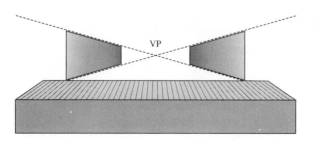

FIGURE 15.3 **Perspective.**
Behind the Renaissance forestage, a vanishing point (VP) was the apparent meeting place of lines (dotted) that, by defining the tops and bottoms of "returns" (scenic faces at angles to the front of the stage), created an illusion of greater depth than the actual theatre offered. Look again at Figure 15.2.

In 1545 an Italian, Sebastiano Serlio, published *Dell'Architectura,* an interpretation of Vitruvius that dominated theatre architecture and design for the next century. Vitruvius, of course, had described the circular, outdoor Roman theatre. But wealthy Italians wanted plays done indoors in wealthy homes. Thus, when the first indoor theatres were designed, the task was to adapt Vitruvius to rectangular spaces and to accommodate them to linear perspective.

An early solution was the *Teatro Olimpico,* which had five onstage doorways (corresponding to Vitruvius's five stage openings), but with a vista in perspective constructed behind each doorway (and each with its own vanishing point). This early solution used a Roman façade and doorways, and it satisfied the Italian demand for perspective. Its multiple vanishing points satisfied its patrons, a wealthy gentlemen's academy: With five vanishing points, there were five "perfect" places to sit.

Later theatres used a proscenium arch that framed and separated the false perspective. Some had other arches farther upstage, each increasing the illusion of depth. In such theatres, a single vanishing point meant only one "perfect" place to sit.

Production Practices: Illusionism

Vitruvius' scanty descriptions of tragic, comic, and satyric scenes became, in Serlio's books, detailed illustrations in false perspective. A brief comparison of Vitruvius and Serlio will show their differences.

Of the satyric scene, Vitruvius said, "Satyric scenes are decorated with trees, caverns, mountains, and other rustic objects delineated in landscaped style." Of the same scenes, Serlio (as early translated into English) said, "The Satiricall Scenes are to Represent Satirs,

FIGURE 15.4 **Teatro Olimpico.**
The Teatro Olimpico was an early compromise between a Roman façade stage and the Renaissance passion for perspective. Each of five doors (two shown here) framed a three-dimensional vista in false perspective, giving each member of the audience a view down at least one.

FIGURE 15.5 Teatro Farnese.

The Teatro Farnese offered a different compromise between a Roman theatre and emerging Italianate architectural conventions. A Roman-style semi-circular seating area was shoe-horned inside a rectangular building, and the elaborate façade of Roman theatres appeared to the sides of a new proscenium arch. The scale of the building is grand, in the manner of Roman outdoor theatres, as the human figures suggest.

FIGURE 15.6   Serlio.

Combining Vitruvius's writings on the Roman theatre with the Renaissance interest in perspective, Serlio created his own ideal scenery for tragedy, comedy, and pastoral (satyric). (Courtesy of Rare Books and Special Collections, Bowling Green State University.)

wherein you must place all those things that be rude and rusticall." He then went on to quote Vitruvius as calling for "Trees, Rootes, Herbs, Hils, and Flowers, and with some countrey houses. . . . And for that in our dayes these things were made in Winter, where there were but fewe greene Trees, Herbs, and Flowers to be found; then you must make these things of Silke, which will be more commendable than the naturall things themselves."

In the remainder of his book, Serlio provided tips on the use of colored lights, fire effects, fanciful costumes, and the use of pasteboard figures in a perspective setting. Serlio's scenography was thus the basis for what we now call *Italianate staging*.

Italianate Staging.   With certain modifications related to place and date, Italianate settings throughout Europe shared the following features during the sixteenth, seventeenth, and early eighteenth centuries:

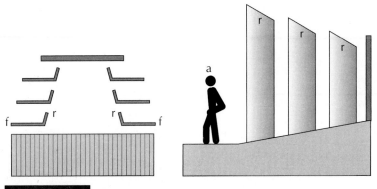

Serlio's Theatre.
Serlio's settings were meant to emphasize depth through false perspective.
Pairs of flats with angled returns (f, r) receded toward a common vanishing
point. The stage floor was raked (angled) upward to accommodate the false
perspective line of the bottoms of the returns. Actors (a) worked in front of
the scenery rather than in it, where they would have destroyed the illusion,
because as the scenery seemed to shrink, the actor would not have done so.

1. Scenery painted in *single-point perspective* (all objects recede to the same vanishing point), as calculated from one seat toward the back of the orchestra (usually the seat of the most important noble or patron)

2. Scenery consisting of *wings*, which were paired flats (wooden frames covered with fabric and painted), each pair closer together as they were farther from the audience, so that the lines of the inner edges of the flats receded toward the vanishing point. The setting culminated upstage in a *backdrop* or a *shutter*, a pair of wings pushed together. Shutters could be opened to reveal even deeper perspective space, or pierced to make a *relieve* through which greater depth was glimpsed

3. Scenery placed behind both a *proscenium arch* and the actors, forming a background rather than an environment to surround them

4. A *raked stage*, slanted upward from front to back to increase the sense of depth. Sometimes only the stage behind the proscenium arch was raked, sometimes the entire stage, causing the actors to climb or descend (hence our terms "upstage" and "downstage")

5. Machinery and rigging hidden overhead by *borders*, framed or unframed fabric painted like sky, clouds, leaves, and so on

Movable Scenery: Torelli.　Having developed this system, Italian artists set about almost at once to give it movement, to shift scenery, and to allow rapid changes of place. The most effective system was shown in 1645 when Giacomo Torelli astonished audiences with fluid, fast, apparently magical changes. The secret was his *chariot-and-pole* system. Small wheeled wagons ran on tracks under the stage, each with a pole that extended

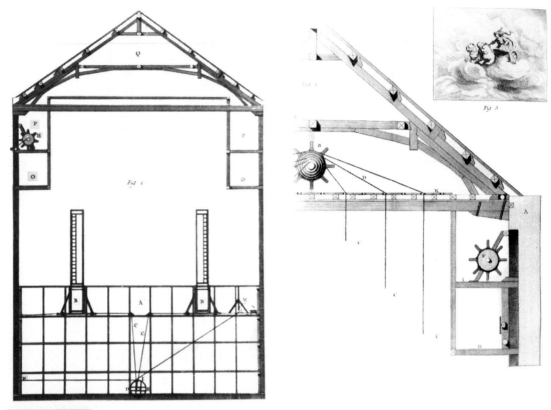

FIGURE 15.8   Special Effects Machines.

Renaissance theatres moved scenery by means of a system of the sort first devised by Torelli. By linking several winches, the chariot-and-pole system could move scenes at the same time that the clouds and cloud machines moved. (From Diderot's *Encyclopédie*, courtesy of Rare Books and Special Collections, Bowling Green State University.)

through a slit in the stage high enough to support a flat. The idea was elegant and simple: As the chariots moved, so the flats moved; pulling a chariot toward the center brought a flat into view; pulling the chariot away from the center caused a flat to disappear. With the chariots harnessed by ropes and pulleys to the same winch, stage mechanics could turn one wheel to change an entire setting. Torelli—no stranger to self-promotion—earned the title "The Great Wizard" by coordinating these changes with special effects (flying, lightning, explosions).

Contradiction in Mainstream Theatre

A contradiction clearly existed between the ideals of theory—the unities of time, place, and action, and an avoidance of the supernatural—and the ideals of scenic design, whose artists increasingly emphasized rapid change of place and spectacle. This tension was resolved by keeping an austere style for Neoclassical plays while expending creativity and money on operas, ballets, and lavish *intermezzi* (entertainments given between the acts of a Neoclassical play)—a way of having cake and eating it at the same time.

By the mid-seventeenth century, Italian opera had become the most popular (and spectacular) form of entertainment in Italy. As it was exported to the rest of Europe, so were its scenic techniques. (In London, remember, Davenant had staged *operas* after the theatres were closed in 1642; even in English, the word probably signified as much about scenery as it did about music.)

An Alternative Theatre: Commedia dell'Arte

Neoclassical dramas and elaborately staged operas were primarily the entertainment of the noble, the wealthy, and the educated. Among other classes, another, very different kind of dramatic entertainment flourished in Italy: the *commedia dell'arte* ("professional playing"). Although neither the origins nor the sources of *commedia* are well understood, its major characteristics were well established by 1550, and Italian troupes were touring western Europe by 1600.

Commedia players—both male and female—worked from a basic story outline (*scenario*) within which they improvised much of their dialogue and action. Each actor in the troupe played the same stock character in almost every scenario and therefore wore the same costume and mask, reused the same bits of comic business (*lazzi*), and even repeated some of the same dialogue from scenario to scenario. Most troupes had ten or twelve members; each troupe had one or two sets of young lovers (*innamorati*) and a number of comic "masks" (characters)—Capitano (the captain), Pantalone (the merchant), Dottore (the doctor), and several *zanni* (servants) like Arlecchino (Harlequin), Brighella, Scaramuccio, and Pulcinello. Male actors outnumbered female. Both mask and costume became traditional for each character (except the lovers, who wore no mask).

Organized as sharing companies, such troupes toured constantly as they tried to scratch out a living without the protection or the financial support of noble houses. Although the influence of *commedia* extended throughout Europe, its ephemeral nature militated against its leaving a lasting record (especially scripts), although this popular Italian comedy has been revived and imitated in many more recent cultures.

Thinking About Commedia

The avant-garde director and playwright Alfred Jarry (1873–1907) said that an actor *"should use a mask to envelop the head, thus replacing it by the effigy of the CHARACTER."* Invent a modern set of *commedia* characters for a contemporary acting troupe of four. They should represent common types today (e.g., nerd, politician). After naming each character, sketch (or describe carefully) their costumes and masks: What traits should go with the type? What nose? Hairstyle? Eyes and mouth? Color and cut of fabric, etc.?

FIGURE 15.9 **Commedia dell'Arte.**

Pulliciniello.   Sig.ª Lucretia.

Troupes had both males and females, masked and unmasked characters. Shown here, Lucretia, one of the female lovers (unmasked) and one of the most popular masked characters, a servant.

Italy: Eclipse

Despite Italy's unquestioned leadership in dramatic theory and scenic display, and in spite of its unique popular comedy, by 1750, except for opera, Italy was no longer a world leader in theatre. Both England and France had outstripped their teacher and had attained an international reputation by the end of the seventeenth century, and both achieved a lasting acclaim never given the Italians, from whom they drew.

Theatres in the East

With the appearance of the prophet Muhammed in the late sixth century C.E., a new religion, Islam, spread rapidly from the Arabian peninsula: north into the Near East; west along all of Mediterranean African and down the East African coast; and east into India and Southeast Asia. For complex reasons, the world of Islam was hostile to theatre (although not to storytelling, puppetry, and dance). As well, it drastically limited the public life of women, including their appearance on the stage.

Islamic peoples developed a highly sophisticated literature, especially in Persian and Arabic, along with other arts; theatre, however, was largely ignored until the nineteenth century. Turkey was an exception.

The Seljuk Turks, who were Muslim but not Arabic, conquered what was left of the Byzantine Empire, taking Constantinople in 1453. After centuries of spasmodic war, the Turks soon occupied parts of modern Romania, Bulgaria, Greece, Turkey, and the eastern Mediterranean coast. They thus became the last heirs of what was left of Rome in the East—and perhaps of its theatre.

This Turkish empire had a popular theatre, a comic form called *orta oyunu* that persisted into the twentieth century, disappearing after World War I. Although its origins

Links to More About Theatre

Pierre Louis Duchartre, *The Italian Comedy: The Improvisation, Scenarios, Lives* . . . 1966. Lavish and fascinating.

Scaramouche. Old but fun.

are unknown, some scholars suggest that it may have been a continuation of Byzantine mime.

Orta oyunu was performed by traveling troupes that included actors, dancers, and musicians. At the head of each was an actor who played Pisekar, the central figure; opposite him was Kavuklu, his comic foil. Men played women's roles, as was true in most medieval theatres then dominating northern Europe. Playing usually in the open with-

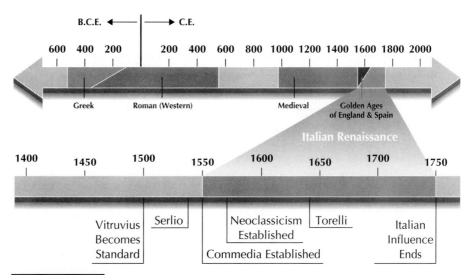

FIGURE 15.10   Timeline.

The Italian Renaissance began about one hundred years before the Golden Ages of Spain and England. By c. 1550 (when religious drama was being outlawed), Neoclassicism, Italianate staging, and *commedia* were already established. Italy's theatrical influence had evaporated by 1750, but Italy continued to dominate opera.

out scenery, the actors relied on mimicry, comic exaggeration, and comic business and gesture. The performance was popular in subject and language and was free of formal theatre structures, using only an open space with a tent or cloth enclosure. Much of the form's popularity came from the use of the same characters over many years, even many generations.

Orta oyunu thus shared several traits with *commedia dell'arte*—comic regional types, improvisation, stock costumes, and characters. These similarities may suggest a common root (Byzantine mime or Roman farces so popular at the turn to the Common era) or they may be simple coincidence. Whatever its origin, orta oyunu did not survive the modernization of Turkey after World War I.

In the fifteenth century, too, Japan was developing a strong and lasting comic theatre, *Kyogen*. An offshoot of Noh, Kyogen is performed between the dramas of a Noh cycle, which seems a contradiction, for Kyogen mocks the very austerity and aristocratic spirituality that make Noh what it is. The reason usually given for Kyogen's placement within Noh is this: Commoners wrote Kyogen at a time when they were attending Noh performances, and Kyogen expressed their attitudes. Kyogen is funny, dealing with the universals of comedy. Its most typical character is a comic servant who serves a feudal lord and is, of course, smarter than he. Although Kyogen used a Noh stage, it used neither its orchestra nor its chorus.

KEY TERMS

Check your understanding against this list. Brief definitions are in the Glossary; page references there will direct you to the appropriate pages. (Persons are page-referenced in the Index.)

border	perspective
chariot and pole	purity of genres
comedy	raked stage
commedia dell'arte	scenario
confidant	shutter (backdrop)
decorum	single-point perspective
illusionism	three unities
Italianate staging	tragedy
Kyogen	verisimilitude
lazzi	wings

The Triumph and Decline of Neoclassicism

When you have completed this chapter, you should be able to

- Explain the significance of the production of *Le Cid*

- Discuss the different performances likely to be seen in the public and the court theatres of France

- Sketch events leading to the formation of the *Comédie Française*

- Explain how sentimentalism affected French drama and theatre

- Discuss the relationship between French theatre and English Restoration theatre

- Describe the major conventions of English Restoration theatre

- Name major kinds of drama existing during the English Restoration

- Suggest how changes in English law facilitated the beginnings of English-speaking theatre in the American colonies

French Theatre from Its Beginnings through Its Golden Age

The ideas and practices of the Italian Renaissance reached France early, but France, being politically unstable, had little energy for developing a strong secular theatre. Its early steps were therefore tentative. Through the early 1600s, its practices remained essentially medieval. Farces performed by traveling actors were the mainstay of a scattered French theatre, and its audiences were famous for their unruliness. At about the time of Shakespeare, the first notable (and extremely prolific) French playwright appeared, Aléxandre Hardy, whose plays resembled those of England's and Spain's Golden Ages (many characters and sprawling actions). Like those of his contemporaries, Hardy's plays used simultaneous settings and emblematic costumes. Although his audiences were more genteel than those of the earlier farces and included women as well as some people from the court, his theatre was still a pretty rough place.

FIGURE 16.1 French Theatre in the early 1600s.
French theatre remained mostly emblematic and simultaneous, with scenery still scattered rather than gathered in one place.

With increasing political stability, Paris became France's theatrical center. The first professional acting troupe established itself there permanently in 1625. Its theatre was the Hotel de Bourgogne, a space built seventy-five years earlier for the production of religious plays (just as they were being banned). When rival professionals began to settle in Paris, however, they chose indoor tennis courts for their theatres. Long and narrow, these roofed buildings had seats along one side and a covered structure at one end—the rest was open. A theatre converted from a tennis court thus had a long, narrow auditorium with a small stage at one end, probably with an upper level (as in both London and Madrid) and some sort of "inner stage" below. Usually, shallow boxes were set along both sides of the auditorium with bleacher-like seats at the end opposite the stage. Between the bleacher-like seats and the stage were benches. The resulting theatres were small and intimate, holding six or seven hundred people. Staging conventions remained basically medieval.

Thus, at a time when the English and Spanish theatres were well into their Golden Ages and Italian theatre was revolutionizing theory and scenery, the French theatre was only just establishing itself.

By the 1630s, however, French theatre and its audience were sufficiently important to make them a focus of government interest. Because the French court of the time was closely linked by marriage and policy to Italy, Italian practices became the model for France, in theatre as elsewhere. In theatre, Italian practice meant promoting Neoclassicism and Italianate staging.

FIGURE 16.2 Italian Influence on French Theatre.

By the 1630s, Italian conventions encroached on French practice: notice the backdrop in single-point perspective and the placement of scenic pieces. But some medieval influence was still visible, as shown by the simultaneous representation of different places, stage right and stage left.

A number of well-educated men began to write for the theatre. Chief among them was Pierre Corneille, whose play *Le Cid* (1636) marked a turning point. Based on a Spanish play of the Golden Age, *Le Cid* was reshaped by Corneille to bring it closer to Neoclassical ideas but not into strict conformity with them: The original six acts were reduced to five; its several years were compressed into a single day; the many locales were squeezed into a single town. Still, the play had a happy ending, and its numerous incidents strained Neoclassical verisimilitude. The recently formed French Academy—itself an example of aggressive Neoclassicism, a literary society supported by those in power—praised *Le Cid* where it conformed to the rules but condemned it where it strayed. French playwrights, including Corneille, got the message: Critical acclaim (and approval from those in political, financial, and social power) would come from lining up with Neoclassicism. After 1636, Neoclassicism would dominate French drama for more than a hundred years. In 1641, the first Italianate theatre was built in Paris. Giacomo Torelli (see pp. 298ff.) was brought to Paris in 1645 to install a chariot-and-pole system. His productions marked the acceptance of all Italianate scenic practices in Paris: almost immediately, the tennis-court (public) theatres had to adapt or die; they installed some form of Italianate scenery. Thereafter, simple Neoclassical settings competed with lavish operas, ballets, and *machine plays,* plays written specifically to exploit the new scenery.

Italian theory and staging played out differently in France, however. The triumph of Neoclassicism was manifest primarily in the French *public* theatres, where a distinct French style of drama developed, one both austere and terse. The triumph of Italianate staging, on the other hand, found its fullest expression in the *court* theatres, where plays from the public theatres were restaged with ballet interludes, movable scenery, and gorgeous costumes, and where king and courtiers played heroes of romance and mythology in purpose-written entertainments that moved out into parks and gardens, sometimes with mock tournaments and battles. Italianate scenery in the public theatres was more modest but shared the basic visual conventions of the court.

Both the court and the public theatres reached their peak during the reign of Louis XIV, a king who drew power to himself as the sun attracts the planets. Calling himself "The Sun King," Louis XIV declared, "I am the state," and he believed it. Absolute power, ego, and show were summed up in the word *gloire,* which carried over from war into theatre; it also extended to the building of great follies, such as Louis's palace at Versailles, where he surrounded himself with France's nobility. When Versailles opened, the court withdrew from Paris. Louis pursued an aggressive campaign of national self-display, not only through military adventures but also through the arts, including theatre.

Theatres benefited. They got both royal subsidy and royal patronage, but not enough to survive without public support, and so they were sometimes in the position of serving two masters at once. Their position became even more complex when, with the opening of Versailles, the court moved there, leaving the public still in Paris. Still, this robust theatre played for court and public, men and women. (Favored male audience members even sat on the stage.) At its best, this theatre offered great variety and superb quality, satisfying an audience that became the most demanding and sophisticated in Europe—and which replaced Italy's as the model for Europe.

FIGURE 16.3 Italianate Scenery in France.

In 1642, encouraged by Cardinal Richelieu, a French court theatre attempted this Italianate production of *Mirame*. It was a precursor of the magic of Torelli.

In addition to the continuing dominance of Neoclassicism and enthusiasm for Italianate staging, the pinnacle of French theatre meant

- The emergence of two great playwrights to join Corneille
- The expansion to five permanent professional theatres in Paris, later reduced to three, with strict government control through monopolies

Although Pierre Corneille continued writing, his fame was eclipsed by that of Jean Racine. Born three years after the first production of *Le Cid*, Racine was educated by Jansenists, a Catholic sect with an overriding preoccupation with sin and guilt, concerns that permeated Racine's major plays. Trained in the classics, Racine based his only comedy, *The Litigants*, on Aristophanes' comedy *The Wasps*, and his most esteemed tragedy, *Phèdre* (*Phaedra*), on Euripides' *Hippolytus*.

Phèdre is a model of Neoclassicsm. Because the play's major conflicts occur within the character Phèdre, the Neoclassical requirements for unity are easily accommodated; and because Phèdre's passion leads to her downfall, Neoclassical commitment to the punishment of evil is satisfied. *Phèdre*, unlike *Le Cid*, is Neoclassical through and through, and its achievement in plot, character, and diction placed it among the masterpieces of dramatic literature. France had accomplished what England would not: lasting and popular drama based on Neoclassical theory.

The **Story** of the **Play**

Jean Racine, *Phaedra* (*Phèdre*), 1677

In Troezen, Hippolytus, son of Theseus, the king of Athens, is about to set out to look for his long-absent father; he confesses he is doing so partly to avoid Aricia, whom he loves despite "glorying in his chastity."

Phaedra, Theseus' wife and Hippolytus' stepmother, is said to be "dying in her nurse's arms." She appears—weak, distraught—but the mention of Hippolytus rouses her, clearly causing pain. She confesses to her nurse, Oenone, that she loves him and is dying of that love.

Word comes that Theseus is dead. Phaedra can now confess her love to Hippolytus; however, his thoughts are of Aricia, whom he tells he will support as a claimant to the Athenian throne. Phaedra tells Hippolytus she loves him, begs him to kill her.

However, Theseus suddenly returns; the rumor of his death is wrong. Phaedra is guilt-stricken, horrified, frightened, but her nurse advises her to protect herself by accusing Hippolytus of having tried to seduce her. Given permission by the frantic Phaedra, the nurse then does so; Theseus confronts his son, who refuses, as a matter of honor, to tell his father the truth about Phaedra. Theseus asks Neptune to avenge him on Hippolytus.

Phaedra learns that Hippolytus loves Aricia and rages. Hippolytus and Aricia vow to marry and to flee.

Hippolytus rides off alone in his chariot. A messenger brings the news that Neptune has sent a monster from the ocean that so terrified Hippolytus's horses that they have dragged him to his death.

The nurse drowns herself. Phaedra commits suicide.

French comedy found its genius in the actor-dramatist Molière. At about the time that theatres were closing in England, Molière was leaving home to join a traveling theatrical troupe in France. By 1660, he was head of the troupe, wrote most of its plays, and had firmly established it as a favorite of Louis XIV. Perhaps the greatest comic writer of all times, Molière used his own experiences as an actor as well as his knowledge of Roman comedy, Italian *commedia,* and French farce to create comedies that ridiculed social and moral pretentiousness.

Molière's comedy typically depicts characters made ludicrous by their deviations from decorum. Although his dialogue is often clever, verbal elegance and wit for their own sake do not form the core of his plays; instead, the comedies depend heavily on farcical business (such as *commedia's lazzi*) and visual gags. Of his more than twenty plays, the best known are probably *Tartuffe, The Miser,* and *The Imaginary Invalid,* whose

The Story of the Play

Molière, *Tartuffe*, 1669

Orgon, a well-to-do bourgeois, has made a religious zealot, Tartuffe, a pampered guest in his house. Orgon is obsessed by Tartuffe—will hear no wrong of him, cannot do enough for him—despite Tartuffe's being despised as a hypocrite by Orgon's brother, Cléante; his wife, Elmire; his son, Damis; and the witty servant, Dorine. Cléante pleads that Orgon use moderation and restraint, but Orgon is unmovable. Orgon tells his daughter, Mariane, that he wants her to marry Tartuffe, but Mariane loves Valère and is disgusted by Orgon.

Tartuffe tries to make love to Elmire; he is overheard by Damis, who tries to expose him to Orgon. Tartuffe turns the accusation upside-down by saying he is too humble and too pious to defend himself. Orgon turns against his son and throws him out of the house, swearing he will strike him out of his will and make Tartuffe his sole heir. He urges Tartuffe to be with Elmire constantly to show Orgon's faith in him.

Elmire, disgusted, tells Orgon that until then she had passed off men's advances as something a wife dealt with herself, but his actions toward Damis are too much: she will show him the truth about Tartuffe. She hides Orgon under a table, then calls Tartuffe into the room and pretends to welcome his advances. Tartuffe is eager, lustful; he wants "tangible proof" of her feelings. Elmire coughs to get Orgon's attention, but he doesn't come out from under the table. She asks about Tartuffe's piety; he tells her that he can "remove Heaven's scruples" about adultery. She keeps coughing. Finally, unable to get Orgon to come out, she sends Tartuffe to make sure nobody is nearby, then all but pulls Orgon out. He is stunned. Elmire is sarcastic: "What, coming out so soon? Why don't you wait until the climax?"

Orgon, his obsession ended, confronts Tartuffe and tells him to leave the house, but Tartuffe instead orders Orgon and the family out: Tartuffe owns the house through Orgon's deed of gift. Worse, Tartuffe has private papers that Orgon entrusted to him that can ruin Orgon with the government.

A process server arrives, threatening Orgon's arrest. The police follow, but they arrest Tartuffe instead—the king knows the truth of Tartuffe's hypocrisy and is just.

leading role Molière was playing when he was stricken. Denied last rites by the Church because he was an actor, he was granted Christian burial only through the direct intervention of Louis XIV.

By 1660, there were five permanent, professional troupes in Paris, including Molière's, a *commedia* troupe from Italy, and the opera, music, and dance troupe headed by Jean-Baptiste Lully. All were sharing companies and *all included women*.

France had no householders—actors who, in England, owned parts of the theatre building. Only the most talented actors settled in Paris as members of these troupes; the rest still toured.

Within fifteen years, however, government control and a tendency toward centralization affected the acting companies. With Molière's death, his troupe was joined with two others to form the *Comédie Française,* which became France's national theatre. Membership in this sharing company was fixed; therefore, new members could not be elected until others had retired or died. Because of its financial rewards, including a substantial pension for retired members, the list of applicants was long.

The *Comédie Française* was granted a monopoly on the (legal) performance of tragedies and comedies in Paris. Lully's company held a monopoly on musical entertainments and spectacles. The Italian troupe—after a short banishment for a political indiscretion—got exclusive rights to what came to be called comic operas. Thus, less than a century after the free-wheeling days of the first professionals, French theatre was rigidly structured, with three legal troupes that were expected to continue their traditions, not to initiate the new. The result was a highly polished but conservative theatre—and the suppression of competition.

The life of French actors, even those settled in Paris, was not easy. Some troupes were granted royal subsidies, and the king tried to improve their reputation and social acceptability by royal edict. Nonetheless, French actors were denied civic and religious rights throughout most of the seventeenth and eighteenth centuries, a situation that led many actors to adopt pseudonyms (e.g., Molière) in order to spare their families.

Acting style was formal, more concerned with fidelity to theatrical tradition than to everyday life. Great emphasis was placed on vocal skill, necessary in part because of the highly poetic, even rhetorical quality of the plays. Actors were conservative in their approach to their craft. They apprenticed or hired into a company and learned to act from other actors, whom they sought to emulate. Once trained, they tended to specialize in

Thinking About **French Neoclassicism**

"As the function of a comedy is to represent in general all men's failings, and principally those of our contemporaries, it's impossible for Molière to create any character which doesn't suggest someone in our society; and if he is to be accused of having in mind all the people who may have the failings he indicates, he'll certainly have to give up writing plays."

—Brécourt in *The Versailles Impromptu,* by Molière

Evaluate this statement in light of Neoclassical views of comedy. How well do these views describe contemporary comedies that appear on stage, screen, or television? How sympathetic are you personally to Brécourt's position?

FIGURE 16.4   **French Actors.**

An artist's imagined view of all major comic actors through the time of Louis XIV. Included are Molière (*far left*), several characters from commedia, and some of the early farceurs (for example, Gros Guillaume—Fat Willy—*center back*).

a limited range of roles throughout their career, a trend that became more pronounced with time.

By the early 1700s, French acting was highly conventionalized and growing still more conservative. As the eighteenth century moved toward 1750, some new kinds of plays began to appear, their traits seemingly driven by two forces: a changing set of moral values and a reaction against Neoclassical dramaturgy.

As Louis became both more conservative and more religious with advancing age, the whole culture shifted toward conservativism, adopting a set of values now called *sentimentalism*. According to this view of the world, each individual is basically good. This doctrine contrasted with the previous, Neoclassical, view that human existence was a continuing struggle between good and evil. According to the sentimentalist, evil came about through corruption; it was not part of human nature at birth. Sentimentalism thus implied that, although people might not be perfect, they were perfectible. Literature should therefore show virtuous people acting virtuously in their daily lives. Heroic behavior and ethical perfection need not be restricted to some idealized world of pastoral poetry or exotic tragedy.

Sentimentalism affected both serious dramas and comedies. Voltaire tried to introduce Shakespearean features to the French plays, including more spectacle and wider-ranging subject matters, but his efforts were mostly frustrated. (Shakespeare remained almost unknown on the French stage until the 1800s.) Molière's ideal of social sanity as a basis of comedy was replaced by virtue, and audiences wept at comedies as much as they laughed.

Design likewise began to change. Although the basic conventions of costume remained unchanged (contemporary rather than historical), the costumes themselves were prettified and sentimentalized, even in *commedia.* In scenery, the introduction of *angle perspective* (moving the vanishing point away from the center and toward the side) and of multiple vanishing points not only allowed actors to work closer to the scenery but also increased the number of "perfect" seats in the audience, suggesting the acceptance of more than one perception or "truth." But, in a contrary trend, the new preference for monumental interiors that disappeared overhead, indicating palaces that dwarfed the human beings who occupied them, was a probably unconscious reflection of the still powerful French court and French government.

Acting, too, grew ever more conservative. The earlier tendency of actors to specialize in certain kinds of roles became gradually more rigid until, by 1750, clearly defined *lines of business* emerged. New actors or actresses were hired as *utility players* and gained their experience by playing a great number of small and varied roles. They then declared

Scena della Festa Teatrale in occasione degli Sponsali del Principe Elettorale di Baviera.

FIGURE 16.5 **Angle Perspective.**
Moving the vanishing point to the sides changed the relationship between actor and scenery. The scale of the setting also changed, seeming to dwarf actors as never before. (Collections of the New York Public Library, Astor, Lenox, and Tilden Foundations.)

a specialty in a specific kind of role: a "walking" lady or gentleman (third line); a specialist in low comedy, or "stage eccentric" (second line); or a hero or heroine (first line). Once committed to a particular line of business, actors did not stray far from it, regardless of age.

Along with lines of business came a practice known as *possession of parts,* an agreement that an actor who played a role in the company possessed that role for as long as he or she remained in the company. Both practices placed a premium on tradition—and, often, on age—and inhibited innovation.

Acting style depended heavily on vocal power and versatility and on formality and elegance rather than "truth to life." For example, some actors apparently intoned or chanted the poetic and lyrical passages of tragedies, much as the recitative of opera is delivered today, and many actors played for *points,* expecting to receive applause for passages particularly well delivered (in which case, the actor might repeat the passage).

With no outlet for the talents of the many actors and writers who did not get into the *Comédie Française,* and with dwindling enthusiasm for Neoclassicism, French men and women began to work in illegal theatres—that is, theatres other than the monopolies. Joining jugglers, dancers, and others who had worked at fairs for centuries, theatrical troupes began to play outside the law, practicing all kinds of tricks to avoid open conflict with the monopolies. From the experiments of these "illegitimate" theatres came a robust alternative to the government theatres—a theatre that was strictly commercial, one supported by a paying audience. Housed in the fairs (it would move to the boulevards in the next century), this theatre aimed to be entertaining and to attract the largest number of spectators possible, their money paying the actors and providing the spectacle.

English Restoration Theatre and Beyond (1660–c. 1750)

We left the English theatre at the moment when another Stuart king was being restored to the throne (1660), hence the name of the period—the Restoration. During the years that the English theatre had been closed, William Davenant had produced his few "operas," introducing Italianate staging to the English public for the first time. (It had long been in the court, remember.)

With the return of king and court from France, English theatres reopened in 1660. Their model, however, was not the theatre of Shakespeare's London; it was now the theatre of Paris. The English theatre now included such French traits as

- Women actors, who quickly assumed all female roles except witches and comic old women, which continued to be played by men (as in Molière's company). The presence of women on stage encouraged, fairly or not, the risqué reputation of Restoration theatre.
- Conventions of Italianate staging
- Newly designed theatre buildings that met the needs of Italianate staging

■ New, French-inspired producing arrangements. The king granted two monopoly patents, one to Davenant and another to Thomas Killigrew, thus limiting London to only two "legitimate" theatres. Although often challenged, these patents were re-affirmed through most of the 1700s.

When theatres first reopened in 1660, they used either old theatre buildings that still stood, or they adapted tennis courts, as in France. As new theatres were built, however, they blended Shakespearean and French features. The auditorium was divided into box, pit (now with benches), and gallery. Favored audience members now sat on the stage it-self, as in France. The stage itself comprised both a proscenium arch with a raked stage behind it and a forestage that thrust into the pit. Most scenery was located behind the proscenium arch, where grooves were installed to facilitate scene changes, but most acting took place on the forestage, which was roughly the size of the area behind the proscenium. Early Restoration playhouses were intimate, with as little as thirty feet from forestage to rear boxes.

Staging conventions were Italian by way of France. Wings, borders, and shutters formed stock sets appropriate for comedies, tragedies, and pastorals. For costumes,

FIGURE 16.6 **English Restoration Theatre.**
This conjectural reconstruction shows a deep forestage, a proscenium arch, and scenery in single-point perspective, perhaps an attempt to combine earlier Shakespearean practice with contemporaneous Italianate conventions. (From Richard Leacroft, *Theatre and Playhouse*, Methuen Publishing Limited.)

most actors wore a sumptuous version of contemporary fashion. Acting depended heavily on vocal power and versatility and on formality and elegance rather than "truth to life." Lines of business and possession of parts determined which actors played which roles, contributing in England as in France to an increasingly conservative style of acting. Lighting was still by candle, and so audience and actors were equally visible.

Dramas of the Restoration likewise showed French influence. Plays written during the age of Shakespeare continued to be produced, but they were often adapted to bring them into closer accord with Neoclassical theory. Newly written plays differed in both content and form from the Elizabethan. The worlds they embodied were those of a highly artificial, aristocratic society, probably influenced by life at Louis XIV's court, and their dramaturgy more closely reflected continental Neoclassicism than Shakespeare.

Most famous today are the Restoration "comedies of manners," plays whose witty dialogue and sophisticated sexual behavior reflect the highly artificial, mannered, and aristocratic society of the day. The heroes and heroines are "virtuous" if they succeed in capturing a lover or tricking a husband. "Honor" depends not on integrity but on reputation, and "wit," the ability to express ideas in a clever and apt way, is prized above all. The admirable characters in the plays are those who can operate successfully within an intricate social sphere; the foolish and laughable are those whose lack of wit or upbringing denies them access to social elegance. In short, the comedies depict the mores and

FIGURE 16.7 **Restoration Drama: Comedy.**
A comedy of wit and sex, *The Country Wife,* by William Wycherley, is still popular with audiences. In production here at Wake Forest University Theatre. (Director, James Dodding; designers, Mary Wayne-Thomas [scenery], Deborah Dale [costumes], and Jonathan Christman [lighting]. Photograph by Bill Ray III.)

conventions of a courtly society where elegance of phrase and the appearance of propriety were more highly prized than morals and sincere feelings. Among the most famous authors of Restoration comedies were William Congreve, whose *The Way of the World* is still produced, and William Wycherley, whose *The Country Wife* can still titillate and amuse.

"Heroic" tragedies presented a conflict between love and duty. In a world far removed from that of the Restoration comedies, tragic heroes were flawless and heroines chaste. The dialogue was based on "heroic couplets," two-line units of rhymed iambic pentameter. The idealization and formality of this kind of tragedy made it unusually susceptible to parody, and so burlesques of it soon appeared.

Succumbing both to the onslaught of burlesque and to the changing tastes of audiences, heroic tragedies declined in public favor, their place being filled by Neoclassical tragedies like John Dryden's *All for Love,* a rewriting of Shakespeare's *Antony and Cleopatra* that brought it closer to the principles of Neoclassicism.

Restoration audiences were small (c. 650) and fairly cohesive—young, courtly, and self-confident. Regularly in attendance were royalty and the upper aristocracy, many of them veterans of exile in France with the king. Some women in the audience wore masks, as much to increase their attractions as to hide them. This theatre was a place to be seen as well as to enjoy the plays. Within fifteen years, however, non-courtiers began to take up theatre as a leisure-time activity in ever-larger numbers, causing a shift in audience taste.

The Rise of Sentimentalism

In England as in France, the coming of the eighteenth century brought with it a change of values. Between about 1700 and 1750, society steadily grew more conservative, middle-class, moralistic, and sentimental.

The amoral tone of the Restoration comedy of manners became offensive to many, and in its place came the view that drama should teach morality. At first, the change was merely in the plays' endings: Young lovers philandered and cuckolded throughout four acts of the play but, in the fifth, repented and declared their intention to lead a moral and upright life henceforth.

By the 1730s, however, heroes and heroines were becoming embodiments of middle-class values, struggling cheerfully against adversity until, at the end, their courage and persistence were rewarded. Prized especially were characters able to express their insights into human goodness in pithy statements (*sentiments*). Thus, the label *sentimental hero* implied not only one who embodied virtue but also one whose speech was rich in sentiments. The audiences of the day experienced "a pleasure too exquisite for laughter," and so *sentimental comedy* dominated English comic drama by the middle of the eighteenth century—a clear break with Neoclassicism.

Heroic and Neoclassical tragedy were increasingly replaced by a kind of serious drama alternately called *domestic tragedy* and *middle-class tragedy.* George Lillo's *The London Merchant* (1731) was also a major break with the Neoclassical ideal: A middle-class hero is led astray by love and is ultimately punished. Although the play aimed to teach morality by showing the punishment of evil, it was nonetheless a far cry from strict Neoclassicism because it was written in prose, featured a middle-class hero, and dealt with affairs of the heart and the marketplace rather than affairs of state.

None of these plays, however, satisfied the English taste for scenic splendor and spectacular effects. Thus, opera and a number of so-called minor forms developed to provide outlets for visual display. Native English opera was gradually replaced by spectacular Italian opera, whose popularity soared in the eighteenth century. As well, English *pantomimes* combined elements of *commedia dell'arte*, farce, mythology, and contemporary satire with elaborate scenes of spectacle in short *afterpieces,* that is, short entertainments to be performed after the evening's play. Often, the dialogue was merely an excuse for major scenes of transformation, in which Harlequin, by a wave of his magic wand, changed places and people into new and dazzling locales and characters. Because new scenery was often commissioned for pantomimes, many innovations in the design and execution of settings in England can be credited to pantomime.

Such changes in drama were accompanied by changes in production and performance practices. As more middle-class people came into the audience, existing theatres were enlarged, and new theatres built larger; within a hundred years the intimate theatre of the Restoration had been superceded by those seating 1,500 or more. Theatres began to commission painters to provide new settings for some plays (especially those

FIGURE 16.8 **Illusionism's Growing Influence.**
Philippe Jacques de Loutherbourg's Eidophusikon (c. 1782) was a model theatre in which the designer tried out new techniques of scenery and lighting as he tried to achieve more real-seeming scenes. Consider its similarity to a modern movie theatre. (From a watercolor by Edward Francis Burney. Photograph © The British Museum and reproduced with permission.)

FIGURE 16.9 **Fair Theatres.**

During the eighteenth century, in England as in France, commercial theatres grew up at fairs as an alternative to the state-supported, monopoly theatres established in the major cities. At London's Bartholomew Fair (shown here) were many entertainments, including theatre. (Collections of the New York Public Library, Astor, Lenox, and Tilden Foundations.)

featuring familiar locations), and these painters, adopting new techniques for suggesting depth, made it possible for actors to work closer to scenery than before. Increased emphasis on scenery led to a gradual decrease in the size of the forestage and a need for more space behind the proscenium arch. As a result of these shifts, by 1750 there was little difference in appearance between English and continental theatres.

By the middle of the 1700s, then, English theatres, like French, had adopted the conventions of Italianate staging, Neoclassical drama, and formal acting. In both, women were now on stage and in the audience. Both cultures had developed theatrical centers in their capital cities, where their kings maintained monopolies over a strictly limited number of theatres. Actors talented and experienced enough to perform in the monopoly theatres lived good lives; others, however, lived precariously, working in small cities and towns and touring outlying areas.

Although some acting troupes continued to be organized as sharing ventures, some performers by the early eighteenth century preferred a fixed salary that they could augment by *benefit performances*. For *benefits*, the designated actor received all of the profits from the evening, a sum that occasionally equaled or exceeded a year's salary. Similar patterns were visible throughout much of western Europe.

By the early 1700s, European audiences (including those of a just developing German theatre) had already begun to tire of the austerity of Neoclassical dramas. As audiences became increasingly middle class, sentimentalism and spectacle began to be prized; both found expression in opera, ballet, and new dramatic forms. When monopoly theatres disdained the innovations, commercial theatres sprang up to house them, first at the fairs of London and Paris (hence, *fair theatres*) and later in London's West End and Paris's boulevards. Actors who found themselves squeezed out of the monopoly theatres played there or toured the provinces.

From among the many English actors and actresses who found themselves squeezed out of the London theatre came the beginnings of theatre in the United States. Rather than touring rural England, William and Lewis Hallam chose to assemble a company (mostly families) and sail to a very distant English province, an outpost of the new world. In 1752, the troupe arrived in Virginia and, after building a theatre, opened with Shakespeare's *The Merchant of Venice*. This group (although reorganized and enlarged after the death of Lewis Hallam and renamed The American Company in recognition of America's break with England) toured the towns of the east coast with almost no competition until the 1790s. Its repertory, acting styles, and production conventions were English, with appropriate adjustments made for the needs of almost constant touring.

Theatres in the East

At a time when France was entering its Golden Age and England, Spain, and Italy were ending theirs, major dance dramas were developing in India and Korea. Because of the great importance of movement, especially highly controlled and traditional movement, many forms of theatre in the east have close affinities with dance. Some are even called

FIGURE 16.10 Kathakali.
One of the rich variety of theatre-dance forms of India.
(Photograph courtesy of Farley Richmond.)

dance drama or *dance theatre* because the dance elements are so strong. Several include story and impersonation, like the one illustrated here.

A spectacular example of dance drama is called *Kathakali,* which had its origins in southern India in the seventeenth century. Kathakali, like many Indian dramatic types, uses stories from the *Ramayana* and the *Mahabharata.* These are sung by one group of performers while others dance to the accompaniment of loud, fast drumming. No raised stage is used and there is no theatre structure: Performers work outdoors on a flat earth square about sixteen feet on a side. The only light is an oil fire. There is no scenery. While the singers recite the text and the drummers pound, the dancers, in astonishing makeup and elaborate but almost abstract costumes, mime, sign, and dance, impersonating characters with intricate hand symbols, facial expressions, and body movements.

Most spectacular of Kathakali elements is the makeup, which can take all day to apply. The entire face is colored, then decorated with lines and planes of other intense colors. False "beards" of rice paste are built up; the eyes are reddened by the insertion of a special seed. In this theatre of the demonic and the divine, such utterly nonrealistic makeup is essential.

All Kathakali performers are male, and the dancers' training takes many years.

FIGURE 16.11

Theatre in Korea.
Masks for a government official, his wife, and a couple of tradesmen, four of the eight characters typical of this Korean play from the 1600s. Of folk origin, the plays often depict the commoners' resentment of the ruling classes. (Photographs courtesy of Elbin Cleveland.)

From about the same time in Korea came a mask play called *kamyonkuk* or *talchum* (*kamyon* and *tal* both mean mask; *kuk* is drama and *chum* is dance). Of folk origin, the talchum embodied commoner's resentment of the ruling classes, using eight masked, stock characters. It remains a principal form of traditional theatre in Korea.

Japan was developing its most popular theatre of all: *Kabuki*. Although related to Noh, the far more robust and spectacular Kabuki quickly established itself as distinct. Whereas Noh is a theatre of resignation and withdrawal from the world, Kabuki is a theatre of confrontation and an embracing of the world. Paradoxically, Kabuki grew quickly strong in part because of early censorship: The temporary suppression of music and dance led to the writing of many new, diverse, and action-driven scripts, and the banning of first women and then young men from the stage produced an intricately conventionalized and arresting style of acting.

In its mature form, Kabuki featured long, fully developed actions that unfolded in many acts, with many characters and scenes. The stories came from diverse sources, and they were often heroic and "romantic." The controlling convention, however, was illusionism, with Kabuki directly imitating contemporary (seventeenth-century) Japanese life.

FIGURE 16.12 Japanese Kabuki, Early and Modern.
The engraving from the 1800s shows clearly the traditional stage for Kabuki, a raised walkway through the audience. The recent production suggests more clearly the spectacular action and gorgeous costumes that mark this form. (Contemporary production photograph courtesy of the Japan Information and Culture Center, Washington, D.C.)

Kabuki also developed its own theatre and production style. Two raised walkways, connected by a third at the rear, ran through the audience to a large raised stage, which featured spectacular scenery, trap doors, and a front curtain. (After c. 1750, there was even a revolving stage, the first in the world.) The costumes were complex, beautiful, and spectacular, featuring some costumes (called *hikinuki*) constructed so that at a gesture they

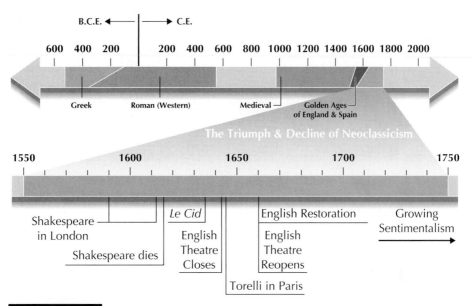

FIGURE 16.13 Timeline.

The Golden Age of French Theatre did not commence until those of England, Spain, and Italy were nearing their ends. Once under way, however, French theatre, like France itself, came to dominate Europe, changing English theatrical practices to bring them closer to continental practice after 1660.

Links to More About Theatre

 Molière, *The Versailles Impromptu,* Molière's play about himself and his troupe, rehearsing under pressure.

 Website of the house of Molière, now the state theatre of France.

<www.fix.co.jp/Kabuki/Kabuki.html> "Kabuki for Everyone."

<http://foires.net/o1d.shtml#royale> Fascinating page of a rich site on Parisian fair theatres and tennis courts. In French, but you can get around, knowing that "jeu de paume" is a tennis court and "iconographie" will lead to more images.

could change completely, turning themselves inside out to reveal, for example, a man in armor where a woman had stood. Makeup, though elaborate, was essentially illusionistic. Within the male-only companies, some actors specialized in female impersonation, raising it to a high art with their meticulous attention to detail. Indeed, despite its spectacular scenery and costumes, Kabuki was an actor's art most of all, with the greatest actors declared national treasures, as if they were great paintings or great buildings.

KEY TERMS

Check your understanding against this list. Brief definitions are in the Glossary; page references there will direct you to appropriate pages. (Persons are page-referenced in the Index.)

afterpiece

angle perspective

benefit

domestic tragedy

fair theatre

Kabuki

Kathakali

lines of business

machine play

pantomime

possession of parts

sentimental comedy

sentimentalism

utility player

c h a p t e r 17

Successful Failure: Theatre and Reform, 1750–1960s

When you have completed this chapter, you should be able to

- Describe the split that came to Western theatre in the late 1700s

- Explain ways in which Romanticism differed from Neoclassicism

- List several major traits of Romanticism and explain how those traits expressed themselves in theatre and drama

- Sketch the arrangement of audience areas in the theatre before and after Wagner

- Compare (that is, identify similarities and differences) Romanticism and Realism

- Compare Realism and Naturalism

- Describe changes in acting in the shift from Romanticism to Realism

- List and define briefly the major avant-garde theories and play-types from c. 1890s–c. 1960

- List and describe briefly the major avant-garde theatres and movements from c. 1890s–c. 1960

History is filled with contradictions, none, perhaps, greater than those of the theater from the mid-eighteenth century until the mid-twentieth. On the one hand, theatre in Europe and America achieved a popularity never before equalled; on the other, people in those same places tried with increasing energy to reform, restore, improve, or save it. These attempts split both theatre and drama into a commercial strand and a something else that was later called the *avant-garde* (advance guard—the term was, significantly, a military one). Because the two strands developed along different, although connected, paths, we are treating them in two chapters; this one deals with the avant-garde from the mid-eighteenth to the mid-twentieth centuries. The next chapter deals with the commercial theatre and the ways in which it used avant-garde experiments.

How did this contradictory process start? As we have seen, by the early 1700s the theatre had begun to lose its ties to the old monarchies. At the same time, the audience base started growing, first into the middle and then into the working class, with the result that the theatre's potential audience grew, but not necessarily for the old kind of theatre. England had had its Glorious Revolution in 1688, ending the Restoration period, and thereafter Parliament shared power with a king who ruled less by divine right than by the negotiated consent of the governed. In France, Louis XIV died in 1715 after seventy-two years of first nominal, than actual absolute power, and he was replaced by a corrupt regime that was wiped out by the revolution of 1789. The monopolies that had tied the theatres to power weakened, and in their place came large audiences who had not power, but money, which they used to buy entrance to new, "illegitimate," commercial theatres (e.g., of the fairs and boulevards).

By the mid-1700s, theatrical energy was shifting to these commercial theatres, which offered new kinds of plays in spectacular settings, leaving the monopoly theatres to traditional practices and traditional audiences. As a result, theatre flourished, but the more popular it became, the farther it got from the old center of power. A series of reformers began to try to steer it back—the subject of this chapter. They usually couched their pleas in terms of art, not of literal connections to central power, often asking for a return to "serious" drama and theatre—a language that now looks like an unconscious recognition of what was really happening.

Germany's experience was different from England's and France's. "Germany" was still a hodgepodge of small states, duchies, and principalities, linked by little except language. Despite a glorious tradition of music, it had no permanent theatres at the beginning of the 1700s. Such traveling players as there were played idiotic low comedy or blood-and-thunder bombast for (powerless) low-class audiences. In 1725, however, Johann Gottsched (a Neoclassicist and playwright) and Carolina Neuber (head of an acting troupe) introduced the first "serious" German drama and theatre; other permanent theatres quickly sprang up, sixty-five of them by 1800. But they were not located in a central capital that was also a nexus of absolute power; they were spread all over the German cultural area. German theorists and artists were not so much reformers, then, as innovators: they were trying to assert a cultural centrality that German theatre had never known, and they used the language of art and seriousness. They tilted toward English models. (They knew Shakespeare from touring seventeenth-century English companies; Gottsched promoted French ideas but failed.)

Thus started, in all three countries, the accelerating movement that tried to reconnect theatrical art with power and with the elite that wielded it. Major waves of would-be reform came at the turn of the nineteenth century (*Romanticism*), in the last quarter of the nineteenth century (*Realism*), and throughout the first two-thirds of the twentieth century (all kinds of *isms*). All had impact on the popular, commercial theatre. All failed. Theatre never recovered its ability to "validate the center of power."

Overall, reformers mistook their goal. For one thing, the nature of power shifted under their feet: it decentralized. As the old structures weakened, the center of cultural power got unclear. Think of 1640 and of our own time as the extremes: Cardinal Richelieu could mandate rules of art for all French-speaking culture; in twenty-first-century America, cultural power is spread from New York to Hollywood, with other centers in sports, e-commerce, universities, and many other locations, as well as individuals as diverse as Madonna and Bill Gates. The one place where cultural power does *not* center any more is the national capital—there has been an almost complete separation between cultural and political power, although, in Richelieu's day, the two were identical.

The role of money as a measure of importance also changed. Increasingly from the 1700s on, wealth became available to the middle class, and great wealth began to rival inherited social position as a source of cultural power. In our time, wealth has outstripped inherited position; it is its own cultural czar.

Theatrical innovators—reformers—then, were often a generation behind these changes. They saw their own declining centrality, but they tried to aim their demands for seriousness and art at a world that was going or already gone. The commercial theatre, however, was happy to sweep up such innovations as pleased its audience.

FIGURE 17.1 German Popular Theatre.
Before the influence of Neuber and Gottsched, German theatre was dominated by stock comic figures like Hanswurst (shown here with sword) and blood-and-thunder romances.

First Wave: Romanticism, 1750–1850

Background

The Declaration of Independence.

Frankenstein.

"'Beauty is truth, truth beauty,'—that is all/Ye know on earth, and all ye need to know."

Art—with a capital A.

The Rights of Man.

What do these things have in common?

There are two answers: first, they fall into the same hundred years and, second, they are expressions of *Romanticism,* a cultural shift so radical that a later observer said that it "destroyed Neo-classicism."

What was Romanticism?

The period from about 1750 to about 1850 was "the world turn'd upside-down." Major political revolutions happened in the Americas and France; the industrial revolution began; demographics changed as population migrated from country to city and across oceans and borders to North America, Australia, and South America. Steam power, mass communications (high-volume printing, cheap newspapers), railroads, and photography came into being. Nations for the first time supported compulsory education. The international slave trade was outlawed by Britain, the ban enforced by its navy.

It was out of this turmoil that the cultural and intellectual cluster we call Romanticism came into being.

The Nature of Romanticism

We now tend to think of Romanticism as a set of theoretical ideas.

It is better to think of it as a set of effects, which were then articulated as theoretical ideas by several people in several countries at more or less the same time, those ideas then becoming causes in their turn. And it is wise to remember that these were political ideas as well as ideas about society, psychology, art, and the nature of the world; that they were only secondarily about the theatre; and that the ideas were not necessarily consistent. One critic much later suggested that we should speak of romanticism*s* (plural), not one Romanticism.

Nonetheless, long after the fact we can see certain common interests:

■ *Rebellion.* Romanticisms were revolutionary. In art, Romanticism wanted to overturn Neoclassicism. In politics, equality and the idea of a social contract binding government and governed were Romantic. Socially, early feminism, personal religion, and opposition to slavery were Romantic. *Romanticisms hated a status quo that inhibited equality and individualism.*

- *Art with a capital A.* Creative and intellectual Romantics all but invented the idea of Art as a special activity. The Artist was a special being—a creative genius able to see truths hidden from others.

- *Nature.* Natural feelings were more reliable than reason or authority. Civilization and education corrupted nature. Children, savages, and peasants were uncorrupted, therefore nearer innocence. Nature was a window through which the child and the artist could see Truth.

- *Anti-industrialism.* Art and beauty were "sublime;" factories were "dark Satanic mills." Cities were unnatural and corrupting. Early industrialists were seen by Romantics as greedy bean-counters without souls—the opposite of the Artist. Industry was ugly (noise, smoke, buildings) and therefore the opposite of Beauty (another way to Truth).

- *Uniqueness.* Truth was also found in the particular, not the general. To establish uniqueness was to establish identity.

People at the time did not necessarily see these five ideas clearly. Political activists saw mostly their own impatience with top-down government; artists saw their own disgust with top-down "rules;" middle-class people saw their own distaste for slavery or

DOLBY'S BRITISH THEATRE.

—

FATHER AND SON.

I. R. Cruikshank, Del.   *White, Sculpt.*

Ant. She's mine—approach and die !
Paul. Thine ! miscreant, tremble !
  [*Music.---they fight a decided combat---*ANTOINE *strikes* ROSEN.
   FORD *a violent blow.*

ACT II. SCENE 2.

FIGURE 17.2 **Romanticism: Nature and the Savage.**
"Picturesque" outdoor scenes and exotic noble savages were important aspects of Romantic theatre.

slums or dreadful working conditions. Many literate people picked up the jargon of Romantic art—"sublime," "picturesque," "grotesque"—and, insofar as they used it, they were "Romantic," but the spread of the jargon probably had more to do with mass communications than with commitment. And romanticisms created their own opposites: after the French Revolution, the top-down government of Napoleon; after the British ban on the slave trade, the American Civil War.

But the romanticisms have a contemporary feel to them. If you could step back right now into the world of 1740, you would find its culture and its behavior alien, but if you could step back into the world of 1820, you would find some of it familiar—ideas about individualism, freedom of choice, human rights, the environment. To be sure, you'd have to land among the right people—mostly upper-middle-class and educated—but if you did, you would see why Romanticism is still important: it was the beginning of our world.

Romanticism in the Theatre

The effects on the theatre were significant, if erratic. Romantic theatre artists disdained Neoclassicism *and* frivolous theatre and tried to reform both. They began slowly and unevenly, and they were rejected by conservative theatres, above all the *Comèdie Française;* yet contradictorily, perhaps, it was in the monopoly theatres where the Romantics wanted to see their ideas applied—that, after all, was where the connection with power had been.

Yet where their ideas crept in partly unnoticed were the boulevard, fair, and non-monopoly theatres, because the ideas were "in the air"—they had come, after all, from the same causes that let ordinary people see and think in new ways, including in the theatres as audiences. International trade and imperialism, for example, created a knowledge of exotic places, and so they began to show up in plays and settings. The new interest in childhood and primitivism brought children, common people, Native Americans, peasants, and Africans to the stage, both as hot topics for hack playwrights and as real concerns of intellectuals. Plays were set in newly detailed scenery of forests, dungeons, jungles, caves, both because new plays required them and because visual artists were themselves now more interested in nature and detail. The new faith in feelings brought plays that appealed to emotions rather than intellect to audiences already attuned to sentimentalism, to emotional religious sects, and to new novels about the emotions. (Matthew Lewis's *The Monk,* for example, was a page-turner about wild emotional states, sex, satanism, and necrophilia. It was tremendously popular and was adapted early and often for the stage.)

In England, most of all, then in Germany and America, Shakespeare was elevated to a cultural icon. His plays were performed from London to the California gold fields; they were read aloud in Hamburg drawing rooms and around the fires of the fur-trapping "mountain men." With the Bible, Shakespeare became a binding force of English-language culture that gave it a frame of reference, a common elevated language, and a common rhythm that lasted well into the twentieth century. In France, however, where Neoclassicism persisted longer, Shakespeare was not seen on the stage until an English company brought the plays in the 1830s.

Perhaps the most important outside force acting on the theatre, however, was demographic. Migration and urban growth meant that for the first time a mass audience existed. Industrial employment meant that for the first time large parts of the working class could afford the theatre. These changes affected the size of theatres, which got bigger; the nature of the drama, which got more sensational; and the business organization of the companies, which got more commercial as the old monopolies withered or ossified. (See Chapter 18.)

Romantic Attempts at Reform

The most conscious efforts to put Romantic ideas into effect in the theatre came in dramatic theory and drama. Especially in Germany, a distinct body of "serious" Romantic plays was written and is still in the German repertory. A recognizable gap appeared, however, between "important" (serious, literary) plays and popular ones in France and England. Partly, this was the gap between the old monopolies and the new, mostly commercial theatres; partly it was the gap between self-aware "Art" and what was called hackwork. Over the long haul, Art lost, in good part because it would not see the theatre itself as art; rather, the theatre was a corrupted thing that had to be reformed.

In Germany, however, Romantic drama found its home. Germany produced a seminal theoretical work, Gotthold Lessing's *Hamburg Dramaturgy* (1770), which rejected French Neoclassicism as a model and recommended instead Shakespeare.

FIGURE 17.3   **Size of Romantic Theatres.**
Buildings got larger after 1750, with the audience in box, pit, and gallery seating. Here, the English artist Thomas Rowlandson's rendering of Covent Garden Theatre in the early 1800s; the play appears to be Shakespeare's *Henry IV*, Part I.

Lessing wrote specifically of art and genius, recommended natural language, praised sentimental comedy and domestic tragedy, and argued for heroes who were human beings, not aristocratic or royal titles. He also wrote several plays, including so-called philosophical dramas, the most lasting—as a literary, not a theatrical, work—*Nathan the Wise*.

Hamburg Dramaturgy, and especially its urging of Shakespeare as a model, in turn influenced young German radicals calling themselves the "Storm and Stress" (an in-your-face term of the day, from a play written by one of them), including two who were to become German classics: Johann Wolfgang von Goethe, whose *Faust* is an acknowledged literary, but not theatrical, masterpiece, and whose novel *The Sorrows of Werther* ("spleen, morbid sentimentality, romantic melancholy, and disgust of life," according to one critic) gave Romantics a myth hero and even a costume; and Friedrich Schiller, whose commitment to liberty showed in *The Robbers* and *William Tell*, both successes that led to many imitations. The subjects of these plays tell us much about self-aware Romanticism—love and loss; liberty; the fight against despotism; free will and wisdom. So do the kinds of characters—robbers, rebels, lovers, questioners. Perhaps most significant is the form of the plays, whose authors demanded the right to roam freely in time and space (like Shakespeare) and not be limited by "the unities," and their poetry, which was intense, usually unrhymed, and rhythmic—neither everyday speech nor Neoclassical artifice.

In England, however, attempts to create a serious body of Romantic drama labored too closely in the shadow of Shakespeare, and a false Shakespearism ruined many plays. Too, serious English Romantics refused to meet the needs of the theatre, including pleasing the audience, which they thought was the problem, not the solution. Even when England's great poets tried seriousness in the theatre, therefore, they usually failed; Byron did write a tragedy that worked, *Werner*, a lurid tale of revenge and despair, but it barely escaped the trap into which most serious Romantic drama

FIGURE 17.4   **The Inside of the State Theatre, Hamburg, Germany.**
The rendering of the interior is crude (the people are erratically out of scale), but this theatre in the early 1800s had a pit orchestra; box, pit, and gallery seating; and a large candelabra in the audience area. German theatre had developed rapidly in a half-century.

FIGURE 17.5 **Romantic Shakespeare.**
During the 1800s the international appetite was for Shakespeare.
France was an exception: Shakespeare was not seen in Paris until
the 1830s. Shown here, the American Edwin Forrest as King Lear.

fell—that of mistaking the most extreme moments of Shakespearean tragedy for the tragedy itself. English Romantics who wanted to bring a new seriousness to the theatre were not alone in thus failing to find a dramaturgy to match the emotional expression in which they believed; the resulting plays therefore often lacked internal probability and had long passages of great dullness separating moments of incredible bombast. Romantic language pushed the envelope and sometimes became wild, torrential, overblown—a verbal diarrhea to match the emotional diarrhea of its heroes. Few of these plays have lasted, and no wonder; rather, what has lasted have been Italian operas made from them, where music supplied the quality that the spoken dramas couldn't.

In Paris, Romantic dramas made it to the boulevard theatres in 1790 but were shut out of the now-hidebound *Comèdie Française* until 1830, when Victor Hugo's self-aware *Hernani* was staged and caused a riot. Hugo won, but it was like mating with a corpse. The *Comèdie* was belatedly revived by the energy of Romanticism, but the movement itself ran out of steam a few years later, so watered down in the popular theatres by that time that storm, stress, and riot fizzled.

Drama had been caught in a contradiction: serious literary Romantics wanted to create Art for a sensitive, therefore limited, audience; the theatres wanted to bring in the largest possible audience. The extreme Artistic position was "closet drama," plays written to be read, not staged. Neither closet dramas nor bad poetic tragedies could restore the theatre to its Neoclassical position, obviously.

Romanticism was pretty well over as a movement by the 1840s. It had succeeded in destroying Neoclassicism; it had planted its flag at the *Comèdie Française*; the English monopoly "patents" had died of old age; and German theatre had had what one source calls its Golden Age. Romantic drama had not reformed the theatre, however.

What persisted was Sentimentalism, which had adapted itself to trivialized Romanticism and which matched Victorian taste, which was middle-class, fussy, and "moral." What the Romantics left most conspicuously to the future, however, was the image of the Artist—special, gifted, emotional—and of Art, which entered Victorian culture as a kind of secular religion (so long as it was moral and approved by experts).

An Aftershock: Richard Wagner

Richard Wagner is now known as an opera composer. His influence on modern theatre, however, has been enormous for two innovations: the idea of unity and a unifying artist; and a separate, classless audience space.

The Master Artwork

Wagner had a huge ego and knew he was a genius in the Romantic mold. His concept of a unified theatrical production meant a "master artwork" conceived and executed by a "master artist" who would run the whole show (ideally, Richard Wagner himself). The idea would go far to establish the director in the modern theatre.

The Separated Audience

In 1876, Wagner got his own theatre at Bayreuth. It epitomized his ideas: several "nesting" proscenium arches between audience and actors, not just one; a hidden orchestra pit; steam jets between audience and playing area to emphasize a "mystic chasm"—the separation of the master artwork from the audience.

Perhaps more importantly, Wagner put his audience in the dark and got rid of box, pit, and gallery. Now, the audience sat in a fan-shaped orchestra that was "classless," and every seat had an equally good view of the stage. Called *continental seating,* the arrangement became standard in the twentieth century.

The effect was in one sense a democratic one, but it had the autocratic effect of putting the entire audience in the same passive surrender to the stage—no catcalls from upper galleries, no bored aristocrats whispering in boxes. It was a top-down theatre space for an art in which the master artist gave and the audience received, both suited culturally to a Germany that had just been unified under the top-down leadership of Otto von Bismarck.

FIGURE 17.6 **Wagner, the Theoretician.**
This is the interior of Wagner's theatre at Bayreuth, an important influence on the future
of theatre architecture and audience seating: he eliminated box, pit, and gallery and put
the emphasis on the proscenium arch.

Second Wave: Realism, 1850–1950

The phenomenal popularity of commercial theatres in the nineteenth century did little
to satisfy reformers. What they saw was a theatre with a huge audience, doing productions that used the best technology of the day, all of which seemed to them wasted; some
saw it as wasted in sheer over-production; others saw it as wasted on triviality. Again, a
call for "seriousness" would come; this time, however, the buzz-word would be not Romanticism, but Realism.

The idea that art should show real life was hardly new. It was implicit in Renaissance
theory, explicit in every portrait or still life. It was explicit in *Hamburg Dramaturgy*. And
a literal rendering of life became concrete with the invention of photography (about
1840). In the theatre, local color and scenic detail dated to the eighteenth century, as did
the prototype of the *box set,* an imitation of a room with side walls rather than wings;
it was common by the end of the Romantic period. In drama, commercial playwrights
were writing "problem plays" that seemed to examine real-life issues. Acting was "real"
enough by the 1830s that Walt Whitman said that Charlotte Cushman's performance as
a woman dying of a severe beating was "too real."

Why, then, a new theatrical radicalism that called itself Realism?

Because the pre-Realisms mentioned above were inconsistent; because the plays, including "problem plays," were more trendy than serious; because acting was obviously acting, not being; because box sets, with their painted canvas walls, were obviously sets; because the theatre, the radicals said, was all about laying on *stuff* and not getting serious.

The Realists got serious.

By the 1850s, problems of inequality, industrialization, and urbanization were well known and widely discussed. Urban poverty was on the rise and with it urban crime. Fear of political instability (a legacy of Romanticism) led toward repression, which fanned dissatisfaction. For some, it was the best of worlds, but for many it was the worst; the tension is part of what we mean by the word "Victorian"—the middle- and upper-class ability to maintain awareness of problems while using apparent ignorance as a coping mechanism ("Nice people don't mention such things").

Science was offering new theories that threatened old ideas: Charles Darwin proposed evolution, which left humanity without uniqueness and apparently at the mercy of environment. At century's end, Sigmund Freud proposed the unconscious, which jerked the feet from under good intentions and double standards. One effect of both was to dislodge humankind from the philosophical pedestal on which it had rested since the middle ages; another was to displace Romantic ideas, especially their optimism and their faith in Nature as a window on the ideal. Instead, it became "Nature red in tooth and claw." At the same time, "social Darwinism" gave oppressors a response to do-gooders: social inequity was merely a survival of the fittest.

FIGURE 17.7 **Industrialization.**
The factory system created wealth but crowded workers into towns and cities. Romantics saw it as an enemy.

The impact on serious art, including theatre, was to turn it toward question and challenge of the status quo.

Realism and Naturalism

Realists—and their more extreme relatives, Naturalists—believed that truth resided in the material objects observable in the physical, external world. They were also objectivists: They believed that truth could be discovered through the application of scientific observation and could be replicated by a series of objective observers, not by Romantic art.

According to the Realists and the Naturalists, the function of art, like that of science, was the betterment of humankind, and the method of the artist should be that of the scientist. Plays should be set in contemporary times and places, for only they could be observed firsthand by the playwright. As the highest purpose of art was the betterment of humanity, the subject of plays should be contemporary life and its problems.

While sharing with Realists a belief in science as a solver of problems, the Naturalists differed in their definition of what problems most needed attention and in their hope for the future. The Naturalists stressed the problems of the poor and tended to be pessimistic about their solution. According to the Naturalists, people were victims, not actors in life. Their destiny was controlled by factors like heredity and environment, over which they had little influence. Because the Naturalists attempted to give the impression that their plays were an actual record of life, the dramas often appeared formless and unstructured, traits that gave rise to the phrase "a slice of life" to describe some Naturalists' plays.

Despite the period's interest in the mass of people, and despite democratizing forces, this was an era of self-defined great men (and a few women). Forceful people—remember Wagner—tried to change the world. The master artist appeared in several guises.

Georg II, Duke of Saxe-Meiningen

One of the earliest creators of realistic staging was Georg II, Duke of Saxe-Meiningen (fl. 1870s–1880s). In some ways, the duke was merely perfecting and popularizing ideals of staging promulgated much earlier; nonetheless, it was he who influenced later Realists.

Saxe-Meiningen objected to many practices of the commercial mainstream because they resulted in productions that lacked unity (internal consistency) and seemed artificial. For the duke and his court theatre, the art of the theatre was the art of providing the illusion of reality; he therefore sought methods of production that would lead to "an intensified reality and [would] give remote events . . . the quality of actuality, of being lived for the first time." To this end, the duke stressed accurate scenery, costumes, and properties; lifelike acting; and unity.

FIGURE 17.8 Realism and Naturalism.

Above, Chekhov's *Three Sisters* at the Moscow Art Theatre, a middle-class setting; *below,* *L'Assomoir* in Paris—a lower-class setting, a commercial laundry. (Photo of *The Three Sisters* from Sayler, *The Moscow Art Theatre Series of Plays;* from *Le Théâtre.*)

Production Practices

The duke believed that all elements of a production required coordination. The setting must be an integral part of the play, and so he encouraged his actors to move *within* the setting rather than merely playing in front of it (as was currently fashionable). If actors were to move within an environment, the scenic details had to be three-dimensional rather than painted, and so actual objects were used in the settings. Simultaneously, the duke strove to provide several levels (e.g., rocks, steps, and platforms), so that the scenic design would not stop abruptly at the stage floor. In these ways, he did much to popularize the use of three-dimensional staging.

Historical accuracy in both scenery and costumes was important. To increase accuracy, he divided each century into thirds and differentiated among various national groups within each period. He used authentic fabrics instead of the cheaper substitutes often seen in commercial theatres of the day.

Acting

There were no stars in Saxe-Meiningen's group. Each member of the company was eligible to play any role; and each member, if not cast as a major character, was required to play in crowd scenes, something commercial stars never did. Each actor in a crowd scene was given lines and actions, and put into a group led by an experienced actor.

FIGURE 17.9 Saxe-Meiningen as Director.

The new stage Realism—individualized crowd members, varying levels, varied postures and arm positions. The funeral oration in *Julius Caesar*.

Actors were to avoid parallel lines on stage, to make crosses diagonally rather than parallel with the curtain line, to keep one foot off the ground whenever possible (by placing it on a step or by kneeling on one knee), and not to copy his neighbor's stance. Actors were told to look at one another rather than the audience, to react to what was said and done onstage, and to behave naturally, even if it meant delivering a line while not facing the audience. Makeup was based on historical portraits. These practices now seem obvious, but in the 1870s they were startling.

Influence

Beginning in 1874 (eight years after the duke took over the theatre), the Meiningen company began touring western Europe and Russia. The troupe gave more than 2,800 performances in thirty-six cities. From these performances came its international reputation and its influence.

André Antoine and the Théâtre-Libre

André Antoine, an amateur actor, abhorred the commercial theatres of Paris, disapproved of the way actors were trained at the Paris Conservatoire (France's leading school for actors), objected to the scenic practices of the major theatres, and decried the flimsiness of contemporary popular drama. What was needed, Antoine concluded, was a theatre where new and controversial plays could get realistic productions. Thus, when an amateur group to which he belonged balked at producing a new play, Antoine undertook the production himself and, spurred by early success, became the full-time director of his own new theatre in 1887. He named it the Théâtre-Libre (Free Theatre) and described it as nothing less than "a machine of war, poised for the conquest of Paris." It was, among other things, an alternative, or avant-garde, theatre. It is worth noting the differences between Antoine and Saxe-Meiningen at this point:

- Antoine was far more interested in new plays
- Antoine faced tough government censorship
- Antoine had to make a theatre from scratch

Plays

Although Antoine produced a wide range of plays at the Théâtre-Libre, he seemed most comfortable with plays in the Realistic and Naturalistic styles. Because Antoine organized his theatre as a subscription ("members only") house, he was able to bypass threats of censorship. Consequently, he was able to introduce to Parisians a wide range of French and foreign authors whose works were considered too scandalous for production in major theatres.

Production Practices—The "Fourth Wall"

Antoine believed with the Naturalists that environment influenced human behavior, so he made his settings as believable and lifelike as possible. He designed a room and then decided which "wall" of the room was to be removed so that the audience could see in. Antoine also used actual, three-dimensional objects rather than their painted substitutes. For one play, he brought real sides of beef on his stage; for another, real trees and birds' nests; and for another, a real student's actual room furnishings. The attention that he paid to realistic detail and his reliance on actual objects led to his being called by many the father of naturalistic staging. Jean Julien, a contemporary of Antoine's, seemed to sum up the goal of Antoine: "The front of the stage must be a fourth wall, transparent for the public, opaque for the player."

Acting

Antoine believed that actors should appear to be people, not actors. Antoine wanted his actors to say their lines naturally, just as one might engage in a conversation with friends and, at the same time, to move about the furniture and accessories as in real life. Sincerity and conviction were the qualities he sought, and so he advised his actors to ignore the audience and to speak to one another in conversational tones—in short, to try to *be,* rather than to *act,* the characters in the play. Perhaps for these reasons, Antoine often used amateurs who had not received conventional training for the commercial theatre and who were therefore more receptive to the experimental style of naturalistic acting.

Influence

The major contributions of Antoine and the Théâtre-Libre were

- To popularize acting techniques leading toward naturalness on stage
- To gain acceptance for scenic practices now known as "fourth-wall realism," with all that implies about scenic detail and literal objects
- To introduce a new generation of playwrights (both French and foreign) to the theatregoing public of Paris
- To establish a model for a censor-free theatre

The most significant experimental theatre of its day, the Théâtre-Libre gave rise to a number of similar noncommercial theatres throughout the world. Called the *independent theatre movement,* this blossoming of small theatres in several countries almost simultaneously gave the impetus to, first, an international idealism and then an ultimate acceptance of Realism as the mainstream of the commercial theatre, an acceptance completed by early in the twentieth century.

Konstantin Stanislavski and the Moscow Art Theatre

When the Meiningen company toured Russia in 1885 and 1890, Konstantin Stanislavski and Vladimir Nemirovich-Danchenko saw it. They decided to establish a new kind of theatre in Moscow whose goals were to remain free of the demands of commercialism, to avoid overemphasis on the scenic elements of production, and to

FIGURE 17.10   **Stanislavski and the Moscow Art Theatre.**
Maxim Gorki's *The Lower Depths,* a Naturalistic play set in a flophouse. Stanislavski, *center,*
on the table. (From Oliver Sayler, *The Moscow Art Theatre Series of Plays.*)

reflect the inner truth of the play. For this theatre, Nemirovich-Danchenko was to select the plays and handle the administration, while Stanislavski was to serve as the production director.

Acting and Directing

By 1917, Stanislavski had developed, from personal experience and observation of others, his major ideas for training actors, ideas that he codified in a series of books that
have since been translated into more than twenty languages (the dates are for the American editions): *My Life in Art* (1924), *An Actor Prepares* (1936), *Building a Character*
(1949), and *Creating a Role* (1961). Together, these books represent what has come to be
called the Stanislavski "system" of actor training, although Stanislavski himself insisted
neither that his was the only way to train actors nor that his methods should be studied and mastered by everyone.

As a director during the early years of the Moscow Art Theatre, Stanislavski worked
in a rather autocratic fashion, planning each detail of his actors' vocal inflections, gestures and movements. But as his interest in the problems of the actor grew, and as his
actors became more skillful, he abandoned his dogmatic approach and became an interpreter and helper to the actors. His ideal became for the director and the actors to
grow together in their understanding of the play. Only after the group had grasped the
psychology of the roles and the complex interrelationships (often a three-month
process) did the actors begin to work on the stage.

Influence

What began in 1898 as an experiment in external Realism and was by 1906 an experiment in psychological Realism had become an established tradition in Russia by the time
of the Russian Revolution (1917). Because a number of Russians trained in "the system"

left their country after the revolution, the teachings of Stanislavski came to the attention of the outside world.

Plays and Playwrights

Realism in the drama began tentatively and cautiously. Although other writers had presaged Realism, it was the Norwegian Henrik Ibsen who launched Realism as a major artistic movement.

Ibsen

With plays like *A Doll's House* (1879), Ibsen assumed his controversial role as an attacker of society's values. Structurally, his plays were fairly traditional: They told a story and moved logically from event to event, just as well-made plays had done for years. But their content was shocking: When individuals came into conflict with society, they were no longer assumed to be guilty and society blameless. Indeed, social customs and traditional morality were exposed by Ibsen as a tangle of inconsistencies and irrelevancies. Questions like the proper role of women, the ethics of euthanasia, the morality of business and war, and the economics of religion formed the basis of serious probings into social behavior. Theatrical producers throughout the world who believed that drama should be involved in the social issues of the day applauded the Norwegian dramatist, and soon other artists began to translate, produce, and, later, emulate his plays.

Shaw

In England, George Bernard Shaw became one of Ibsen's most vocal and influential supporters. Unlike many Realists, Shaw always retained his sense of humor; he almost always wrote comedies (e.g., *Major Barbara*, 1905), and their popularity did much to ensure the final acceptance of Realistic drama in England before the close of World War I.

Chekhov

Anton Chekhov scored his first success in 1898 when *The Seagull* was produced at the Moscow Art Theatre. Chekhov's plays differed from those of Ibsen and Shaw in their tendency toward poetic expression and symbolism. His manipulation of language, with measured pauses and artful repetitions, produced a sense of reality as well as music and allusion. In some ways, he foretold the Russian Revolution by depicting the isolation of the aristocracy and its inevitable extinction.

Naturalistic Playwrights

Émile Zola called for "living characters taken from real life," who spoke everyday language and offered "a material reproduction of life"; he called for playwrights who scientifically analyzed and faithfully reported the social problems of the world with a view to their correction.

The *Story* of the Play

Henrik Ibsen, *A Doll's House*, 1879

Nora Helmer is a married woman and a mother, but some of her behavior is childlike, and her husband Torvald, a priggish bank manager, treats her as a charming toy (and, implicitly, a sexual toy). When an old friend of Nora's, Mrs. Linde, comes to ask if Torvald can give her a job at the bank, Nora confesses that she is not so childish as she appears: she has "saved Torvald's life" by borrowing money when he was ill to send him to recuperate in Italy. Torvald does not know of the debt, which she has been repaying from her household money, so that Torvald thinks she is a spendthrift, as well.

Her creditor is Krogstad, who works at Torvald's bank and is going to be fired; he demands that Nora intercede for him or he will reveal to Torvald not only her borrowing but also the fact that she forged her now-dead father's signature to the note.

Krogstad is fired; his job is to go to Mrs. Linde. He demands again that Nora help him get a better job at the bank; when she cannot, he leaves a letter for Torvald in the letterbox. Nora, recognizing that the truth must come out, believes that Torvald will stand by her, even share the blame; she tells Mrs. Linde that there will be a "miracle." Still, waiting for her husband to find the letter, she becomes more and more frantic, talks of suicide; she dances for her husband a tarentella that becomes wild, manic.

Krogstad and Mrs. Linde meet at Nora's and recognize each other—they are former lovers who now decide to reconcile. Krogstad says he will retrieve the letter, but Mrs. Linde tells him that "this unhappy secret must come out."

After a party, Nora tries to keep Torvald from the letter. Torvald is sexually aroused; he calls her his "most precious possession." He reads the letter and his mood flip-flops: she has "ruined his happiness, threatened his future." They will have to go on living together "for public appearances," but she will not be allowed to raise his children. Nora's "miracle" does not happen.

The maid brings another letter. Torvald reads it and cries, "I am saved!" Krogstad has sent him the forged note to destroy and said he will keep silent.

Nora has become quieter and quieter. Now, she sits her husband down at the table and, in a lengthy scene, explains how wronged she has been. "I have been your doll wife, Torvald." Finally, she leaves him and the children—coolly, calmly—telling him that her first duty is to herself. She goes out; Torvald cries out her name, then says that there is still hope—and there is the sound of the house's outer door slamming.

Among the most successful playwrights in the Naturalistic style were Gerhart Hauptmann and Maxim Gorky. Hauptmann's *The Weavers* (1892) uses a group protagonist to show the devastation that comes to already impoverished workers when industrialization threatens their way of life. Gorky's *The Lower Depths* (1902), by depicting

Anton Chekhov.
Chekhov's *Uncle Vanya* at the Moscow Art Theatre. Contrary to what the photo suggests, this is a
comic scene—the man with the gun shouts "bang!" (From Oliver Sayler, *The Moscow Art Theatre
Series of Plays.*)

the seemingly hopeless lives of people living in a flophouse, explores whether religion
or political reform offers the best chance for change.

The Third Wave: Avant-Gardism, 1890–1960

Although the Realists were themselves innovators, another group reacted against them
almost immediately. The split deepened as a trivialized Realism was taken over by the
commercial theatre, and Art again dictated that serious people would revolt against both
Realism and its commercial adaptation.

But what was wrong with Realism?

In essence, the objections to it boiled down to three: first, Realism wasn't *theatrical.*
The audience was shut out; a separate world existed beyond the fourth wall, with actors
behaving as if the audience wasn't there. It was too much like life. Second, Realism was dull:
The language was mundane, the characters flat, the action—if truly lifelike—boring.
Third, Realism had to struggle to be significant—if no more was at stake than the fate of
one ordinary individual, what was the larger meaning?

These objections to Realism coalesced around a view that Realism was inimical to Art, a view that is one of the bases of the avant-garde ideas in all the arts called modernism. (Significantly, major Realists didn't talk much about Art.) We know modernism best in painting (Picasso, "Cubism") and in literature (Joyce), but it was also a force in the theatre, where it believed that the theatre had to be "re-theatricalized," that innovation itself was valuable, and that form or style was as important as content so long as both were *artistic.*

Many modernist attempts followed to re-theatricalize the theatre. In one direction, they redefined theatrical space by throwing out the proscenium arch and the picture-frame stage; in another, they threw out the box set and detailed settings, replacing them with varying kinds of stylized or abstract scenery, including settings of ramps, stairs, and levels. Others tried to re-theatricalize acting by throwing out "ensemble" and "inner truth" and going for a style that was bigger, more external, more physical and symbolic. None replaced Realism but several modified it.

Reactions against Realism

Impressionism (fl. 1890s) was a style that sought to capture fleeting moments of awareness that were believed to constitute the essence of existence. By reproducing these glimpses, art could provide insights into the truth that lay underneath the external world—the opposite of Realism. Probably the playwright who wrote most successfully in the style was Maurice Maeterlinck. In short plays like *The Intruder* (1890), Maeterlinck presented a world far removed from reality. Subjectivity permeates the plays, which are typically moody and mysterious, hinting at a life controlled by unseen and inexplicable forces. The actions seem hazy, distant, out of focus; indeed, in the theatre, the plays were often played behind gauzes (scrims) or clouds of fog, and they moved between patches of light, dark, and shadow. Some of Impressionism's techniques were adopted by Realists like Ibsen (in his later plays), Chekhov, and Tennessee Williams.

Symbolism (fl. 1890s) had two major figures. Adolphe Appia believed that artistic unity was the fundamental goal of theatrical production and that lighting was the ele-

FIGURE 17.12 **Impressionism.**
Maurice Maeterlinck's *The Bluebird.* Balance, dreamlike costumes and setting, and the weirdly unrealistic details like the long fingernails show the departure from Realism.

ment best able to fuse all others into an artistic whole. Like music, light was capable of continual change to reflect shifting moods and emotions within the play, and light could be orchestrated by variations in its direction, intensity, and color to produce a rhythm to match the dramatic action. Because he found an aesthetic contradiction between the three-dimensional actor and a two-dimensional floor set at right angles to two-dimensional painted scenes, Appia gave the stage floor and scenery mass. He solved the problem in part by devising three-dimensional settings composed of steps, ramps, and platforms, among which the living actor could comfortably move.

Like Appia, Gordon Craig opposed scenic illusion and favored instead a simple visual statement that eliminated inessential details and avoided photographic reproduction. His emphasis was on the manipulation of line and mass to achieve, first, a unity of design and, ultimately, a unity for the total production. Although Craig placed less emphasis on the importance of the actor and the text than Appia, they agreed on the importance of the visual elements of the production. Perhaps it would not be an injustice to designate Appia as the formulator of the theories that Craig later popularized. Appia and Craig influenced the New Stagecraft and then commercial theatrical design.

Expressionism (fl. 1910–1930s) usually focused on political and social questions in a stage world close to nightmare. Plays unfolded in a world of bizarre and garish colors, jagged angles, and oddly proportioned objects. Actors moved in mechanical or puppetlike ways and often spoke in disconnected or telegraphic conversations. They bore names of types rather than people: The Mother, The Son, The Cipher. Conventional ideas of time and space collapsed. Ernst Toller, whose best-known work was *Man and the Masses* (1921), was a leading Expressionist.

FIGURE 17.13 Symbolism: Appia and Craig.
Left, a setting by Adolphe Appia; *right,* a sketch for a setting by Gordon Craig.

FIGURE 17.14 **Expressionism.**
If Impressionism resembled a dream, Expressionism resembled a nightmare. Here, Ernst Toller's *Man and the Masses*. (From *The Theatre*.)

Expressionism has been influential for three reasons:

- Many of the techniques were adapted and used in film (*The Cabinet of Doctor Caligari*).
- Techniques were adapted by Realistic playwrights, notably Eugene O'Neill and Arthur Miller.
- It was an influence on "epic theatre" (see pp. 352–354).

Constructivism (fl. 1920–1935), the practice of Vsevolod Meyerhold, paralleled that of the German Expressionists. Although early in his career Meyerhold directed experimental works for Stanislavski, during the 1920s he devoted himself to developing a theatrical art suitable for a machine age. He relied on two major techniques: biomechanics and constructivism. *Biomechanics* was a training system and performance style for actors based on an industrial theory of work: They were to be well-trained "machines" for carrying out the assignments given them, and so they needed rigorous physical training in ballet, gymnastics, and circus techniques. *Constructivism* was a theory of visual art in which scenery did not attempt to represent any particular place but provided a "machine" on which actors could perform. In practice, sets designed for Myerhold were combinations of platforms, steps, ramps, wheels, and trapezes. A goal of both biomechanics and constructivism was to retheatricalize the theatre.

FIGURE 17.15 Constructivism.

Although associated with the name of a director, Vsevolod Meyerhold, Constructivism was a visual style in which settings were seen as machines, their construction as visible as that of a car's engine. (From *Theatre Arts.*)

Absurdism appeared just after World War II, when several new playwrights were grouped together by critics and given the name *Absurdists*. *Absurdism* (fl. 1940s and 1950s) was itself a blend of earlier *Dadaism* (fl. 1920s), with which it shared an emphasis on life's meaninglessness and art's irrelevancy, and a commitment to irrationality and nihilism as appropriate responses to life and living. With *Surrealism* (fl. 1920s), it viewed the source of insight as the subconscious mind. Most important, with *Existentialism* (fl. 1930s and 1940s), it sought an answer to the question: What does it mean to exist and to be? The answer was a moral code based on a consistent atheism with human beings adrift in a world without order or purpose: Each person must define his or her own value system and then act accordingly.

Absurd, then, meant not *ridiculous* but *without meaning.* Absurdists abandoned story and dramatic unity based on causality. The plays were often constructed as a circle (ending just where they began, after displaying a series of unrelated incidents) and as the intensification of a single event (ending just where they had begun but in the midst of more people or more objects). Usually, the puzzling quality of the plays came from the devaluation of language as a carrier of meaning: In the plays, *what happens* on stage often transcends and contradicts *what is said* there. Absurdists included Samuel Beckett, who won the Nobel Prize; Eugène Ionesco; and Edward Albee; they influenced later playwrights like Harold Pinter.

FIGURE 17.16 Surrealism.

Dream, distortion, mockery, and childlike representation marked Surrealism. Here, Apollinaire's *The Breasts of Teiresias.* (From Huntley Carter, *The New Spirit in the European Theatre, 1914–1924.*)

Brecht and Artaud

Although these styles have influenced today's theatre, the theories and practices of Bertolt Brecht and Antonin Artaud have probably been more influential than others. These two theorists operated from quite different sets of assumptions about the nature of theatre and the purpose of art, but they shared a disdain for Realism. It may be useful to think of Brecht as developing from Expressionism and Artaud from Impressionism and Surrealism. Together, their theories can help account for much experimentation of the 1960s and 1970s.

Bertolt Brecht and Epic Theatre

Bertolt Brecht believed that theatre should educate *citizens* (participants in a political system) in how to bring about socially responsible change. He saw theatre as a way of making a controversial topic easier to consider. His commitment to a socially responsive theatre doubtless came, in part, from his being both Jewish and leftist at a time when Hitler was rising to power in Germany.

Traditional German theatres, whether those of Wagner or Saxe-Meiningen, had sought an illusion that allowed the members of the audience to believe in and identify with the onstage actions. As Brecht was a Marxist and viewed theatre as an instrument for change, he objected to a theatre that mesmerized its audiences and made them passive. Brecht therefore tried to redefine the relationship among the theatre, its audience, and society. He proposed that if he jarred audiences out of their identification with the action, he would succeed in forcing them to think about what they saw onstage. He sought, therefore, alternately to engage and estrange his audiences, a technique he called *Verfremdungseffekt* (usually translated as the *alienation effect* or, simply, the *A-effect*).

Epic Theatre

The complex of staging and playwriting used by Brecht came to be called *epic theatre.* "Epic" captured many of the qualities that Brecht prized: the mixing of narrative and dramatic episodes, the telescoping of time and place, and the spanning of years and countries (similar to epic poetry).

Although Brecht was not the first to use either these techniques or the term *epic* (Erwin Piscator had been active in the same kind of experimentation several years earlier), Brecht popularized the term and the practices through his own plays, his theoretical

FIGURE 17.17 **Bertolt Brecht.**

The Threepenny Opera, with music by Kurt Weill, a Brechtian revision of the English "ballad opera" *The Beggar's Opera* by John Gay. Here, at Syracuse University in 1996. (Directed by Rodney Hudson, courtesy of Syracuse University Department of Drama.)

writings (particularly the "Little Organon for the Theatre," 1948), and his productions at the Berliner Ensemble, after 1954 East Germany's most prestigious theatre.

Antonin Artaud and the Theatre of Cruelty

Although Antonin Artaud was an actor, director, playwright, poet, and screenwriter, it was as a theorist that he made his greatest impact. *The Theatre and Its Double,* a compilation of Artaud's major essays, was published in France in 1938 but was not translated into English until the late 1950s. Because Artaud believed that important ideas came not from logical reasoning or rational thinking but from intuition, experience, and feelings, he developed his ideas through images and metaphors:

- *The Theatre as Plague.* Comparing theatre to a plague, Artaud said, "It appears that by means of the plague, a gigantic abscess, as much moral as social, has been collectively drained, and that like the plague, the theatre has been created to drain abscesses collectively." He declared that theatre caused people to confront themselves honestly, letting fall their individual masks and confessing their social hypocrisies.

- *The Theatre and Its Double.* Western theatre had lost its magic and its vibrancy and had become merely a pale imitation, a *double,* of the true theatre (that is, the Eastern theatre). Artaud proposed "a theatre in which violent physical images crush and hypnotize the sensibility . . . as by a whirlwind of higher forces."

- *The Rejection of Language.* Artaud wanted to remove the script from the center of his theatre, for he believed that words and grammar were insufficient carriers of meaning. Truth came instead from spiritual signs whose meaning emerged intuitively and "with enough violence to make useless any translation into logical discursive language." Artaud wished to substitute gestures, signs, symbols, rhythms, and sounds. Theatre was intuitive, primitive, magical, and potentially powerful.

- *The Centrality of Audience.* Artaud dismissed notions of art as a kind of personal therapy for the artist. Theatre was good only when it returned the audience to the subconscious energies that lay under the veneer of civilization and civilized behavior. Whereas Brecht tried to make audiences *think* about a social or political issue, Artaud wanted to make them experience a spiritual awakening, to participate in something that might be called a communion (in its real sense of a coming together).

- *The Theatre of Cruelty.* Artaud called for a *theatre of cruelty.* To achieve it, Artaud developed a number of techniques seldom used in commercial productions. He wanted to bombard the senses. He experimented with ways of manipulating light and sound: In both, he adopted the abrupt, the discordant, the sudden, the shrill, the garish. Lights changed colors quickly, alternated intensity violently; sound was sudden, often amplified. Scenery was subservient to the other elements of production, with the audience placed in an environment created by actors, lights, sound, and space (Artaud preferred barns and factories to conventional theatres). The actors were encouraged to use their bodies and their voices to provide scenery, sounds,

FIGURE 17.18 **Theatre of Cruelty.**
Artaud's ideas underlay the "theatre of cruelty" of the 1960s, especially the production of *Marat/Sade* directed by Peter Brook, its "cruelty" embodied in a threat of assault on the audience by the actors; although fictitious, that threat seemed real enough to break the long-established bond of "safety" for the audience. Here, *Marat/Sade* at the University of South Carolina. (Directed by Richard Jennings.)

and visual effects and not to be bound by notions of psychological realism and character analysis. Actors were to address the senses of the spectators, not merely their minds.

Artaud's theories, in many forms and with many distortions, were appropriated and applied after 1960 by theatre artists, movie-makers, and especially rock musicians. Whatever one may think of his pronouncements, it is clear that, although long in coming, their acceptance has been widespread.

Avant-Garde Theatres and Movements

The Art Theatre Movement

Reactions to Realism and to commercial theatre came in the form of new kinds of theatres as well as the new theories and plays just discussed. Just as the Realists had started the first "independent" theatres, reactions against those very theatres brought a proliferation of "art" theatres, soon followed by other radical or "experimental" or "little" theatres into the 1960s. Taken as a group, they can be called the avant-garde.

Early creators of such art theatres included

- *William Poel*, an antiquarian who reacted against late Victorian production by staging Shakespeare and other Elizabethans in supposedly authentic ways—a bare-stage *Hamlet* in 1881, for example. He founded the English Stage Society in 1895 to recreate the Elizabethan stage. Poel influenced both modern thinking about Shakespeare and the popularity of the thrust and arena stages.

- *Aurélien Lugné-Poë* had acted for Antoine, but he turned to nonrealistic production with Paul Fort at the Théâtre d'Art (1891) and then alone at the Théâtre de l'Oeuvre (1893). Lugné-Poë staged "experimentally," seeking new styles, especially for Symbolist works.

- *Jacques Copeau*, an actor-director who founded the Vieux Colombier theatre and "cleared out the wings and old picture frame" by building a permanent setting of levels, an inner below, and an upper balcony. Although Copeau staged mostly the traditional French repertory, his productions rejected realistic scenery. Copeau founded a school that influenced modern French, English, and American theatre; one of the *Comédie-Française* theatres is now called the Vieux-Colombier.

- *Alexander Tairov*, at Moscow's Kamerny ("Chamber") Theatre after 1915. Determinedly anti-realistic, he had no one style of his own and was called "Cubist" for his modernism. He staged a wide variety of plays in several non-representational ways, anticipating the eclecticism of later directors and the "heretical" approach to classics.

FIGURE 17.19 The Vieux-Colombier.
This influential theatre had a permanent setting of arch, "above," and openings; it was meant to serve the spare style of its originator, Jacques Copeau. (From *Theatre Arts*.)

FIGURE 17.20 **Tairov at the Kamerny.**
Alexander Tairov's production of Shaw's *Saint Joan* in Moscow, 1925—a
distinctly nonrealistic staging of a work of Realism. (From *Theatre Arts.*)

The "art theatre movement" was an after-the-fact term for this very mixed bag, which included these theatres as well others as different as the Abbey in Dublin, Ireland. The "art" of the art theatres was still partly Romantic but existed against the background of a changed culture, that of turn-of-the-century Europe—imperialist, stuffy, class-conscious, money-conscious—and foregrounded a somewhat superficial, sometimes glib, sentimentalized belief in the power of beauty to improve life. That belief was mostly elitist, as were the art theatres.

The art theatre came a bit late to America. When it did, it was bound up culturally with several other fashions: the civic pageant, which was also genteel and "artistic;" the first programs in "theatre arts" at colleges and universities; and the New Stagecraft.

The New Stagecraft was an avant-garde tendency in stage design that favored simplified, sometimes abstract settings; nonrealism; lighting as a major design component; and alternatives to the proscenium stage. European in origin and based heavily on the ideas of Appia and Craig, it surfaced in America when Sam Hume (a designer who had been working at the Moscow Art Theatre) organized a New Stagecraft exhibition in Boston and New York in 1914–1915. It was, in fact, the future: designers like Norman Bel Geddes, Robert Edmond Jones, and Lee Simonson made the New Stagecraft dominant in American design by 1930.

The first American art theatres arrived more or less with the New Stagecraft; that they soon became known as "little" theatres was significant (that is, they attracted small audiences). The Abbey Theatre's American tour of 1911 seems to have inspired them: the Chicago Little Theatre began in 1912, the Boston Toy Theatre and the Wisconsin Dramatic Society about the same time, and by 1925 there were little theatres "from Maine to

FIGURE 17.21 **American Art Theatre.**
The Provincetown Playhouse in its 1917 theatre on Macdougall Street, New York City. The extreme smallness of the space is noteworthy for this influential theatre. (Photo courtesy of Brown Brothers.)

California, sophisticated Greenwich Village to the open spaces of Vancouver. . . .'' Amateur, artistic, and mostly elitist, their most famous example was the Provincetown Players, which had started in a shack in the art colony at Provincetown, Massachusetts, in the summer and moved to New York's Greenwich Village in 1915. The Provincetown staged the early plays of Eugene O'Neill and included people as diverse as journalist John Reed and poet Edna St. Vincent Millay; people from it helped found the Theatre Guild (see p. 389).

The little theatres became a movement and an influence because they quickly had a voice: their organ was *Theatre Arts Magazine,* which gave national distribution to their ideas. It described individual theatres, kept readers up on what was going on in Europe and at home. By 1930, however, *Theatre Arts* was turning toward the New York–based commercial theatre for its copy. The little theatres still existed, but many had used up their enthusiasm for art and had become community theatres. Art and Beauty had not proved potent at either paying the bills or solving social problems, and no wonder: they were ideas from before "the War"—World War I—and the cynicism and striving of the 1920s was not congenial to them, nor, in much of America, was the provincialism then being lampooned in *The New Yorker.* The Depression and the rise of fascism in Europe finished Art and Beauty as ideas with power, not least because those ideas were associated with German culture.

Thinking About the Avant-Garde

> "The theatre is a humble materialistic enterprise which seeks to produce riches of the imagination, not the other way around."
> —Charles Ludlam (1943–1987), avant-garde playwright and director.

Study the illustrations in this chapter. In what ways has the imagination been called on to reduce "material riches" in the avant-garde productions?

The fading of *Theatre Arts* magazine marked the death of the little-theatre movement but not of avant-gardism in America. Much of the same energy went into leftist theatre in the 1930s, but it appeared again after World War II in new forms.

The post–World War II innovators in America were partly like the older ones—that is, committed to a reformist art—but different in that some were overtly political. "Political" here, however, must be taken in a large sense, for it included not only the politics of the anti–Vietnam War movement, but also the emergence of groups that had until then been unidentified or invisible—African Americans, Asian Americans, Latinos, women, homosexuals.

The now-old-fashioned arts reformers were again trying to make theatre important and serious—that is, to claim a place for it near cultural power. The political reformers

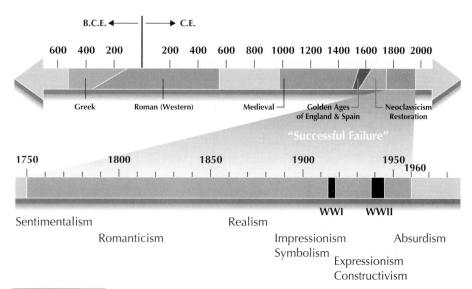

FIGURE 17.22 Timeline—the "isms."

Building on the sentimentalism of late Neoclassicism, Romanticism flourished in the early 1800s, giving way to Realism by the late 1800s. Thereafter came a flurry of other "isms," each striving to reposition theatre in its culture.

Links to More About Theatre

Shari Benstock, *Women of the Left Bank: Paris, 1900–1940*, 1986.

C. D. Innes, *Avant Garde Theatre, 1892–1992*, 1993.

Cheryl Black, *The Women of Provincetown*, 2001.

<pages.nyu.edu/~jgk2598/provincetown.html> A site about the Provincetown Playhouse.

were trying to use the theatre to carry vivid messages, to raise consciousness, to incite action. Both kinds, in the process, tried to rethink the relationship of theatre to life; of theatre to commerce; of actors to audience; and of text to performance.

These avant-garde groups remained vital for a while, many getting new life from resistance to the Vietnam War. However, they never pulled the theatre at large closer toward the cultural center, and, indeed, by the 1970s it was evident that that center was somewhere else. American culture had changed seemingly overnight in the 1950s, actually over a much longer period that culminated in the enormous importance of Elvis Presley, rock, and popular music itself. Seemingly suddenly, a pounding music derived from a mostly hidden black source *was* American culture, and the European icons that had so long dominated were eclipsed. History itself fell off the charts as a way of knowing. By the 1970s, the common coin was not Shakespeare and the Bible and the European canon, but television and advertising and rock 'n' roll. Art, the secular religion that was going to save humanity, lost all definition and crumbled into Andy Warhol's "Art is whatever you can get away with."

The theatre persisted after c. 1970 as a moderately successful kind of commerce. It had offshoots in other activities but it had no avant-garde. Consciously or not, people who might once have tried to reform it now recognized that it was an impotent activity—an entertainment, a business, a way of life for a few, an artifact.

KEY TERMS

Check your understanding against this list. Brief definitions are in the Glossary; page references there will direct you to appropriate pages. (Persons are page-referenced in the Index.)

absurdism

A-effect

art theatre movement

avant-garde

biomechanics
box set
constructivism
continental seating
epic theatre
Existentialism
Expressionism
Impressionism

independent theatre movement
master art work
Naturalism
Realism
Romanticism
Surrealism
Symbolism
theatre of cruelty

Commercialism

When you have completed this chapter, you should be able to

- Sketch the ways in which theatre business reflected changing business practices outside theatre

- List and explain the major traits of melodrama

- Compare Romantic and Realistic melodrama

- Name some major writers of serious and comic drama from the mid-eighteenth to the mid-twentieth centuries

- Discuss the emergence of American musical theatre and name some of its major plays and practitioners

- Describe the changing theatre buildings and scenic practices during the period

- Trace the major lighting changes during these years

- Discuss problems affecting Broadway by WWII along with some strategies being tried to ameliorate them

The last chapter covered three major attempts to reform the theatre between 1750 and about 1960. This chapter covers exactly the same period but looks at another movement—the rise and triumph of commercialism. It took place at the same time and showed some of the same characteristics as Romanticism, Realism, and the artistic movements, but without their ideological underpinnings. It came to dominate the theatre, even to be what most people meant by "theatre."

The years from 1750 to 1960 were the period of commercialization—the triumph of capitalism and the glorification of wealth. "Captains of industry" made fortunes in railroads, steel, oil, textiles, canals, road-building, manufacturing, mass communications. Such fortunes were possible because of industrialization, increasing population, and empire—from the mid-eighteenth century to the mid-twentieth, European nations colonized and then lost South Asia and Africa. New technologies made long-distance transport, mass production, and mass consumption possible. New ideas of business organization and new laws made big business and big fortunes possible, so that Mark Twain called the last decades of the nineteenth century "the Gilded Age."

These same two hundred years saw also the transformation of a large swathe of North America from a sprinkling of French, English, and Spanish colonies to an independent nation that became, after World War II, one of the world's two great powers. Spared the damage from the war that wrecked Europe, the United States became the engine that drove its rebuilding; in the process, the United States became the leader of world capitalism and the commercialization of culture.

The theatre took part in this historical movement. It could not ignore the new working-class audience that poured into cities, or the expanding middle class that occupied new urban developments, or the more distant audiences now reachable by railroad and steamship. Nor could it ignore profits, now possible on a scale never imagined by Shakespeare or Molière. By 1900, American commercial theatre was one of the most successful of all time; therefore, we draw many of our examples from the United States. Many of the trends discussed in this chapter were seen throughout the West.

What Is Commercialism?

The fully developed commercial theatre (i.e., after c. 1860) was one in which profit was the primary goal, with income from ticket sales the principal source. Capitalization came either from individual wealth or from limited companies created for the purpose. The creators of theatre—actors, directors, designers—became salaried employees.

At first glance, it might seem that the theatre had always been commercial—an enterprise to make money by selling tickets. Commercial pressure on theatre, however, was long muted by support from a crown, from aristocrats, from local governments, or from the church. Starting before 1750, however, those subsidies declined and the need to pursue profit increased.

As these commercial pressures increased, theatres organized themselves differently. Earlier sharing companies that had toured or located in small cities had led perilous lives: when income went down, all the shares went down; collecting capital was difficult;

and most sharing companies were lucky if they owned decent costumes, much less scenery or a theatre. To reduce these risks, actors came to prefer salaries to shares, even though this change made them employees rather than part owners. This shift, however, required a changed business organization. In some companies, a leading actor now managed the company (the *actor-manager*), made decisions once made by the group of sharers, and paid the others; in other, somewhat later companies, a director managed (director-managers, ultimately *producers*).

Through the 1700s, theatre companies tended to stay together in one place or in a few places reachable by horse. Changes in technology broke this pattern. By the early 1800s in the United States, for example, actors were playing a circuit of theatres up the Mississippi River from New Orleans, something possible only with steam power. With paved roads and an expanding rail system after the 1840s, national and even international stars could move fairly quickly between cities, where they usually played with resident companies. This *star system* brought William Macready, for example, from London to both America's cultural backwaters and Paris, where he introduced Shakespeare to French audiences. However, the star system had the unhappy effect of eroding the quality of the resident actors, who now merely supported the visitor. Stars later began to travel with their own supporting actors and then their own production units; somewhat later still, lesser actors formed *combination companies* (that is, complete producing units) to travel the nation and the world. Combination companies were common by 1900, and the combination system was then the norm.

The theatre was also affected by the way the rest of the society did business. The late nineteenth century saw money and power increasingly concentrated in fewer hands. Monopolies were created as large businesses swallowed small ones, until few rivals remained, marking the age of the robber barons and the great "trusts" in the United States. Bigger business created its own reactions: working people organized to get safer conditions, more money, more power.

Theatre was part of all this. Since Shakespeare's day, entrepreneurs had owned theatre buildings; by the 1800s, a businessman might own several theatres in different cities and send companies from one to another, creating a circuit. Toward the end of the nineteenth century, one group in the United States, the Theatrical Syndicate, realized that if they could own all the theatres they could control all theatre, including ticket pricing and actors' salaries. They bought buildings, organized them into circuits based on transportation routes, centralized the booking of combination companies in New York (causing actors to have to live there), and created a near-monopoly by the early twentieth century. It effectively ended the tradition of stock or sharing companies. ("Summer stock" was a pale remnant through most of the twentieth century.) Not surprisingly, actors and then other theatrical workers organized. Actors Equity staged its first strike in 1916.

Theatre's increasing commercialization had other consequences. As theatre depended more and more on ticket sales and was managed more and more by business people, profit trumped art, committing the theatre to popular culture because it caused theatre to rely on a mass audience. When, then, movies and later television became the entertainment of choice for that audience, the theatre lost its hold on mass consciousness. By 1960, the theatre was no longer central to either popular or high culture. It existed as a hybrid of the two, essential to neither.

Drama in the Commercial Theatre

Since the mid-eighteenth century, as many as twenty thousand plays have been staged in commercial theatres around the world. Of this number, few have ever been revived. Most of the best plays from the period were first done in subsidized or in independent or art, not commercial, theatres; of the rest, we have to remember that timeliness and subject matter were often more commercially important than quality. This is not to say that plays from the commercial theatre were bad; it is to say that they had their own goals. Above all, commercial plays had to be *accessible*—without signals that would offend a mass audience, including challenge, moral shock, and political innovation (all of which could be found in the plays of the last chapter).

As will be seen, the dominant dramatic genre of the period was *melodrama*, which was hugely popular but usually trivial; its nineteenth-century type has gone out of fashion and is even found funny now, so it is seldom revived. Comedy has fared better, perhaps because commercial comedy has sometimes not been so closely tied to a moment. Musical theatre, at least as conceived after the mid-twentieth century, has been more durable, and revivals are now staples in London and New York.

FIGURE 18.1 Melodrama.
The genre dominated the hugely popular theatre of the 1800s and early 1900s and moved seamlessly into movies and then television. This is an advertising poster for a melodrama of 1909. (Courtesy of the New York Historical Society, New York City.)

Major Changes

Three major cultural changes can be seen as underlying the shifts in drama after 1750:

■ *The Rise of Sentimentality. Sentimentality* is the arousing of feelings out of proportion to their cause—"easy tears." Most often, too, the cause is situation or type rather than particular character, calling up a stereotype to which the feelings are already attached—the helpless child, the threatened virgin, the faithful dog. Sentimentality is related to Sentimentalism: both have strong ideas of good and evil; both believe in love, happiness, and virtue; both use lots of words and overblown language to express themselves. Both emphasize male values that suited the age of commercialism: family, fidelity, loyalty, work, obedience to superiors. Sentimentalism, however, was a literary idea; sentimentality is a social or personal attitude.

To audiences new to the city, sentimentality was a satisfying response to stereotypes that called up a lost rural life. To the rising middle class, sentimentality allowed for easy tears that cost nothing: a businessman could weep over a hungry child, applaud the happy ending, and then go home and ignore servants who had emigrated from the Irish famine only months before.

Sentimentality gave quick access for audiences not interested in subtlety. It encouraged identification. It was safe. Usually, it was socially conservative. By contrast, as unsentimental a playwright as George Bernard Shaw was subtle, alienating (through laughter), unsafe, and socially disruptive. It is no accident that his comedies triumphed by turning sentimentality on its head.

■ *The Shift from the Active to the Acted-On.* Sentimentalism, unlike earlier drama, was concerned with victims as much as with heroes. Sentimentality found its easiest stereotypes among such victims. The result was a 180-degree turn from heroic drama to what one critic has called "losers' stories." The focus became victimization and the reaction to it instead of heroic effort in the face of opposition—Tennessee Williams's Blanche Dubois, for example (see p. 374). It is worth noting, however, that such victims were usually presented as single cases and were not generalized to cause the audience to think about a real social problem: the rural virgin threatened by the evil young aristocrat was not connected to issues of poverty and exploitation or to the many real-life urban prostitutes who had started as farm girls and gone to the city to earn money.

■ *The Collapse of Genre.* With the end of the "rules" of Neoclassicism, the idea of genre started to crumble. Tragedy pretty much ceased to exist except as "closet drama," because the ideas that had defined it had died. Melodrama took its place. Comedy became little more than a play with a happy ending or a funny play with gags. There have, nonetheless, been attempts to revive the old generic distinctions, most of all that of tragedy. In the twentieth century, Eugene O'Neill rewrote the *Oresteia* by substituting Freudian pathology for the gods and the fates; the result was certainly somber but, because Freudian psychology lacked the power of the gods and the fates, unconvincing. Arthur Miller has argued that *Death of a Salesman* is a tragedy, with a common man substituted for the aristocratic tragic hero. Again, the argument is not persuasive: *Salesman* is a fine play, meaningful and deeply serious, but it re-

FIGURE 18.2 Sentimental Victims. Melodrama throve on victimization. Here, two stereotypical victims, the mother and the weeping child—in a snowstorm, no less.

mains a mostly realistic picture of a small man being broken on the wheel of false hopes—no heroic imperfection, no divine manipulation, no poetry, no chorus, no self-understanding, and a suicide that is made trivial by its motive—an insurance policy. Most of all, the question of genre was irrelevant: midway through the twentieth century, in a mass culture, what was the point of calling up a dramatic theory that hadn't had power for two hundred years?

Serious Drama

Romantics revived Shakespeare, finding in his work the breadth and the emotional power they prized. From the 1770s until well after 1900, his plays remained among the most often-produced in the world. Playing Shakespeare's tragic roles became the test of an actor. A great Hamlet or a great Juliet was an international star. Lines from the plays were common in everyday speech; the characters were role models: it was Shakespeare, along with the Bible, that gave a changing society connectedness. Attempts to imitate Shakespeare were generally unsuccessful, however; what audiences wanted in new plays was something emotional, prosaic, and spectacular.

Melodrama

Melodrama was the most popular dramatic genre of the period. What audiences loved was its exploitation of unquestioned good and evil, with the good always under threat from the evil but triumphing at the end. Almost as important was melodrama's sentimentality. Both the good/evil dichotomy and the sentimentality in which it was enveloped typified a period looking for stability in a time of great change.

That said, what has to be remembered is how enjoyable melodramas were (and still often are, at least in the reading). They were full of energy, whipping from adventure to adventure; they had thrills, emotions, and a good deal of laughter—many of the melodramas were full of comic sequences. Their workmanship was often clumsy, their coincidences transparent, their language overblown—but they gave enormous pleasure.

Melodrama means "music drama," a term taken from the widespread use of music within the plays. Melodramas used emotional music (still used in movies and television) to push mood and to announce surprise (loud crash of music) or to build suspense (tense, unsettling music). Music also appeared as *signature music*, the same theme played whenever a certain character entered or left or performed some audience-arousing feat. (The scores later written for silent movies did the same.) A pit orchestra was essential to early melodrama; some melodramas also used vocal songs.

Melodrama presented a simplified moral universe in which good and evil were clear and were embodied by easily recognizable characters. Physical attractiveness typified the hero and heroine (often in love with each other); costume also announced their character types (see, for example, Figure 18.3). Helping the hero was the comic man (and sometimes comic woman), who often saved the hero and frustrated his enemies. It was evil, however, that propelled the action in the person of a villain, also recognizable by costume and physique (older, heavier) and sometimes by social rank—a nobleman or landowner. He initiated the action by threatening the hero or heroine; he or she escaped, often saved by the comic man; and the villain threatened again, and again there was an escape, and so on. The structure was thus episodic, progressing by threat and escape, each more extreme than the last until the final incident, when hero and heroine might move from certain death to happy marriage within minutes. By the end of the Romantic period, this action was being played out in three acts rather than the Neoclassical five.

Many Romantic melodramas also depended on spectacle—fires, explosions, drownings, earthquakes—as threats to the good characters or as obstacles to the villain. Many also featured animals—"equestrian dramas" (horses) and "canine melodramas" (dogs). (Movies such as *Lassie Come Home* and *National Velvet* thus had a long pedigree.) Romantic interest in the sea and the navy during the Napoleonic Wars gave rise to "nautical melodramas." These, and "rustic" (rural) melodramas, "gothic" melodramas (sometimes medieval, often what we would call horror, e.g., *The Vampire*) and others filled the theatres. After 1850, middle-class theatres increasingly played Realistic melodramas, and Romantic melodramas increasingly became the fare of the lower-class theatres, but it is important to remember that Romantic melodrama persisted right through the period and moved seamlessly into silent movies. The term "neo-Romantic" is sometimes used to describe this later use of Romantic elements.

Stock Types.
The villain drove the action of melodrama; the comic man often frustrated him, saving the hero or heroine for another attempt by the villain.

Two playwrights of Romantic melodramas were international favorites between 1750 and 1850, August Friedrich von Kotzebue and René Charles Guilbert de Pixérécourt. Pixérécourt set the fashion for canine and disaster melodramas, and, because his staging requirements were so demanding, staged his own plays and was thus also important as an early director.

Realistic melodrama began to appear about 1850. Theoretical realism would not appear in the avant-garde theatres until the 1870s, but it had precursors that went back to the 1700s. The box set (1830s) was a step toward realistic interiors; photography and improved printing made "real" views of the world familiar. As well, the end of Romanticism and the rise of a practical-minded business class shifted attention from the exotic and the never-never to the familiar and the utilitarian, and particularly to the middle-class drawing room and the issues of money and status (including moral status and "belonging" in society). "Gentlemanly melodrama" became a feature of middle-class theatres. It was less lurid in language and incident than Romantic melodrama, its incidents themselves more carefully linked by cause and effect. Less reliant on violent spectacle, it put melodrama into middle-class costume but kept the action of threat and

FIGURE 18.4 **Spectacle.**
Fires were great theatre; so were volcanoes, ships, trains, and disasters of all kinds. Melodramas were advertised by woodcuts such as this one. (From Stanley Applebaum, *Advertising Woodcuts from the Nineteenth Century Stage.*)

escape—for example, a well-to-do woman threatened with revelation of her past—but sometimes extended the single threat and its resolution across the whole play. So common that they became a cliche satirized in Wilde's *Importance of Being Earnest* were scenes of the finding of a long-lost child or the reunion of long-separated mothers, brothers, sisters, or children. Such scenes derived from Greek New and Roman comedy; that comic root symbolizes the importance to melodrama of the satisfying ending.

Most Realistic melodramas remained wedded to victims, sentimentality, and social conservatism. Strains of Romanticism persisted in them—big speeches, excessive gestures of self-sacrifice or love. No matter how realistic melodramas might get, however, they remained a form of Romantic wish-fulfillment, driven by an idea of how the audience wished people behaved rather than by how they knew they behaved. In essence, the wish-fulfillment was the wish for social and cultural stability as defined by a patriarchal, commercial society—the idea that long-lost children should be united with their parents, that erring wives should be saved from themselves, that bankrupt fathers should be rescued by secret benefactors. It was this social conservatism that kept melodrama from truly attacking social problems (as Realistic avant-garde drama did). Despite many plays about laboring people in laboring settings—mines, factories, ships, farms—and despite a recurring tendency to make the villain an owner or a boss or an aristocrat, melodramas did not suggest that poverty or bad working conditions or prostitution had

The **Story** of the **Play**

Augustin Daly, *Under the Gaslight,* 1867

In an upper-class New York drawing room, Laura Courtland, engaged to Ray Stafford, is confronted by the villainous Byke. Laura tells her flighty cousin Pearl to tell Ray the truth that Byke threatens to reveal: Laura is not a real Courtland, but an adopted former street-child. Ray decides to break off the engagement, writes Laura a letter, then crumples the letter and shoves it into a pocket, saying he loves her. Later, however, at a gathering at swank Delmonico's Restaurant, the letter falls out and sneering society women read it and banish Laura. This time, Ray fails to stand by her and she goes, an outcast.

Three months later, Laura is living incognito in a basement with Peachblossom, a street-child. Byke and his female accomplice, Old Judas, try to kidnap them but are foiled by Snorkey, a one-armed Civil War veteran who leads Ray to Laura. Ray pleads for a second chance, but Byke and Old Judas return and kidnap the women, then try to get Laura to a New Jersey hideout from a Hudson River pier.

Snorkey and a gang of street boys thwart them; Laura is thrown into the river, and Ray dives in after her.

Some time later, at an elegant country house, Ray is now engaged to Pearl. Laura is a reclusive guest, but she flees, still loving Ray. In a nearby woods, Snorkey overhears Byke and Old Judas plotting to murder Laura and rob Pearl. At a railroad, the fleeing Laura is exhausted and arranges to spend the night locked in a signal shed; Snorkey appears, but Byke captures him and puts him, tied, on the railroad track. Laura hacks her way out of the locked shed with an axe and rescues Snorkey, just as the train roars by.

Back at the country house, Byke is stealing Pearl's jewels when Laura, Ray, and Snorkey catch him. Byke announces that Pearl, not Laura, is the adopted child thief; Laura is a real Courtland. Peachblossom announces that Old Judas has been killed in an accident. Ray switches his engagement from Pearl back to Laura, and Snorkey is to marry Peachblossom.

systemic causes; rather, the cause was always the villain—an individual, an evil boss or corrupt factory owner or seducer.

Probably the most important melodrama in the world was *Uncle Tom's Cabin* (first version 1852), based on the novel by Harriet Beecher Stowe. Before the age of copyright, it was pirated, adapted, and translated without permission wherever there were theatres. The play remained strong through World War I (1914–1918), when more than a dozen companies were still touring it in the United States. Some actors

FIGURE 18.5 Realistic Melodrama.

Real places and real details modified the exoticism of Romantic melodrama, but the reliance on thrills remained: here, the heroine smashes her way out of a shed with an axe, just in time to save the comic man from an oncoming locomotive—itself a real device then new to the stage. (From Stanley Applebaum, *Advertising Woodcuts from the Nineteenth Century Stage.*)

spent their lives touring the play, and "Tomming" was a recognized actors' term. First staged at the pivot between Romantic and Realistic melodrama, it included an escape across an ice-clogged river by a runaway slave pursued by dogs; a dead child being carried to heaven by angels; and virtuous Uncle Tom being beaten by the villain, Simon Legree.

Most melodramas, both Romantic and Realistic, were written by hacks hired by the theatres. Buffalo Bill Cody, for example, toured for years in hack melodramas about the West before he started the Wild West Show. Gentlemanly melodramas, on the other hand, were sometimes written by quite eminent but now forgotten literary people. An author important to subsequent playwrights was the Irish-American Dion Boucicault, who demanded a percentage of box-office receipts instead of a flat fee, thus starting the practice of *royalties*. By 1866, the first international copyright agreement was made, partly because of Boucicault, allowing playwrights to share the spoils of commercialism.

Melodrama remained a dominant genre into the last third of the twentieth century, although toned down in its excesses of both action and language by Realism. It is still, for example, the genre of soap opera and the suspense thriller, as well as of many plays where an unquestioned assumption of goodness is threatened by unquestioned badness, with goodness and badness more recently defined not in moral terms but in terms of

FIGURE 18.6 **The Most Famous Melodrama in the World.**
Uncle Tom's Cabin toured the world for generations. Here, it is being played in Paris about 1900. (From *Le Théâtre*.)

power—the sensitive loner oppressed by heartless prudery, the AIDS victim oppressed by small-minded fear.

Other Serious Drama

"Great" plays have been rare in commercialism. Where important serious plays have been produced in commercial theatres, they often were by playwrights who had made their reputations elsewhere. George Bernard Shaw came out of the independent theatre. Eugene O'Neill, the majority of whose plays were done at the Provincetown Playhouse and the Theatre Guild, came late to Broadway. Edward Albee has moved back and forth between Off-Broadway and Broadway but first established himself in Europe and Off-Broadway. The commercial theatre has generally wanted challenging or "difficult" playwrights to prove that they can win an audience elsewhere before risking money on them.

In the United States, however, two playwrights of real challenge and difficulty appeared in the commercial theatre just before the middle of the twentieth century: Tennessee Williams won the Drama Critics Circle Award for his first major Broadway production, *The Glass Menagerie* (1945), a wistful memory play reminiscent of the impressionists and Chekhov. *A Streetcar Named Desire* (1947) won both the Pulitzer Prize and the Drama Critics Circle Award and established Williams as a major American playwright.

Arthur Miller is, like Williams, a Realist of sorts, but whereas Williams's work tended toward the dreamlike and impressionistic, Miller's moved in harsher, more expressionistic ways. *All My Sons* (1947) told of an American businessman who knowingly sold inferior products to the American military in order to turn a profit. In *Death of a*

The **Story** of the **Play**

Tennesee Williams, *A Streetcar Named Desire*, 1947

Blanche Dubois arrives at her sister Stella's apartment in a New Orleans slum, having come because she has nowhere else to live: she is trying to find a safe haven. Blanche is outwardly a Southern belle, ridiculously genteel; within, she is a wounded sufferer—of alcoholism, of loneliness, of despair. She is appalled by Stella's surroundings and by her husband, Stanley Kowalski, whom she calls "common."

Stanley, however, is much more than common. He is a patriarch (Stella is pregnant); he is also a materialist, a Philistine, and a brutal realist. He sees, correctly, that Blanche threatens his relationship with Stella (a mutually powerful sexual one) and his "possession" of Stella.

Stanley's friend Mitch is attracted to Blanche, and Blanche sees in him a last chance to find a protected place for herself. She and Mitch seem headed toward marriage, but Stanley tells Mitch what he has learned from other men about Blanche's past: that she was fired from a teaching job because she seduced a seventeen-year-old; that she was notorious for one-night stands in cheap hotels. Blanche tells Stella more truths about herself: that she nursed their mother through the horrors of a lingering death; that she lost the family home, Belle Reve, because she had no money; that the "sensitive young man" she has often talked about so romantically was in fact her husband, whom she found in bed with another man and who, when she said he disgusted her, killed himself.

Mitch fails to appear for a date; he has abandoned her because of what Stanley told him. Stanley buys Blanche a bus ticket out of town. Then, when Stella is in the hospital having the baby, Stanley rapes Blanche (the extent of her acceptance a matter of performance).

Some time later, Stella is home again. Blanche is disoriented, hallucinating that an old boyfriend is coming to save her. Instead, a doctor and nurse called by Stella come to take her to a mental institution. She goes on the doctor's arm, murmuring, "I have always depended on the kindness of strangers."

Salesman (1949), realistic scenes are interspersed with scenes remembered by the disordered protagonist, Willy Loman. *Death of a Salesman* won both a Pulitzer Prize and the Drama Critics Circle Award.

Comedy

Perhaps, given the loosening of generic ideas, we ought to speak of "comic plays" rather than "comedy," at least as it used to be understood. "Plays with happy endings" might better define many plays of the period between 1750 and 1960, except that most melo-dramas had satisfying endings, and so "comedy" must be understood to include a wide range of plays from farce to non-melodramas with happy endings and a light tone.

As with serious plays, Shakespeare was a dominant figure. His romantic comedies, with their stellar female roles, offered the nineteenth-century culture female models who were attractive, often witty, virtuous, and ultimately subservient to males—Viola, Ros-alind, Isabella, Beatrice, Portia. They became nineteenth-century icons throughout Europe and America.

Early comic plays of the Romantic period, created in either monopoly theatres or theatres in transition to commercialism, partook of the older sentimental comedy but often made gentle fun of Sentimentalism itself. They kept the five-act structure of Neo-classicism, even some of the character types and stock scenes of Restoration comedy, but their characters were mostly less aristocratic and their concerns more middle class. In England, the leading comic authors before 1800 were Richard Brinsley Sheridan (*The School for Scandal*) and Oliver Goldsmith (*She Stoops to Conquer*). Both are still revived.

The most popular comic playwright in Europe and America before 1850, however, was Eugène Scribe, who created more than three hundred plays for Parisian theatres, in-cluding the Comédie Française (after *Hernani* had made a place for Romantic drama there). Their translation and international production made French comedy a model for

FIGURE 18.7 **Shakespearean Comedy.**
Like Shakespeare's serious plays, his comedies were popular across Europe and America in the 1800s, providing great roles for actors and giving the culture several female role models. Here, *The Merchant of Venice* in a typically antiquarian setting— lavish details, explicit imitation of the real Venice.

the world. Scribe's technique—for example, careful preparation, meticulous networks of relationships, apparent chains of cause and effect—gave the impression of tight causality when, in fact, the plays were built around multiple lines of action that touched mostly by chance or coincidence. The expression *the well-made play* was applied to these techniques, first as a compliment and later (twentieth century) as a term of contempt. Nonetheless, it worked brilliantly for Scribe's audiences and served as an example to writers such as Ibsen. In a few plays, Scribe used these techniques to touch on contemporary problems, reviving the term *problem play*. Problem plays, although technically comedies, at least acknowledged contemporary social flaws; their resolutions, however, avoided suggesting how society could correct itself. (Ibsen's *A Doll's House* is, at base, a problem play, but its ending, in which a wife leaves her domineering husband and her children, slamming the door on them with "a sound heard all over Europe," could never be found in Scribe: it is too socially revolutionary.) Scribe could also write witty dramatic prose and sparkling farce.

The most popular comic playwright of the Realistic period was the French Victorien Sardou, who is best remembered for such well-made plays as *A Scrap of Paper*, in which the insignificant thing of the title became the major factor in the dénouement. These plays sometimes seem like well-oiled machines that run themselves rather than being driven by their characters (a charge made against all well-made plays). The same could be said of the farces of Eugène Labiche (*The Italian Straw Hat*) and Georges Feydeau (*A Flea in Her Ear*)—complicated, rapid-fire actions that set the example for "French bedroom farce," an equally mechanical type in which sets of lovers, angry husbands, wives, and would-be lovers go in and out of bedroom doors like toy trains going around tracks.

In England, Oscar Wilde wrote perhaps the best, and still the most often revived, light comedy since the Restoration, *The Importance of Being Earnest*, an apparently frivolous look at upper-class mores and duplicity. George Bernard Shaw then dominated European and American comedy until the 1930s. A Realist and a socialist, Shaw was paradoxically both the best comic playwright of the period and the most serious one as well, his plays full of verbal fireworks and the collision of real ideas—poverty, industrialism, war, nationalism—although their subjects were ostensibly the old ones of love, marriage, and money. Noel Coward continued verbal, elitist English comedy of wit through World War II. The three playwrights continue to be widely revived around the world.

In the United States, George S. Kaufman and Moss Hart created off-beat characters and a more democratic approach to comedy, but they remained socially conservative and somewhat sentimental. They wrote large-cast plays that commercial Broadway could still afford, even in the Great Depression. However, as costs rose, casts shrank, and by the time Neil Simon began to dominate Broadway in the 1960s, smaller casts were the rule. Simon's mixture of gags and sentiment has made him the most produced American playwright of his time.

Musical Theatre

Music has always been part of the theatre; as we have seen, it was a major component of melodrama. Various kinds of "ballad opera" marked the pre-Romantic period (e.g.,

Gay's *The Beggar's Opera*). By the early nineteenth century, *operetta* (romantic, story-based play with music) was popular in Paris; in London, the works of William S. Gilbert and Arthur Sullivan (*The Pirates of Penzance*) dominated British musical theatre in the last quarter of the nineteenth century. In working-class areas, "music halls" grew out of public houses (saloons), and "music hall" became a term for lower-class musical variety, which included a master of ceremonies, songs, comedians, and dancers. In America, the similar vaudeville and burlesque were established during the first half of the nineteenth century. Burlesque, originally a comic form for mixed audiences (e.g., *Po-Co-Hon-Tas*, a send-up of a fashionable play about Native Americans) became overwhelmingly a male entertainment after Lydia Thompson's "British Blondes" toured America in 1869. Thereafter, burlesque featured spectacle, song, dance, and female bodies. "Striptease" was added after World War I, pushing burlesque to the outskirts of respectability. Vaudeville, on the other hand, flourished as a family entertainment and served as an example and a recruiting league for the Broadway *revue*, a non-story mix of comedy, music, and dance with opulent spectacle and lots of more or less clothed female bodies (e.g., the many *Ziegfeld Follies*). Many of the stars of vaudeville moved to radio and the movies in the 1930s when vaudeville itself died, done in by movies and the Depression.

Musical theatre in America, however, took another direction. Incorporating songs and dance into story in new ways, it became the outstanding theatrical export of a nation that itself was coming to dominate the world with its popular culture.

The American Musical

As a distinctly American musical form developed after about 1900, the American musical separated itself from European operetta on the one hand and the musical revue, on the other. From its beginnings, nonetheless, it had a double appeal in music and spectacle; the latter was often the female body, gorgeously costumed, often dancing—the "chorus girl."

Composers.   Most of the top Broadway composers of the first half of the twentieth century wrote for operetta or revue (or both), even while (perhaps unconsciously) helping to create the new, story-based, integrated form that became American musical comedy. They worked with *lyricists* (writers of words to songs) and *librettists* (writers of the play or "book"). These composers included

- Victor Herbert (1859–1924), *Babes in Toyland,* 1903; *The Red Mill,* 1905; *Naughty Marietta,* 1910 (operettas)
- Jerome Kern (1885–1945), *Oh, Boy!,* 1917; *Sally,* 1920; *Show Boat,* 1927
- Sigmund Romberg (1887–1951), *Blossom Time,* 1921; *The Student Prince,* 1924; *The Desert Song,* 1926
- Irving Berlin (1888–1989), *Music Box Revue,* 1921; *Annie Get Your Gun,* 1946; *Call Me Madam,* 1950
- Cole Porter (1891–1964), *Anything Goes,* 1934; *Red, Hot and Blue!,* 1936; *Kiss Me, Kate,* 1948

FIGURE 18.8 The American Musical—the 1930s.

Ethel Merman (*center*) was one of the great stars of the period of American musicals that was star-dominated. Here, she is seen in Cole Porter's *Anything Goes* on Broadway. (BETTMAN/Corbis)

- George Gershwin (1898–1937), *Lady, Be Good,* 1924; *Strike Up the Band,* 1930; *Of Thee I Sing,* 1931 (first Pulitzer Prize for a musical); *Porgy and Bess,* 1935
- Richard Rodgers (1902–1979), *Garrick Gaieties,* 1925, 1926; *On Your Toes,* 1936; *Pal Joey,* 1940; *Oklahoma!,* 1943; *Carousel,* 1945; *The Sound of Music,* 1959

A slightly later group of composers (with their lyricists, librettists, and directors) brought the integrated story musical to its optimal form:

- Frederick Lowe (1901–1988), *Brigadoon,* 1947; *My Fair Lady,* 1956; *Camelot,* 1960
- Jule Styne (b. 1905), *Gypsy,* 1959; *Funny Girl,* 1964
- Leonard Bernstein (1918–1990), *On the Town,* 1944; *Candide,* 1956; *West Side Story,* 1957

Neither these composers' backgrounds nor their music was entirely "American," however. Herbert was born in Ireland, Romberg in Hungary, Berlin in Russia, Lowe in Germany, Styne in England. Their musical training was often European and classical, not American and popular—Gershwin with a private teacher; Romberg, Herbert, and Lowe in Europe; Kern at the New York College of Music and in Europe; Porter at Yale and Harvard. What distinguished their music as the century progressed, however, was the adoption of rhythms that were the rhythms of popular dance music. Such music had its roots in nineteenth-century black musical forms that, by 1900, had their own literature and their own artists and that were known throughout America. Probably popularized in theatrical types that were themselves patronizing to blacks (e.g., the minstrel show, blackface vaudeville acts, "coon singing"), this music—cakewalk, ragtime—was already in the American grain by the time the American musical was ready to begin its evolution. Over the next half-century, jazz, blues, and then rock were also welcomed. Such music's creators, however, were not adequately credited, and black composers rarely made it to Broadway. (Exceptions included Will Marion Cook and Eubie Blake.)

This new American music was sung by new American characters. The characters of operetta had been stock European figures, usually with upper-class backgrounds (Romberg's *Student Prince* is typical); the characters of the new musical were untitled—although sometimes rich—and American.

Lyricists. Essential to such change were the lyricists who wrote the words to the songs and, sometimes, the scripts of the musicals. With increasing frequency, the top composers were associated with the same lyricists in musical after musical, and the lyricists clearly shaped the tone and often the style of the music. In no composer is this clearer than Richard Rodgers. Until 1940, his lyricist was the witty and inventive Lorenz Hart, and their musicals show Hart's unsentimental mind (*Pal Joey*). Rodgers later connected with Oscar Hammerstein II, and the musicals became more romantic, sometimes saccharine—*The Sound of Music,* for example. Hammerstein had had much the same effect on Jerome Kern, with whom he collaborated after 1925; the result was *Show Boat,* a more serious and sentimental musical than Kern's earlier work with others. George Gershwin, on the other hand, worked throughout his career with his brother Ira. Frederick Lowe had his greatest successes when teamed with Alan J. Lerner (*Brigadoon* and after). Cole Porter wrote his own lyrics.

Melody and Song. Both the operetta and the revue faded after the 1920s; the "book musical" (drama with music, but not operetta, first seen in the second decade of the twentieth century) took their place. Still usually frivolous and with songs often more stuck in than developed from the action, such musicals were meant as entertainments whose scripts were excuses for glorious melody. As a result, they produced many of the great songs of the American theatre. Jerome Kern, for example, poured out beautiful melodies seemingly endlessly; George Gershwin, in his short life, wrote many songs that became "standards." What is perhaps most significant about these composers is that they were primarily *song*-writers. Many of them wrote songs on order for a moment in a script ("song cue here!")—love songs, novelty songs, Southern songs, patter songs, "show-stoppers." These songs became part of the national cultural life at a time when many middle-class homes had a piano, and sheet music was sold at the five-and-dime. Songs were detached from the musicals and popularized via sheet music and radio, and they were sung and played in nightclubs and supper clubs—and in homes.

The Integrated Musical. Only gradually did a more serious dramatic purpose appear, foreshadowed in *Show Boat,* fully realized in *Pal Joey* and *Oklahoma!.* The movement

FIGURE 18.9 **The American Musical—the Zenith.**
George Gershwin's *Porgy and Bess*, shown here in a 1950s production, pushed the musical
into opera. Gershwin himself bridged what had been a gap between classical and popular
music, writing both magnificent show tunes such as "I've Got Rhythm" (and some hack ones
such as "Mammy," written by the young Gershwin for Al Jolson) and symphonic music such
as "An American in Paris." Much of Gershwin's music owed a debt to jazz and other African-
American music, which he acknowledged. (Photo courtesy of Brown Brothers.)

thereafter—that is, after 1940—was toward a serious comedy with a happy ending,
usually centered on romantic love, mostly dealing with contemporary people, and having song arising from character and moving the plot along (integrated). The appearance
of serious social content was sometimes important (*West Side Story*), but it was a rare
musical that dealt so harshly with tough subject matter that it demanded a downbeat
ending (*Gypsy*).

Gender and Race.   It should be noted that all the composers and lyricists named above
were white men; so were most musical producers and directors. (A few white women—
Dorothy Fields, Betty Comden—were notable lyricists; Mary Rodgers was a composer.)
Many of the composers and lyricists were also European immigrants or children of immigrants; most revered European culture but were caught up in American commercial
culture. Their assumptions were reflected in the musicals, which, until at least the 1970s,
were mostly about a white America obsessed with romantic love and material success.
The "glorification of the American girl" was a very white-male undertaking.

Mostly invisible but essential to the music were black musicians of both sexes. Although individual white composers often acknowledged a debt to African American
music, the industry did not, and some black musicians resented such cooptings as
Gershwin's *Porgy and Bess*—a white's version of Southern black life, using the white's

version of black music. Yet, Gershwin's work is now an American classic, and one that has provided great roles for black musical performers. Since the 1970s, the imbalance has somewhat corrected itself.

Theatres and Production Practices

As we have seen, the most important factor in the development of commercial theatre was demographic: a larger and larger potential audience as cities grew and population increased. In the nineteenth century, theatre became the most popular public art in Europe and America, at least equal to contemporary movies or television. Satisfying this huge audience changed theatre buildings, scenery, acting, and costumes. The number and capacity of theatres increased; so did the size and complexity of stages and support areas. (The forestage, however, shrank.) At the same time, detail in scenery, costumes, and acting increased as a result of the shift from hearing to seeing plays.

The eighteenth-century division between "legitimate" (monopoly) and "illegitimate" (proto-commercial fair and boulevard) theatre became a more complex segmentation by class and by taste within commercialism itself, with the remnant monopoly theatres (e.g., the *Comédie Française*) holding a bastion a little apart. By the late 1800s, cities had become enormous and public transport was needed to get from one part to another, deepening the division between middle-class and working-class theatres. At the same time, the economic thrust toward profiteering and monopoly made producers and theatre-owners the new masters of the theatre, able (briefly, as it turned out) to dictate what would be played and who would play it, and centralizing the theatre nationally while maintaining far-flung circuits.

Physical Theatre

With Romanticism, theatres had begun to expand and multiply as early as the late eighteenth century. London's Covent Garden Theatre, for example, doubled its capacity between 1730 and 1793. The first Chestnut Street Theatre in Philadelphia (1794) seated 1,200 but was quickly enlarged to 2,000. More than thirty theatres were built in Germany in 1775–1800, thirty-five more by 1850.

The standard configuration remained box, pit, and gallery until almost the end of the nineteenth century. However, as seeing the play became dominant in the Romantic age of spectacle, the audience was banned from the stage and the best seats shifted from boxes to the orchestra (the old pit). As Romanticism gave way to Realism, however, theatres tended to become more intimate, with Continental seating and well-defined proscenium stages without forestages. Smaller theatres for Realistic plays had relatively simple scene-shifting facilities, but those designed for spectacle had advances made possible by new technology—elevator stages, powered turntables.

Overall, these physical changes after 1750 were democratizing ones—removing a favored elite from the stage, bringing the best seats down among the audience, adopting Wagner's model of a theatre where all seats were equally good. At the same time, much of what was staged in the Romantic period was less verbal and more visual, muting the old upper-class reliance on language as a mark of class. However, as theatres themselves stratified socially, the lower-class ones moved still farther away from language—music hall, variety, vaudeville, and burlesque—and the now middle-class ones in places such as London's West End and New York's Broadway tended toward a drama that relied on language, albeit in prose instead of poetry. New theatres built for Realism were more intimate, again built for hearing as much as for seeing.

Production Practices

In 1750, scenery comprised wings, drops (painted fabric hung from overhead to the stage floor), borders, and ground rows (low, free-standing flats on the stage floor), the whole arrangement called *wing-and-drop scenery*. It adapted well to Romanticism, with the edges of wings, borders, and ground-rows cut into the shapes of leaves, branches, and other natural objects; wings set at angles and sometimes set asymmetrically; and drops giving distant landscape and sky or imitations of walls, room interiors, and such things as caves. Three-dimensional details were added only where so-called *practicables* were needed—a bridge that actors actually crossed, for example. Increasingly after 1750, scenery and special effects were governed by the desire to represent reality pictorially; hence the term *pictorial illlusionism*. Increasingly, too, the level of detail was raised to particularize settings (not simply "a room in a palace" but a particular room in a par-

FIGURE 18.10 **Theatre of the Late 1700s.**
"Inside View of the New Theatre, Philadelphia," showing box, pit, and gallery; a sizeable forestage with stage doors; and wing-and-drop scenery. (Courtesy of the Library Company of Philadelphia.)

FIGURE 18.11 **Romantic Scenery.**
Dominated by the "practicable" (the bridge on which actors are moving), this scenery
has uneven silhouettes, broken lines, and distant, natural vistas.

ticular building.) Historical and geographical detail were also added; by 1850, even in
America (which lagged behind Europe), historical accuracy in costumes and sets was so
popular that a term, *antiquarianism,* was used for it. By the 1880s, antiquarianism had
become so entrenched that productions of Shakespeare sought to reproduce the real
Juliet's tomb for *Romeo and Juliet,* the real Ardennes forest in France for the Forest of Arden in *As You Like It.* Costumes for such productions were copied from period paintings
and museum collections.

With the emergence of Realism in the commercial theatre, scenery became still
more three-dimensional and detailed—a literal copy of a restaurant, for example. By
1900, as well, audiences often sat in darkened auditoria, following Wagner's model, increasing their attention to the stage and increasing the sense of a stage "picture" framed
by the proscenium. The now-unused forestage shrank to a narrow "apron," scarcely big
enough for anything but so-called "cross-overs"—brief scenes in front of a curtain
while scenery was changed behind it.

Lighting

Eighteenth-century lighting was still done by candles or oil lamps. Various attempts to
improve it with lenses and such things as liquid-filled bottles didn't work; the principal

lighting was from candelabra hung over the stage. They lighted only certain areas, however, and then not well, probably causing actors and designers to use contrasting makeup and bright or glittery costumes; candelabra also inhibited the use of overhead scenery. After 1830, lighting in big, urban theatres was often done with gas, the audience area lighted by enormous central clusters of gas lights that generated so much moisture as a by-product that a fog could develop near the ceiling. Gas and, later, limelight (a chemical caused to incandesce by heat) allowed for crude spotlighting, with other principal lighting from footlights along the front of the stage and border-lights overhead.

About 1880, the first electric lights appeared in theatres (the first all-electric theatre was the Savoy in London, home of Gilbert and Sullivan). Electricity made the artistic manipulation of light finally possible, and it extended the life of theatre buildings by reducing the risk of fire that had plagued theatres until then. Electric control also coincided with the darkening of the house, changing the visual relationship between audience and performance.

Actors and Acting

Commercial theatregoers loved great acting as much as they loved spectacle and sentimental shlock. Steam, gas, and then electric power made national and then international stardom possible: stars had their names and pictures in publications read by thousands, thanks to steam-powered printing machines.

Stars became identified with a role they played over and over: England's Henry Irving played a now-forgotten melodrama, *The Bells,* for thirty-four years; Eugene O'Neill's father, James, was identified with the role of the Count of Monte Cristo all his life; Joe Jefferson was identified with Rip Van Winkle. Such stars could become rich; it is said that Sarah Bernhardt had an income equal to that of her nation's prime minister.

Perhaps because of its enthusiasm for individuality and "genius," Romanticism also produced oddities—child stars who played adult roles, female stars who played men's (so-called breeches) roles. More important, Romanticism created a space and then an appetite for spectacular acting. Edmund Kean started a new age when he appeared in London in 1814, abandoning dignity and control in favor of flamboyance and passion. To see Kean act was to "read Shakespeare by flashes of lightning," a contemporary said. Romantic acting was thereafter marked by passionate outbursts and novel interpretations. In melodrama, differing levels of passion were seen, and, just as there were blood-and-thunder melodramas and "gentlemanly" melodramas, so, too, there were blood-and-thunder theatres (the Bowery in New York in the 1840s) and more genteel theatres (New York's Park Theatre), and actors to suit each. Great actors moved across these extremes: Charlotte Cushman played both the Bowery and the Park, chilling audiences at the first with the death of Nancy Sykes in an adaptation of Dickens's *Oliver Twist* and charming them at the Park in ladylike roles. Probably the greatest American actor of the nineteenth century, she played Romeo, a crazed Scottish witch, a blood-curdling English avenger, and most of the female roles of Shakespeare—all to raves.

The acting style was very vocal, highly gestural, and not often tied to what we would now call motivation and objective. The emphasis on language—big speeches, flowery vocabulary—moved actors toward vocalism. An emphasis on physical illustration of big

FIGURE 18.12 **Romantic Melodrama on the Modern Stage.**
The Vampire gave the theatre that exotic villain 75 years before Dracula and a hundred years before the movies' *Nosferatu*. Nonetheless, it thrilled audiences with some of the same spooky fol de rol—pursuit of a virgin whose blood the vampire wanted to drink; his fear of the sunlight; his eternal life. Here, two scenes show something of the acting style in a modern re-creation (*above*) and the scenery (*below*). (Courtesy of DePauw University. Directed by Susan Anthony.)

FIGURE 18.13 **The Child Actor.**
"Miss Clara Fisher as Lord Flimnap." Child stars played adult roles and were hugely popular. (Hand-colored etching by George Cruikshank. Print collection, Miriam and Ira D. Wallach Division of Arts, Prints, and Photographs, the New York Public Library, Astor, Lenox, and Tilden Foundations.)

moments moved them toward gesture—"physicalization," but not in a way bound by close imitation of life. Many melodramas, for example, included in their stage directions what gesture the actor was to use ("recoils in horror"), and many also ended a big scene or act with the word "tableau," a posed group picture that was to be held to make the maximum impact on the audience. Such posing and holding had no motivation: it was a purely aesthetic device, unconnected to character. In the same way, many of the comings and goings of characters were unmotivated or only thinly motivated. As with the tableaux, the needs of the play overcame the needs of character. By and large, as well, despite powerful superobjectives (the villain's evil, the hero's goodness), individual objectives could not be connected into a through-line because too many deviations and tendencies were necessary to meet the needs of the story.

Subsequent acting, however, moved toward Realism as such plays as the comedies of Scribe provided contemporary roles with less flamboyance. Gentlemanly melodrama of the second half of the nineteenth century also reduced the wilder excesses of earlier melodramas, although blood-and-thunder could still be seen in many theatres. Subsequently, Realism required a still less formal style (see pp. 341–343). In the United States, this style took over an earlier one called *local color acting,* that is, the playing of rural types with identifiable accents and distinctive, often cute, quirks. However, a truly Realistic acting style did not reach the American commercial theatre until at least the 1930s.

The Decline of Commercial Theatre

Shortly after 1900, the theatre was faced with commercial competition of a kind it had never known—the movies. *Birth of a Nation,* the first feature-length film (1915), was a sensation and a box-office hit. Sound came in 1927. By the late 1930s, *Gone With the Wind* was on the way to grossing more than $70 million; vaudeville stars were moving to another new medium, radio; and theatres across America were closing or turning into movie houses. Television became a commercial reality in America in 1948. These new

FIGURE 18.14 **The New Rival—Film.**
Short movies became popular early in the twentieth century, but in 1915,
D. W. Griffith released his feature-length *The Birth of a Nation*. Movies drained the
mass audience out of the theatres, ending stock companies, vaudeville, and most of
the road. This is a still from *Birth of a Nation*, the assassination of Lincoln in Ford's
Theatre, from the souvenir program of 1915. The lavish souvenir program itself
suggests how important this premiere was.

rivals ravaged the American theatrical circuits and the "road," ending vaudeville and burlesque, and driving the last nails into the coffins of stock companies.

The effect on Broadway was also severe and long-drawn-out. At the end of World
War I (1918), Broadway saw two to three hundred productions a year. Costs were reasonable (as little as $2,000 for a small show, rarely more than $10,000). Tickets prices
were low—$3 bought the best seat in the house. Tourists and New Yorkers flocked to the
theatres.

By the end of the 1930s, however, the vigorous commercial theatre of the 1920s was
in trouble. Despite occasional bright spots, Broadway's commercial theatre continued to
decline through World War II and beyond. Increasingly, New York theatres were abandoned, torn down, or converted to movie houses or "girlie shows." Many others were
dark (closed) as often as they were open.

Several other causes may be given for this decline. The Depression (1930s) hit
theatre hard. Theatrical unions grew strong enough to demand higher wages—from a
theatre less able to pay them. After World War II, the price of land in Manhattan soared,
making theatre buildings extremely expensive to rent or to buy. Fire regulations grew
more strict, and the cost of remodeling a building to meet the new codes went up. As the
cost of producing plays escalated, so did ticket prices; therefore, some former patrons

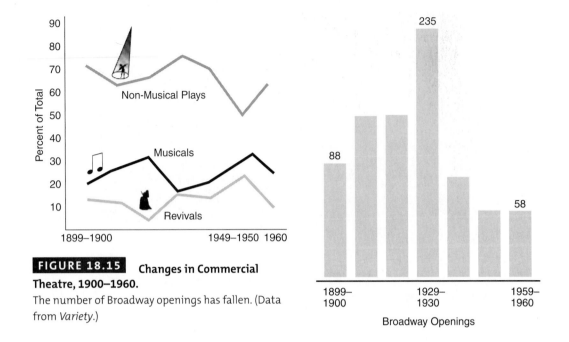

FIGURE 18.15 Changes in Commercial Theatre, 1900–1960.
The number of Broadway openings has fallen. (Data from *Variety*.)

found themselves priced out of the theatre. Clearly, the commercial theatre was in trouble, and its death was regularly—if inaccurately—predicted. It survived, but its glory days lay back before 1900.

Responses to Commercial Theatre

We saw in Chapter 17 that reformers founded little and art theatres, which sought small and elite audiences. However, the triumph of commercialism also spawned attempts to create noncommercial theatres that rivaled the commercial in size and production values. In many cases, these involved government subsidy and pointed toward the foundation of a national theatre in the cultural capital.

Modern Germany has many state- and city-supported theatres; the most influential has been Brecht's Berliner Ensemble (founded 1953). The Comédie Française still exists as a major world theatre, with state support. France and French cities have supported theatres outside the capital as well. The National Theatre of Britain uses Britain's best actors and artists and is subsidized; it grew out of earlier theatres like the Old Vic (London) and the Stratford (England) Shakespeare, now the Royal Shakespeare Company. The United States has had several attempts at mainstream companies with a noncommercial repertory in New York City: the actress Eva LeGallienne's Civic Repertory (1926), for example, and several companies at Lincoln Center more recently.

Thinking About Commercialism

Sometimes I worry about being a success in a mediocre world.

—Lily Tomlin

In a commercial theatre, the most successful play is the one that makes the most money; that is, profit defines success. To assure profit, Broadway tends to produce plays that have already succeeded somewhere else—in London,

in previous Broadway seasons, in regional theatres or Off-Broadway, as a movie. Using *Variety* and a Sunday *New York Times*, make a list of plays currently playing on Broadway. Using clues provided in the ads and whatever other resources you need, answer these two questions: Where did each production come from? How successful does it seem to be? (Successful plays tend to have longer runs.)

However, the United States has developed no national theatre in either the political (Washington) or the cultural (New York) capital. Instead, some organizations have made more modest efforts to offer productions not limited by a need for maximum profit. The first was the Theatre Guild in the 1920s, which supported works by American playwrights dealing with serious artistic or political issues (e.g., Eugene O'Neill) and serious (and at the time still controversial) foreign playwrights such as Ibsen and Shaw. Its early success almost persuaded Broadway that a commercial-sized audience existed for serious drama. By the Depression, however, the Guild was losing ground; as its own finances became precarious, it moved toward commercial practice. By the 1940s, the Theatre Guild was almost indistinguishable from the Broadway producers against whom it had originally rebelled.

In the 1930s, another new organization, the Group Theatre, was at first a militant voice for non- or anti-commercial theatre in New York, driven by a strong leftist slant. Its repertory focused on social issues, especially poverty and oppression. Perhaps more important was its popularizing of an Americanized version of Stanislavski's acting techniques (the American Method), which became the American Realistic style and dominates American stage and film. The Group Theatre also popularized a design style now called Simplified or Selective Realism. Financial and political problems ended the Group during World War II.

Launched in 1935, the Federal Theatre Project (FTP) was a program of the federal government aimed at aiding theatre artists who had been thrown out of work by the Depression. Part of the program's excitement came from its national character (units were established in almost every state); part came from its commitment to cultural diversity (there were, for example, both Jewish and black theatre companies); and part came from its innovative artistic practices. In New York, for example, the first *living newspaper* in the United States premiered. A kind of staged documentary, living newspapers soon spread throughout the country, dramatizing society's most pressing problems: housing, farm policies, venereal disease, war. During an anticommunist

FIGURE 18.16   **The Federal Theatre Project.**
The United States has never had a national theatre, but in the 1930s, the Works Projects
Administration ran the Federal Theatre Project to create jobs for theatre workers.
Hundreds of productions played all over the country. Here, Shaw's *Androcles and the
Lion* in a New York City production. (The National Archives of the United States.)

government probe, however, living newspapers were denounced as communist plots.
In 1939 the government failed to appropriate money for the FTP, and so ended the
nation's first far-reaching experiment in support of the arts. Before its demise, however,
the FTP introduced a number of major new artists and theatres, among them Orson
Welles.

The regional theatre movement is usually dated from 1947, when Margo Jones
opened a professional theatre in Dallas, Texas. Her goal was not only to decentralize the
theatre (to bring professional productions to the heartlands of America) but also to encourage the production of original and classic plays. She nurtured the talent of Tennessee Williams, for example. Before Jones's death in 1955 there were professional
theatres in Washington, D.C.; Houston, Texas; and Milwaukee, Wisconsin. With the
1960s came a surge of such theatres in places like Minneapolis, Los Angeles, Baltimore,
New Haven, and Louisville. In a departure from current New York practices, some of
these theatres built spaces without proscenia, preferring theatres in the round (e.g.,
Dallas and Washington, D.C.) or thrust stages (e.g., Minneapolis).

The Off-Broadway movement is usually said to have begun in 1952, when Tennessee
Williams's *Summer and Smoke* (first produced by Margo Jones in Dallas) became the
first major hit in a theatre located below Forty-second Street in thirty years. From then
through the 1960s, Off-Broadway served as a showcase for new talent and for plays
whose experimental style or controversial subjects made them unsuitable for the big
business of Broadway. Off-Broadway, however, finally succumbed to the pressures of
commercialism, and today it is little more than a tryout space for Broadway.

The Theatres of Colonialism

The major commercial powers in Europe established colonial empires in Asia and Africa in the eighteenth and nineteenth centuries. Missionaries, soldiers, settlers, and administrators went out from European centers to rule the new colonies. Their theatres went with them, both as professional companies that toured from the European base and as amateur theatres done by resident Europeans, mostly, for other Europeans. In both cases, it was national classics (Shakespeare, Molière) and plays of the commercial theatre that traveled. It was this theatre that the colonized peoples came into contact with, and it was this theatre, if any, that they later encountered in schools and universities.

European empires in Asia and Africa did not end until shortly after the middle of the twentieth century. At that time, the new nations, formerly colonies, were pulled in conflicting directions—toward the previous colonizer because of ties of language, governmental culture, education, and religion; away from the colonizer because of histories of oppression and rebellion; toward Soviet Marxism, which exploited their resentment of colonialism; toward capitalism, which promised wealth. When they got their independence, the new countries immediately had to cope with conflicts between old and new, tribal and colonial, traditional and modern. Complicating these tensions were others: the countries were in many cases impoverished, with no industrial base, and they had to build their own governments on a colonial framework, sometimes with no help from the old colonial power. They wanted to display to themselves and the world their new independence, but they still had financial and cultural ties with Europe. And some, like India and Pakistan, were torn by civil war.

All such forces buffeted and shaped post-colonial theatres, which thus became complicated mixes of indigenous forms, Western commercialism, Brechtian epic, and new ideas that tried to make theatre do its part in bringing former colonies into the developed world. At the end of the colonial period, most colonial theatres were still tied to the commercial theatre of the colonial power through the very idea they held of theatre itself and through their awareness of the European repertory. They were pushed away from these things, however, by distrust of the old colonial powers, by new self-assertion, and by desires to recover and celebrate their non-European past through indigenous forms.

The Indian sub-continent had Hindu, Buddhist, and Muslim cultures that long pre-dated colonialism, and a history that long pre-dated Europe's, with highly developed written languages and arts. (The Sanskrit play *Sakuntala,* for example, had been enthusiastically praised by German Romantics.) It also had rich indigenous theatrical forms (see pp. 321–322). Twentieth-century India maintained its traditions of indigenous theatre and added a minor, Westernized theatre. Bridging the two was Rabindranath Tagore (fl. 1890s–1920s), colonial India's Nobel laureate, but his vision of a native drama that provided a modern fusion of poetry, music, and movement was never realized. India's greatest commercial performance after independence was its booming film industry in "Bollywood" (Bombay).

Africa, with its mostly oral history and mostly tribal cultures, also had indigenous performances in some areas, but it was in a much weaker position than India. What we see in Africa through 1960, therefore, is only the beginning of a modern African theatre. The transition from colonial to post-colonial, c. 1920–1960, was marked by

- Adoption of European commercial theatre forms that were suitable for simple production and traveling
- Adaptation of indigenous theatre forms, using local language and culture, for professional touring
- Emphasis on the university drama department as the hothouse for a later national drama

In West Africa, these took several forms. *Concert party* was a British theatre term for a kind of traveling vaudeville with simple production values. Starting in the 1920s, both Ghanians and Nigerians developed this into a national form; the leading figures were Ishmael Johnson in Ghana and Hubert Ogunde in Nigeria. Ogunde built as well on one of Nigeria's dominant tribal traditions, Yoruba, to create *Yoruba opera*. It was rich in music, toured by companies through the Yoruba-speaking regions of Nigeria, where its performances had strong communal impact. Both countries also had universities with British-influenced interest in drama. In the 1950s, Efua Sutherland founded the

Links to More About Theatre

Heller in Pink Tights. Touring the Old West with Sophia Loren.

Funny Girl. Barbra Streisand as vaudeville star Fanny Brice.

Gerald Bordman, *American Musical Theatre,* 1992 (2nd edition).

Charles Dickens, *Nicholas Nickleby.* No one will ever create a better—or funnier—picture of a fifth-rate theatre troupe.

Henry T. Sampson, *The Ghost Walks,* 1988. "Blacks in show business, 1865–1910." Essential to an understanding of African Americans vis-à-vis the commercial theatre of the period.

<www.eoneill.com> Devoted to playwright O'Neill.

<http://memory.loc.gov/ammem/fedtp/> Library of Congress site chock-full of Federal Theatre Project stuff.

<www.welcometoindia.com> Click on culture, leisure, theatre.

<www.chinavista.com> Click on English, culture, Beijing opera (under music).

Ghana Drama Studio in close connection with the University of Ghana and became important as both playwright and producer. In 1960, however, vigorous theatre still lay mostly ahead for these nations; Nigeria would produce a Nobel-laureate playwright before 2000 (see pp. 416–417). None of the three East African colonies (Kenya, Uganda, Tanganyika) had the indigenous ritual and performance that was found in West Africa, with the result that through c. 1960 such theatre as there was, was university- and European-centered. To the south in Malawi, a slyly subversive but minor theatrical form developed out of military drill and marching. Using bands, martial music, and song and speeches, it became a subtle way to mock the colonial power.

South Africa was at once a more Westernized and a more racially divided colony. With Europeans resident since the seventeenth century, it had a longer and a more intense European contact than most of the rest of Africa. Larger and richer than many African colonies, it was, by the late nineteenth century, a touring destination for commercial theatrical companies also heading for Australia and India. White-dominated South Africa became independent in the 1950s, but, for its black majority, it remained a colony until 1993. Apartheid (racial separation instituted after World War II in imitation of Nazi Germany) kept races apart, with theatre mostly European (white) and done in and for white areas of large cities. The mostly white media advertised and reviewed plays imported or copied from Broadway and the West End and largely ignored black theatre. Nonetheless, a black *township theatre* came into existence before independence, named for the black areas in the cities (townships). Originally nonconfrontational, it highlighted musicals that combined elements of the American musical with indigenous dance and music. The leading figure was Gibson Kente. At least one production, *King Kong* (no relation to the movie) toured internationally.

Theatres of Cultural Imperialism

Even in areas where Europe did not actually take over and colonize, it nonetheless exerted great influence. The cultural pressure was to "modernize," meaning to adopt the practice of the world-dominant cultural power. The result was the creation of European-style commercial theatres, even in Muslim countries such as Egypt and, after the collapse of the Ottoman Empire in the 1920s, Turkey. When the Suez Canal was finished in 1876, for example, the Europeanized Egyptian ruler commissioned Giuseppe Verdi's *Aida* for the opening ceremonies. Both Turkey and Egypt have since developed commercial theatres on the European model.

Theatres in the East

In China, a new theatrical form became dominant at about the same time that Romanticism peaked in the West. Called *opera* by Westerners, it took many local forms, but the best-known and the still-dominant one was *Beijing opera*. It was typified by

- Multiact dramas
- All-male actors

- Song and music almost throughout
- Division of characters into four main types—male, female, painted-face, and clown ("painted face" referring to elaborate makeup of, for example, demons and warriors)
- Reliance on traditional sources for stories and characters

In the 1800s, Beijing opera became enormously popular in China. Although a tradition of itinerant actors continued (troupes rarely stayed at the same theatre for more than a few days), permanent theatres were built. Leading actors moved from theatre to theatre as Western stars did; the repertory was usually so familiar that they could step into a role in any theatre without rehearsal. The performances themselves relied on centuries-old conventions, played in theatres of a single type with

- A raised, pillared stage with audience on three sides and entrances left and right
- No scenery, and only large properties (tables and chairs) that could be used for walls, mountains, etc.
- A nonrealistic acting style that took as much as twenty years of training
- Symbols and signs—a whip to signify riding, running with flags to signify wind
- Remarkable acrobatics, especially in battle scenes (perhaps the precursor of Kung Fu films)

Western accounts describe Beijing opera audiences as noisy but may have reflected either misunderstanding or a corrupt stage in the form's development. All agreed, how-

FIGURE 18.17 **Eastern Theatre.** Beijing opera is now the best-known of Chinese theatre forms, with performances in many parts of China, Taiwan, and Chinese communities in cities like San Francisco. Here, a performance in Taiwan with Yi-Hui Lee. (Photo courtesy of Yi-Hui Lee.)

ever, that Beijing opera, like Kabuki, was an actor's art. One name stands out in Beijing opera of the early 1900s—Mei Lan Fang. A superb actor of female roles, he toured in the West, restored some classical elements of the form, and was a force for its preservation.

However, Western cultural influence also affected China. Anti-traditional ideas were loosed about 1900 with the fall of the last dynasty, and people with new ideas produced China's first Western play—*Uncle Tom's Cabin*. Other Western plays followed, bringing innovations: popular, not classical, language; non-Confucian moral ideas; spoken, not sung, drama; and, after 1924, female actors. A coeducational theatre school was started in 1930. A new Chinese drama emerged, typified by Ts'ao Yu's *Thunderstorm* and *Metamorphsosis* after World War II. With the Communist rise to power in 1949, some Russian influence was seen, and a model revolutionary opera on the Beijing model, *Taking Tiger Mountain by Strategy,* was produced.

FIGURE 18.18 **Eastern Theatre.**
Princess Iron Fan, a Beijing opera performance in China. (Courtesy of the People's Republic of China.)

Similarly, Western influence was felt on Japanese theatre after about 1900. It was only after World War II, however, and the American occupation (which was unsympathetic to Kabuki and traditional forms) that a modern theatre form was established. Junji Kinoshita's *Twilight Crane* (1950) has been called "a milestone in the history of Japanese playwriting," fusing Japanese art with modern ideas.

KEY TERMS

Check your understanding against this list. Brief definitions are in the Glossary; page references there will direct you to appropriate pages. (Persons are page-referenced in the Index.)

actor-manager	royalties
antiquarianism	sentimentality
Beijing opera	signature music
commercialism	star system
concert party	township musical
gentlemanly melodrama	well-made play
integrated musical	wing-and-drop scenery
melodrama	Yoruba opera
producer	

Theatre for a
New Millennium

When you have completed this chapter, you should be able to

- Discuss the history of commercial theatre since 1960

- Identify and discuss the principal noncommercial trends since 1960

- Identify and discuss leading examples of postcolonial African theatre

- Identify and discuss leading avant-garde theatres of the 1960s
  and 1970s

Since 1960, lives in developed countries have been marked by increasing information overload and increasing rate of change. The idea of stability, so essential to the nineteenth century, has all but vanished, victim of two upheavals—that in science, where Einstein and Heisenberg demolished the idea of certainty; and that in technology, which has reduced the idea of a "generation" of common experience from decades to no more than a few years. The great divide has been the coming of the computer and the Internet.

The new technology brought two revolutions: quantity of information and quantity of points of access, the latter of which made it possible for everybody to be in touch from home, from a car, from the street. The results have been, on the one hand, self-definition by groups whose members had before not been able to find each other—ethnic, political, religious, sexual, social—and a shift from "engagement" or direct individual experience to observation or the life of the couch potato—virtual experience.

Since 1960, millions of people have discovered that they were not alone in what they thought an isolated moral or sexual or religious stance. Conservative Christianity, feminism, and the gay rights movement were all enabled by the same technologies, and all became mass movements as a result. The same thing is happening with entities as diverse as Latino politics, Chinese-American consciousness, and American Islam. Electronic communications also "democratized" institutions by making it difficult to hide information or to ignore constituencies; they also gave power to any individual with e-mail. This surfacing of previously hidden identities and invisible individuals created a furor over "political correctness," an outward sign of an increasingly democratic society—that is, one in which everybody has a voice.

FIGURE 19.1   **Cultural Democratization.**
The 1970s musical *A Chorus Line* had a group protagonist, dancing here in the finale. This kind of democratization of culture was typical of the period. (Photograph by Martha Swope.)

The movement toward substitute or virtual experience has been marked by, on the one hand, an interest in "interactivity" and, on the other, an interest in a substitute reality more "real" than Realism. Interactivity gave individuals at last the illusion of control over subject matter (e.g., computer games, computerized narrative) and led, for example, to more interaction between audience and performers. Substitute reality led to a perhaps temporary enthusiasm for "reality TV," shows that seemed unscripted, performed by people without actor training (although close examination suggests that many such shows were in fact carefully scripted and their performers were very self-aware.) Both of these tendencies changed the idea of theatre and its practice.

During the same period, America "won" the Cold War (or the Soviet Union "lost" it) and stood after 1990 as the sole super-power. The United States could not, nonetheless, resolve horrendous contradictions in the world: Americans were overweight and used a disproportionate amount of the world's energy and raw materials, but millions were dying of starvation in the Southern Hemisphere. The United States was rich but was also crime-ridden and violent. American capitalism "triumphed," but huge businesses went bankrupt overnight, the stock market yo-yoed, economies crashed, and states from South America to central Europe questioned the free market. America's popular culture dominated the world, but people in far-flung places hated America enough to blow up the World Trade Center and kill its citizens.

Contradictions, complexities, and uncertainties thus mark the new millennium. Denied by technology the nineteenth-century ability to ignore the unpleasant, people find themselves in a culture that must, like it or not, tolerate opposites and ambivalences. Democratized by forces outside itself, what used to be called *art* finds itself joined by activities that would not formerly have been thought of as art. Hierarchies have been shaken, and "good" and "bad," "high" and "low" have become sometimes meaningless. Culture, like economics, has become global, and, although the flow is mostly from America outward, important elements flow inward, as well.

Postmodernism

Postmodernism is a perhaps crude term for the changes since 1960. Above all, these have been the collapse of hierarchies, the equalizing of individuals and ideas, and the loss of certainty. The assumptions underlying these attributes include

- Loss of belief in objectivity and truth
- Loss of belief in meaning
- Reliance on bottom-up participation rather than top-down dictation
- Belief in differences and shades of meaning rather than black-white opposites

Inevitably, postmodernism has created reactions, which we see in flights toward hierarchy, inequality of ideas, and certainty—most obviously, the recent, powerful rise in fundamental religions all around the world. It may be that the theatre itself, or at least the commercial theatre, represents the same sort of flight.

FIGURE 19.2 **Postmodernism.**

Mixing of periods and radical reinterpretaion of text mark postmodern performance. This is a production of Molière's *Tartuffe* at the University of Missouri. (Directed by Suzanne Burgoyne, scenic design by R. Dean Packard, costume design by James Miller, lighting design by Sandy Harned; photo courtesy of the University of Missouri.)

The Theatre, 1960–2000s

When a society is uncertain, its art is likely to show uncertainty. As a culture looks for a paradigm to explain itself, its art, and therefore its theatre, also seeks a model to try to capture the essence of the age. However, commercialism becomes a counter-force if the theatre is not bound to the culture, as now seems to be the case: that is, when the theatre exists out at the edge somewhere, the commercial need to attract audiences may cause it to offer not what is new and often threatening in the culture but what is old and comforting.

If anything can be said to characterize the theatre, both commercial and non-commercial, of 1960–present, it has been its eclecticism—its tolerance of many diverse styles. The theatre buildings of the period have been variously shaped and located. Theatrical productions have been variously conceived, with wildly different styles. Plays have been of mixed forms, mixed media, mixed theories.

Much of American and European theatre after 1960 continued to be commercial; it was, in fact, the "mainstream." Through the 1970s, however, there was also a strong avant-garde movement. There were also many other noncommercial theatres, some political, some aesthetic. Nonetheless, the loss of the theatre's audience continued, the competition from film and television reinforced by new technologies that kept people at home, online, tuned-in, and out of big cities after dark.

Commercial Theatre

As costs of production continued to rise after 1960, long runs and higher ticket prices got more important. The average ticket cost about ten dollars by 1975, about thirty by 1985, and more than forty-five by 2000. In 1995, the average *regional* theatre ticket cost twenty dollars, with highs of forty-eight. As costs and prices rose, audiences and repertories got more conservative. In the United States, musicals dominated Broadway. An occasional serious drama appeared, but none captured the Broadway audience for long.

At midsummer of 2002, for example, thirty-six productions were playing on Broadway. Twenty-two were musicals; three others were one-person shows, one of them musical. Of the other musicals, fourteen were from former seasons, several from more than five years before; seven were revivals of shows from the 1960s or earlier. Eight were "presold," adapted from works already successful elsewhere—mostly movies. Of the nonmusical plays, three were revivals going back as far as the 1930s; one was adapted from a 1960s movie; and only three were new and original plays—two of them by playwrights whose careers went back to the 1960s. None of the plays in the sample was a nonmusical classic from American or world theatre—no Miller or Williams; no Ibsen or Shaw; no Molière or Shakespeare. The repertory at this point suggested a dearth of serious new playwrights and plays, a reliance on musicals, and a desire to guarantee against failure by adapting works that had succeeded in other media, usually the movies—a reversal from the days when movies were adapted from Broadway hits.

Musical Theatre

Musicals of the early 1960s were mostly optimistic—*Camelot, Mame*—but they gave way to darker works as the era itself darkened. The two following decades were dominated by the composer-lyricist Stephen Sondheim. His lyrics for *Gypsy* and his lyrics and music for *Follies* took a bittersweet look at the musical stage itself. All his work integrated character and song, so that songs often could not be detached from the drama (a great change from the days of Gershwin and Porter, when show tunes became "standards" without reference to the shows from which they came). To some in the audience, the gain in dramatic power was won at the cost of tunefulness and the old zesty, punchy musical show. However, the theatre itself had changed: many fewer shows were being produced, and the age of the star whose name could sell tickets was about over.

Other changes came, as well: *Hair* brought 1960s counterculture and rock to Broadway; in the 1970s, *A Chorus Line* brought a group protagonist and a love affair with dance that lasted into the 1990s. Black composers and performers finally broke through the commercial theatre's glass ceiling.

In the 1990s, spectacle dominated, with dance, dazzling costume, and high-tech effects. A 1980s influx of British musicals (*Cats, Phantom of the Opera*) had started this

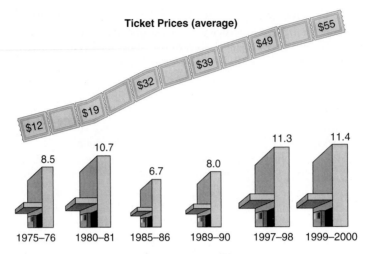

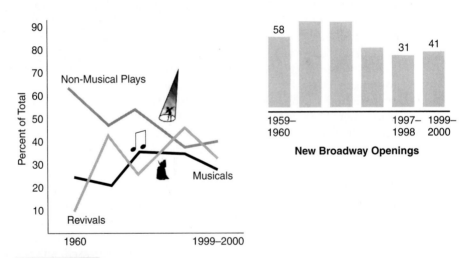

FIGURE 19.3 **Changes in Commercial Theatre, 1960–2000.**

Since 1960, ticket prices have soared as Broadway costs have risen; the number of Broadway openings has declined. (From data in *Variety.*)

trend, which reached its peak with the expensive and elaborate Disney production *The Lion King.* By 2002, it was joined on Broadway by two other Disney productions, a sign of a shift in commercial organization toward the corporate. Much of Broadway musical theatre, however, was by then looking backward (in 2002, revivals of *Oklahoma!,* 1944; *Cabaret,* 1966; *Flower Drum Song,* 1958; *The Boys from Syracuse,* 1938) or toward collage musicals of earlier hits (*Mamma Mia,* from the songs of the 1960s group ABBA).

FIGURE 19.4 **Counterculture on Broadway.**
The musical *Hair* was a 1960s milestone, bringing "hippie" themes and rock. Cutting-edge
when it was done, it now seems rather quaint. (Martha Swope Photo.)

Comedy

Commercial theatre from the 1960s through much of the 1990s relied as well on comedies more than serious drama to ensure box-office revenue. Neil Simon was the most
successful playwright. Major plays of the 1960s (*The Odd Couple*) established him as a
master gag writer and were transferred to movies and television. Throughout the early
1990s, Simon gave more depth to his comedies and, in 1991, won the Pulitzer Prize for
the more or less autobiographical *Lost in Yonkers.* No other American comic playwright
showed either Simon's ability or his staying power, but the British Michael Frayne was
successful with a series of comedies. The best of these, *Noises Off,* was a masterly farce
about the theatre, revived in 2002.

Serious Plays

The proportion of serious plays declined throughout the period. Older playwrights
such as Arthur Miller and Tennessee Williams wrote important plays in the 1960s, and
Miller was still active at the century's end. Edward Albee, first seen Off-Broadway at the
end of the 1950s, towered over most of the period, still winning a Tony in 2002 (*The
Goat*). The outstanding serious drama of the 1990s was Tony Kushner's two-part *Angels
in America,* which won many awards. Black playwrights moved into the mainstream in

FIGURE 19.5   **The Age of Imports.**

The 1980s Broadway was marked by imported British musicals. Here, *Cats*.
(Martha Swope Photo.)

this period, with August Wilson (*Fences, The Piano Lesson*) important from the 1980s on and Suzan-Lori Parks (*Topdog/Underdog*) winning the Pulitzer Prize in 2002.

Globalization

American commercial theatre also got some of its small supply of serious plays from abroad. Mostly, these were British, occasionally Irish; a few regional theatres late in the period did rare productions of African drama, including at least one translated Yoruba opera. However, the few non-American plays that Broadway produced were mostly European. In the 1960s, the German Peter Weiss's *Marat/Sade,* in an English production, was a hit. Later, the plays of British playwright Harold Pinter provided some of the most serious of Broadway drama for two decades. The proportion of serious plays declined, however; after 2000, the few imported plays were mostly comedies.

At the same time, America's best dramas were produced around the world, particularly the plays of Miller, Williams, and Albee, with Tony Kushner's *Angels in America* also a major export.

Retrogression

What is perhaps most significant about Broadway's recent seasons has been the extent to which it looked backward. It did not do so by reviving classics, other than 1940s and

1950s musicals that are in a sense "classics" of the genre, but by reviving successes. It continued to fill a modest number of theatres by doing so, but the total audience for all of Broadway in the new millennium cannot have been more than twelve million people a year—a tiny proportion of the U.S. population.

It is also significant that this retrogression mostly escaped the effects identified as postmodern, including the interactivity, connectedness, and uncertainty discussed above. This escape from contemporary life suggests, perhaps, how irrelevant at least commercial theatre had become by 2000.

Noncommercial Theatre

In the 1960s, a different kind of theatre tried, sometimes desperately, to be relevant. The 1960s saw a powerful counterculture arise, lasting into the 1970s; partly the product of the Vietnam War, partly the product of political leftism, it challenged established values. This counterculture expressed itself in theatre through a new wave of avant-gardism that began Off- and Off-Off-Broadway but quickly decentralized.

Avant-garde theatres included *The Living Theatre,* founded in 1947 by Julian Beck and Judith Malina, which started as an art theatre in New York (the last of the "modernist" theatres), doing such works as Picasso's *Desire* and plays by Bertolt Brecht. In the 1960s, it became a political theatre and reorganized into a commune to promote a revolution through "benevolent anarchy." It toured internationally, becoming famous for involvement of the audience, for performances that turned into protest marches, and for such shock tactics as nudity, moving from modern to postmodern in its style. The *Bread and Puppet Theatre* (1961) toured, handing out bread and using giant puppets that told stories; they played in found spaces and used found materials. After the 1970s, they became a mostly local Vermont phenomenon. *The Open Theatre* (1963), directed mostly by Joseph Chaikin, was a postmodernist influence on theatre practice: it used theatre games and improvisations to make scripts; its techniques included "transformations" (actors transforming themselves into several characters without masks, costume changes, or signs), and actors as environment (by "becoming" objects and moving the sparse scenery). The group dissolved in 1974. Charles Ludlam's *Ridiculous Theatre Company* appeared Off-Broadway in the late 1960s, the best and best-known of the outrageous, camp theatres of the period. Postmodern in its style, it used snippets of dialogue, characters, and events from many sources, including heavy doses of pop culture. Ludlam died in 1987. *Robert Wilson and the Byrd Hoffman School of Byrds* crossed artistic lines into music, dance, sculpture, painting, and film. By manipulating space, time, and sound, Wilson created works with an incantatory, trancelike quality and remarkable visual beauty. Most prominent in the 1970s and 1980s, Wilson remains an important influence on both directing and design.

Street theatre and *guerilla theatre* were also 1960s terms for political performances that went to the audience, the first into the streets, the second in hit-and-run "guerilla" raids on nontheatrical spaces where people could be found. *Happenings,* on the other hand, were non-linear and deliberately meaningless events that tried to re-define what was meant by theatre. All three types often used amateurs and usually had rather low production values.

This new avant-garde remained vital as long as political and social uneasiness did. By the 1980s, however, a reversal had taken place; in this new environment, with the idea of art itself also being undercut, the avant-garde faded. In the 1980s, America got over Vietnam and became an apparently more optimistic and less questioning place: quick wars in Grenada, Panama, and Iraq were popular; society seemed not to want to probe or protest any more. In a sense, there was a contradictory coexistence of new technology and its effects, on the one hand, and nostalgia and retrogression toward "simpler" values, on the other. By the late 1980s, theorists were proclaiming avant-gardism dead. Some individual theatres persisted and still exist, and many styles other than Realism still exist outside commercial theatre, but what appears to have happened to avant-gardism itself is that a social shift undercut its political strength, and the postmodern withering of ideas of art, good art, bad art, and experimental art undercut its aesthetic strength. Avant-gardism is primarily reactive, and, after 1980, there was little to react against: avant-gardism became like kicking a pillow. By the 1990s, the decade of e-commerce and big money, only local vestiges remained.

Major Noncommercial Movements

Related to, but separable from, the avant-garde were three theatre movements directly tied to political movements: black theatre, tied to the Black Power movement; women's theatre, tied to the feminist movement; and gay and lesbian theatre, tied to the gay rights movement. Although these shared many basic assumptions, they differed in several ways.

Black Theatre. Although African-American performers in America date from well before the Civil War, and African-American theatre companies were firmly established within their communities by the end of the nineteenth century, their performers and plays seldom reached commercial theatres in the United States until midway in the twentieth century.

Before the 1960s, most *commercial* plays featuring African-American characters had been written by whites, who often stereotyped and placed them in inferior social positions, where they were patronized by wealthier, wittier, and more powerful white characters. Paul Green's *In Abraham's Bosom* (1926), Marc Connelly's *Green Pastures* (1930), and Carson McCullers's *The Member of the Wedding* (1950), although sympathetic treatments of African-American characters by white playwrights, nonetheless displayed many of the stereotypes.

Public images died hard, but they did die. The French playwright Jean Genet, in *The Blacks* (1959), reversed the traditions of the minstrel show and used African-American actors in white face to display abuses of power. Although many African Americans rejected the play's thesis—that blacks will come to power only by adopting the tactics of their white oppressors—few failed to realize that the play represented a turning point in the portrayal of black people. More important, Lorraine Hansberry's *A Raisin in the Sun* (1959) appeared, an early portrait of African-American family life in which the tensions between women and men were sympathetically and sensitively dramatized; it won the Drama Critics Circle Award.

FIGURE 19.6   Black Theatre.

From its avant-garde surfacing in the 1960s, assertive black theatre moved into the mainstream by the 1980s. This is a scene from George Wolfe's *The Colored Museum* at Hampton University in 1993.

With the racial turmoil of the 1960s and the early 1970s, blacks turned in large numbers to the arts as a way of demanding change and repairing their ruptured society: "Black Art is the aesthetic and spiritual sister of the Black Power concept." The black theatre movement is dated from 1964 and the Off-Broadway production of LeRoi Jones's first two plays, *The Toilet* and *Dutchman,* both of which presented a chilling picture of racial barriers, human hatred, and the senseless suffering that results from racism. Thereafter, the stereotypical stage Negro was increasingly replaced by more honest, if often less agreeable, black characters. Throughout the 1960s and the early 1970s, Jones (now Imamu Amiri Baraka) remained the most militant and best-known black playwright.

Alongside such antiwhite and separatist works were plays depicting the politics and economics of life within the African-American community. Douglas Turner Ward's *Day of Absence* (1967) poked fun at whites as they were outwitted by cleverer blacks, whose disappearance for a single day led to the collapse of the white social structure. Alice Childress's *Mojo* (1970) suggested that African-American men and women could work out their differences and exist happily as equals if they loved and respected one another.

By the mid-1970s, African-American authors felt free to criticize their own community. Ntozake Shange's *For Colored Girls Who Have Considered Suicide/When the Rainbow is Enuf* (1976) explored the double oppression of being black and female and presented a most unflattering portrait of black males, some of whom were portrayed as brutalizing black women as they themselves had been previously brutalized. Originally

FIGURE 19.7   Pulitzer Prize, 2002.

Black theatre became mainstream theatre in the 1970s and 1980s. In 2002, playwright Suzan-Lori Parks was awarded the Pulitzer Prize for *Topdog/Underdog,* shown here in its original New York production at the Public Theatre. (Michal Daniel Photo.)

staged in an African-American theatre, this powerful "choreopoem" eventually moved to Broadway, where it earned a Tony Award.

African-American playwrights then moved into the commercial mainstream. A few of the major authors and their best-known works included Ed Bullins, *The Electronic Nigger* (1968); Lonne Elder III, *Ceremonies in Dark Old Men* (1968); Charles Gordone, *No Place to Be Somebody* (1969); Charles Fuller, *A Soldier's Play* (1981); August Wilson, *The Piano Lesson* (1990); Suzan-Lori Parks, *Topdog/Underdog* (2002).

Among the major theatres dedicated to producing African-American plays for primarily African-American audiences (1960s and after) were the Negro Ensemble Company, the New Lafayette Theatre, and Spirit House (all in the New York area) and the Watts Writers Workshop, the Performing Arts Society of Los Angeles, and the Inner City Cultural Center (in the Los Angeles and San Francisco areas).

With new plays and special theatres came calls for a new criticism. Some African-American critics took the position that their audiences saw and understood art in ways different from whites. Those artists and critics sought an aesthetic that was moral and corrective, one that supported plays that, in a direct and immediate way, affected the lives of African-American theatregoers. An African-American critic explained, "The question for the black critic today is not how beautiful a melody, a play, a poem, or a novel is, but how much more beautiful [that] poem, melody, or play [has] made the life of a single black man."

FIGURE 19.8 **Black Theatre/Women's Theatre.**
Women's theatre took several forms; here, Ntozake Shange's *For Colored Girls . . .* , a
sometimes bitter examination of black men by black women, in its New York production.
(Martha Swope Photo.)

Women's Theatre.   Whereas black theatre and drama arose from the social upheavals
of the late 1950s and 1960s, *women's theatres* were a phenomenon of the 1970s, during
which increasing numbers of people, mostly female, banded together into theatrical
units that aimed to promote the goals of feminism, the careers of women artists, or both.
By the mid-1970s, more than forty such groups were flourishing; by 1980, more than a
hundred had formed. Unlike black theatres, which were usually found in urban settings
and amid high concentrations of blacks, women's theatres sprang up in places as diverse
as New York City and Greenville, South Carolina.

The theatres ranged in size from those depending on one or two unpaid and inex-
perienced volunteers to organizations of professionals numbering into the hundreds.
Budgets, too, varied widely, with some groups existing on a shoestring and the good
wishes of friends, and others displaying a financial statement in the hundreds of thousands of dollars. Organization, repertory, working methods, and artistic excellence were
highly diversified, but the groups all shared the conviction that women had been sub-
jected to unfair discrimination based on their gender and that theatre could serve in
some way to correct the resulting inequities.

Like the African-American theatres, the women's theatres attempted to serve different audiences and to serve them in different ways. Some groups, like the Women's In-
terart in New York City, existed primarily to provide employment for women artists.

Such groups served as a showcase for the works of women playwrights, designers, and directors. Because their goal was to display women's art in the most favorable light, artistic excellence was a primary goal of each production. Critical acceptance by the theatrical mainstream was the ultimate measure of success. But other groups, like the now-defunct It's All Right to Be Woman Theatre (also in New York), believed the problems of women to be so deeply rooted in the society that only a major social upheaval could bring about their correction. Such groups were revolutionary and tended to adopt tactics designed to taunt, shock, or shame a lethargic society into corrective action. These groups cared not at all for the approval of the established critics, because they believed that traditional theatre was a male-dominated, and hence oppressive, institution.

Two techniques in particular came to be associated with revolutionary women's theatres: a preference for collective or communal organization and the use of improvised performance material, much of it uncommonly personal.

During the 1970s and 1980s, three feminist playwrights attracted special attention: Megan Terry (*Approaching Simone,* 1970); Myrna Lamb (*The Mod Donna,* 1970); and Martha Boesing (*Antigone Too,* 1984). By 1990, however, these playwrights had moved to other matters, and women's theatres were in flux. Some had ceased producing, and some had moved away from feminism. Others moved in directions newly pointed by feminism itself—emphasizing differences among women. They renewed explorations of the function of gender in life and art, investigating through performance the ways in which society and theatre construct gender. These new directions (earlier pointed by Caryl Churchill) found expression in the works of playwrights like Simone Benmussa (*The Singular Life of Albert Nobbs*) and Hélène Cixous (*Portrait of Dora*) and in theatre companies like Split Britches and Spiderwoman.

Gay and Lesbian Theatre.   Many American cities had self-aware gay and lesbian communities before the 1960s, but these were largely covert, "in the closet." Homosexual acts were illegal in most of the United States; public homosexual conduct, even language, was sometimes punishable under laws against indecency and obscenity. Thus, plays about homosexuality usually fell under the heading of prohibited speech. The exceptions were guarded, almost coded—for example, Lillian Hellman's *The Children's Hour* (1934). This situation changed in the 1960s, however, as court rulings extended free speech and concepts of privacy.

In 1968, Mart Crowley's *The Boys in the Band* was produced Off-Broadway and became the first homosexual hit comedy in a mainstream venue. Sympathetic to the lives and problems of gay men, Crowley's play made a place in commercial theatre for plays in which homosexuality was acceptable and non-threatening—and funny. Self-deprecating and sometimes self-destructive wit positioned homosexuals as victims, however, and thus ran the risk of sentimentality.

In the 1970s, gay theatre companies found permanent homes in big cities (e.g., Theatre Rhinoceros in San Francisco, The Glines in New York). Sympathetic gay plays became common in mainstream theatre, the more so when the AIDS epidemic became national news, and "AIDS plays" became a subgenre (e.g., *As Is,* 1984). Lesbian theatres surfaced in the 1980s (e.g., Split Britches). Now, some theatres produce both gay and lesbian plays.

FIGURE 19.9 Gay Theatre Into Mainstream.

Surfacing first Off-Broadway, gay theatre by the 1970s in good part lost its identity in mainstream acceptance. Nonetheless, *Angels in America,* a double prize-winner and arguably the best play of the 1990s, was subtitled "A Gay Fantasia on National Themes," for all that it was far more than a gay play. Here, Ron Leibman as Roy Cohn in a performance of "Millennium Approaches," one of the two plays that comprised *Angels,* at the Mark Taper Forum, directed by Oskar Eustis with Tony Taccone. (Courtesy of the Mark Taper Forum. Photo by Jay Thompson.)

As with other political theatres, coherent theoretical bases are elusive. Problems of definition exist: What is a gay play—a play about gay men? By a gay man? Is a negative play about gay men a gay play? When is a woman's play a lesbian play? Where does a play by a gay or lesbian author but with a different subject fit? What of those plays of the past by homosexual authors (e.g., Oscar Wilde, Tennessee Williams) that have no ostensibly homosexual content?

Partly to deal with such problems, the idea of queer theatre and queer studies has evolved. "Queer" is both an umbrella and a political term, a weapon seized from, as it were, "the enemy" and turned around. Queer theatre announces itself and has pride in itself.

Performance Art.   *Performance art* probably began in European art circles at the turn of the century, among the dadaists, and it found echoes in the happenings of the 1960s. Its resurgence in the 1980s made performance art the most energetic expression within the avant-garde. It is a form that defies traditional categories like theatre or dance or painting and that varies widely among its practitioners. As its name suggests, it depends on both performance and art, and despite its diversity it tends to share certain traits:

- A preference for a nonlinear structure, one unified more often by images and ideas than by stories
- An emphasis on visual and aural rather than literary elements
- A tendency to mix elements of several arts, especially music, dance, painting, and theatre

Links to More About Theatre

 David Kerr, *African Popular Theatre*, 1995.

 David Henry Hwang, *M. Butterfly.*

 <www.sehiutiyatrolai.com> In Turkish—hack around.

<www.pbpub.com/bread&puppet/bread.htm> Site of the current Bread and Puppet Theatre.

Although performance art includes many group works, a large proportion of the works are conceived and performed by individual artists working alone, often resembling standup comedians like Lenny Bruce.

Performance art probes the boundaries between life and art and among the several arts. Its frank experimentation has made it controversial not only among those who resist blurring the boundaries of arts but also among those who resent its often graphic portrayal of (to them) repugnant ideas or activities (e.g., feminism, homosexuality, pornography). Performance art is rarely Realistic, but many of its devices (the solo performer, the confessional mode, the lack of deliberate technique) seek to authenticate its reality. In a sense, it is the ultimate reduction of American Realism.

It is also part of the social shift that has made reality TV and tell-it-all interviews popular.

Thinking About Theatre

Gwendolyn Brooks (1917–2000), American poet, suggests that *"Art hurts."* On the other hand, Tommy Tune (1957–), one of today's director-choreographers, believes that theatre's *"only a show. . . ."* Which is closer to your view of what theatre should be? Which is closer to your view of what theatre is in America today? Is it possible to reconcile the two positions?

Noncommercial into Commercial

By the 1990s, except for the work of performance artists and some of the women's theatres, most of the vitality of the avant-garde of the 1960s and 1970s had dissipated. Nonetheless, several of the directions pointed by the avant-garde in the 1960s and 1970s were visible, if modified, in the later commercial theatre, which, after 1980

- Exercised greater freedom with respect to language, dress, and subject; nudity and profanity were readily accepted, and previously taboo subjects were now freely treated—e.g., *Torch Song Trilogy* (1983, homosexuality), *'Night Mother* (1983, suicide), and *As Is* (1985, AIDS)

- Included and awarded prizes to plays by African-American authors—e.g., *A Soldier's Play* by Charles Fuller (Pulitzer, 1982), *The Piano Lesson* (Pulitzer, 1990) by August Wilson, and *Topdog/Underdog* (Pulitzer, 2002) by Suzan-Lori Parks

- Included and awarded prizes to plays by female playwrights in larger numbers than before—e.g., Margaret Edson, *Wit* (Pulitzer Prize, 1999)

Global Theatre

By 1960, many nations around the world had theatre as part of their cultures. Many, such as Turkey, had state-supported national theatres as well as commercial theatres in larger cities. Language limited the internationalization of these theatres, however; many nations continue to have active, sophisticated theatres that are little known outside their own boundaries.

FIGURE 19.10 **Global Theatre: Turkey.**
Since the creation of the modern Turkish state in the 1920s, Turkey has created a sophisticated theatre. This is a scene from *Butun Menekseler Annem Kokar,* directed by Semih Sergen, at the Turkish State Theatres, Ankara. (Courtesy of the Turkish Tourism Office, Washington, DC.)

The collapse of the Soviet Union also changed the theatres of several countries. Where, before 1989, there had been state-supported theatres with varying degrees of censorship, there were then theatres with little or no censorship and, often, less state support. Some Communist-era theatres survived intact—for example, the Moscow Art Theatre. Others, like the Berliner Ensemble, found their status lowered. Some playwrights in formerly Communist countries complained that there was suddenly nothing to work *against*, the Communist regimes having inspired a good deal of creative satire and nonrealistic drama to evade censorship. In others, new freedoms led artists down new paths: the playwright Waclaw Havel, who had done prison time under Communism, became president of the new Czech Republic.

There was some crossing of international boundaries. Foreign plays such as *Marat-Sade* (originally German) had a huge impact in England and America. The play's director, Peter Brook, became an international figure, directing in Iran as well as Britain and the United States. The Polish director-theorist Jerzy Grotowski had considerable influence in the 1960s and 1970s as director and teacher. International festivals in places as far apart as Scotland, Costa Rica, and Iran (which held a festival of Islamic theatre in the 1990s) brought together productions from all over the world. Japan did a commercial production of a musical version of *Gone With the Wind*. At the same time, the great "museum" theatres—Kabuki and Noh in Japan, Kathakali in India, Beijing opera in China—maintained their places and were seen by increasing numbers of foreigners, with their art internationalized by tours and by replication by foreign artists—Beijing opera

FIGURE 19.11 **Globalization of Theatre.**

Increasingly since the 1960s, plays have crossed boundaries and cultures. Here, Samuel Beckett's *Waiting for Godot* in 1999 at the Echo Theatre Company, Seoul, Korea. (Courtesy of Seoul Performing Arts Festival, Seoul, Korea.)

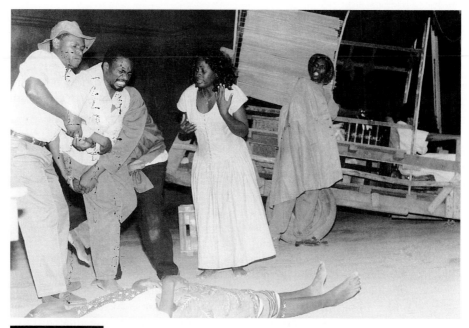

FIGURE 19.12   African Theatre.

Bertolt Brecht has been an important influence on some African theatre. Here, his *Mother Courage and Her Children* at Makerere University, Uganda. (Photo courtesy of Jessica Kaahwa.)

in San Francisco, Noh and Kabuki at the Institute for Advanced Study in the Theatre Arts in New York.

Africa was a special case. Still achieving independence in 1960, it was a complex of new countries that were working out often separate solutions to the conflicts between colonialism and nation status. South Africa was different still, burdened with apartheid for decades after independence, yet closer to European theatre because of its long history and large European population.

African universities were important to the theatre after 1960 because many had created departments of drama, often with advanced degrees. These sometimes, as in Botswana, provided the only live theatre to be seen; thus, unlike American colleges and universities, African institutions were central to the country's theatre rather than peripheral. Indeed, where university theatre was strong, African theatre tended to be strong.

Makerere University in Uganda, for example, was at independence a center for British-influenced theatre in East Africa, educating students and audiences in Uganda, Kenya, and Tanzania. The three had a common regional language, Kiswahili, and a common, although brief (1890–c. 1960) European colonial history. Their post-colonial histories proved so different, however, that their theatres have evolved separately: Tanzania became socialist and for years oriented itself toward China more than Europe; Uganda suffered horrendous internal oppression from the 1960s on and distanced itself from Europe; and Kenya kept its European ties while becoming a one-party state. Uganda stabilized in the 1990s after terrible internal wars, and Makerere University again became an important center for theatre; both Uganda and Kenya now have national theatres, Uganda's strong enough to produce a satire on the country's recent history, *Thirty Years of Bananas.*

It was also partly from the universities that a new South African theatre came. In academic venues, multi-racial casts were sometimes possible, even under apartheid; there, as well, both whites and blacks opposed to apartheid could seek ways to express their dissatisfaction. From such sources, as well as from small amateur groups would evolve both black and bi-racial theatres in the large cities, with plays written to meet demands not usually associated with dramaturgy—small casts to dodge the problem of curfews, episodic structure to allow rehearsal of scattered bits when actors were not able to travel from the townships. Several professional theatres thus developed in major cities, the best-known being the Market in Johannesburg. Undergirded by scholarship and criticism in the universities, and extended professionally by a government-funded film industry (jobs for actors, directors, and technical people), the South African theatre had strong black, white, and interracial companies by the end of apartheid (c. 1992).

Elsewhere in Africa, however, theatres tended to use amateur rather than professional actors and to work in a variety of performance spaces because of a lack of dedicated ones. Practicality dictated both traits (budgets were often limited), but they were also influenced by such indigenous practices as rituals and by paratheatrical forms such as dancing. More important, perhaps, many African nations developed a different idea of the purpose of theatre, seeing it less as an art or an entertainment and more as something that should "do its work in the world," as George Bernard Shaw said all theatre should. The principal African thrust in this direction has been *theatre for development* (see p. 419).

Drama, too, was affected by the unique African experience. At independence, African playwrights were writing Western-style plays in both formerly French (francophone) and British (English-speaking) Africa. Few were known outside of Africa, however, not least because they could find neither production nor publication overseas. At the same time, writers often had trouble at home if they chose the former oppressors' language instead of a local one; thus, not merely was the content of plays sometimes political, but the very language in which the playwright wrote was also political. Nor was the life of an outspoken writer in many post-independence African countries easy: not only could self-censorship block performance, but government repression could also cost playwrights their freedom—or even their lives. The Nigerian playwright Ken Saro-Wiwa, for example, was executed in 1996 for anti-government activity.

Nonetheless, a highly varied African drama has emerged. Three outstanding African dramatists can serve as examples.

- Wole Soyinka, a Nigerian, winner of the Nobel Prize for Literature in 1986. Soyinka's first play was produced while he was at the Royal Court Theatre in London; his later plays, including both those on African themes and those oriented toward European

FIGURE 19.13 **South Africa.**

South Africa developed a vigorous theatre scene despite apartheid; the fully integrated Market Theatre of Johannesburg was one of the most important. Here, the Market's 1986 production of Mbongeni Ngema's *Asinamali!,* directed by Ngema, on tour at the Mark Taper Forum, Los Angeles. (Courtesy of the Mark Taper Forum. Photo by Laine McCall.)

culture, have gained him international acclaim and got him into trouble with his government (*The Trials of Brother Jero, Death and the King's Horseman*). Soyinka ultimately went into exile to escape government repression, although he made a brief return in 1998 after the government changed. Despite Soyinka's international reputation, he suffers a typically African criticism from some quarters: he writes in English, not an African language; he sometimes uses non-African models (e.g., his own version of Euripides' *The Bacchae*). To some, he is "too European"—although if he did not write in English and did not have a European literary orientation, it is unlikely he would be known.

■ Athol Fugard, who is white, is the most famous of South African playwrights (*Master Harold and the Boys, The Captain's Tiger*). An actor as well as a writer, he acted in and directed his own small-cast, anti-apartheid plays. Most had mixed-race casts and were realistic in style. Fugard was able to dodge government censorship with comedy, obliqueness, and a lack of preaching: his plays presented apartheid in individual, often superficially funny, cases. Fugard's career has been a long one, spanning the worst of apartheid and its aftermath.

FIGURE 19.14   Athol Fugard.
Fugard was the most important South African playwright through the apartheid years and after, dealing with censorship and restrictions through guile and artistic genius; his plays were also staged at the Market. Here, *Sizwe Bansi Is Dead,* in a South Carolina State University production directed by Frank Mundy and designed by Robert A. Osei-Wusu. (Courtesy of South Carolina State University.)

- Ngugi wa Thiongo of Kenya wrote both plays and novels about the problems of independence and Kenya's casting-off of colonialism. He was particularly interested in the problems of his own Kikuyu people. Plays such as *I Will Marry When I Want* (written with Ngugi wa Mirii, 1980) had powerful—and dangerous—implications for policy in independent Kenya, made more so by Ngugi's sometimes writing in Kikuyu when the government was trying to downplay tribal cultures. As a result, Ngugi had difficulties with the government; his theatre company was forbidden to play in 1982, and he was in detention for several years. He decided to live outside the country and left Kenya.

  Many other African playwrights, as their nations moved away from their colonizers and their literature, came to share traits that set their plays apart from Western drama. Much influenced by Brecht's epic theatre, these included

- An epic quality: large casts, sweeping themes, loosely structured plots, free-ranging space and time
- A didactic purpose

- A mixture of Realism and nonrealism, with music, dance, and drumming
- An extensive use of recognizable cultural elements, for example, proverbs, gestures, history, symbols, rituals
- An openness to dramatic symbolism and symbolic characters

A few such African plays have been produced in American universities and regional theatres. It is unlikely, however, that they will find a place in the commercial theatre.

Theatre for Development

Much world theatre of the last twenty years has reacted against remnants of colonialism. One example is theatre for development—that is, a use of theatre to define and help solve local problems. Originally conceived as a top-down educational form in which an elite (government or university) would develop a script, rehearse actors, and send them out to perform, it is now conceived cooperatively. The top-down model is now seen as paternalistic, "Western," and "colonial."

Instead, a few actors now go into a village to live. With local people, they develop and rehearse a script in the local language about a local problem (AIDS, marriage laws, pollution). Everybody is encouraged to participate, including watching rehearsals. Everybody is invited to contribute. Discussion follows public performance, but the process itself is seen as more important than the performance. Theatre thus becomes a way of studying a problem, devising a solution, and showing how to effect it—a way of "performing" real life to understand it.

KEY TERMS

Check your understanding against this list. Brief definitions are in the Glossary; page references there will direct you to appropriate pages. (Persons are page-referenced in the Index.)

black theatre movement	Ridiculous Theater Company
guerilla theatre	street theatre
happening	theatre for development
performance art	transformation
postmodernism	women's theatre
revival	

Glossary

(Discussion will be found on the page or pages indicated, where appropriate.)

abstraction: An artistic depiction that is different from a literal, photographic representation of the thing depicted, usually by being more generalized, less particular. (65–67)

absurdism: A style of drama popularized in France after World War II that viewed human existence as meaningless and treated language as an inadequate means of communication. Major authors include Samuel Beckett and Eugène Ionesco. (35)

academy: A group formed to further a specific artistic or literary end; for example, the French Academy and the rhetorical academies of the Renaissance. (308)

acting: Creation of a character in action, through impersonation, for an audience. In formal acting, the actor seeks the truth of theatrical convention; in realistic acting, the actor seeks the truth of everyday life. (125–149)

action: According to Aristotle, a causally linked sequence of events, with beginning, middle, and end; the proper and best way to unify a play. More popularly, the single and unified human process of which a drama is the imitation. To some modern critics, an interaction (between dramatic protagonist and others). (40–41)

actor-manager: A starring actor who is head and nominal artistic director of a company; for example, Sir Henry Irving in the late nineteenth century in England. (364)

Actors Equity: See *union.*

actos: Very short, politically significant playlets. Term associated with Chicano theatre, particularly the work of El Teatro Campesino.

A-effect: See *Alienation.*

aesthetic response: Audience reaction to art object as art, not as idea, meaning, and so on; implies some idea of "beauty." (8)

aesthetics: Study of the nature of beauty.

afterpiece: A short play that followed the main attraction. (319)

agent: Professional who represents theatre artists for a percentage of their income. (80–82)

agitprop: Short for *agitation propaganda.* A kind of political drama popular in the 1920s and 1930s in America. Phrase subsequently used to describe all didactic drama whose social stance was unusually militant.

alienation: Customary, but perhaps misleading, translation of the German *Verfremdung,* "to make strange." Term now almost always associated with Bertolt Brecht's epic theatre, which aims to distance the spectator from the play's action in order to force conscious consideration of the political and social issues raised by the play. Shortened often to A-effect. (352–353)

amphitheater: In Roman theatre, a large public space for paratheatrical entertainments, like animal fights. (248)

alley stage: Performance-area shape that puts audience on each side with the performance area, usually a long rectangle, between. (88, 90)

angle perspective: Multipoint perspective; results when several vanishing points are located away from the center of the stage so that vistas appear toward the wings. (314)

angle wing: Wings consisting of two parts hinged together, one rectangular flat placed parallel with the proscenium arch and one (called the return) placed at an angle to it in order to increase the sense of distance. (On a raked stage, the return is not a rectangle but a trapezoid.) (299)

antagonist: The opponent in an *agon,* or contest; in drama, either of two opponents in conflict, or the character who opposes the protagonist. (44)

antiquarianism: The study of the details of past civilizations, often with a view to reproducing historically accurate settings onstage. Movement was popular toward the end of the eighteenth century and is viewed as a precursor to Romanticism. (383)

applause: Positive response to performance by clapping hands. (2)

apron: That part of a stage that extends in front of the proscenium arch. (87)

arena (stage) theatre: A theatre in which the audience completely surrounds the playing area. Also called *theatre in the round.* (88–90)

art: Activity done for its own ends, separable from both life and practicality, although it may be applied to very practical as well as aesthetic purposes. (7–8)

art theatre: A theatrical movement of the late nineteenth and early twentieth centuries that tried to separate itself from commercial theatre and the reliance on box-office. (355–358)

atellan farce: A short, rustic, improvised, and often bawdy play especially popular in Rome during the first centuries B.C. and A.D. Possibly the forerunner of the *commedia dell'arte* (see entry).

audition: A session at which a theatre artist, usually an actor, displays his or her craft in order to secure a job. (145)

auditorium: "Hearing place"; audience section of theatre.

autos sacramentales: Vernacular religious plays of sixteenth- and seventeenth-century Spain.

avant-garde: Art thought ahead of the mainstream, experimental. (328)

balance: On the proscenium stage, the visual equalizing of the two halves of the stage picture as seen from the audience. In any stage moment, the attempt to achieve a sense of equal weight among the people and objects on stage. More a metaphor than an actuality. (174–175)

balcony: Elevated audience area. (277)

ballad opera: A "minor" form of musical drama especially popular during the eighteenth and nineteenth centuries in England and featuring political satire interlarded with familiar tunes for which new and topical lyrics were devised; for example, John Gay's *The Beggar's Opera.* (376)

beat: A rhythmic unit in a play; defined variously by different actors and directors. (179)

Beijing opera: Traditional Chinese theatrical form, spectacular, nonrealistic. (393–395)

benefit: A performance, the profit of which is set aside for a particular actor, company member, or cause. In the eighteenth and nineteenth centuries, a primary means of supplementing an actor's annual salary. Now, any performance done for charity. (320)

biomechanics: The concept and the complex of techniques devised by Vsevolod Myerhold to train actors so that their bodies could be as responsive as a machine. (350)

black theatre movement: A theatre movement of the 1960s and after, primarily for black audiences, actors, and playwrights, originally connected with the Black Power Movement, a political ideology. (406–408)

blocking: Stage movement for actors, given in rehearsal (usually) by the director. (168)

body language: Communicable emotional states understood from posture and other conscious and unconscious use of the body. See also *gesture.* (137)

book: 1. The spoken text of a play or musical; early musicals with stories and dialogue were called *book musicals.* 2. Several flats hinged together and folded together form a *book of flats.* 3. To *book* a production is to schedule a performance of it.

booth: Temporary structure for fairs, etc; *booth stage* has playing area in front of curtained booth. (90)

border: Curtain, or less often flats or cutouts, suspended at intervals behind the proscenium arch to mask the overhead rigging. Particularly important in Italianate settings. (298)

boulevard: Historically the permanent home of the old fair theatres of eighteenth-century Paris, and later of the illegitimate houses where melodrama and comic opera flourished during the nineteenth century. Now refers to the district of the commercial theatres in Paris and means roughly what the word *Broadway* implies in the United States. (320)

box: Historically the favored, and most expensive, seats in a theatre. Made by sectioning off parts of a gallery, boxes were spacious and outfitted with armed chairs, in contrast to the crowded galleries, whose seats consisted of backless benches, and to the pit, where originally no seats were provided. (316)

box, pit, and gallery: Eighteenth- and nineteenth-century arrangement of audience with a ground-level pit, up to five levels of boxes or galleries surrounding it, with the cheapest seats at top. (316)

box set: Interior setting represented by flats forming three sides (the fourth wall being the proscenium line); first used around 1830 and common after 1850. (337)

breeches role: Role in which an actress portrays a male character and dresses like a man, presumably adding sexual titillation to dramatic interest. (384)

Broadway: In popular parlance, the area of New York City on and adjacent to the street named Broadway, where the commercial theatre of America is concentrated. (90–93)

burlesque: In eighteenth- and nineteenth-century theatre, a form of "minor" drama popular in England and featuring satire and parody. In America of the late nineteenth century and the twentieth century, a kind of entertainment originally dependent on a series of variety acts but later including elements of female display (including striptease) in its major offerings. After moving to the fringes of respectability by the 1940s, burlesque disappeared in the United States by the late 1950s. (377)

business: Activity performed by actor(s) at given points in a performance; for example, the *business* of lighting a cigarette or cooking a meal. See also *lines of business.*

byplay: Business that takes place alongside the primary action and that is slightly different from it; for example, in *Tartuffe,* Orgon's behavior under the table while Tartuffe is trying to seduce Orgon's wife.

Byzantine: "Of Byzantium," the eastern Roman Empire, c. 300–1453. (248–250)

CAD: Computer-aided design. Use of powerful computer programs to draft, elevate, rotate, color, etc., designs. (191, 192)

casting call: Public announcement of auditions or interviews for casting of a play. (165)

catharsis: Aristotle cited as the end cause of tragedy "the arousal and catharsis of such emotions [pity and fear]," a statement popularly understood to mean that

tragedy "purges" fear and pity from the audience; but alternative interpretations suggest that tragedy arouses and satisfies such emotions within its own structure and characters. Highly controversial and elusive concept. (231)

causality: Belief that human events have causes (and therefore consequences); as a result, events are seen as joined in a chain of cause and effect.

causal plot: Plot of linked, internally consistent cause and effect. (42–43)

cazuela: In Spanish Golden Age theatre, the women's area. (287)

centering: Actor's term for localization of human energy source in the body, usually in the abdomen. (133)

character: One of Aristotle's six parts of a play, the material of plot and the formal cause of thought; an agent (participant, doer) in the play whose qualities and traits arise from ethical deliberation. In popular parlance, the agents or "people" in the play. (43–45)

chariot and pole: An elaborate system for changing elements of the scenery simultaneously. Devised by Giacomo Torelli in the seventeenth century, the system involved scenery attached to poles that rose through slits in the stage floor from chariots that ran on tracks in the basement and depended on an intricate system of interlocking ropes, pulleys, wheels, and windlasses for their simultaneous movement. (299)

chorus: In Greek drama of the fifth century B.C., a group of men (number uncertain) who sang, chanted, spoke, and moved, usually in unison, and who, with the actors (three in tragedy and five in comedy), performed the plays. In the Renaissance, a single character named *Chorus* who provided information and commentary about the action in some tragedies. In modern times, the groups that sing and/or dance in musical comedies, operettas, ballets, and operas. (216–217)

City Dionysia: The major religious festival devoted to the worship of the god Dionysus in Athens. The first records of tragedy appeared at this festival in 534 B.C., and so it is called the home of tragedy. See also *festivals.* (216)

classical: Specifically refers to that period of Greek drama and theatre from 534 B.C. to 336 B.C. (the advent of the Hellenistic period). Loosely used now to refer to Greek and Roman drama and theatre in general (a period dating roughly from the sixth century

B.C. through the sixth century A.D., about twelve hundred years). (210)

climax: The highest point of plot excitement for the audience. (43)

cloak and sword play *(capa y espada):* Romantic Spanish plays of love and dueling—swashbucklers. (287)

closet drama: Plays written to be read, not performed. (336)

comedy: A form (genre) of drama variously discussed in terms of its having a happy ending, dealing with the material, mundane world, dealing with the low and middle classes, dealing with myths of rebirth and social regeneration, and so on. (49–50)

comedy, middle: See *middle comedy.*

comedy, new: See *new comedy.*

comedy, old: See *old comedy.*

comedy of manners: Refers most often to seventeenth- and eighteenth-century comedies whose focus is the proper social behavior of a single class. (317–318)

comic opera: A "minor" form of musical drama popular first in the eighteenth century and characterized then by sentimental stories set to original music. Later used to mean an opera in which some parts were spoken (in contrast to "grand opera," where everything was sung). (312)

commedia dell'arte: Italian popular comedy of the fifteenth through seventeenth centuries. Featured performances improvised from scenarios by a set of stock characters and repeated from play to play and troupe to troupe. See also *lazzi.* (300–301)

community theatre: Theatre performed by and for members of a given community, especially a city or town. Usually amateur, with sometimes professional directors, designers, and business staff. (99–100)

complication: Ascending or tying action. That part of the plot in which the action is growing tenser and more intricate up to the point of *crisis* (turning point), after which the action unties and resolves in a section called the *dénouement* (see entries). (41)

composition: Arrangement of visual elements for aesthetic effect. (174, 175)

concert party: British touring form, mixed song, comedy; adapted to African types in Ghana and Nigeria. (392)

confidant(e): In drama, a character to whom another leading character gives private information. (44)

conflict: Clash of characters, seen either as objectives that create obstacles for each other, or as actions, neither of which can succeed unless the other fails. (42)

confraternity: In France, a religious brotherhood, many of which sponsored or produced plays during the Middle Ages. One, the Confraternity of the Passion, held a monopoly on play production in Paris into the 1570s. (262)

constructivism: A nonrealistic style of scenic design associated with Vsevolod Myerhold and marked by the view that a good set is a machine for doing plays, not a representation of familiar locales. Incorporated simple machines on stage and often revealed the method of its own construction. (350–351)

continental seating: First devised by Wagner in the late nineteenth century for his theatre at Bayreuth; eschews a central aisle in favor of entrances and exits at the end of each aisle. (336–337)

convention (dramatic, theatrical): A way of doing things agreed on by a (usually unstated) contract between audience and artists; for example, characters' singing their most important feelings and emotions is a *convention* of musical comedy. (63–65)

copyright: Legal concept of intellectual property rights. (123)

Corpus Christi: A spring festival established in the fourteenth century in honor of the Christian Eucharist, at which medieval cycle plays and cosmic dramas (see entry) were often performed. Also see *festivals.* (259)

corrales: Spanish theatres of the late Middle Ages, sited in open courtyards among houses. (286)

cosmic drama: Long dramatic presentations popular in the Middle Ages that depicted religious events from the Creation to the Last Judgment. Short plays were combined until the total presentation could last several days or weeks and occasionally a month or more. See also *cycle play.* (261)

court theatre: A theatre located at the court of a nobleman. After the Renaissance, Italianate theatre, whose perspective was drawn with the vanishing points established from the chair of the theatre where the ruler sat, making his the best seat in the house. (283ff.)

crisis: Decisive moment at the high point of a rising action; turning point. (42)

criticism: The careful, systematic, and imaginative study and evaluation of works of drama and theatre (or any other form of art). (1)

cue: Immediate stimulus for a line, an action, or an effect.

culture: The set of beliefs, values, and life style of a group. (24)

cycle play: Medieval (especially English) dramas covering the "cycle" of history from the creation of the world to doomsday. See also *cosmic drama*. (261)

dadaism: Art movement of the first third of the twentieth century that rejected logic and tradition; often satirical, sometimes intentionally contradictory, silly. (351)

decision: In Aristotelian criticism, the most highly characterizing trait of a dramatic agent; the trait that translates idea into action and thus, in Aristotelian terms, unites with plot (in the sense here of action). See also *plot* and *action*. (41)

declamation: A style of verbal delivery that emphasizes beauty of sound, speech, and rhetorical meaning rather than the realistic imitation of everyday speaking. (244)

deconstruction: A strategy in criticism for finding unintended meanings in a work. Popularized by Jacques Derrida, postmodern strategies have been adopted by feminists and Marxists for social as well as poetic analyses of scripts and performances.

decorum: In Neoclassical theory, the behavior of a dramatic character in keeping with his or her social status, age, sex, and occupation; based on the requirements of *verisimilitude* (see entry). (293)

dénouement: That part of the plot that follows the crisis (turning point) and that includes the untangling or resolving of the play's complications. (42)

determinism: Philosophical stance undergirding Naturalistic drama that asserts that human behavior and destiny are determined by factors, especially heredity and environment, largely beyond human control.

deus ex machina: Literally, "the god from the machine," a reference to a deity who flew in at the conclusion of some Greek tragedies (particularly those of Euripides) to assure the play's appropriate outcome. Popularly, any ending of a play that is obviously contrived. (228)

dialect: Regional or ethnic speech, sometimes necessary for an actor in a particular role. (139)

dialogue: Character interaction through language. (116)

diction: In Aristotle, one of the six parts of a play; also called language; the formal cause of music, the material of thought; the words of a play. Popularly the proper and clear formation of the play's words. (47)

didacticism: "Teaching." In the theatre, plays are didactic when they emphasize ideological content rather than artistic form.

dimmer: Instrument for controlling the intensity of light by manipulating the amount of electricity that reaches individual lamps. (198)

Dionysia: A Greek religious festival in honor of the god Dionysus. The City Dionysia and the Rural Dionysia both included drama as a part of the celebration, but the city festival was clearly the dominant one of the two. See also *festivals*. (216)

diorama: Distant scene viewed through a cutout or other opening in scenery. Also, a three-dimensional arrangement of figures and painted scenes.

discovery: According to Aristotle, any passage from ignorance to knowledge within a play, by means of (for example) sign, emotion, reasoning, action. Good discoveries grow out of suffering (awareness) and lead to reversal (change of direction). (41)

discovery space: Permanent or temporary space in the Elizabethan (Shakespearean) playhouse that permitted actors and locales to be hidden from view and then "discovered" (or revealed) when needed. Location, appearance, and even invariable existence of the space are hotly disputed. (278)

dithyramb: A hymn of praise, often to the god Dionysus, performed by a chorus of men or boys; a regular part of the religious festival of Athens after 509 B.C. (213)

domestic tragedy: A serious play dealing with domestic problems of the middle or lower classes. In the eighteenth century, a reaction against "regular" or Neoclassical tragedy. See also *purity of genres*. (318)

double: 1. To play more than one role. 2. *The Theatre and Its Double,* an influential book by Antonin Artaud, calls the Western theatre merely a shadow or *double* of the (to him) true and vital Eastern theatre.

downstage: That part of the stage closest to the front. In early Italianate theatres, the stage floor was raked (slanted) up from the front to the back; therefore, to move forward on the stage was literally to move "down the stage." (299)

drama: 1. In the eighteenth century, a serious play (*drame,* in France) that dealt with domestic issues and thus failed to conform to the standard Neoclassical definition of tragedy. 2. Any serious play that is not a tragedy. 3. The literary component of performance, the *play*—often contrasted with the *theatre.*

dramaturg: Dramatic advisor and researcher for theatre or production. (78–79)

dress rehearsal: A final rehearsal in which all visual elements of production, including costumes, are used. Typically a rehearsal that strives to duplicate, insofar as possible, an actual performance. (180)

drop: Backdrop. Large curtain, usually of painted canvas, hung at the rear of the stage to provide literal and visual closure for the stage setting. (299)

dual-issue ending: Double ending. Ending of a play when good is rewarded *and* evil is punished. Associated with melodrama particularly.

eccyclema: In classical Greece, a machine used to thrust objects or people (often dead) from inside the scene house into view of the audience. Probably some sort of wheeled platform that rolled or rotated through the *skene's* central door. (227)

eclectic(ism): Gathering of materials from many sources; popularly a mixture of styles and methods. In twentieth-century theatre, the idea that each play calls forth its own production style. (400)

educational theatre: Theatre by and (in part) for students in an elementary, secondary, or collegiate setting. (97–99)

emblem: A device (usually an object or picture of object) used as an identifying mark; something that stands for something else. In the Middle Ages, a key stood for St. Peter, a crooked staff for a bishop. (252)

empathy: "Feeling into" another's state.

encore: Part of performance repeated in response to audience applause. (22)

ensemble: A performing group. Also, a group acting method that emphasizes unity and consistency of performances.

environment: The visual and spatial surrounding of the play, influenced by such matters as mood and visual meaning. (162–163)

environmental theatre: 1. Theatre whose performance is the audience's environment, so that the performance surrounds some or all of the audience and the line between performance space and audience space breaks down. 2. Theatre done in nontraditional space.

ephemeral art: Art that cannot be repeated exactly. (4)

epic theatre: Term originated by Erwin Piscator and popularized by Brecht to describe a theatre where the audience response is objective, not subjective, and where such narrative devices as film projections, titles, and storytelling are used. See also *alienation.* (353–354)

epilogue: A short scene that comes at the conclusion of the main line(s) of action.

episodic plot: Plot whose incidents are connected by idea or metaphor or character, not by cause and effect. (43)

existentialism: A philosophical system that lies at the root of Absurdism (see entry) and whose basic assumptions are the absence of transcendental values, the isolation of humans and their acts, and the lack of causality in the universe. (351)

experimental theatre: Any theatre whose methods or goals depart markedly from the mainstream of its day; thus, in the eighteenth century, Romanticism was experimental; in the heyday of American Realism, Absurdism was experimental.

exposition: Necessary information about prior events, or a part of a play given over to communicating such information; because it is a "telling" and not an enacting of narrative, it is usually nondramatic. (40)

expressionism: A style of theatre popular in Europe after World War I and typified by symbolic presentation of meaning, often as viewed from the standpoint of the main character; distortions of time, space, and proportion are common. (349–350)

façade stage: One that puts the actors in front of a neutral (nonrepresentational) surface. (210)

fair theatre: "Illegitimate" theatres in France and England performed at large, periodic fairs. (315)

farce: Form of comedy "stuffed" with laughs that arise not from verbal wit or human profundity but (usually) mechanics: business, mix-ups, mistaken identities, etc. (50)

feminist criticism: Analyses of plays and productions in terms of gender and the consequent effects on audiences and society. (77)

feminist theory (of theatre): An attempt to explain the effects of gender in the workings of theatre and drama and, through them, on society and culture. (74)

festivals: In Greece, religious worship took place in private and at major public festivals. In and around Athens, there were four festivals devoted to the god Dionysus. At three of these, records of drama appeared during the fifth century B.C. At the festival of no other gods can such records be found. See *City Dionysia, Rural Dionysia,* and *Lenaia.* During the Middle Ages, there were Christian festivals at which dramas were often produced. See also *Corpus Christi.*

flat: A structure upon which scenery is painted, consisting of a wooden frame and canvas covering; usually of a size to be carried by one or two persons for shifting. Used in both Italianate staging and box sets (see entries). (299)

floodlight: Broad-beam stage instrument that "floods" a large area with light. (198)

flying: Method of handling scenery for quick shifting by raising it out of sight over the stage with one of various systems of ropes, pulleys, counterweights, machines, and so on. Also, the illusion of flight in actors and properties through the use of concealed wires and the same system of ropes and pulleys.

focus: The point or object that draws the eye of the audience to the stage picture. (173)

foil: A minor character intended to set off another character through contrast. (44)

follow spot: Powerful, hard-edged lighting instrument mounted so that an operator can "follow" action with the light. (198)

footlights: Light sources arranged along the front of a stage (between actors and audience) to throw light upward from stage level to eliminate shadows from harsh overhead lighting. Rarely used with modern lighting systems, but standard equipment with candle, oil, gas, and early electrical systems (c. 1650–1920). (198)

forestage: That level part of the stage in front of the scenery, especially in Renaissance stages, which used a slanted floor for forced perspective in the scenic area. See also *Apron.* (87)

formalism: 1. Strict adherence to established ways (forms) of doing things. 2. In scenic design, use of nonrepresentational shapes and forms as the design base. 3. In criticism, attention to matters of dramatic form and structure as distinct from philosophical and sociological issues.

fourth wall (Realism): Nineteenth-century concept of a completely Realistic performance space that the audience looked into through a removed or invisible "wall" (the proscenium plane). (342–343)

French scene: Scene division between entrance or exit of major character(s). (179)

front of house: Activities relating to production that transpire in front of the curtain: e.g., promotion and publicity for performances, house management, box office sales. (79)

functionalism: Aesthetic or artistic method that focuses on the function of objects (scenery, for example) instead of on prettiness.

gallery: The highest audience areas in nineteenth-century theatres (box, pit, and gallery), hence, the cheapest seats; the balconies. (316)

gatekeeper: Somebody who has power to admit or deny access to jobs, production, performance, etc. (73)

gel: In stage lighting, a medium for coloring the beam of light. (198)

generic criticism: Criticism by identification of genre (comedy, tragedy, etc.) (49–50)

genre: In dramatic criticism, a category of plays: comedy, tragedy, melodrama, farce. Popularly, any category. (49)

gentlemanly melodrama: Later melodrama for middle-class audience with upper-middle-class subjects and settings. (369)

gesture: In one sense, any human act that conveys meaning (i.e., a speech is a gesture). In a more limited sense, a planned physical movement that conveys meaning, like waving a hand or pointing a finger.

given circumstances (of characters): In Stanislavskian vocabulary, those aspects of character that are beyond the character's or actor's control: age, sex, state of health, and so on. (142)

given circumstances: Basic facts that define the world of the play; conditions of place, period, social level, and so on. (62–63)

glory: In medieval and Renaissance art, a cloud or sunburst in which divinities appeared. In the theatre of those periods, a flown platform made to look like a cloud or sunburst. (265)

Golden Age: The great age of any culture. In Spain, the period c. 1550–1650, the greatest age of Spanish drama; in France, the age of Louis XIV; in England, the age of Elizabeth and Shakespeare.

gradas: Covered bleacher-style seats at ground level in the Spanish *corrales* (see entry).

Graeco-Roman period: That period in Greece and Greek lands when Roman domination had arrived, usually dated from c. 100 B.C. to the fall of the Western Roman Empire, c. A.D. 550. In theatre architecture, those Greek theatres that were remodeled to bring them in closer accord with the Roman ideals. (Not to be confused with Roman theatres built in Greek lands.) (236)

Griot: West African storyteller.

groove: A shallow channel in the stage floor in which a flat rode, for quick scene changes; a bank of several grooves would allow one flat to be pulled aside while another was pushed on in its place, seemingly in the same plane. (316)

ground plan: The "map" of the playing area for a scene, with doors, furniture, walls, and so on indicated to scale. (165)

ground row: A piece of scenery at stage level, often used to hide stage-level machinery or lights or to increase the sense of distance. (382)

guerrilla theatre: Didactic political theatre done in nontheatrical spaces—streets, factories, subways—without previous announcement; hit-and-run performances like guerrilla attacks. (405)

guild: Religious and, sometimes, trade or professional organization in the Middle Ages that became the producers of civic medieval theatre. (262)

hamartia: Aristotle's concept of error or failure of judgment by the tragic hero (sometimes translated inaccurately as "tragic flaw"). (231)

hanamichi: In the Japanese Kabuki theatre, a walkway through the audience used by actors to get to and from the stage. (324)

happening: Quasi-theatrical event of the 1960s, done outside the commercial theatre, usually done in nontraditional spaces and having no plot (in the Aristotelian sense); often, audience members moved through the event at their own rates and in their own sequences. (405)

happy idea: The basic premise on which a particular Greek old comedy was based. For example, the *happy idea* in *Lysistrata* is that women can prevent war by withholding sex. (422)

hashigakari: In the Japanese Noh theatre, a walkway at the side of the stage for the actors' entrances and exits. (271)

heavens: 1. Area above the stage: in the Elizabethan theatre, the underside of the roof that extended over the stage. 2. In the nineteenth century, the highest gallery.

Hellenistic Age: 1. That period of Greek history dating from the coming of Alexander the Great (c. 336 B.C.). 2. In theatre architecture, those Greek theatres built during the Hellenistic period. (229ff.)

hero: 1. A figure embodying a culture's most valued qualities (for example, Achilles in *The Iliad*) and hence the central figure in a heroic tragedy. 2. Popularly the leading character in a play or, more precisely, the leading male character in a play. 3. In melodrama, the male character who loves the heroine. See also *protagonist.*

heroic: Of or relating to a hero; by extension, exalted. *Heroic couplets* are two lines of rhyming iambic pentameter, probably an English attempt to reproduce the French Alexandrine, the approved verse for Neoclassical tragedy. *Heroic acting* stressed the vocal and physical grandeur of the actor. *Heroic tragedy,* popular during the seventeenth and eighteenth centuries, customarily treated the conflict between love and duty and was written in heroic couplets.

high comedy: Comedy of intellect and language, usually emphasizing upper-class characters and concerns. See also *comedy.*

high culture: The culture of the social and intellectual elite; the idea implies education, tradition, hierarchy. (24)

hikinuki: In Japanese Kabuki performance, the sudden transformation of a costume into a completely different one. (324)

hireling: In professional companies of the Renaissance and after, an actor or technician hired by the shareholders, to work for a set wage at a set task. (280)

hit or flop: Supposed condition of a commercial theatre that has no middle ground and no economic tolerance for plays that may earn back their costs slowly. (92)

householder: Member of an acting company who owns a share of the theatre building itself. (280)

humanism: That philosophy that believes that people should be at the center of their own deepest concerns. (274)

idea: In Aristotelian criticism, the moral expression of character through language; more generally, the intellectual statement of the *meaning* (see entry) of a play or a performance. (45–47)

identification: Audience attitude in which the audience member believes that important elements of himself or herself are to be found in a dramatic character; the audience "identifies" with the character. A suspect theory.

illusion of the first time: An expression used by an English critic (late nineteenth century) to describe the effect of good realistic acting: That is, the event seems to be happening for the first time *to the character.*

illusionism: Scenic practices (with analogs in acting, directing, and other theatre arts) that rely on a belief in the theatrical imitation of the real world. (290)

imagination: In acting, inventive faculty of the actor. (See also *instrument.*) More generally, that faculty of mind or feeling, usually thought to be nonlinear, imagistic, metaphorical, and playful. (131)

impersonation: Pretending to be another. (11)

Impressionism: A style of art that sought truth in fleeting moments of consciousness. Prevalent in the drama and theatre of the 1890s, Impressionism was noted for its moody and mysterious quality. (348)

improvisation: Acting technique or exercise emphasizing immediacy of response and invention rather than rehearsed behavior. (141)

independent theatre movement: In nineteenth-century Europe, the appearance of noncommercial theatres in several countries more or less simultaneously, most of them amateur or nontraditional and able to operate outside the usual censorship, "independent" of commercial demands. (343)

instrument: The actor's physical self. See also *imagination.* (131)

integrated musical: Musical with songs and dances that are organic parts of story and character. (139ff.)

interlude: A kind of dramatic fare performed between other events, as between the courses of a banquet. Important during the Middle Ages and the Renaissance and connected with the rise of the professional actor. (266)

intermezzi: Italian entertainments usually given at courts and presented between other forms of entertainment. See *interlude.* (301)

Italianate staging: A kind of staging developed during the Renaissance in Italy and marked by a proscenium arch and perspective scenery arranged in wing and shutter. (298ff.)

Kabuki: Traditional Japanese theatre of great spectacle and powerful stories, often heroic and chivalric or military. (323–325)

Kathakali: Traditional Indian dance-drama form. (322)

kuttambalam: Theatre type used by an Indian *Kuttiyattam* (which see): square, roofed stage with audience on three sides. (288)

Kuttiyatam: Indian theatrical form, derived from Sanskrit drama. (288)

Kyogen: Japanese theatre form: comic interludes between parts of a Noh performance. (304)

Latin music drama: Medieval dramas performed inside churches by clergy. The dramas unfolded in Latin rather than the vernacular and were sung rather than spoken, thus the name. Also called liturgical drama. (258)

laughing comedy: Specifically, comedy dating from the late eighteenth century and intended to restore the comic (laughing) spirit to the comedies of the age—in contrast to the then-popular sentimental or tearful comedies. (See entry.)

lazzi: Stock bits of business designed to provoke a particular response, usually laughter, from the audience. Associated particularly with the *commedia dell'arte* and the French farce of the seventeenth century. (301)

Lenaia: One of three major Athenian religious festivals devoted to the public worship of the god Dionysus at which drama was recorded. The home of comedy. See also *festivals.* (216)

light plot: The lighting designer's graphic rendering of the arrangement of lights and their connections. (198)

lines of business: A range of roles in which an actor would specialize for the major part of his or her acting career. Particularly important during the seventeenth and eighteenth centuries. (314–315)

little theatre movement: In the early twentieth-century United States, the appearance of noncommercial theatres throughout the country dedicated to art; many became community theatres. (357ff.)

liturgical: Associated with the liturgy (the rites of worship) of the church; in drama, the kinds of plays that were done inside churches as part of the religious services and thus were performed in Latin, by the clergy, and were usually chanted or sung rather than spoken. Liturgical drama is also called Latin music drama. (257)

long run: Uninterrupted sequence of performances of the same play, "long" by comparison with that of others like it: A dozen performances would have been a long run in the seventeenth century; on today's Broadway, a long run can last years. (92)

Lords' room: Expansive space close to the tiring house in Elizabethan theatre. (277)

low comedy: A kind of comedy that depends for its humor primarily on situation, visual gags, or obscenity. See also *comedy.*

ludi: 1. In Rome, festivals or *ludi* were given for public worship of a variety of gods and on various public occasions like military victories and the funerals of government officials. As drama was often included as a part of the festivals, they are important in a history of Roman theatre. 2. Early medieval term for plays. (239)

machine play: Any play written especially to show off the special effects and movable scenery in a theatre. Especially popular during the Neoclassical period, when regular plays obeyed "unity of place" and so had few opportunities for elaborate scenic changes. (308)

mansion: The particularized setting in the medieval theatre that, together with the *platea,* or generalized playing space, constituted the major staging elements of the theatre. Several mansions were placed around or adjacent to the *platea* at once—thus "simultaneous staging." See also *platea.* (257)

masque: Spectacular theatrical form, especially of the Renaissance and the Neoclassical periods, usually associated with *court theatres* (see entry) or special events. Emphasis was put on costumes and effects, with much music and dancing; amateur actors frequently performed. For example, Ben Jonson's many court masques. (283–285)

master artist: A term, coined by Richard Wagner, to identify the person responsible for the unification of a complex work of art like a music drama; someone who controls every aspect of a performance. (336)

master art work: *Gesamtkunstwerk.* Both term and concept popularized by Richard Wagner, who argued that such a work would be the artistic fusion of all major artistic elements, including music, into a single work under the artistic supervision of a single master artist. (336)

master of secrets: That craftsman/artist of the medieval theatre charged with the execution of special effects in the dramas. (265)

meaning: Intellectual content suggested or inspired by a play or a performance. All plays have meaning, however trivial, and most plays and performances have several meanings. Best thought of as "range of meaning" or "world of meaning." (45–47)

mechane: Machine, or *machina.* In classical Greece, a crane by means of which actors and objects could be flown into the playing area. (227–228)

mediator: One who comes between—in theatre, somebody who stands between audience and performance, affecting audience perception. (73)

mediated performance: Any performance in which audience perception is affected by an outside entity, particularly medium, e.g., film, television. (4–5)

medieval: That period of world history dating roughly from the fall of the Western Roman Empire (c. A.D. 550) to the fall of Constantinople and the beginning of the Renaissance (c. 1450). In drama, the period between 975, the first record of drama, and c. 1550, when religious drama was outlawed in many countries throughout Europe. (255)

melodrama: Literally "music drama." A kind of drama associated with a simplified moral universe, a set of stock characters (hero, heroine, villain, comic relief), rapid turns in the dramatic action, and a dual-issue ending. Leading form of drama throughout the nineteenth century. (50)

method: The American version of Stanislavski's "system" of actor training. (142–143)

Middle Ages: An early name for the period dating roughly from the fall of Rome to the Renaissance. (255)

middle comedy: That transitional kind of Greek comedy dating from c. 404 B.C., the defeat of Athens by Sparta, to 336 B.C., the beginning of the Hellenistic Age. Less topical than Greek old comedy, middle comedy dealt more with domestic issues and everyday life of the Athenian middle class. (229)

milk an audience: When a performer tries to evoke responses from an audience beyond that which it seems inclined to give. (21–22)

mime: 1. A kind of drama in which *unmasked* actors of both sexes portrayed often bawdy and obscene stories. In Rome, it became the most popular kind of drama after the first century A.D. 2. Form of silent modern theatre. (246–247)

miracle play: Medieval play treating the lives of saints. (259)

modernism: Name for art of a period (roughly 1890–1950) identified by radical experimentation with form and nonrealism. (348)

monopoly: Legal control or exclusive domination of a theatrical locale; the courts of both France and England in the late seventeenth century, for example, granted licenses to a limited number of theatres that thus gained *monopolies.* (312, 316)

morality play: Allegorical medieval play, like *Everyman,* that depicts the eternal struggle between good and evil that transpires in this world, using characters like Vice, Virtue, Wisdom, and so on. (259)

motivation: In Stanislavskian vocabulary, the internal springboard for an action or a set of behaviors onstage. (142)

music: One of Aristotle's six parts of a play: the material for diction. Popularly, the kind of art form having harmony and rhythm. (48)

musical: An American musical comedy, a form traceable to the mid-nineteenth century and now typified by a spoken text or *book* (see entry) with songs and (usually) dances and a singing-dancing chorus. (377ff.)

musicians' gallery: A space for musicians. In the Elizabethan theatre it is above the stage. (278)

mystery plays: Usually drawn from Biblical stories, these medieval plays were often staged in cycles, treating events from the creation to the last judgment. Often staged in connection with Christian festivals, some mysteries were quite elaborate and took days or even weeks to perform. (259)

myth: Story with a religious or magical base, featuring a myth hero who typifies important features of the culture, for example, the myth of Oedipus (ancient Greece) or the myth of Skunniwundi (Native American). In a less precise sense, some critics speak of the myth behind or imbedded in a work of narrative art and even of a dream, that is, the culturally important pattern that can be found there.

naturalism: A style of theatre and drama most popular from c. 1880 to 1900 that dealt with the sordid problems of the middle and lower classes in settings remarkable for the number and accuracy of details. Practitioners included Émile Zola, André Antoine, and Maxim Gorky. See also *determinism.* (339ff)

Natyasastra: Ancient Indian (Sanskrit) work on theatre aesthetics. (234)

National Endowment for the Arts (NEA): Federally (U.S.) funded arts-support entity. (102)

Neoclassicism: A style of drama and theatre from the Italian Renaissance based loosely on interpretations of Aristotle and Horace. Major tenets were verisimilitude, decorum, purity of genres (see all of these entries), the five-act form, and the twofold purpose of drama: to teach and to please. (292ff.)

neoromanticism: Literally, "new Romanticism." A style of theatre and drama of the late nineteenth century that sought to recapture the idealism and exoticism of early nineteenth-century Romanticism. A reaction against the pessimism and sordidness of the Realists and the Naturalists. (368)

new comedy: That form of Greek comedy dating from the Hellenistic and Graeco-Roman periods and treating the domestic complications of the Athenian middle class. A major source for Roman comedy. (230)

noble savage: A manifestation of *primitivism* (see entry) that depicted a romanticized view of primitive people and led to an artistic presentation of Native Americans, African slaves, and so on as major figures in art. (331)

Noh: Austere, poetic drama of medieval Japan, based in Zen Buddhism. (269–270)

Obie: Awards given annually to performers, playwrights, designers, and productions that made significant contributions to the Off-Broadway theatre scene. Name comes from the first letters of Off-Broadway.

objective: In Stanislavskian vocabulary, a character's goal within a beat or scene; the goal of a motivation. (143)

obstacle: Barrier, difficulty; in acting, something preventing the reaching of an objective. (143)

Off-Broadway: Popularly, those small, originally experimental but now often quite commercial theatres that are located outside the Times Square/Broadway area. Theatres with a seating capacity of fewer than three hundred that pay lower wages and fees than the larger Broadway houses. (93–94)

Off-Off-Broadway: Popularly, the very small nontraditional theatres located in churches, coffee houses, and so on that fall considerably out of the commercial mainstream. Theatres with highly limited seating capacities that may be granted exemptions from a wide variety of union regulations and scales. (94)

old comedy: That form of Greek comedy written during the Classical period (see entry) and featuring topical political and social commentary set in highly predictable structural and metrical patterns. (222–224)

onkos: The high headdress of the Roman, and perhaps Hellenistic Greek, actor. (232)

orchestra: 1. That area of the Greek and Roman theatre that lay between the audience area and the scene house. 2. Originally the circular space where actors and chorus danced and performed plays; later a half circle that was used as a seating space for important people and only occasionally as a performance area. 3. In modern times, the prized seating area on the ground level of a theatre and adjacent to the stage.

organic: Suggesting growth from a definable beginning; developing naturally.

orta oyunu: Traditional Turkish comic theatre form. (302–303)

pacing: Apparent rate of performance; partly a matter of speed with which the performance goes forward, but also related to intensity of action and complication and the artistic ways (actor's intensity, for example) that the action is realized. (176)

pageant: In the medieval period, a movable stage, a wagon on which plays were mounted and performed in parts of England, Spain, and occasionally Continental Europe. By extension, the plays performed on such wagons. (262–265)

pageant wagon: See *pageant.*

pantomime: In the Roman theatre, a dance/story performed by a single actor with the accompaniment of a small group of musicians, particularly during the Christian era. In the eighteenth and nineteenth centuries, a "minor" form of entertainment marked by elaborate spectacle and often featuring *commedia* characters and a scene of magical transformation.

paratheatrical: Related to or parallel to the theatrical. Used to refer to activities tangential to theatre: circus, parades, and so on.

patent: An official document that confers a right or privilege to the bearer. In several countries during the seventeenth and eighteenth centuries, only men who held patents from the king could open and operate theatres. (316)

patio: Ground-level audience area in the Spanish *corrales* (see entry). (287)

performance: In life, the execution of an action (or the action executed) or a behavior taken in response to a stimulus. In art, the action of representing a character in a play, or, more generally, any public presentation. (113)

performance art: An avant-garde form that blends several arts (most often music, painting, dance, and theatre) into a visual, more than literary, expression of an often very personal truth. (411–412)

performance criticism: Analysis and explanation of performance (rather than of drama alone). (541)

performance theory: Systematic description of the nature of performance (rather than of written drama alone). (73)

performing art: Any art that depends on a live performer in the presence of a live audience, for example, theatre, dance, opera, musical concerts. (14)

periaktoi: Stage machines in use by the Hellenistic period in Greece. An early method of scene changing that consisted of a triangle extended in space and mounted on a central pivot so that when the pivot was rotated, three different scenes could be shown to an audience. (242)

period movement: Actors' movements imitative or suggestive of the way people moved, or are thought to have moved, in another historical period. (137)

perspective: Simulation of visual distance by the manipulation of size of objects. (295)

phallus: Simulation of the male sex organ. In Greek old comedy and satyr plays, phalluses were enlarged and otherwise made prominent for purposes of comic effect. (234)

phonetic: Relating to the human voice and human speech; symbolizing (in letters or pictures, for example) precise human sounds, as in the phonetic alphabet.

physical theatre: The theatre building: its architecture and decorations, including the audience, stage, and backstage areas.

pictorialism: Directorial use of the proscenium stage's potential for creating pictures for both aesthetic and ideological ends. (382)

picturization: Directorial creation of stage groupings ("pictures") that show or symbolize relationships or meanings; storytelling through stage pictures. (169)

pit: 1. Area of the audience on the ground floor and adjacent to the stage. Historically an inexpensive area because originally no seats were provided there and later only backless benches were used. By the end of the nineteenth century, a preferred seating area (now called the orchestra section). 2. Now refers often to the area reserved for members of the orchestra playing for opera, ballet, and musical comedy.

plague (as metaphor): For Antonin Artaud, theatre is like a plague in its ability to rid society of corruption. See *theatre of cruelty.* (354)

platea: The unlocalized playing area in the medieval theatre. See also *mansion.* (257, 262)

plot: 1. In Aristotle, one of the six parts of a play and the most important of the six; the formal cause of character; the soul of tragedy; the architectonic part of

a play. 2. Popularly the story of a play, a novel, and so on. (40–43)

point of attack: The place in the story where a dramatic plot begins. Typically Greek plays, like *Oedipus Rex,* have a late point of attack, and medieval and Shakespearean plays, like *King Lear,* have an early point of attack. (40–41)

political theatre: The kind of theatre devoted to achieving political and social rather than artistic goals. (101)

possession of parts: During the seventeenth and especially the eighteenth centuries, the practice of leaving a role with an actor throughout a career. Under the system, a sixty-year-old woman playing Juliet in Shakespeare's tragedy was not unheard of. (315)

postmodernism: A critical approach that doubts the possibility of objectivity and that favors, consequently, the open acknowledgement of socially constructed meanings and investigates the implications of those meanings. (74)

presentational: Style of performance and design that lays emphasis on *presenting* a theatrical event to an audience. Contrasts with representational (see entry), which stresses the reproduction of life on stage for an audience that merely looks on.

preview: Public performance given prior to the official opening of a play, often to test the audience's response. (180)

primitivism: Interest in life and societies of primitive people; associated in particular with the Romantic movement of the late eighteenth and early nineteenth centuries. (332)

private theatre: In Elizabethan and Stuart England, indoor theatres that were open to the public but were expensive because of their relatively limited seating capacity. Located on monastic lands, these theatres were outside the jurisdiction of the city of London. Initially they housed children's troupes, but later the regular adult troupes used them as a winter home. (278–279)

probability: In drama, the internally closed system that allows each event in a play to seem likely and believable for that play (for example, the appearance of God in a medieval cycle play).

producer: Executive who arranges financing and who oversees a commercial production. (32)

prologue: In Greek drama, that part of the play that precedes the entrance of the chorus. In other periods, a short introductory speech delivered by an actor, either in or out of character, to set the scene, warm up the audience, defend the play, or entertain.

properties: Objects used on stage—furniture, cigarettes, dishware. (191)

proscenium (arch, theatre): Theatre building in which the audience area is set off from the acting area by a proscenium arch that frames the stage, protects the perspective, masks the backstage area, etc. The audience views the onstage action from one side only. (87, 88)

protagonist: In Greek theatre, the first (or major) actor, the one who competed for the prize in acting. Later, the leading character in any play (the "hero"). (44)

psychological realism: A kind of theatre that relies on a view of human behavior as defined by late nineteenth- and twentieth-century psychology. (344)

public relations: The business of causing the public to understand and esteem an event, institution, or cause. In theatre, it usually includes activities like advertising plays, developing essays for programs, designing posters, and inducing the public to have goodwill toward the theatrical organization before and after, as well as during, a specific production. (79–80)

public theatre: In Elizabethan and Stuart England, outdoor theatres like the Globe. Because larger than the indoor theatres, public theatres tended to be relatively inexpensive and so attract a general audience. (277–278)

purity of genres: Neoclassical tenet that elements of tragedy and those of comedy could not be mixed. The injunction was not merely against including funny scenes in tragedy but also against treating domestic issues or writing in prose, these elements being of the nature of comedy. (293–294)

Quem Quaeritis: A liturgical trope that opens, "Whom do you seek?" and that has early connection to drama, most especially in Ethelwold's *Regularis Concordia,* where the trope is accompanied by directions for staging. (256)

raisonneur: In drama, a character who speaks for the author. (44)

raked stage: Stage slanted up from front to back to enhance the perspective. Stages began their rakes either at the front of the apron or at the proscenium line. (298)

rasa: Important element of Sanskrit aesthetic theory—the inducing of an appropriate emotion in the audience. (235)

Realism: The style of drama and theatre dating from the late nineteenth and early twentieth centuries that strove to reproduce on stage the details of everyday life with a view to improving the human and social condition. (357ff.)

regional theatre: Theatre outside New York City in the United States and Canada; term usually restricted to professional, nontouring companies. (95–97)

register: A written, official version of a medieval cycle play. By seizing a register a person could prevent the production of a play. (268)

rehearsal: The practicing of plays, either whole or in part, in order to improve their performance. (179–180)

Renaissance: Literally, "rebirth"; refers to a renewed interest in the learning and culture of ancient Greece and Rome. Beginning in Italy, the Renaissance spread throughout Western Europe from c. 1450 to c. 1650. (274–276)

rendering: Theatrical designers' finished drawings or paintings intended to show how the item(s) will look when built and placed on the stage. (191)

repertory: A set group of performance pieces done by a company. Also, the practice in such a company of alternating pieces so that they are done *in repertory.* Loosely, a resident professional theatre company in the United States, a *repertory theatre.*

representational: A style of performance and design that lays emphasis on re-creating onstage aspects of daily life; the audience members are thought of as passive onlookers. Contrasts with *presentational* (see entry), a style that stresses *presenting* an event *for an audience.*

Restoration: The period of English history that dates from 1660, when King Charles II was restored to the throne. (315)

reversal: According to Aristotle, a change in the direction of action or in the expectation of character. Reversals result in complex plots, preferred for tragedies over simple plots. (41)

reviewer: A person who views an artistic event and then writes his or her descriptive evaluation of it for immediate publication. (77–78)

revival: A new production of a play after its initial run. (91)

rhythm: Regular and measurable repetition. (176ff.)

Ridiculous Theatre Company: Charles Ludlam's innovative, postmodern group, important as both early gay theatre and exponent of cultural montage. (405)

rigging: The combination of ropes, lines, pulleys, pipes, and so on that permits the manipulation of scenic units backstage. (190)

ritual: Any oft-repeated act that has a specific goal. *Ritual theory:* a theory that asserts that drama derived from religious rituals (in Greece, for example, religious rituals devoted to the worship of the god Dionysus). (6–7, 214)

road: A complex of theatrical circuits for travelling and performing plays outside of New York City. *Road show:* production for the road. (93)

Roman: A period in theatre and drama dating from c. 364 B.C.E. to c. 550 C.E. and customarily subdivided into the Republican period (c. 364 B.C.E.–27 B.C.E.) and the Empire (c. 27 B.C.E.–c. 550 C.E.). (237ff.)

Romanticism: A style of theatre and drama dating from c. 1790 to c. 1850 and marked by an interest in the exotic, the subjective, the emotional, and the individual. Began in part as a reaction against the strictures of Neoclassicism; grew out of the eighteenth century's sentimentalism (see entry). (330–339)

royalties: Payments made to authors (and their representatives) for permission to reproduce, in text or in performance, their artistic products (plays, designs, etc.). (122–123)

run-through: A kind of rehearsal in which the actors perform long sections of the play (or the whole play) without interruption, usually for the purpose of improving the sense of continuity, shaping the whole, and so on. (179)

Rural Dionysia: One of three Athenian festivals devoted to the public worship of the god Dionysus at which drama appeared. See also *festivals.* (216)

Sanskrit drama: Drama of ancient India, e.g., Kalidasa's *Sakuntala.* (235–236)

satyr play: A short, rustic, and often obscene play included in the Dionysian festivals of Greece at the conclusion of the tragedies. (217)

scaffold: In medieval staging in England, the localizing structure in or near the *platea.* See also *mansion.* (262)

scenario: In general, the prose description of a play's story. In the *commedia dell'arte,* the written outline of plot and characters from which the actors improvised the particular actions of performance. (300)

scrim: Mesh used in scenery; becomes transparent when lighted from behind, opaque when lighted from the front; useful for transformations, misty effects, and so forth. (348)

script: Play text. See also *text* and *book.*

secular plays: Plays that treat matters of this world rather than the next. Often used in discussions of the Medieval period to distinguish between religious and worldly plays. (266ff.)

secularism: Belief in the validity and importance of life and things on earth. Often contrasted with spiritualism, other-worldliness, or religiosity. The Renaissance period was marked by a rising *secularism.* (274)

semiotics: The study of signs, things that stand for other things. When applied to language, art, and criticism, semiotics focuses attention on the meanings that audiences create from the words or images of a playscript or a performance. (74)

sense memory: Recall of a sensory response—smell, taste, sound—with both its cause and the actor's reaction; important to the creation of a character's behavior in some theories of acting. (141)

sententiae: Pithy, short statements about the human condition. Associated with the tragedies of Seneca and with those of his successors in the Renaissance. (244)

sentimental comedy: A kind of comedy particularly popular during the eighteenth century in which people's virtues rather than their foibles were stressed. The audience was expected to experience something "too exquisite for laughter." Virtuous characters expressed themselves in pious "sentiments." (318)

sentimentalism: Prevalent during the eighteenth century, sentimentalism assumed the innate goodness of humanity and attributed evil to faulty instruction or bad example. A precursor of the Romanticism of the nineteenth century. (313)

shareholder: Member of a sharing company who owned a part of the company's stocks of costumes, scenery, properties, and so on. Sharing companies were the usual organization of troupes from the Renaissance until the eighteenth century (and beyond), when some actors began to prefer fixed salaries to shares. (280)

sharing company: One made up of shareholders. (3)

shite: In Noh theatre, the protagonist. (269)

shutter: Large flat, paired with another of the same kind, to close off the back of the scene in Italianate staging; an alternative to a backdrop; sometimes used for units at the sides. When pierced with a cutout, it became a "relieve" and showed a *diorama* (see entry). (296)

sight lines: Extreme limits of the audience's vision, drawn from the farthest and/or highest seat on each side through the proscenium arch or scenery obtruding farthest onstage. Anything beyond the sight lines cannot be seen by some members of the audience. (190)

signature music: Music associated with certain characters or certain types of characters, particularly in the melodramas of the nineteenth century. Stage directions indicate "Mary's music," "Jim's music," and so on. (368)

silhouette: The outline of a body or costume—its mass. (196)

simultaneous staging: The practice, particularly during the Middle Ages, of representing several locations on the stage at one time. In medieval staging, several *mansions* (see entry), representing particular places, were arranged around a *platea*, or generalized playing space. (257)

single-point perspective: A technique for achieving a sense of depth by establishing a single vanishing point and painting or building all objects to diminish to it. (295–296)

skene: The scene house in the Greek theatre. Its appearance can first be documented with the first performance of the *Oresteia* in 458 B.C. Its exact appearance from that time until the first stone theatre came into existence (probably in the late fourth century B.C.) is uncertain. (225)

slice of life: Critical notion closely associated with Naturalism and used to describe plays that avoided the trappings of Romanticism and the obvious contrivance of well-made plays in favor of a seemingly literal reproduction of daily life on the stage. (339)

socialist realism: The realism associated with the former Soviet Union, in which the problems of society were shown as solvable by application of socialist principles.

soliloquy: An intensely emotional passage, often lyric, delivered by a person onstage alone.

spectacle: One of Aristotle's six parts of a play, the part of least interest to the poet but of most importance in differentiating the dramatic form from the narrative and the epic. In everyday parlance, all visual elements of production and, by extension, particular plays, scenes, or events in which visual elements predominate. (48)

spine: In Stanislavskian vocabulary, the consistent line that connects all elements of a character through a play. See *through line.* (143)

spotlight: Stage light with hard-edged focus intended to highlight a person or object in their beams. (198)

stage left: The left half of the stage as defined by someone standing onstage facing the audience. (170–171)

stage right: The right half of the stage as defined by someone standing onstage facing the audience. (170–171)

standing ovation: An audience stands and claps in order to show supreme approval of a performance. (22)

star: Dominant actor whose name and presence draw an audience.

star system: Company organization in which minor characters are played by actors for the season, while central roles are taken by *stars* (see entry) brought in for one production; still common in opera, sometimes seen in summer theatres. (364)

stock company: Theatre company in which actors play standardized roles and (originally) owned shares of stock in the company. (364)

Storm and Stress: *Sturm und Drang;* a theatrical movement in Germany during the 1770s and 1780s that was marked by its militant experimentation with dramatic form, theatrical style, and social statement. (334)

story: Narrative; coherent sequence of incidents; "what happens." A general, nontechnical term that should not be confused with *plot.* (40, 58–59)

street theatre: Theatre, often political, that takes place outside traditional theatre spaces and without traditional theatrical trappings. (405)

strip lights: Series of lights connected together and located overhead or in the wings; usually used to bathe the stage in light; *also* light border. (198)

style: 1. Distinctive combination of elements. 2. In Aristotelian terms, the way in which the manner is joined to the means. 3. Particulars of surface, as distinguished from substance. 4. "The way a thing is done" in a time and place. (65ff.)

subtext: In Stanislavskian vocabulary, action "between the lines," implied but not stated in the text.

suffering: According to Aristotle, an awareness. The material out of which discoveries are made.

superobjective: In Stanislavskian vocabulary, the "life goal" of the character. (143)

surprise: An unexpected discovery or event. In dramatic surprise, the surprise, although unanticipated, must be seen in retrospect to be quite probable. (59)

Surrealism: A style popular immediately following World War I that rejected everyday logic in favor of a free expression of the subconscious (or dream) state. (351)

suspense: An increasing sense of expectation or dread, provoked by establishing strong anticipations and then delaying outcomes. (59)

symbolism: A style of theatre and drama popular during the 1890s and the early twentieth century that stressed the importance of subjectivity and spirituality and sought its effects through the use of symbol, legend, myth, and mood. (348–349)

take a bow: To appear in front of the audience to acknowledge its applause, usually at the end of a play. Women customarily curtsy and men bow. (21)

take an encore: From the French *encore*, meaning *again*. A performer repeats a part of a performance or offers an additional piece in performance at the insistence of an audience, which claps until the encore is begun. (22)

technical director: The person charged with coordinating backstage activities preparatory to production, including the coordination required to transform the scenic designer's vision into finished settings. (192–195)

technical rehearsal: Rehearsal devoted to the practice and perfection of the various technical elements of the show (lighting, sound, flying, trapping, and so on). (180)

tendencies: In Stanislavskian vocabulary, aspects of an actor's performance that digress from the *through line* (see entry). (143)

text: The written record of a play, including dialogue and stage directions; a playscript.

theatre of cruelty: Phrase popularized by Antonin Artaud to describe a kind of theatre that touched the basic precivilized elements of people through disrupting normal "civilized" expectations about appearance, practice, sound, and so forth. (354–355)

theatre for development: Use of theatrical techniques for both community involvement and community instruction. (419)

theatre history: Theatre's past. Also, a study of the theatre's traditions, including its plays, performers, designers, buildings, and methods of payment. Also, a field of scholarly endeavor devoted to such studies.

theatre in the round: See *arena theatre.*

theory: Any systematic attempt to explain a phenomenon. (73ff.)

three unities: In Neoclassical (Western) dramatic theory, the unities of time, place, and action. (294)

through line: In Stanislavskian vocabulary, a consistent element of character running through a scene or a play. (143)

thrust stage: Dominant kind of staging during Shakespeare's time in England that is being revived in many contemporary theatres. Also called *three-quarter round* because the audience surrounds the action on three sides as the stage juts into the audience area. (87–88)

timing: Actor's sense of tempo and rhythm. (176)

tiring house: The building from which the Elizabethan platform, or thrust, stage extended. A place where the actors attired themselves. (227)

Tony: Annual awards made by the directors of the American Theatre Wing in memory of Antoinette Perry to recognize outstanding contributions to the current New York theatrical season.

township musical: Apartheid-era musical from segregated South African area ("townships"). (393)

tragedy: In popular parlance, any serious play, usually including an unhappy ending. According to Aristotle, "an imitation of a worthy or illustrious and perfect action, possessing magnitude, in pleasing language, using separately the several species of imitation in its parts, by men acting, and not through narration, through pity and fear effecting a catharsis of such passion." At this point in theatrical history, almost indefinable. (49)

transformation: 1. Technique popularized in the 1960s whereby an actor portrayed several characters without any changes in costume, makeup, or mask, relying instead on changing voice and body attitudes in full view of the audience. 2. In medieval and Renaissance theatre, seemingly magical changes of men into beasts, women into salt, and so on. 3. In English pantomime, magical changes made by Harlequin's wand. (405)

trap: Unit in stage floor for appearances and disappearances; varies from a simple door to complex machines for raising and lowering while moving forward, backward, and sideways. (265)

trope: An interpolation in a liturgical text. Some believe medieval drama to have been derived from medieval troping. (256)

turkey: A play expected to fail, so called because of the earlier practice of opening such plays during Thanksgiving week.

unified art work: A work in which all elements are brought together to form an artistic whole; associated with the theories of Richard Wagner. See *master artwork*. (336)

union: An alliance of persons formed to secure material benefits and better working conditions. Major theatrical unions are USAA (United Scenic Artists of America, for designers); Equity (Actors Equity Association, for actors); IATSE (International Alliance of Theatrical Stage Employees, for theatre technicians). (364)

unit set: A single setting on which all scenes may be played.

unity: Cohesion or consistency. When applied to a text, it refers to the method of organizing: unity of plot, unity of character, unity of action. When applied to design, it refers to how well all the visual elements fit together to achieve an artistic whole.

upstage: The sections of the stage closest to the back wall. Comes from a time when stages were raked, or slanted, from the front to the back, so that upstage meant quite literally walking up the stage toward the back wall. (299)

utility player: Actor hired to play a variety of small roles as needed. (314)

vaudeville: 1. In America in the nineteenth and twentieth centuries, vaudeville was popular family entertainment featuring a collection of variety acts, skits, short plays, and song-and-dance routines. 2. In France in the eighteenth and nineteenth centuries, *vaudeville* referred to *comédie-en-vaudeville*, short satiric pieces, often topical, that were interspersed with new lyrics set to familiar tunes and sprinkled with rhyming couplets (*vaudevilles*). The form in France is roughly equivalent to the *ballad opera* (see entry) in England. (377)

verisimilitude: Central concept in Neoclassical theory and criticism. Literal meaning is "truth-seemingness," but used historically, at a time when *truth* referred to the general, typical, categorical truth. Not to be confused with "realism." (292)

villain: Character in melodrama who opposes the forces of good (represented by the hero and the heroine) and who, at the play's end, is punished for his evil ways. Typically the villain propels the action of a melodrama. (368)

vocal folds: Tissue in the throat over which air passes to make sound; incorrectly called *vocal cords*. (138)

vomitory: Audience entrance (Roman audience) into middle of auditorium through passage under part of audience area. (88)

wagon: Wheeled platform that moves on and off a stage, particularly a proscenium stage; also, in medieval theatre, a movable scenic unit and playing area, or pageant (see entry).

waki: In Noh theatre, the second character, usually a confidant. (269)

well-made play: A play written by or in the manner of Eugène Scribe and marked by careful preparation, seeming cause-and-effect organization of action, announced entrances and exits, and heavy reliance on external objects or characters to provide apparent connections among diverse lines of action. Now often used as a term of derision. (376)

wing and drop: An illusionistic arrangement, common from the Renaissance through the nineteenth century in Europe and the United States, of paired wings along the sides and a drop along the back of the stage. See *wings;* see *drop.* (299, 282)

wings: 1. Scenic pieces (*flats*) placed parallel to the stage front, or nearly so, on each side of the stage; combined with overhead units for "wing-and-border" settings. 2. The offstage area beyond the side units of scenery—"in the wings." (From which is derived *wing space,* the amount of room offstage at the sides.) (299)

women's theatre: A theatre whose repertories and practices are devoted to the advancement of women. Such theatres offer some combination of theatre by women, for women, and about women. (409)

wright: "Maker," as in playwright. (105)

yard: Another name for the pit in the Shakespearean theatre; where patrons stood on the ground in front of the stage. (277)

Yoruba opera: Nigerian theatrical form. (392)

zanni: In *commedia dell'arte,* the group of comic servants that includes Arlecchino, Trufaldino, etc. (301)

INDEX

Note: This is primarily an index of names, terms, and titles. Historical subjects within periods (e.g., Elizabethan acting) are not so indexed but can be located using the appropriate headings (e.g., acting). Technical and historical terms are also listed in the glossary (which is not indexed). The color section is not indexed. References on successive pages appear with the page number followed by ff. (e.g., action, 40ff.).